FAST TRACK TO A 5

Preparing for the AP* Psychology Examination

To Accompany
Psychology
8th and 9th Editions
by Douglas A. Bernstein, Louis A. Penner, Alison Clarke-Stewart, and Edward J. Roy

William James
Milford High School, Highland, Michigan

Michael McLane
Sterling Heights High School, Sterling Heights, Michigan

WADSWORTH
CENGAGE Learning

Australia • Brazil • Japan • Korea • Mexico • Singapore • Spain • United Kingdom • United States

*AP and Advanced Placement Program are registered trademarks of the College Board, which was not involved in the production of, and does not endorse, this product.

ISBN-13: 978-1-111-34758-1
ISBN-10: 1-111-34758-1

Wadsworth
20 Davis Drive
Belmont, CA 94002-3098
USA

Cengage Learning is a leading provider of customized learning solutions with office locations around the globe, including Singapore, the United Kingdom, Australia, Mexico, Brazil, and Japan. Locate your local office at: **www.cengage.com/global**

Cengage Learning products are represented in Canada by Nelson Education, Ltd.

To learn more about Wadsworth, visit **www.cengage.com/wadsworth**

Purchase any of our products at your local college store or at our preferred online store **www.cengagebrain.com**

Printed in the United States of America
2 3 4 5 6   20 19 18 17 16

CONTENTS

ABOUT THE AUTHORS

WILLIAM JAMES teaches at Milford High School in Highland, Michigan, and has also taught Educational Psychology at Lansing Community College. He earned a Bachelor degree in Psychology from Alma College and a Master of Teaching from Wayne State University. In 2003 he initiated and developed AP Psychology for his school and district. Since the inception of the AP Psychology program, he has had a passing rate of 90 percent. In 2010 he was a recipient of the APA/TOPSS (Teachers of Psychology in Secondary Schools) Excellence in Teaching Award. William has been a College Board reader for the AP Psychology examination since 2005.

MICHAEL MCLANE teaches at Sterling Heights High School in Sterling Heights, Michigan. He earned his Bachelor degree from Eastern Michigan University and a Masters in the Art of Teaching from Marygrove College. In 2000, he initiated and developed the curriculum for AP Psychology for his school and district. In addition to teaching AP Psychology, he also teaches Transitional Psychology, a course that he wrote and implemented, as well as Psychology 1. He has been a Presenter at several AP National College Board Conferences, and in 2007 was a recipient of the APA/TOPSS (Teachers of Psychology in Secondary Schools) Excellence in Teaching Award. Michael has also been a reader for the AP Psychology exam since 2006.

PREFACE

Psychology has always been a popular subject to study. There is not a day, nor a situation, where the content of psychology cannot be applied. People have found that the more they learn about the theories and concepts of psychology; the more they learn about themselves and others. This gained understanding leads to improved thinking skills, expanded viewpoints and opinions, and a more productive lifestyle. In short, psychology is a great discipline to study, but more importantly, it is an excellent discipline to apply.

William wishes to thank his wife Jamie for the support and patience she has shown during the writing process of this review book. He would also like to thank his mother for her support and his father for instilling in him a desire and passion for teaching; without his words of advice and affirmation none of this would have ever been possible. William would also like to thank his high school principal Mike Krystyniak for his support in fostering a wonderful AP program, and his coauthor Mike McLane for the opportunity to work alongside him in producing this study guide. Finally, William would like to thank his students, both past and present, for increasing his passion in teaching AP Psychology.

Michael would like to thank his wife, Tracy, and his family for their support and encouragement throughout his teaching career. He would especially like to thank his mother for "pushing" him to become a teacher; he acknowledges the memory of his father, whose words of advice are often underlying points in his lectures. Michael also thanks the staff of Sterling Heights High School and Warren Consolidated Schools for providing a learning environment which has allowed him to develop and grow as a teacher. He would also like to thank his mentor, Dan Bolla, as well as his coauthor, William James, whose knowledge and dedication has helped to make this an excellent reference book. Lastly, Michael would like to thank his past and present students, to whom this book is dedicated, who have helped him become a better teacher.

We would both like to thank Margaret Lannamann, our project manager, for her organization and assistance in this project. Finally, we would like to thank our reviewer, Chris Eadie, whose keen eye and attention to detail helped make this review book complete.

William James
Michael McLane

Part I

Strategies for the AP Examination

PREPARING FOR THE AP* PSYCHOLOGY EXAM

An Advanced Placement course is a challenging yet stimulating class. Whether you are taking an AP course at your school or online, or you are working on the AP course independently, the stage is set for a rewarding intellectual experience. As the school year progresses and you burrow deeper and deeper into your coursework, you will learn the psychological perspectives, broad concepts, and personalities that have shaped psychology. Fleshing out that knowledge with additional information and examples is thought-provoking and exciting.

But as spring approaches and the College Board examination begins to loom large on the horizon, Advanced Placement can seem downright intimidating, given the enormous scope of information that you need to know to score well. If you are intimidated by the College Board examination, you certainly are not alone.

The best way to succeed on an AP exam is to master it, rather than let it master you. If you manage your time effectively, you will meet one major challenge—learning a considerable amount of material in the time remaining. In addition, if you can think of these tests as a way to show off how well your mind works, you will have an advantage— attitude *does* help.

This book is designed to put you on a fast track to a successful score. Focused review and practice time will help you master the examination so that you can walk in better prepared, more confident, and ready to do well on the test.

WHAT'S IN THIS BOOK

This book is keyed to *Psychology*, 8th and 9th editions, by Douglas A. Bernstein, Louis A. Penner, Alison Clarke-Stewart, and Edward J. Roy. However, because it follows the College Board Topic Outline, it is compatible with all psychology textbooks.

In the newly released 9th edition there is an increased amount of material on applied psychology, which will provide a greater understanding of the basic research in psychology. Readers will also note the continued balance between current and classic psychological research, demonstrating the growth and development of psychology over the years.

This book is divided into three sections. Part I offers suggestions for getting yourself ready for the exam, from signing up to take the test and sharpening your pencils to organizing a free-response essay. At the end of Part I, you will find a diagnostic test. This test has all the

---

*AP and Advanced Placement Program are registered trademarks of the College Board, which was not involved in the production of, and does not endorse, this product.

3

elements of the AP Psychology examination (100 multiple-choice and two free-response questions), except that here the questions are organized according to the College Board Topic Outline. (In the actual AP test, and in the two Practice Tests that come at the end of this book, the questions are not ordered according to content area.) Because the diagnostic test is organized by content areas, you should be able to identify in which areas you need the most practice. When you go over the answers at the end of the test, a cluster of wrong answers in one content area will show you where to focus your attention. Page references at the end of each answer indicate where you will find the discussion on each particular question in both the 8th and 9th editions of *Psychology*.

Part II is made up of 14 chapters, given below. Each of the subject areas is listed in the College Board content outline. The percentages indicate how many multiple-choice questions will be devoted to each content area.

Chapter 1	Research Methods	8–10 %
Chapter 2	Biological Psychology	8–10 %
Chapter 3	Developmental Psychology	7–9 %
Chapter 4	Cognition	8–10 %
Chapter 5	Motivation, Emotion, and Stress	6–8 %
Chapter 6	Sensation and Perception	6–8 %
Chapter 7	States of Consciousness	2–4 %
Chapter 8	Learning	7–9 %
Chapter 9	Testing and Individual Differences	5–7 %
Chapter 10	Personality	5–7 %
Chapter 11	Abnormal Psychology	7–9 %
Chapter 12	Treatment of Psychological Disorders	5–7 %
Chapter 13	Social Psychology	8–10 %
Chapter 14	History and Approaches	2–4 %

These chapters are not a substitute for a textbook and class discussions, but they offer review and help you prepare further for the exam. At the end of each chapter, you will find fifteen multiple-choice and two free-response questions based on the content of that chapter. Again, you will find page references at the end of each answer directing you to the discussion on each particular point in the 8th and 9th editions of *Psychology*.

Part III offers two complete AP psychology examinations. At the end of each test, you will find the answers, explanations, and references to the 8th and 9th editions of *Psychology* for the 100 multiple-choice and two free-response questions. Following the answers and explanations is a worksheet you can fill in to calculate your score and compare it to the scores of students who took the exam in 2007.

SETTING UP A REVIEW SCHEDULE

If you have been steadily doing your homework and keeping up with the coursework, you will be in good shape. The key to preparing for the examination is to begin as early as possible; don't wait until the exam is just a week or two away to begin your studying. But even if you've done all that—or if it's too late to do all that—there are other ways to pull it all together.

To begin, read Part I of this book. You will be much more comfortable going into the test if you understand how the test questions are designed and how best to approach them. Then take the diagnostic test and see where you stand.

Set up a schedule for yourself on a calendar. If you begin studying early, you can chip away at the review chapters in Part II. You'll be surprised—and pleased—by how much material you can cover in half an hour a day of study for a month or so before the test. Look carefully at the sections of the diagnostic test; if you missed a number of questions in one particular area, allow more time for the chapters that cover that area of the course. The practice tests in Part III will give you more experience with different kinds of multiple-choice questions and the wide range of free-response questions.

If time is short, reading the review chapters may not be your best course of action. Instead, skim through the chapter reviews to re-familiarize yourself with the main ideas. Spend the bulk of your time working on the multiple-choice and free-response questions at the end of each review. This will give you a good idea of your understanding of that particular topic. Then take the tests in Part III.

If time is *really* short, go straight from Part I to Part III. Taking practice tests repeatedly is one of the fastest, most practical ways to prepare.

BEFORE THE EXAM

By February, long before the exam, you need to make sure that you are registered to take it. Many schools take care of the paperwork and handle the fees for their AP students, but check with your teacher or the AP coordinator to be certain that you are on the list. This is especially important if you have a documented disability and need test accommodations. If you are studying AP independently, call AP Services at the College Board for the name of an AP coordinator at a local school who will help you through the registration process.

The evening before the exam is not a great time for partying—nor is it a great time for cramming. If you like, look over class notes or skim through your textbook, concentrating on the broad outlines, rather than the small details, of the course. You might also want to skim through this book and read the AP Tips. This is also a great time to get your things together for the next day. Sharpen a fistful of number 2 pencils with good erasers for the multiple-choice section; collect several black or dark-blue ballpoint pens for the free-response questions; make sure you have a watch and turn off the alarm if it has one; get a piece of fruit or a granola bar and a bottle of water for the break; make sure you have your Social Security number and whatever photo identification and admission ticket are required. Then relax, and get a good night's sleep.

On the day of the examination, it is wise to eat breakfast—studies show that students who eat a healthy breakfast before testing earn higher grades. Be careful not to drink a lot of liquids, thereby necessitating a trip to the bathroom during the test. Breakfast will give you the energy you need to power you through the test—and more. Remember, cell phones are not allowed in the testing room. You will spend some time waiting while everyone is seated in the right room for the right test. That's before the test has even begun. With a short break between Section I and Section II, the psychology exam lasts for over two and a half hours. Be prepared for a long test time. You don't want to be distracted by a growling stomach or hunger pangs.

Be sure to wear comfortable clothes; take along a sweater in case the heating or air-conditioning is erratic. Be sure, too, to wear clothes you like—everyone performs better when they think they look better.

You have been on the fast track. Now go get a 5!

TAKING THE AP PSYCHOLOGY EXAM

The AP Psychology exam consists of two sections: Section I is made up of 100 multiple-choice questions; Section II contains 2 free-response questions. You will have 70 minutes to complete the multiple-choice portion. The questions are then collected, and you will be given a short break. You then have 50 minutes for the free-response questions. You must answer both questions. Some AP exams allow you to choose among the free-response questions, but psychology is *not* one of them. Keep an eye on your watch and devote 25 minutes to each free-response question. Please note that watch alarms are *not* allowed.

Below is a chart to help you visualize the breakdown of the exam:

Section	Multiple-Choice Questions	Two Free-Response Questions (Essay)
Weight	66 2/3 % of the exam	33 1/3 % of the exam
Number of Questions	100	2
Time Allowed	70 minutes	50 minutes
Suggested Pace	40-45 seconds per question	25 minutes per question

STRATEGIES FOR THE MULTIPLE-CHOICE SECTION

Here are some rules of thumb to help you work your way through the multiple-choice questions:

- **Multiple-Choice Scoring** Each correct answer is worth 1 point, and because of a recent change to AP exam scoring, you will no longer lose points for incorrect answers. Therefore, it is worthwhile to answer every question, even if you have to guess. There are five possible answers for each question. If you cannot narrow down the choices at all, you have a 20% chance of guessing correctly. If you can eliminate even one response, it will improve your chances of guessing correctly. Your best strategy is to go through the entire multiple-choice section, answering all questions to which you know the answers. If you skip a question, be careful to skip that line on the answer sheet as well. Then go back and work on the questions you skipped. Leave yourself enough time to fill in answers—

even if they are guesses—on all unanswered items before the time expires.

■ **Progressively harder** Though there is no clear, definitive organization to the multiple-choice questions, there are some patterns that emerge that you may want to note. As the test progresses, the questions may seem to become longer and more difficult. Approximately the first third of the exam will consist of define and apply questions, the middle third of the exam will consist of apply and relate questions, and the final third of the exam will consist of analyze and evaluate questions. Pace yourself accordingly, using the allocated time of 70 minutes. In other words, try to spend about 30 seconds per question at the start of the multiple-choice section so you have more time per question toward the end, when the questions become more challenging.

■ **Read each question carefully** Pressed for time, many students make the mistake of reading the questions too quickly or merely skimming them. By reading each question carefully, you may already have some idea about the correct answer. You can then look for that answer in the responses. Careful reading is especially important in EXCEPT questions (see the next section which describes the types of multiple-choice questions).

■ **Eliminate any answer you know is wrong** You can write on the multiple-choice questions in the test book. As you read through the responses, draw a line through every answer you know is wrong.

■ **Read all of the possible answers, then choose the most accurate response** AP examinations are written to test your precise knowledge of a subject. Sometimes there are a few possible answers but one of them is more specific and therefore the correct response.

■ **Avoid absolute responses** These answers often include the words "always" or "never." For example, the statement "The occipital lobe always processes light" is incorrect because in cases of traumatic brain injury in young children the brain can and often does adapt to compensate.

■ **Mark and skip tough questions** If you are hung up on a question, mark it in the margin of the question book. You can come back to it later. Make sure you skip that question on your answer sheet as well.

■ **Working backward** Some students find it beneficial to glance through the exam to get an idea of how to pace their per-question time allocation. Other students find it beneficial to work backward, as they may find that some of the more difficult questions help identify questions found at the beginning. If you decide to work backward, be sure to fill in the correct ovals. If you do decide to start from the beginning of the test, be careful not to spend too much time on the early questions, since questions toward the end of the exam become more difficult. Remember, your goal should be to finish the entire exam.

TYPES OF MULTIPLE-CHOICE QUESTIONS

There are various kinds of multiple-choice questions. Here are some suggestions for how to approach each one.

CLASSIC/BEST-ANSWER QUESTIONS

This is the most common type of multiple-choice question. It simply requires you to read the question and select the correct answer. For example:

1. Which psychologist is considered the founder of American behaviorism?
    (A) Sigmund Freud
    (B) Harry S. Sullivan
    (C) William James
    (D) Wilhelm Wundt
    (E) John B. Watson

Answer: E. This question has only one correct answer. John B. Watson is considered the father of American behaviorism.

EXCEPT QUESTIONS

In EXCEPT questions, all of the answers but one are correct. The best way to approach these questions is to treat them as true/false questions. Mark a T or an F in the margin next to each possible answer. There should be only one false answer, and that is the answer you should select. For example:

1. All of the following are considered symptoms of major depressive disorder EXCEPT
    (A) lack of energy
    (B) loss of appetite
    (C) continued interest in activities
    (D) prolonged feelings of despair
    (E) suicidal thoughts

Answer: C. A person with major depressive disorder does not have a continued interest in daily activities.

ANALYSIS/APPLICATION QUESTIONS

1. Jim is having a difficult time forming and maintaining commitments in relationships. His last relationship ended because Jim did not seem to know what he wanted in his life, which affects what he wants from other people. According to Erik Erikson, which psychosocial conflict is Jim presently experiencing?
    (A) Trust versus mistrust
    (B) Initiative versus guilt
    (C) Generativity versus stagnation
    (D) Identity versus role confusion
    (E) Autonomy versus doubt/shame

Answer: D. According to Erikson, a person tries to find his or her place in life during adolescence, to figure out exactly who he or she is. This explains why adolescents may switch peer groups, trying to find where and with whom they fit in. When adolescents are unable to find their sense of self-identity, role confusion occurs.

FREE-RESPONSE QUESTIONS

There are two mandatory free-response questions on the AP Psychology examination, and you will have 50 minutes to answer them. The questions can cover multiple content areas and typically involve multiple chapters. Be prepared to combine several topics and psychological perspectives within your answers.

Some free-response questions may ask you not only to define but also to apply the topics presented within the question. Some questions may ask you to *only* apply your knowledge of the identified terms, concepts, or theories. Be sure to read both questions and identify what they are asking.

Typically one of the questions will be primarily devoted to a particular chapter (i.e., psychological disorders, learning, human development) and the other will ask you to synthesize multiple chapters or concepts into one answer. In other words, one question will be more specific, whereas the other question will be much broader in nature.

Essays for free-response questions can be written in any order. Whether you write the essays in or out of order, make sure you put the number of the question in the upper corner of each page of your essay booklet. In addition, questions are sometimes broken into parts, such as (a) and (b). When this is the case, label each part of your response.

These are not traditional essay questions. Free-response questions in AP Psychology do not require either an introduction or conclusion or a thesis; these elements are not counted and waste valuable time for you and the reader who is grading your free-response question. Many of these questions may be written in a short-answer format. Bulleted responses in complete sentences are accepted.

Although this may sound easier than writing a traditional essay, it is important that you know the material well because these are targeted questions. Even if you do not feel you know what the question is asking, try to answer it as best you can; each individual part of a question is scored separately.

Examination readers want specifics, so don't use words such as "things" or "stuff," or general "pop" psychology terms that you have heard on television. Readers are looking for accurate information presented in clear, concise prose. You can't mask inadequate information, even with elegant prose.

You will have a 50-minute block for this section, so watch your time. In most cases, you should allow 25 minutes for each question. Spend 5 minutes reading the question and jotting down a few words on each point you want to cover in your answer. Then spend 15 minutes writing your response. Save the last 5 minutes to read over your response to make sure you have covered each point in enough detail. If 25 minutes have passed and you aren't finished with a question, leave some space, and start a new question on the next page. You can come back later if you have time.

VOCABULARY FOR FREE-RESPONSE QUESTIONS

In answering the free-response questions, carefully read each question and do exactly what it asks. It is important to note the word choices used in the questions.

- **Define** means to state the meaning of a word or phrase or to give a specific example. For instance, if a question asks you to define "heuristics," the response should be along the lines of "A heuristic is a general rule of thumb used to help reach a decision." Definitions are usually just one sentence.
- **Identify** means to select a factor, person, or idea and give it a name. For instance, if a question asks you to identify one advantage of a case study, a possible response is "One advantage of a case study is that it allows the researcher to gain an in-depth view into a rare condition or disorder."
- **Explain why/explain how** means to give a cause or reason. Explanations usually include the word *because*. For instance, if a question asks you what are some disadvantages of using a case study, one possible response is "One disadvantage in using a case study is that the researcher cannot generalize to the wider, more general population because the event or disorder being studied does not occur often enough or is rare."

SCORING FREE-RESPONSE QUESTIONS

These questions are scored using a rubric that assigns points for each part of the answer. For example, if Part (a) requires you to identify and explain two factors, that part of the response will be worth 4 points (1 point for each identification and 1 point for each explanation). If Part (b) requires you to identify and explain one factor, that part of the response will be worth 2 points (1 point for the identification and 1 point for the explanation), for a total of 6 possible points on the question.

FREE-RESPONSE QUESTION

1. After the first psychology test, Dr. Border is interested in knowing whether lectures improve student academic performance on the second test. Design a study that would provide Dr. Border with adequate data to address his question. Be sure to address each of the following in your answer:
   - Independent variable (IV)
   - Dependent variable (DV)
   - Sampling of participants
   - Assignment of participants
   - Possible outcome of experiment
   - Potential confounding variables

SCORING (6 POINTS POSSIBLE)

- Independent variable (IV) (point 1)
  - The independent variable (IV) in this experiment is the lecture.
- Dependent variable (DV) (point 2)
  - The dependent variable (DV) in this experiment is the performance on the test.
- Sampling of participants (point 3)
  - The sampling of participants refers to which group of people will be targeted for the experiment. For example, if the experiment pertains to women between the ages of 18 and 25, then only women within this parameter will be selected. This allows the researcher the opportunity to study a selected group from Dr. Border's classes.
- Assignment of participants (point 4)
  - How participants are assigned to either the experimental or the control group.
  - Randomly selecting participants allows all participants the same chance of being assigned to a particular group.
- Possible outcome of experiment (point 5)
  - The possible resulting effects of the experiment must be mentioned (either the scores improved or they did not improve after the lectures).
  - As long as the result is supported, it doesn't matter what outcome or result is mentioned.
- Potential confounding variables (point 6)
  - Variables that may influence the experiment and cannot be accounted for or controlled.
  - Some possible confounding variables are the level of participants' education, different student cognitive skills, individual motivation, Dr. Border's lecturing abilities; no mention of a double-blind study.

SAMPLE FREE-RESPONSE ANSWER #1

The <u>independent variable (IV)</u> would be the lectures. The <u>dependent variable (DV)</u> would be how much the subjects' academic performance increased, if at all. Researchers would <u>randomly assign</u> participants to either the lecture group (the experimental group) or the non-lecture group (the control group) by assigning each subject a number and then randomly selecting numbers out of a hat. Participants should be selected from one psychology class, with equal numbers of males and females, to obtain a solid <u>sample</u> size. A <u>possible outcome of the experiment</u> would be that those who listened to lectures would receive higher scores on the second psychology test. One possible <u>confounding variable</u> would be each student's prior knowledge and exposure to psychology.

All points were scored in this sample response.

Score: 6/6

SAMPLE FREE-RESPONSE ANSWER #2

Independent variable (IV) is how much the subjects' academic performances increased. Dependent variable (DV) is which group participants were assigned to (lecture or non-lecture).

Assignment of participants must be done in a random manner to control for potential experimenter bias. The sample size must be adequate enough to represent the population the researcher is studying, and therefore must include both males and females. A confounding variable is any variable that cannot be controlled for. In this experiment the amount of prior knowledge cannot be controlled for and thus could influence the results.

Points 1 and 2 were not scored because they were wrongly identified. The remaining points all scored.

Score: 4/6

SAMPLE FREE-RESPONSE ANSWER #3

Independent variable (IV) is the variable that is manipulated.

Dependent variable (DV) is the measurement or outcome of the independent variable.

Sampling of participants, random sampling would enable all participants an equal chance of being selected for the experiment.

Assignment of participants, random assignment of individuals for each group gives each participant an equal chance of being assigned to a particular group.

Possible outcome of the experiment would be the findings of the research.

Confounding variables are variables that are uncontrollable and may affect the outcome of the experiment.

No points were scored because the individual simply defined each term and did not apply the terms, as requested.

Score: 0/6

FINAL WORDS OF ADVICE

This book is designed to prepare you for the AP psychology exam, but it is also meant to instill a relationship between you and the material that will last a lifetime. In order to accomplish this, you must be able to not only memorize terminology and theories, but also apply and relate the information to everyday experiences.

Throughout this book, certain terms are in bold; their definitions are italicized, and examples are given that are meant to explain any difficult concepts. You will notice that there are "Nuts and Bolts" sections throughout each chapter as well. These sections are provided to help you remember the vocabulary and concepts, and to help you further understand each concept by tying in common knowledge and experiences with psychological theory. There are also AP Tip boxes to offer hints about multiple-choice or free-response questions that may appear on the exam.

A DIAGNOSTIC TEST

This diagnostic test will give you some indication of how you might score on the multiple-choice portion of the AP Psychology exam. (Of course, the exam changes every year, so it is never possible to predict a student's score with certainty.) This test will also pinpoint your strengths and weaknesses on the key content areas covered by the AP exam.

PSYCHOLOGY
Section I: Multiple-Choice Questions
Time—70 minutes
Number of Questions—100

MULTIPLE-CHOICE QUESTIONS

1. Multiple sclerosis (MS) is a degenerative disease of the nervous system associated with
    (A) an excess of dopamine in the synapse
    (B) a deficiency of serotonin
    (C) a degeneration of the axon terminal
    (D) a degeneration of the myelin coating the axon
    (E) overstimulation of the neuron

2. Evolutionary psychologists would most likely say which area of the brain was the last to form?
    (A) The midbrain
    (B) The hindbrain
    (C) The forebrain
    (D) The cerebellum
    (E) The amygdala

3. Grady was in a violent car accident that left him unable to comprehend spoken words. Which area of his brain was most likely damaged in the accident?
    (A) Broca's area
    (B) Motor cortex
    (C) Pons
    (D) Cerebellum
    (E) Wernicke's area

4. During neural transmission, the term "threshold" refers to
    (A) the point at which a neuron fires
    (B) the period of neural transmission, during which a neuron is waiting for stimulation
    (C) the time after a neuron has fired but before it can fire again
    (D) the period of excitation that a neuron must reach before it is able to fire
    (E) the period during which a neuron contains negatively charged ions that are waiting for stimulation

5. Moments after his mountain biking accident, Mark said that he felt fine and was experiencing no pain. Which neurotransmitter helped Mark cope with his pain?
    (A) Dopamine
    (B) Serotonin
    (C) Endorphins
    (D) GABA
    (E) Acetylcholine

6. A deficiency in which neurotransmitter has been linked to Parkinson's disease?
   (A) GABA
   (B) Dopamine
   (C) Acetylcholine
   (D) Endorphins
   (E) Serotonin

7. The left hemisphere of the brain is primarily responsible for controlling which of the following?
   (A) The right side of the body
   (B) The left side of the body
   (C) The creativity of a person
   (D) The body's circadian rhythm
   (E) The body's production of hormones

8. A researcher interested in understanding how gambling affects the brain shows study participants pictures of playing cards, dice, and casino chips while recording the participants' brain activity. Which of the following would be used to measure the amount of brain activity in response to these items?
   (A) Magnetic resonance imaging (MRI)
   (B) Computerized axial tomography (CAT) scan
   (C) Intracranial stimulation (ISC)
   (D) Positron emission tomography (PET) scan
   (E) Electrocardiograph (EKG)

9. Olivia is having trouble sleeping through the night, so her doctor prescribes medication to help her. Olivia is most likely taking medication that affects which hormone?
   (A) Testosterone
   (B) Melatonin
   (C) Serotonin
   (D) Cortisol
   (E) Dopamine

10. Which of the following receives information from neighboring neurons?
    (A) Dendrite
    (B) Synaptic cleft
    (C) Axon terminal
    (D) Axon
    (E) Myelin

11. Cognitive psychologists classify learning as
    (A) the overt action displayed by a subject
    (B) the mental processes that allow the subject to connect the stimulus with the response
    (C) a function necessary to the survival of a species
    (D) the unconscious thoughts produced by the id and regulated by the ego and the superego
    (E) the connection between a reflex and the response the reflex generates

12. Larry has successfully trained his dog to sit on command. If Larry wants to continue having his dog sit on command for the longest time possible, what type of reinforcement schedule should Larry keep the dog on?
    (A) Continuous reinforcement
    (B) Partial reinforcement
    (C) Fixed-interval
    (D) Fixed-ratio
    (E) Stimulus-response

13. Rhonda works at a car dealership. She receives a commission for each car she sells. The amount is proportional to the price of the car. What type of reinforcement schedule is Rhonda working on?
    (A) Fixed-interval
    (B) Fixed-ratio
    (C) Variable-interval
    (D) Variable-ratio
    (E) Primary reinforcement

14. Political advertisements often use classical conditioning to influence viewers' perceptions of a candidate. Each time a rival candidate is shown, a negative word that elicits a feeling of anger appears on the television screen. What is the conditioned stimulus in such ads?
    (A) The negative word
    (B) The rival candidate
    (C) The feeling of anger
    (D) The television advertisement
    (E) The number of times a commercial airs

15. According to the principles of positive punishment, the presentation of an aversive stimulus will have what effect on behavior?
    (A) It will decrease future incidences of the behavior.
    (B) It will increase future incidences of the behavior.
    (C) It will only be displayed under certain conditions.
    (D) Higher order conditioning will begin to limit the behavior.
    (E) It will have no effect on behavior.

16. In classical conditioning, the conditioned stimulus is
    (A) any previously unconditioned stimulus that elicited a response
    (B) any previously conditioned stimulus that has been associated with another stimulus
    (C) the result of a previously neutral stimulus being repeatedly successfully paired with an unconditioned stimulus
    (D) the result of the presentation of a primary reinforcer on a fixed-interval schedule
    (E) the result of observational learning

17. In an experiment, a dog is exposed to a series of electrical shocks that are painful but that will cause no permanent damage. According to the principles of learned helplessness, the dog will eventually
    (A) reduce the amount of shocks it receives if it learns to avoid the pain
    (B) experience a higher-order conditioning response to the shock itself
    (C) learn to avoid the shock by escaping from the situation
    (D) stop trying to escape the shock because its behavior has no control over the outcome
    (E) display what it has learned from watching other dogs receive the electrical shock

18. Which of the following is NOT considered a secondary reinforcer?
    (A) Food
    (B) Praise
    (C) Money
    (D) A promotion
    (E) An automobile

19. Dr. Knight believes that a person can overcome a fear of spiders if he watches the reaction of another person holding a spider. Dr. Knight most closely follows which psychological perspective?
    (A) Psychobiological
    (B) Psychodynamic
    (C) Humanistic-existential
    (D) Behavioral
    (E) Drive-reduction

20. Reiko decides not to cheat on a test because she is fearful that if she is caught she will be sent to detention. According to Lawrence Kohlberg, Reiko is functioning at what level of morality?
    (A) Preconventional
    (B) Conventional
    (C) Postconventional
    (D) Preoperational
    (E) Concrete

GO ON TO NEXT PAGE

21. Jerry is a freshman in high school and has very few friends. He recently joined the swimming team, but then quit because he thought the coach was mean. Jerry decided to audition for the school play instead. According to Erik Erikson, what psychosocial stage of development is Jerry currently experiencing?
    (A) Trust versus mistrust
    (B) Industry versus inferiority
    (C) Intimacy versus isolation
    (D) Identity versus role confusion
    (E) Generativity versus stagnation

22. Which of the following best illustrates Jean Piaget's concept of conservation?
    (A) Gwen wants to give her brother a doll for his birthday because she likes dolls.
    (B) Mark thinks the sky is crying every time it rains.
    (C) Andrea believes that if everyone would recycle, the planet would be a better place.
    (D) Heather closes her eyes and sits in the middle of the room during a game of hide-and-seek.
    (E) There are three pieces of pizza left. Six-year-old Billy is still hungry. Billy takes two pieces and gives the remaining piece to his three-year-old brother. To convince his brother that they have the same amount of pizza, Billy cuts his brother's piece of pizza into two slices.

23. Lawrence Kohlberg conducted research on the moral development of individuals. He interviewed the same subjects every three years until they were 18 years old. Kohlberg was using what type of research methodology?
    (A) Cross-sectional
    (B) Longitudinal
    (C) Experimental
    (D) Correlational
    (E) Stratified

24. Any agent that may delay or harm the development of a fetus is known as a(n)
    (A) teratogen
    (B) impairment
    (C) noxious substance
    (D) critical period
    (E) depressant

25. Which psychologist believed that children are capable of higher cognitive tasks if they are guided by an adult, also known as the zone of proximal development?
    (A) Jean Piaget
    (B) Lawrence Kohlberg
    (C) Noam Chomsky
    (D) Lev Vygotsky
    (E) Howard Gardner

26. When asked to decide which toy he wanted to play with, five-year-old Harrison pointed to a truck. When asked why, he replied, "Because my mommy says that big boys don't play with dolls!" This is an example of the environmental impact parenting has on
    (A) maturation
    (B) gender roles
    (C) conservation
    (D) egocentrism
    (E) object permanence

27. Dr. Tallway believes that children learn language based on reinforcement they receive. Which psychologist would most likely agree with Dr. Tallway?
    (A) Howard Gardner
    (B) Jean Piaget
    (C) B.F. Skinner
    (D) L.L. Thurstone
    (E) Noam Chomsky

28. Dr. Cleveland is studying the cognitive development of males and females. She gives subjects an assortment of puzzles and allows them to engage in "free-play" for one hour. Study results show that boys over the age of 12 prefer puzzles that have more than 500 pieces, whereas girls under the age of five prefer puzzles that have only ten pieces. Dr. Cleveland used which type of sampling to conduct her experiment?
    (A) Longitudinal study
    (B) Stratified sample
    (C) Case study
    (D) Correlational study
    (E) Kinship study

29. Derek goes to a dealership to purchase a new car. He tells the dealer that he is only interested in purchasing a blue car, so the first step is to eliminate all cars that are not blue. Derek is using which problem-solving strategy to help him choose a car?
    (A) Representativeness heuristic
    (B) Means-end heuristic
    (C) Availability heuristic
    (D) Central route to persuasion
    (E) Conformity

30. While packing for vacation, George realizes to his frustration that he doesn't have a suitcase. His older sister tells him to use an empty garbage bag instead. George's inability to think of using a garbage bag in this manner is due to
    (A) functional fixedness
    (B) insight
    (C) incubation
    (D) divergent creativity
    (E) object permanence

31. Units such as "ed" or "pre" are examples of the smallest unit of language that has meaning, also known as
    (A) a phoneme
    (B) a morpheme
    (C) syntax
    (D) semantics
    (E) displacement

32. Joan is a highly skilled painter who has been compared to master artists such as Picasso. Her paintings are full of vivid colors and sharp lines that have no direct pattern. Which type of creativity does Joan display?
    (A) Convergent
    (B) Simplistic
    (C) Divergent
    (D) Displacement
    (E) Sublimation

33. Samantha is attempting to solve a lengthy math problem on a test. Which problem-solving strategy would most likely be beneficial to her?
    (A) An algorithm
    (B) A heuristic
    (C) A prototype
    (D) A concept
    (E) An alternate

34. Which of the following best demonstrates the Sapir-Whorf hypothesis of language?
    (A) Infants around the world begin to babble at about the same age.
    (B) Joe is a three-year-old toddler who refers to all four-legged animals as "doggies."
    (C) Clare's parents clap and cheer for her each time she says a word correctly.
    (D) Frank calls his soft-drink "soda," but his friend who lives in another state calls it "pop."
    (E) Gloria is 14 months old and has a vocabulary of approximately 20 words.

35. Jan was at a cookout when she noticed three bright lights in the sky. After staring at the bright lights, she noted that they resembled a triangle. Which Gestalt principle best explains why Jan saw a triangle?
    (A) Closure
    (B) Figure-ground
    (C) Proximity
    (D) Similarity
    (E) Selective attention

GO ON TO NEXT PAGE

36. The concept of top-down processing is best illustrated by which of the following?
   (A) A puzzle upside down without looking at the picture
   (B) The apparent movement of a stationary point of light in a dark room
   (C) A picture of your favorite actor/actress
   (D) A scoreboard displaying fireworks after a team hits a homerun
   (E) Being unable to remember your own phone number after receiving a new one

37. Dr. Randall is using a list of words to conduct research on the effect sleep has on memory retention. The less time a subject spends in REM sleep, the more errors she makes in recalling the list of words, whereas if the subject spends more time in REM sleep, she will make fewer errors recalling the list. Dr. Randall concludes that REM sleep and memory retention have
   (A) a negative correlation
   (B) a positive correlation
   (C) no correlation
   (D) a skewed distribution
   (E) a test-retest

38. Which of the following correlation coefficients indicates the strongest relationship between two variables?
   (A) +0.56
   (B) +0.78
   (C) -0.88
   (D) -0.72
   (E) -0.10

39. For his psychology research methods class, Tim is conducting an experiment on the effects of chocolate on mathematical ability. The first study group receives ten pieces of chocolate and then takes a math test. The second group receives no chocolate before taking the same test. After the study, Tim concludes that chocolate increases mathematical ability. Identify the independent variable in Tim's study.
   (A) The score on the math test
   (B) Chocolate
   (C) The time of day
   (D) The highest math class completed
   (E) The assignment of participants to experimental groups

40. A confounding variable is
   (A) what is being measured in an experiment
   (B) any variable that changes during an experiment
   (C) a way of identifying potential experimenter bias
   (D) any variable that cannot be controlled by the experimenter
   (E) a way of measuring the relationship between two variables

41. In order to avoid experimenter bias, it is important for an experiment to be conducted with which of the following types of procedures?
   (A) Placebo
   (B) Debriefing
   (C) Deception
   (D) Transparency
   (E) Double-blind

42. According to APA ethical guidelines, psychologists conducting experiments must obtain informed consent by human subjects, treat subjects with respect and concern, protect subjects from potential physical or psychological harm, allow subjects to abandon the experiment at any time, and
    (A) expose the subjects to deception to ensure accurate data
    (B) allow subjects to determine the assignment groups
    (C) debrief subjects after the experiment is completed
    (D) allow subjects to deceive the experimenter
    (E) expose all subjects to the same experimental conditions

43. A recent survey of psychology students indicated that 85 percent of respondents felt that psychology was the most beneficial class they had taken in college. This type of statistical result is known as
    (A) inferential statistics
    (B) deceptive statistics
    (C) hindsight bias
    (D) dependable statistics
    (E) descriptive statistics

44. Dr. Paulson, a social psychologist, is interested in the behavioral patterns of subjects standing in line to purchase lunch. Which method of research should Dr. Paulson use to conduct his study?
    (A) Survey
    (B) Case study
    (C) Inferential statistics
    (D) Naturalistic observation
    (E) Double-blind procedure

45. Jonas is taking a placement test for his honors English class. According to the honors English teacher, students who perform well on the test will perform well in class. The placement test is therefore said to have good
    (A) criterion validity
    (B) construct accuracy
    (C) standardization
    (D) test-retest
    (E) face validity

46. Howard Gardner's research on multiple intelligences states that
    (A) intelligence is genetically inherited
    (B) subjects don't lose all of their cognitive abilities after a traumatic brain injury
    (C) intelligent people are more likely to succeed in all areas of life
    (D) as a person ages, fluid intelligence increases
    (E) once a person is labeled gifted he or she begins to display higher cognitive functioning

47. Horace is shown a photograph and instructed to construct a plausible story about the subject of the photograph. Horace is most likely taking the
    (A) Rorschach Inkblot Test
    (B) Thematic Apperception Test (TAT)
    (C) Minnesota Multiphasic Personality Inventory (MMPI)
    (D) Stanford-Binet Intelligence Scale version 3 (SB3)
    (E) Wechsler Adult Intelligence Scale (WAIS)

48. According to the DSM-IV-TR, a person is considered mentally retarded if he has an IQ below
    (A) 50
    (B) 100
    (C) 85
    (D) 70
    (E) 115

GO ON TO NEXT PAGE

49. The Advanced Placement Psychology exam is designed to predict how well a high school student would have done in an introductory psychology course in college. Because studies have shown that students who score above a 3 on the exam would have passed a college psychology class, the exam is said to contain high
    (A) construct validity
    (B) criterion validity
    (C) standardization
    (D) face-validity
    (E) test-retest

50. The three measures of central tendency are
    (A) mean, median, and mode
    (B) validity, reliability, and standardization
    (C) mean, reliability, and predictability
    (D) marketability, test-retest validity, and skewed distribution
    (E) normal curve, validity, and reliability

51. Which of the following best illustrates the concept of conformity?
    (A) Jared is punctual for his first class of the day because he knows that he will get detention if he's not there on time.
    (B) Mr. Lowe asks Erica to turn in her homework at the end of the hour.
    (C) Kyle faces forward while riding on an elevator and avoids eye contact with the other passengers.
    (D) Gloria gives an answer when called on during biology class.
    (E) David follows a recipe when making his favorite cookies.

52. In Stanley Milgram's classic study on obedience, approximately what percentage of participants administered the maximum voltage?
    (A) 50 percent
    (B) 30 percent
    (C) 90 percent
    (D) 65 percent
    (E) 85 percent

53. According to evolutionary psychologists, aggression occurs because
    (A) of the unconscious desires resulting from a weak ego
    (B) it serves a purpose in advancing the survival potential of a species
    (C) humans prefer order to chaos and follow orders given by authority figures
    (D) of the desire for a person to reach self-actualization
    (E) it is modeled after observing the behavior of others

54. In a classic experiment, Albert Bandura concluded that
    (A) a child will model aggressive acts if he or she sees them performed by adults
    (B) aggression is the result of a conflict between two opposing thoughts
    (C) a person will attribute the failure of others to dispositional factors
    (D) aggression that is rewarded will continue
    (E) unconscious thoughts and desires influence our daily lives

55. On her way to school, Carley notices that a car is stuck in a ditch. However, she does not stop to see if anyone in the car is in need of assistance. According to studies conducted on bystander intervention, Carley would be more likely to stop if she
    (A) were late to her appointment
    (B) noticed that others were stopping to offer assistance
    (C) had other people in her car with her
    (D) were in a good mood
    (E) had recently broken up with her boyfriend

56. After failing his psychology test, Don told his teacher that he thought the test was unfair because it included questions that had been covered in previous chapters. According to social psychologists, Don is displaying
    (A) the fundamental attribution error (FAE)
    (B) self-efficacy error (SEE)
    (C) actor-observer bias
    (D) self-handicapping
    (E) self-serving bias

57. Hiroto does not like working in a group because he feels that the other group members are lazy and unmotivated, whereas he is motivated to obtain a passing grade. According to social psychologists, Hiroto is displaying
    (A) the actor-observer bias
    (B) the self-efficacy effect
    (C) a fundamental attribution error
    (D) group polarization
    (E) groupthink

58. The tendency to attribute one's actions to situational factors while attributing another's actions to dispositional factors is known as
    (A) social loafing
    (B) an actor-observer bias
    (C) a fundamental attribution error
    (D) a self-serving bias
    (E) social facilitation

59. A group of high school students took part in an experiment designed to measure the influence that in-group bias has on group decision making. All the students knew they were being observed for this experiment and therefore did not display in-group bias. The resulting effect of group members' changing their behaviors because they were participating in an experiment is known as
    (A) social facilitation
    (B) groupthink
    (C) deindividuation
    (D) the Hawthorne effect
    (E) self-serving bias

60. At a school assembly, Rick observed students throwing paper airplanes at the school principal. According to the theory of deindividuation,
    (A) Rick is less likely to throw a paper airplane
    (B) Rick would be more likely to throw a paper airplane
    (C) students who can throw farther would be more likely to participate
    (D) Rick is less likely to offer help in identifying the students who threw the airplanes if he is in a good mood
    (E) students are more likely to attribute their actions to their own weak superegos

61. When they first met, Ron didn't like Tyler very much. However, after they had spent an entire year in the same study group, the two became close friends. Which social psychology theory best explains this friendship?
    (A) The mere-exposure effect
    (B) The Hawthorne effect
    (C) The fundamental attribution error
    (D) Self-serving bias
    (E) Confirmation bias

62. Andy believes that all athletes are unintelligent and should not be allowed to take advanced placement classes. Andy's beliefs are an example of
    (A) the actor-observer bias
    (B) the Pygmalion effect
    (C) the mere-exposure effect
    (D) a stereotype
    (E) the just-world hypothesis

63. The belief that behavior is determined by a person's choices based on their perceptions about the world is most clearly supported by what approach?
    (A) Behavioral
    (B) Psychodynamic
    (C) Humanistic
    (D) Cognitive
    (E) Evolutionary

GO ON TO NEXT PAGE

64. Dogs have a tendency to become aggressive when other dogs enter their territory. Which psychological approach would account for this aggression as a sign of protection and survival?
(A) Behavioral
(B) Psychodynamic
(C) Humanistic
(D) Cognitive
(E) Evolutionary

65. When Thomas first put on his glasses, he complained that they bothered his nose. Throughout the day, he complained less and less, and finally stated that he had gotten used to them. Thomas was not bothered as much by his glasses because of
(A) sensory adaptation
(B) transduction
(C) Weber's law
(D) perception
(E) selective attention

66. Which of the following specialized cells are located in the retina and detect different wavelengths of light?
(A) Cilia
(B) Olfactory receptor cells
(C) Photoreceptors
(D) Bipolar cells
(E) Ganglion cells

67. Jenny was asked to write a paper on how the brain and the nervous system influence human behavior. Jenny would best be served by interviewing a
(A) biological psychologist
(B) cognitive psychologist
(C) personality psychologist
(D) developmental psychologist
(E) psychodynamic psychologist

68. Scott complained that he can never hear his teacher during lectures. Scott's teacher and his parents met and determined that Scott did not have a hearing deficit, but rather a lack of interest in the class. This is referred to as
(A) sensitivity
(B) response criterion
(C) Weber's law
(D) sensory adaptation
(E) accommodation processing

69. Lani's music teacher is amazed at how well Lani can identify a variety of musical notes. Lani's ability to differentiate among notes is referred to as
(A) accommodation
(B) difference threshold
(C) selective attention
(D) perceptual set
(E) transduction

70. Paradoxical sleep is referred to as
(A) NREM stage 1
(B) NREM stage 2
(C) NREM stage 4
(D) REM sleep
(E) sleep apnea

71. Nightmares occur during _____ sleep, and night terrors occur during _____ sleep.
(A) REM; NREM stage 1
(B) REM; NREM stage 2
(C) NREM stage 4; REM
(D) REM; NREM stage 4
(E) NREM stage 3; NREM stage 4

72. Addictive drugs affect the "pleasure center" area of the brain. Which neurotransmitter is associated with that part of the brain?
(A) Endorphins
(B) Dopamine
(C) GABA
(D) Glutamate
(E) Serotonin

73. Homeostasis is
    (A) the detection of energy from the environment
    (B) a diminished sensitivity to an unchanging stimulus
    (C) the tendency to maintain and regulate an internal bodily state
    (D) a fixed and innate behavior
    (E) the amount of arousal needed to enhance performance

74. At a dance, Jon complained that he was bored and wanted to find somewhere more interesting to go. Which theory of motivation would explain Jon's desire to go elsewhere?
    (A) The drive-reduction theory
    (B) The instinct theory
    (C) The hierarchy of needs
    (D) Competence motivation
    (E) The arousal theory

75. According to the drive-reduction theory, a _____ produces a psychological state referred to as a

    _____.
    (A) need; drive
    (B) drive; need
    (C) sensation; perception
    (D) perception; sensation
    (E) thirst; drink

76. Brandon wasn't motivated to study for the AP psychology exam. His mom intervened and promised Brandon a new car if he could earn a 5 on the exam. Suddenly, Brandon was motivated to study. The promise of a car is an example of which type of motivation?
    (A) Drive-reduction motivation
    (B) Intrinsic motivation
    (C) Extrinsic motivation
    (D) Achievement motivation
    (E) Instinct theory of motivation

77. Jody was involved in a serious car accident and suffered a severed spinal cord. Which theory of emotion would suggest that Jody will not be able to experience emotions as a result of no physiological input?
    (A) The Cannon-Bard theory of emotion
    (B) The two-factor theory of emotion
    (C) The cognitive-mediational theory of emotion
    (D) The James-Lange theory of emotion
    (E) The facial feedback hypothesis

78. As two potential applicants wait for a job interview, one tells the other how nervous she is, while the second responds by saying that he is excited. These differing responses could be explained through which theory of emotion?
    (A) James-Lange
    (B) Cannon-Bard
    (C) Facial feedback hypothesis
    (D) Weber's law
    (E) Cognitive appraisal

79. Jill has to choose between two classes she really doesn't want to take. Which type of conflict is Jill experiencing?
    (A) Approach-approach
    (B) Avoidance-avoidance
    (C) Approach-avoidance
    (D) Alternative-alternative
    (E) Alternative-avoidance

80. According to Sigmund Freud, the id operates according to the _____ principle and the ego operates according to the _____ principle.
    (A) libido; thanatos
    (B) eros; libido
    (C) pleasure; reality
    (D) reality; pleasure
    (E) eros; thanatos

GO ON TO NEXT PAGE

81. Julie is having a hard time recalling the events that surrounded her childhood abuse. Her psychoanalyst believes that Julie is utilizing which defense mechanism?
    (A) Rationalization
    (B) Projection
    (C) Regression
    (D) Repression
    (E) Compensation

82. Who suggested that archetypes are stored in the collective unconscious?
    (A) Carl Jung
    (B) Sigmund Freud
    (C) B.F. Skinner
    (D) Karen Horney
    (E) Alfred Adler

83. A factor analysis identifies
    (A) a cluster of traits that predict one another
    (B) the average of a distribution
    (C) the middle number within a distribution
    (D) the most frequently occurring number in a distribution
    (E) biological predispositions to certain traits and averages

84. David's parents only express their support for David's activities when he is successful. When David is not successful, his parents seem distant and unaffectionate. David's parents are expressing
    (A) unconditional positive regard
    (B) sympathetic reasoning
    (C) conditional positive regard
    (D) selective attention
    (E) authoritative parenting

85. According to the diathesis-stress model, psychological disorders develop because of the type and combination of stress in addition to a person's
    (A) explanatory style
    (B) genetic predisposition
    (C) cognitive ability
    (D) maladaptive behavior
    (E) sense of right and wrong

86. Recently Dennis has shown symptoms that include fatigue, apprehension, and anxiety in a variety of different situations. These symptoms most likely describe
    (A) a mood disorder
    (B) an obsessive-compulsive disorder
    (C) a dissociative disorder
    (D) paranoid schizophrenia
    (E) a generalized anxiety disorder

87. After Tim's son died, Tim experienced a period in which he lost the ability to walk. A doctor would most likely identify this as
    (A) bipolar disorder
    (B) phobia
    (C) conversion disorder
    (D) hypochondriasis
    (E) generalized anxiety disorder

88. Jon's friends are concerned about his behavior. They all agree that Jon has been acting oddly. He doesn't show an interest in any of the activities that he previously enjoyed and he frequently complains of being tired. Jon still attends school and work, but doesn't make a lot of effort. Jon may be experiencing
    (A) a major depressive disorder
    (B) generalized anxiety disorder
    (C) obsessive-compulsive disorder
    (D) a dysthymic disorder
    (E) a cyclothymic disorder

89. During the winter months, Tony doesn't feel like himself. He feels tired, lacks interest in various activities, and loses weight. During the summer months, Tony doesn't feel this way. Tony would most likely be diagnosed with a(n)
    (A) obsessive-compulsive disorder
    (B) posttraumatic stress disorder
    (C) seasonal affective disorder
    (D) conversion disorder
    (E) cyclothymic disorder

90. Neologisms are
    (A) words used by schizophrenics that have meaning only to them
    (B) false beliefs that are characterized as delusions
    (C) false sensory images
    (D) mixed-up words in a sentence
    (E) a person's thoughts of paranoia and a belief that everyone is out to get them

91. The abuse of cocaine could result in symptoms that resemble
    (A) dissociative disorders
    (B) schizophrenia
    (C) a conversion disorder
    (D) an obsessive-compulsive disorder
    (E) anxiety disorders

92. Jill was diagnosed with autism early in her life. Recently, her doctors noticed that she has developed a habit of memorizing numbers in the phonebook. Jill may be exhibiting
    (A) catatonic schizophrenia
    (B) a mood disorder
    (C) a dissociative disorder
    (D) Asperger's disorder
    (E) a bipolar disorder

93. Danny's psychiatrist informed Danny that in his most recent session he exhibited several distinct and separate personalities. Danny's psychiatrist has diagnosed him with
    (A) paranoid schizophrenia
    (B) residual schizophrenia
    (C) a dissociative identity disorder
    (D) dissociative fugue
    (E) a generalized anxiety disorder

94. In dream interpretation, a psychoanalyst would be most interested in which part of a person's dream?
    (A) Manifest content
    (B) Latent content
    (C) Any underlying determinants
    (D) Freudian slips
    (E) Guilt content

95. Juan realized that he directed most of his therapy session. Which therapeutic approach stresses that the patient should direct the session?
    (A) Psychoanalytic
    (B) Humanistic
    (C) Behavioral
    (D) Biomedical
    (E) Social-cognitive

96. June was told by her therapist that if she wanted to conquer her fear of snakes, she would have to face her fear. When June inquired how, the therapist told her that gradually she would have to associate her fear of snakes with a more pleasant state of mind when a snake was present. This process is referred to as
    (A) flooding
    (B) dream interpretation
    (C) token economy
    (D) systematic desensitization
    (E) empathy

97. Which factor would a cognitive therapist identify as an explanation for depression?
    (A) Feelings of worthlessness
    (B) Unconscious conflicts
    (C) Repeated failures resulting in learned helplessness
    (D) Incongruence experienced within the self-concept
    (E) Environmental factors outside the individual's control

98. When first developed, Tardive dyskinesia was a possible side effect associated with
    (A) antidepressant medications
    (B) antianxiety medications
    (C) psychosurgery
    (D) ECT
    (E) antipsychotic medications

99. Xanax has been prescribed to treat
    (A) bipolar disorder
    (B) major depression
    (C) seasonal affective disorder
    (D) agoraphobia
    (E) specific phobias

GO ON TO NEXT PAGE

100. Juanita is concerned that she might not be able to afford therapy. She is also concerned about being in a one-on-one setting with a therapist. Which type of therapy would be most advantageous for Juanita?

(A) Group therapy
(B) Client-centered therapy
(C) Psychoanalysis
(D) Rational emotive therapy
(E) ECT

STOP

END OF SECTION I

IF YOU FINISH BEFORE TIME IS CALLED, YOU MAY CHECK YOUR WORK ON THIS SECTION. DO NOT GO ON TO SECTION II UNTIL YOU ARE TOLD TO DO SO.

PSYCHOLOGY
Section II
Time: 50 minutes

1. In an effort to improve academic performance, administrators at Central High School conducted a pilot study that would pay students each time they successfully passed a district-wide standardized test.

   Twenty students—five from each grade—were assigned to the pilot study and divided into two groups. After two standardized tests were administered, the results showed that students who received money for passing tests scored significantly higher on all tests than those students who did not receive money. Administrators concluded that offering money for passing tests increased student performance.
   a. In relation to the study described above, identify each of the following:
      - Identify the independent and dependent variables.
      - Identify the reinforcement schedule that was implemented.
      - Identify one potential flaw in the study, and explain how you would correct it.
   b. In relation to student performance, explain how each of the following might be affected by paying students for academic success.
      - Intrinsic motivation
      - Learned helplessness
      - Expectancy effect (Pygmalion effect)

2. What a person experiences depends largely on sensation.
   a. Identify the sensory receptors and locations for each of the following senses:
      - Vision
      - Audition
      - Gustation
      - Olfaction
      - Touch
      - Kinesthetic
      - Vestibular
   b. Explain how the following terms affect the process of sensation.
      - Perceptual set
      - Retinal disparity
      - Relative size

END OF EXAMINATION

ANSWERS FOR MULTIPLE-CHOICE QUESTIONS

Using the table below, score your test.

Determine how many questions you answered correctly and how many you answered incorrectly. You will find explanations of the answers on the following pages.

1. D	2. C	3. E	4. D	5. C
6. B	7. A	8. D	9. B	10. A
11. B	12. B	13. D	14. B	15. A
16. C	17. D	18. A	19. D	20. A
21. D	22. E	23. B	24. A	25. D
26. B	27. C	28. B	29. C	30. A
31. B	32. C	33. A	34. D	35. A
36. C	37. B	38. C	39. B	40. D
41. E	42. C	43. E	44. D	45. A
46. B	47. B	48. D	49. B	50. A
51. C	52. D	53. B	54. A	55. D
56. E	57. C	58. B	59. D	60. B
61. A	62. D	63. C	64. E	65. A
66. C	67. A	68. B	69. B	70. D
71. D	72. B	73. C	74. E	75. A
76. C	77. D	78. E	79. B	80. C
81. D	82. A	83. A	84. C	85. B
86. E	87. C	88. D	89. C	90. A
91. B	92. D	93. C	94. B	95. B
96. D	97. A	98. E	99. D	100. A

1. Answer: D. The myelin covers and protects the axon (specifically, white matter contained in the brain and spinal cord) and the information stored inside. Multiple sclerosis (MS) causes the myelin to degenerate, which results in physical and cognitive impairment (*Psychology*, 8th ed. pp. 63, 66–67/9th ed. pp. 67–68).

2. Answer: C. The "newest" and most advanced part of the human brain is the forebrain, which is seen in cognitively advanced species. The forebrain houses areas of the brain associated with critical thinking skills, planning, and inhibitions, all within the prefrontal cortex. In addition, the forebrain contains such areas as the cerebrum (all the lobes) and the limbic system (*Psychology*, 8th ed. pp. 79–80/9th ed. pp. 82–83).

3. Answer: E. Wernicke's area is responsible for the comprehension of speech (turning words into thoughts), whereas Broca's area is responsible for the production of speech (turning thoughts into words) (*Psychology*, 8th ed. pp. 86–87/9th ed. pp. 89–90).

4. Answer: D. For a neuron to "fire" it must reach a certain level of excitation (–55mV). If a neuron does not reach the threshold it will not "fire" or send an electrochemical impulse down the

axon to the axon terminal, which releases neurotransmitters (*Psychology*, 8th ed. pp. 62–64/9th ed. pp. 66–67).

5.   Answer: C. Endorphins are peptides and the body's natural painkillers. They are released to assist the body in fighting off the sensation of pain (*Psychology*, 8th ed. p. 98/9th ed. pp. 101–102).

6.   Answer: B. A dopamine deficiency has been linked to Parkinson's disease, whereas an excess of dopamine has been linked to schizophrenia. A deficiency of acetylcholine is associated with Alzheimer's disease and paralysis of the muscles, whereas an excess produces convulsions (being unable to control the shaking and contraction of muscle fibers). A serotonin deficiency has been linked to depression. A deficiency in GABA has been implicated in a variety of anxiety-based disorders (*Psychology*, 8th ed. p. 97/9th ed. pp. 100–101).

7.   Answer: A. The brain's left hemisphere is responsible for controlling functions on the right side of the body. The left hemisphere is also implicated in speech production, logic, and mathematical analysis. The right hemisphere is responsible for controlling functions of the left side of the body, as well as for both recognition of faces and creativity (*Psychology*, 8th ed. p. 88/9th ed. pp. 91–94).

8.   Answer: D. A PET scan involves the injection of a small amount of a radioactive substance which, when injected into the body, is processed by the brain. The area responsible for a given task or thought then becomes active. Researchers use PET scans to measure which areas of the brain are responsible for cognitive functioning for given tasks. Note that a fMRI also measures cognitive functioning; however, because that was not an option here, the answer would have to be a PET scan (*Psychology*, 8th ed. p. 72/9th ed. p. 74).

9.   Answer: B. Melatonin is a hormone produced by the pineal gland, located within the brain. The amount of melatonin the brain produces increases as exterior light begins to decrease. Melatonin is one hormone responsible for making human beings sleepy (*Psychology*, 8th ed. p. 342/9th ed. p. 344).

10. Answer: A. The dendrite receives information in the form of neurotransmitters from the adjacent axon terminal (*Psychology*, 8th ed. p. 62/9th ed. p. 66).

11. Answer: B. Cognitive psychologists believe that a mental representation between a stimulus and its response is what allows the subject to predict and perform the desired behavior needed for a response to occur (*Psychology*, 8th ed. p. 5/9th ed. pp. 5–6).

12. Answer: B. Partial reinforcement schedules are important for establishing a behavior because of the unpredictability of the reward. If a reward is given continuously the person or animal will have a difficult time making the connection between the

reward and which behavior will be rewarded. It must also be noted that partial reinforcement is less susceptible to extinction (*Psychology*, 8th ed. pp. 211–214/9th ed. p. 215).

13. Answer: D. A variable-ratio schedule of reinforcement occurs when an operant is reinforced after a behavior is performed a varying number of times. Since Rhonda's check is directly related to the number of cars she sells, her reinforcement (being paid) is contingent upon the number of cars she sells, and the reinforcement is therefore on a variable-ratio schedule (*Psychology*, 8th ed. p. 212/9th ed. p. 214).

14. Answer: B. A conditioned stimulus is established when a neutral stimulus is repeatedly paired with a unconditioned (unlearned) stimulus. The unlearned stimulus produces an unlearned response (in this case, the negative word elicits anger), and after several pairings the conditioned stimulus (the rival candidate) produces the conditioned response (anger). After repeated exposure to the advertisement, viewers will, in theory, associate anger with the rival candidate and consequently view the candidate unfavorably (*Psychology*, 8th ed. p. 198/9th ed. p. 201).

15. Answer: A. Punishments decrease behavior, while reinforcers increase behavior. Positive means that a stimulus is added, whereas negative implies that a stimulus is removed. Positive punishment implies that an aversive stimulus is added, and the resulting effect will be a decrease in behavior (*Psychology*, 8th ed. pp. 215–217/9th ed. pp. 217–218).

16. Answer: C. After repeatedly pairing an unconditioned (unlearned) stimulus that produces an unconditioned (unlearned) response with a neutral stimulus, the neutral stimulus will become the conditioned (learned) stimulus, which evokes a conditioned (learned) response (*Psychology*, 8th ed. p. 198/9th ed. p. 201).

17. Answer: D. Learned helplessness occurs when subjects believe that no matter what actions they take, they cannot change the outcome. Believing that the outcome is inevitable, the subject simply gives up and succumbs to it (*Psychology*, 8th ed. pp. 221–223/9th ed. pp. 223–224).

18. Answer: A. Secondary reinforcers are not necessary for survival, but are enjoyable due to the association with a primary reinforcer (things that *are* necessary for survival). Food is clearly a primary reinforcer, as human beings need it to survive (*Psychology*, 8th ed. p. 211/9th ed. p. 213).

19. Answer: D. Behavioral psychologists study people's overt actions. By watching another person's reaction to a spider, the subject will see the overt actions or behavior of that person while encountering the feared object (*Psychology*, 8th ed. pp. 19–20/9th ed. pp. 21–22).

20. Answer: A. Preconventional morality is when a person bases decisions on what is right and wrong, as well as on the hedonistic principle (doing what benefits that person directly). In this case, Reiko is basing her decision on gaining a reward or avoiding a punishment (*Psychology*, 8th ed. pp. 499–500/9th ed. p. 506).

21. Answer: D. During the adolescent years, individuals try to find an identity, including where they belong in society. Adolescents may change peer groups in an effort to find the group they feel they can identify most closely with (*Psychology*, 8th ed. p. 485/9th ed. p. 490).

22. Answer: E. According to Jean Piaget's stage theory on cognitive development, conservation occurs when the child understands that a change in mass does not necessarily mean a change in overall volume. The child who understands the principle of conservation realizes that liquid in a short, fat glass that is poured into a tall, skinny glass retains the same volume (*Psychology*, 8th ed. p. 471/9th ed. p. 476).

23. Answer: B. A longitudinal study is used to observe a group of individuals over a long period of time. Tests are typically given to individuals before the experiment starts, then periodically throughout the experiment, which usually lasts for many years *Psychology*, 8th ed. pp. 393–395/9th ed. pp. 400–402).

24. Answer: A. A teratogen is any agent that may negatively affect the fetus. These agents may cause severe physical and/or cognitive delays or impairments (*Psychology*, 8th ed. pp. 460–461/9th ed. p. 469).

25. Answer: D. Lev Vygotsky thought that Piaget's stages of development did not take into account a child observing or directly working with another, older person. By watching such a person engaged in a task, the child is more likely to achieve the task earlier than the timeframe Piaget had proposed (*this material does not appear in the 8th ed. text*/9th ed. pp. 481–482).

26. Answer: B. Gender roles are influenced by numerous factors: parents, the media, and other environmental elements (*Psychology*, 8th ed. pp. 490–492/9th ed. pp. 496-498).

27. Answer: C. B. F. Skinner believed that all behavior, whether related to language or not, is determined by the reinforcement the individual receives Therefore, learning a language is the direct result of positive reinforcement from others (*Psychology*, 8th ed. pp. 315–316/9th ed. pp. 320–321).

28. Answer: B. A stratified sample uses all segments (age and gender) of the population for the experiment. The reason for using a stratified sample is to reach a more general conclusion that can be applied to all segments of the population (*this material does not appear in either textbook edition*).

29. Answer: C. Availability heuristics is a problem-solving strategy that relies on the most current or easily accessible information pertaining to the problem (*Psychology*, 8th ed. pp. 294–295/9th ed. p. 299).

30. Answer: A. Functional fixedness hinders problem solving because it doesn't allow the individual to think of using an object for anything other than its original purpose (*Psychology*, 8th ed. pp. 290–300/9th ed. p. 305).

31. Answer: B. The smallest unit of language that has meaning is the morpheme. Phonemes are the basic sounds of language and letters (*Psychology*, 8th ed. pp. 310–311/9th ed. p. 315).

32. Answer: C. Divergent creativity allows a person to see multiple angles or approaches when solving a problem or considering a situation. This directly contradicts with convergent creativity in that the latter uses one solution or approach to solve a problem (*Psychology*, 8th ed. pp. 396–397/9th ed. p. 403).

33. Answer: A. An algorithm is a systematic or step-by-step approach to solving a problem. Algorithms take longer when used to solve a problem, but they do guarantee the correct solution to the problem (*Psychology*, 8th ed. pp. 290–291/9th ed. pp. 295–296).

34. Answer: D. According to the Sapir-Whorf hypothesis, language is relative to the culture a person lives in. Environment determines each person's language. If a person lives in a culture that is dependent on time (such as the United States), he will know numerous words for time (*Psychology*, 8th ed. pp. 320–321/9th ed. pp. 325–326).

35. Answer: A. The Gestalt theory of closure states that the human mind fills in any gaps, based primarily on previous experience. The rationale is that human beings understand whole objects clearer than we understand individual parts (*Psychology*, 8th ed. p. 164/9th ed. p. 168).

36. Answer: C. Top-down processing is a Gestalt approach to solving a problem that relies on prior knowledge acquired through experience. This prior knowledge allows a person to have an expectation about what the final product will look like, thereby helping him or her to piece together the individual parts (*Psychology*, 8th ed. pp. 176–177/9th ed. pp. 179–180).

37. Answer: B. A positive correlation occurs when the variables move in the same direction. For example, if the number of hours of sleep increases, so does a person's overall grade point average (*Psychology*, 8th ed. p. 51/9th ed. p. 54).

38. Answer: C. The correlation coefficient is a number that shows the strength between two variables. The closer the number is to the absolute value of one, the stronger the relationship between those variables (*Psychology*, 8th ed. pp. 51–52/9th ed. p. 54).

39. Answer: B. The independent variable is what is being manipulated in the study—in this case, chocolate. The dependent variable is what the study is attempting to measure—in this case, mathematical ability (*Psychology*, 8th ed. p. 41/9th ed. p. 43).

40. Answer: D. A confounding variable is any variable that cannot be controlled for in an experiment and that may affect the outcome of the experiment (*Psychology*, 8th ed. p. 41/9th ed. p. 43).

41. Answer: E. In a double-blind study neither the researchers nor the participants know which treatment participants are receiving, so researcher bias can't influence the outcome of the study (*Psychology*, 8th ed. p. 43/9th ed. p. 45).

42. Answer: C. Debriefing subjects after an experiment is important for any research. It is important to inform the participants what the true goal of the study was (*Psychology*, 8th ed. pp. 55–56/9th ed. pp. 57–58).

43. Answer: E. Descriptive statistics are current statistics about an event. This form of statistics is the most commonly used (*Psychology*, 8th ed. p. 49/9th ed. p. 51).

44. Answer: D. A naturalistic observation occurs when a researcher observes participants in their natural settings. This allows the researcher to gain a real-life example of what he or she is studying. However, the problem with naturalistic observational studies is that the researcher is not directly involved with the experiment and is usually some distance away, and therefore must infer the reasons for the studied behavior (*Psychology*, 8th ed. pp. 34–35/9th ed. p. 37).

45. Answer: A. Criterion validity is a measure of how well a test predicts future outcome (*Psychology*, 8th ed. pp. 373–374/9th ed. p. 380).

46. Answer: B. Howard Gardner said that there are multiple intelligences, and that a person may be intelligent in areas other than the material found on basic standardized tests. Gardner researched people who had suffered traumatic brain injuries and a resulting loss of certain cognitive functions (the ability to do mathematical computations), but were still able to complete other cognitive functions (such as memorize a list of words) (*Psychology*, 8th ed. pp. 391–392/9th ed. pp. 398–399).

47. Answer: B. The TAT is a projective test that attempts to relate information regarding achievement motivation, as well as unconscious conflicts in psychotherapy. According to Henry Murray, the more elaborate and detailed the story, the higher the motivation in the subject (*Psychology*, 8th ed. p. 582/9th ed. p. 586).

48. Answer: D. People who have an IQ below 70 are considered mentally retarded. There are numerous levels of mental

retardation given in the DSM-IV-TR (*Psychology*, 8th ed. p. 398/9th ed. p. 405).

49. Answer: B. Criterion validity refers to the fact that a test accurately measures what it is designed to measure (*Psychology*, 8th ed. pp. 372–373/9th ed. p. 380).

50. Answer: A. The three measures of central tendency refer to the average score (mean), the score in the middle (median), and the most frequently occurring score (mode) (*Psychology*, 8th ed. pp. 49–50/9th ed. pp. 22–23).

51. Answer: C. Conformity is when a person changes a behavior due to real or imagined pressure from others. In this case, Kyle faces forward because everyone else on the elevator is doing so. Compliance and obedience are when a person changes a behavior at the request of another individual (*Psychology*, 8th ed. p. 727/9th ed. p. 733).

52. Answer: D. Approximately two-thirds of all subjects in the Milgram study administered the full range of shocks (*Psychology*, 8th ed. p. 732/9th ed. p. 738).

53. Answer: B. According to evolutionary psychologists, if a behavior persists over time, then it must serve an important function of the survival of an individual or continuation of the survival of a species. Behaviors that do not serve these functions will not be repeated (*Psychology*, 8th ed. p. 737/9th ed. p. 743).

54. Answer: A. Albert Bandura conducted a classic experiment on the effects of violence and behavior. He found that children modeled the same aggressive behavior they saw adults exhibit toward a Bobo doll (*Psychology*, 8th ed. p. 737/9th ed. p. 746).

55. Answer: D. A person who is in a good mood, is not running late, and is cognizant of the bystander effect is more likely to help in an emergency situation (*Psychology*, 8th ed. pp. 747–748/9th ed. pp. 753–754).

56. Answer: E. According to the self-serving bias principle, a person will take credit or believe he personally contributed to the outcome if that outcome was desirable. However, if the outcome is not desirable, the person will blame his failure on the actions or inactions of others (*Psychology*, 8th ed. p. 700/9th ed. p. 707).

57. Answer: C. The fundamental attribution error occurs when someone blames the behavior of another person on internal or dispositional characteristics, disregarding any situational variables that might have influenced the behavior (*Psychology*, 8th ed. p. 699/9th ed. p. 706).

58. Answer: B. According to the actor-observer effect, a person excuses his or her own behavior due to situational/external factors, but explains the behaviors of others based on their

internal or dispositional characteristics (*Psychology*, 8th ed. pp. 699–700/9th ed. pp. 706–707).

59. Answer: D. The Hawthorne effect occurs when subjects in an experiment alter their behaviors because thcy are aware of being observed. This can affect the outcome of the experiment and would be considered a confounding variable (*this material does not appear in either textbook edition*).

60. Answer: B. Deindividuation occurs when an individual loses his sense of self-identity due to the increased feelings of anonymity the crowd gives him. People in large crowds may lose their inhibitions and act in a manner that differs from their normal behavior because of the perception that they will not be singled out from the rest of the crowd (*Psychology*, 8th ed. pp. 723–724/9th ed. p. 730).

61. Answer: A. According to the mere-exposure effect, the more time a person spends around someone new, the more they begin to like him or her (*Psychology*, 8th ed. p. 703/9th ed. p. 710).

62. Answer: D. A stereotype is a generalized belief about a specific group or ethnicity of people and can be either positive or negative (*Psychology*, 8th ed. pp. 707–708/9th ed. p. 714).

63. Answer: C. The humanistic perspective emphasizes free will through consciously making choices that pertain to attaining human potential (*Psychology*, 8th ed. pp. 20–21/9th ed. pp. 22–23).

64. Answer: E. The evolutionary perspective focused on each organism's effort to survive. Charles Darwin believed that nature selects organisms that are best suited for survival; every organism needs to behave in ways that enhance its survival (*Psychology*, 8th ed. p. 18/9th ed. p. 20).

65. Answer: A. Sensory adaptation occurs when sensory receptors become less sensitive because of constant contact with an unchanging stimulus (*Psychology*, 8th ed. pp. 108–109/9th ed. pp. 110–111).

66. Answer: C. Photoreceptors are located in the retina and are designed to detect light energy wavelengths. Cones are an example of a photoreceptor and detect color and sharp details. Rods are another type of photoreceptor and are stimulatcd in dlm light and peripheral vision (*Psychology*, 8th ed. p. 121/9th ed. p. 123).

67. Answer: A. Biological psychologists investigate the role of the brain and the nervous system and how they affect human behavior. For example, a biological psychologist would research how a stroke had affected an individual's functioning (*Psychology*, 8th ed. p. 4/9th ed. p. 5).

68. Answer: B. Response criterion is a person's willingness to respond to a stimulus. Scott chose not to pay attention to his teacher's lecture. If it had been determined that Scott could not hear his teacher because of noise in the classroom, then Weber's law would explain Scott's inability to hear his teacher (*Psychology*, 8th ed. p. 158/9th ed. p. 163).

69. Answer: B. Difference threshold refers to the minimum difference necessary to detect variations between two different stimuli (*Psychology*, 8th ed. p. 161/9th ed. p. 165).

70. Answer: D. REM sleep is referred to as paradoxical sleep because the brain is active, displaying beta waves, while the body is completely at rest, or asleep. The body's inactivity during this stage of sleep can be explained by muscle atonia (lack of muscle tone) (*Psychology*, 8th ed. p. 337/9th ed. p. 340).

71. Answer: D. Nightmares occur during REM sleep, when the brain is active, which is why people often remember their dreams. Night terrors occur during NREM stage 4. Night terrors are experienced mostly by children, who often don't remember anything because the terrors take place when the child is in deep sleep (when, as demonstrated by delta waves, the brain shows the least amount of activity) (*Psychology*, 8th ed. p. 341/9th ed. p. 348).

72. Answer: B. All addictive drugs affect the "pleasure center" of the brain, which affects the regulation of dopamine. Neuropsychologists have linked the pleasure that people report with activity in the dopamine systems (*Psychology*, 8th ed. p. 352/9th ed. p. 357).

73. Answer: C. Homeostasis is the regulation of the internal states of the body. For example, body temperature is regulated by homeostasis (*Psychology*, 8th ed. p. 408/9th ed. p. 417).

74. Answer: E. The arousal theory of motivation suggests that each person has a desired level of arousal that dictates the types of activities he or she pursues. If an activity does not provide enough stimulation, then the person looks for alternatives; if an activity is too stimulating, then the person may back off (*Psychology*, 8th ed. p. 409/9th ed. p. 418).

75. Answer: A. A need is a state of deprivation. Experiencing needs is necessary for the body to survive. When needs are not met, tension is produced in the body; this tension is referred to as a drive. For example, the body's need for water produces thirst, which directs the behavior to satisfy the need (*Psychology*, 8th ed. p. 408/9th ed. p. 417).

76. Answer: C. Extrinsic motivation is based on performing behaviors that attain promised rewards or diminished threats of punishment. Intrinsic motivation is a desire to perform certain behaviors for personal reasons, such as competence (*Psychology*, 8th ed. p. 410/9th ed. p. 436).

77. Answer: D. The James-Lange theory of emotion suggested that emotion is the result of the detection of physiological arousal within the body (i.e., that physiological arousal precedes emotion). Thus, people who experience spinal cord injuries will suffer impairment of their emotional responses. However, there was substantial criticism of the James-Lange theory because people who had suffered spinal cord injuries were still able to experience emotions (*Psychology*, 8th ed. p. 445/9th ed. pp. 449–450).

78. Answer: E. The cognitive appraisal theory suggests that emotions are determined by appraisal of a stimulus as either threatening or nonthreatening. This results in the type of emotion that will be experienced and displayed (*Psychology*, 8th ed. p. 448/9th ed. pp. 454–455).

79. Answer: B. Avoidance-avoidance conflicts occur when each alternative has a negative implication. When a person has to choose between two equally unappealing choices, it is referred to as an avoidance-avoidance conflict (*Psychology*, 8th ed. p. 435/9th ed. p. 443).

80. Answer: C. The id operates according to the pleasure principle, which demands immediate gratification, and is often present at birth. The ego counteracts the id by relying on the reality principle, which considers the reality of the situation, often delaying the id (*Psychology*, 8th ed. p. 553/9th ed. p. 559).

81. Answer: D. Repression is the unconscious blocking of memories, often traumatic ones. Regression, which is often confused with repression, is regressing, or consciously retreating back to an infantile time period to ease present anxiety (*Psychology*, 8th ed. p. 554/9th ed. p. 560).

82. Answer: A. Carl Jung was a neo-Freudian who said that the collective unconscious contains archetypes, universal symbols that enhance survival and are passed through ancestral lines (*Psychology*, 8th ed. p. 556/9th ed. p. 562).

83. Answer: A. A factor analysis is used to identify a group of traits, or items that are related. Raymond Cattell used factor analysis to identify 16 personality traits that could predict one another (*Psychology*, 8th ed. p. 560/9th ed. p. 567).

84. Answer: C. Conditional positive regard, a term associated with the humanistic perspective, is when affection and approval are shown only if certain conditions have been met. David's parents express their approval only when David is successful. If he is not successful, they withhold their affection (*Psychology*, 8th ed. pp. 572–573/9th ed. pp. 578–579).

85. Answer: B. According to the diathesis-stress model, the combination and interpretation of different types of stress and a person's genetic predisposition lead to that person's developing a psychological disorder (*Psychology*, 8th ed. p. 595/9th ed. p. 602).

86. Answer: E. Generalized anxiety disorder is characterized by anxiety displayed in a variety of situations. A person displaying these symptoms does not know when and where feelings of anxiety are going to surface (*Psychology*, 8th ed. p. 605/9th ed. p. 611).

87. Answer: C. A conversion disorder occurs when psychological stress and anxiety are converted to physical symptoms (*Psychology*, 8th ed. p. 610/9th ed. p. 616).

88. Answer: D. Dysthymic disorder is a low-grade form of depression and can last a few years. Major depressive disorder is characterized by extreme symptoms of depression that often lead to impaired functioning and even hospitalization. A person experiencing major depression would have a hard time going to school and work and would likely experience suicidal ideations (*Psychology*, 8th ed. p. 615/9th ed. p. 621).

89. Answer: C. Seasonal affective disorder is characterized by feelings of depression connected to seasonal change. An explanation for this disorder may be linked to the lack of daylight during the winter months. Consequently, light therapy can be an effective treatment for SAD (*Psychology*, 8th ed. p. 619/9th ed. p. 625).

90. Answer: A. Neologisms are words used by a schizophrenic that have meaning only to them. These are often called nonsense words as no one else can understand their meanings (*Psychology*, 8th ed. p. 622/9th ed. p. 628).

91. Answer: B. Cocaine can lead to the development of excessive dopamine receptors and can produce symptoms that are similar to those associated with schizophrenia (*Psychology*, 8th ed. p. 637/9th ed. p. 643).

92. Answer: D. Asperger's disorder is characterized by impaired relationships, repetitive behaviors, and memorization of various facts or activities. It is often found in people with high-functioning autism (*Psychology*, 8th ed. p. 634/9th ed. p. 640).

93. Answer: C. Dissociative identity disorder is characterized by multiple distinct personalities the individual is unaware of. Dissociative fugue involves a moving, or fleeing, to a new place without conscious recall of identity associated with the previous location (*Psychology*, 8th ed. p. 612/9th ed. pp. 618–619).

94. Answer: B. The latent content represents the symbolic portion of the dream and could help the psychoanalyst and patient uncover unconscious motivation and conflicts. The manifest content is the remembered portion of the dream (*Psychology*, 8th ed. p. 647/9th ed. p. 654).

95. Answer: B. Carl Rogers's client-centered approach, based on the humanistic perspective, stresses that the client must direct the session in the hopes that the client will realize the problem

and find a solution on his or her own (*Psychology*, 8th ed. p. 650/9th ed. p. 657).

96. Answer: D. Systematic desensitization is an example of exposure therapy influenced by the behavioral perspective. The technique involves counter-conditioning the unpleasant feelings that are associated with anxiety-provoking stimuli with pleasant, relaxing feelings (*Psychology*, 8th ed. p. 654/9th ed. p. 661).

97. Answer: A. Cognitive therapists believe that a person's thought process and self-defeating attitude contribute to symptoms associated with depression (*Psychology*, 8th ed. p. 658/9th ed. p. 667).

98. Answer: E. Roughly 25 percent of people who used the original antipsychotic medications, chlorpromazine and haloperidol, developed tardive dyskinesia—uncontrollable, repetitive actions (*Psychology*, 8th ed. p. 677/9th ed. p. 683).

99. Answer: D. Xanax has been prescribed to treat anxiety disorders such as agoraphobia (*Psychology*, 8th ed. p. 679/9th ed. p. 685).

100. Answer: A. Group therapy is an effective form of therapy for people who are looking for group support, cost effectiveness, and empathy (*Psychology*, 8th ed. p. 661/9th ed. pp. 667–669).

ANSWERS FOR FREE-RESPONSE QUESTIONS

1. In an effort to improve academic performance, administrators at Central High School conducted a pilot study that would pay students each time they successfully passed a district-wide standardized test.

   Twenty students—five from each grade—were assigned to the pilot study and divided into two groups. After two standardized tests were administered, the results showed that students who received money for passing tests scored significantly higher on all tests than those students who did not receive money. Administrators concluded that offering money for passing tests increased student performance.

   a. In relation to the study, identify each of the following:
   ▧ Identify the independent variable. **(Point 1)**
      i. The independent variable (IV) is receiving money or not receiving money.
   ▧ Identify the dependent variable **(Point 2)**
      i. The dependent variable (DV) is the test scores.
   ▧ Identify the reinforcement schedule that was implemented. **(Point 3)**
      i. Students who received money were on a fixed-ratio (FR) or continuous reinforcement schedule. Each time they passed an exam, they received money.
   ▧ Identify one potential flaw in the study, and explain how you would correct it. **(Point 4 for the flaw and Point 5 for the correction)**
      i. One potential flaw with this study was in the selection of students. The experiment did not indicate whether the students were chosen by random sampling. Failure to use random sampling could impact the results; if the top five students in each grade were selected, that would not produce a representative sample of the population. To correct this flaw, it should be

noted that the experimental/treatment group was based on random sampling to give all students the same chance of being selected.

ii. Another potential flaw was that after the first test students and teachers would know which group they were assigned to; therefore, experimenter and participant bias may be present. This could lead to a self-fulfilling prophecy (for both the teachers and the students). To correct this flaw, students should be paid after the study was completed, and the study should apply the double-blind procedure.

iii. Another potential flaw could be the inclusion of only 20 students. A sample size this small could not be generalized to the larger population.

b. In relation to student performance, explain how each of the following might be affected by paying students for their academic success.

▨ Intrinsic motivation (**Point 6**)

i. Paying students for grades serves as an extrinsic motivator; thus, students would expect to be paid based on performance, ultimately decreasing their internal motivation to succeed.

▨ Learned helplessness (**Point 7**)

i. Students who were not assigned to the experimental group might develop a sense of helplessness in that no matter how they performed on a test they would not receive money, thus decreasing their efforts on subsequent tests.

▨ Expectancy effect (Pygmalion effect) (**Point 8**)

i. Students who were assigned to the experimental group might believe that they would earn the money, thus increasing the time they devoted to studying. Teachers who knew of the study might unconsciously pay more attention to help those students who were assigned to the experimental group, increasing the students' chances of passing the exams.

2. What a person experiences depends largely on sensation.

a. Identify the sensory receptors and locations for each of the following senses:

▨ Vision: Sensory receptors: rods and cones/ located in the retina (**Point 1**)

▨ Audition: Sensory receptors: hair cells (cilia) located in the basilar membrane in the cochlea (**Point 2**)

▨ Gustation (taste): Sensory receptors: taste buds: sweet, salty, bitter, sour; located on the tongue and throughout the mouth (**Point 3**)

▨ Olfaction (smell): Sensory receptors: olfactory receptor cells; located in the nasal lining (**Point 4**)

▨ Touch: Sensory receptor: pacinian corpuscle; located unevenly throughout the body, more sensitivity around face, lips, and hands (**Point 5**)

▨ Kinesthetic: Sensory receptors: proprioceptors; located in the muscles and joints for detecting movement and body position (**Point 6**)

▨ Vestibular: Semicircular canals and vestibular sacs/located in the inner ear (**Point 7**)

b. Explain how the following terms affect the process of sensation.

▨ Perceptual set: (top-down processing) mental predisposition based on past experiences to view stimuli a certain way (**Point 8**)

▨ Retinal disparity: binocular depth cue that points out that slightly different images are produced because of the separation of the right and left retinas (**Point 9**)

▨ Relative size: closer objects appear larger than objects that are farther away (**Point 10**)

Calculating Your Score on the Diagnostic Test

This scoring chart is based on the 2007 AP Psychology released exam. While the AP Grade Conversion Chart is NOT the same for each testing year, it gives you an approximate breakdown.

SCORING THE MULTIPLE-CHOICE SECTION

Use the following formula to calculate your raw score on the multiple-choice section of the exam:

$$\underset{\text{number correct}}{\underline{\hspace{3cm}}} \times 1.00 = \underset{\substack{\text{weighted Section 1 Score} \\ \text{(out of 100)}}}{\underline{\hspace{3cm}}}$$

SCORING THE FREE-RESPONSE SECTION

Question 1 $\quad \underset{\text{(out of 8)}}{\underline{\hspace{2cm}}} \times 3.1250 = \underset{\text{(do not round)}}{\underline{\hspace{2.5cm}}}$

Question 2 $\quad \underset{\text{(out of 10)}}{\underline{\hspace{2cm}}} \times 2.5 = \underset{\text{(do not round)}}{\underline{\hspace{2.5cm}}}$

$$\text{sum} = \underline{\hspace{3cm}}$$

weighted Section II
score (do not round)

YOUR COMPOSITE SCORE

$$\underset{\substack{\text{weighted} \\ \text{Section I score}}}{\underline{\hspace{2.5cm}}} + \underset{\substack{\text{weighted} \\ \text{Section II score}}}{\underline{\hspace{2.5cm}}} = \underset{\substack{\text{composite score} \\ \text{(round to nearest} \\ \text{whole number)}}}{\underline{\hspace{2.5cm}}}$$

AP GRADE CONVERSION CHART

Composite Score Range	AP Grade
113 – 150	5
93 – 112	4
77 92	3
65 – 76	2
0 – 64	1

Part II

A Review of Psychology

1

RESEARCH METHODS

Every day, Americans are inundated by statistics in the media, yet many people fail to question the nature and validity of these figures. Most of us enjoy hearing stories, and we often accept anecdotal stories over scientific facts; but why? Statistics often confuse and bore people, whereas stories are filled with details and, of course, personal accounts. Thinking critically is important in the field of psychology; it allows you to look at stories to see if they are, in fact, valid. Examining studies allows a person to examine the research methods used. However, experiments are not the only type of studies psychology researchers rely on.

CRITICAL THINKING

One of the things psychology stresses is **critical thinking**, *researching with factual information in order to arrive at a valid conclusion.* You should use critical thinking whenever you are faced with a new situation or information. Thinking critically is important when conducting scientific research because it allows the researcher to base any conclusions on facts, rather than on assumptions or half-truths. Scientists must formulate a **hypothesis**, *an educated guess of a specific and testable problem or question,* as the first step in any research. The hypothesis allows the researcher to clearly state the question he or she seeks to answer. In order to test the hypothesis, the researcher must create an **operational definition**, *the definition of how the research will be tested.* Operational definitions help clarify how the researcher plans to test his or her hypothesis. The operational definition allows the researcher to identify the **variables**, *any factor that may influence the outcome.* Once the research is complete, the researcher may formulate a **theory**, *an explanation of the recorded data used to explain a phenomenon.* Note that theories are not created, as hypotheses are; rather, they are an explanation of the results of a hypothesis.

RESEARCH METHODS IN PSYCHOLOGY

Psychologists who take part in research aim to meet four goals: describe a phenomenon, predict future or past behavior, control current or future behavior and thinking, and explain how and why a phenomenon happened. To accomplish these goals, psychologists use five different research methods: naturalistic observations, case studies, surveys/interviews, correlational studies, and experiments, defined below. The first three (naturalistic observations, case studies, and surveys) are examples of a larger category referred to as descriptive studies, whose goal is to describe the experiment.

Research Method	Definition	Example	Advantages	Disadvantages
Naturalistic observation	Watching participants in their natural environment.	Lucinda conducts her research at the local mall and observes how parents interact with their children in a public setting.	The researcher can observe the subject in his or her natural environment.	The researcher may have to infer information based on his or her observations. The researcher cannot control the environment or any outside factors that may influence the outcome.
Case study	An in-depth examination of a rare phenomenon that occurred with an individual, small group, or situation.	Trevor was recently involved in an accident that destroyed a portion of his brain.	The researcher can examine, in depth, the rare occurrence.	The researcher can't generalize his or her findings to the entire population. The event or situation may never occur again, thus making it impossible to formulate an exact theory.

Research Method	Definition	Example	Advantages	Disadvantages
Surveys	The administration of questionnaires or interviews; used to identify attitudes, beliefs, and opinions	Ron calls 1,500 people to hear their opinions on global warming.	The researcher can obtain information from a large number of subjects.	Subjects may lie or deceive the researcher. Subjects who answered may not represent the entire population.
Correlational study	Examining the relationship between two or more variables	Jamal records the GPAs and the number of miles each high school student drives each day to see if the two variables are related.	The researcher can see whether the variables are related.	Just because two or more variables appear to be related does not mean that one variable caused the other variable (correlation does not equal causation).
Experiments	Attempting to prove causation by allowing the researcher to manipulate one or more variables and measure their outcome.	Bailey believes that chocolate improves memory. She administers chocolate to one group but not the other. After a memory test, Bailey records the data and formulates her theory.	The researcher can prove whether one variable causes a particular outcome.	The researcher cannot always account for outside influences (confounding variables) that may impact or skew the overall results. It is also difficult to apply what occurs in a controlled lab setting to the real world.

EXPERIMENTS: AN IN-DEPTH LOOK

Because experiments are the only accurate way to prove cause and effect, psychologists use them in the laboratory setting. Being able to control variables allows psychologists to gain a better understanding of the phenomenon being tested.

There are two variables in most experiments: the **independent variable**, *the variable that is manipulated by the experimenter,* and the **dependent variable**, *the measurable outcome or resulting effect of the manipulated variable.* In every experiment, there are **confounding variables**, *variables that cannot be controlled by the researcher but may influence the results.* Once the independent, dependent, and confounding variables are established, the researcher must select participants for the study. In most experiments, there are two groups of test subjects: the **experimental group**, *the group that receives the treatment,* and the **control group**, *the group that does not receive any treatment.* The control group is often used as a measuring stick, a way to judge the effectiveness of the treatment by comparing its results to the results of the experimental group.

When conducting an experiment, the researcher must take into account some of the following confounding variables. The first variable that may influence the final results is known as **participant bias**, *subjects who act as they believe the experimenter wants them to.* Because participant bias may influence subjects' participation in an experiment, researchers must keep it in mind, as it may skew the final results. Another variable that may impact the results is known as **experimenter bias/expectancy**, *the experimenter's actions influencing the outcome of the experiment.* Psychologists who are conducting an experiment may unknowingly influence their research through their own behavior. One way to control the effects of both of these variables is for the experimenter to use a **double-blind design**, *an experiment design in which neither the experimenter nor the subjects know who is in the experimental and control groups.* In a double-blind study, the people conducting the research know which group receives the treatment and which group does not; however, they are not administering the tests, but are simply looking at the results. Using a double-blind design lessens the chances of participant or experimenter bias.

SELECTING HUMAN PARTICIPANTS

Depending on what the researcher is trying to accomplish, different types of population sampling may occur in a study. A **representative sample**, *selecting participants from the population that closely matches the population being studied,* is necessary when the researcher wants to generalize his or her findings to a larger specific population. For example, if a researcher is studying the effects of sleep on teenage females, he should select a large enough sample of teenage females to be able to generalize his findings to all teenage females. Yet even such a representative sample must include a diverse sample of the more general population to accurately account for the entire population. Another type of sample is known as a **stratified sample**, *categorizing the desired target population and selecting participants that best represent a particular category of interest.* For example, if a researcher is studying the effects of reading on male second-grade students, she must first categorize second-grade students by gender. Once that is completed, the researcher must select only second-grade males who best represent the entire second-grade male population. Stratified samples are useful when researching specific target populations, but do require more work in identifying the categories being considered. Experiments such as those involving twins or adoptee subjects (see Chapter 10 for more information regarding such studies) typically involve stratified sampling.

Nuts and Bolts

Remember that representative samples "represent" a particular segment of the population. A good way to remember what stratified sampling means is to keep in mind that "stratified" means formed into layers, and in conducting stratified research, the researcher is looking at just one of those layers.

Once the experiment design is established, the experimenter must choose subjects through a process known as **sampling**, *selecting participants from a population that the experimenter wishes to study.* To be certain that the sample is not biased, the researcher must use a technique known as **random sampling**, *selecting participants in a manner that ensures that each member of the population has the same possibility of being selected.* Doing so helps avoid a biased sample or **sampling bias**, *selecting participants in a manner that does not allow for all potential subjects to have an equal chance of being selected.* Biased sampling may skew the final results of an experiment because the researcher will have selected participants to ensure that the experiment produces the desired results. After participants are selected using random sampling, the researcher must decide which group each participant will be a part of. Placement of individuals can influence the results of a study; therefore, it is important that the researcher use the method of **random assignment**, *allowing all participants the same opportunity of being placed in a participation group.* Randomly assigning participants to the control or experimental groups helps guard against any bias that may skew the results.

Nuts and Bolts

Remember that "random sampling" refers to how participants are selected, whereas "random assignment" refers to which group participants are assigned to.

STATISTICAL ANALYSIS OF RESEARCH

Like other scientists, psychological researchers rely on raw data to draw conclusions. How a researcher comes to his or her conclusions is often the result of statistical analysis. When analyzing the results, psychologists rely on two types of statistical analysis: inferential and descriptive. These two types of statistics allow the researcher to formulate a conclusion of his or her findings.

DESCRIPTIVE STATISTICS

Descriptive statistics, *data that are used to numerically summarize or describe the results for the targeted population,* help the researcher in describing the results. There are five types of descriptive statistics that are used in psychological research: frequency distribution, measures of central tendency, normal curves, measures of variability, and correlation.

- Frequency distribution
  - **Frequency distribution** is *gathering data and arranging the information to indicate how often a score occurs.* The frequency distribution can be arranged in a bar or line graph. For example, Professor Parrott collects the number of advanced placement classes students in each grade take and displays them in a bar or line graph.
- Measures of central tendency
  - The three measures of central tendency are mean, median, and mode. **Mean** is *the average numerical value of all presented data.* **Median**, *the numerical value that appears in the middle of all presented data,* is used to calculate how many scores are below or above the middle, or 50 percent score. **Mode** is *the numerical value that appears most often in the presented data.* Each of these measures of central tendency is used to describe numerical data.
- Normal curves
  - **Normal distribution** is *data that is arranged in a manner that resembles a normal curve.* In a normal distribution, the mean, median, and mode are the same or nearly identical.
  - **Normal curve** is *a bell-shape/curve or inverted U that graphically represents the occurrence of all the scores in a given set of data.*

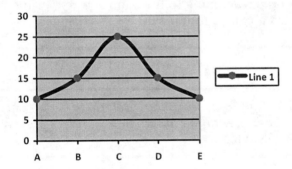

- Measures of variability
  - The variability/spread/dispersion of data in the presented data is arranged in two manners: range and standard deviation. **Range** is *the difference of the numerical value of all given scores arranged from highest to lowest (i.e., the difference between the highest and lowest values within a distribution).* **Standard deviation (SD)** is *the variability between scores and how far each diverges from the average/mean.* The standard deviation formula can be used for numerous psychological experiments, but is most often associated with intelligence quotients (IQs). For more information, see Chapter 9.
- Correlation
  - **Correlation**, *the numerical relationship between two or more variables or factors,* is often used to see how two or

more variables or factors relate to each other. Correlational studies are often represented by a histogram or scatterplot graph. The **correlation coefficient** is *a numerical value demonstrating the strength or weakness of the relationship between two or more variables or factors.* Psychologists use the correlation coefficient to predict how well one variable or factor correlates with another. The correlation coefficient scale is +1.00 to –1.00. The closer the numerical value to +1.00 or –1.00, the stronger the relationship, thus increasing the chances that the two variables or factors are related. A study that has a correlation coefficient of –.89 demonstrates a stronger relationship between variables than a study that has a correlation coefficient of +.70 because it is closer to –1.00. However, it must be noted that just because two variables or factors are correlated does not mean that one variable caused the other to occur (correlation is *not* causation).

▪ **Positive correlation** occurs when *both variables or factors move in the same direction.* For example, suppose Professor Yeld is interested in conducting a study looking at the relationship between the number of Introduction to Psychology classes students attended and the students' final grades. Professor Yeld concludes that the more classes a student attends, the higher his or her final grade will be. Therefore, there is a positive correlation between attending class and the final grade in Introduction to Psychology.

▪ **Negative correlation** occurs when *one variable or factor increases and the other decreases.* This reflects an inverse relationship between the variables. For example, Professor Randal is interested in the effects of alcohol on a person's memory retention. After collecting data, Professor Randal concludes that as the amount of alcohol consumed increases, the person's memory retention decreases. Therefore, there is a negative correlation between alcohol consumption and memory retention.

▪ **Illusionary correlation**, *an incorrect belief that supposes one variable affected the outcome.* For example, Juan believes that every time there is a full moon the night before he takes an exam he will fail that test. Juan's belief that a full moon influences his test scores is an illusionary correlation.

Nuts and Bolts

Remember that the fact that two factors appear to be related does not necessarily mean one caused the other. Also, the closer a number is to +1.00 or –1.00, the stronger the correlation. Think of +1.00 and –1.00 in terms of absolute values (remove the positive or negative sign in front of the number); the number closer to 1.00 is considered the stronger study.

INFERENTIAL STATISTICS

Inferential statistics *allow the researcher to apply his or her results to the general population and infer whether the data can be generalized to the population at large.* For example, if a researcher is interested in comparing shoe sizes for males and females, she would record the height and shoe size of a large sample size (more than 1,000 participants). Once the researcher had collected the data and established a normal curve that shows the heights and shoe sizes of both male and female participants, she might infer that the taller males wear larger shoes than the females. However, is this assumption correct? Can the researcher say for certain that all males who are taller than females wear larger shoes? The answer is no. However, if the conclusion is based on more than chance alone, then the conclusion is said to be **statistically significant**, *the resulting correlation is not influenced by chance.* Results that are statistically significant are considered reliable and valid.

AP Tip

Past free-response questions (FRQs) have focused on different research methods, specifically identifying the pros and cons of each.

ETHICAL GUIDELINES FOR PSYCHOLOGISTS

When conducting research, animal or human, psychologists must adhere to strict ethical guidelines. These guidelines are in place to protect the subjects (animal or human) who participate in any experiment. Researchers must obey the guidelines set forth by the American Psychological Association's (APA) *Ethical Principles of Psychologists and Code of Conduct*, the Association for the Accreditation of Human Research Protection Programs (AHRPP), and their college/university ethics and research committees to conduct any experiment. Studies involving the use of humans conducted within the United States, Canada, and many other countries must be approved by the Institutional Review Board (IRB). The IRB reviews all potential experiments, taking into consideration the knowledge gained versus the potential harm a study might cause. Reviewing each potential experiment is the first step in obtaining permission for the use of humans in research experiments.

When using human participants, it is important that each of the following guidelines be followed:

- Participants must provide informed consent before taking part in an experiment. This means that participants have agreed to be part of the experiment and are aware of what may take place during it.
- Participants must be debriefed and allowed to view the results after the experiment is completed. Debriefing subjects allows each one to know what the researchers were hoping to accomplish.

- The researcher must take necessary measures to ensure the confidentiality of all participants. All identifying information regarding participants who take part in a study is closely guarded.

- Participants who are under the age of majority (minors) must have a parent or guardian present during the experiment. This helps ensure that the participants do not suffer short- or long-term harmful effects.

- No participant may be psychologically or physically harmed. The experimenter must remove any potentially damaging associations before participants are released (the legacy of John Watson's "Little Albert" study, discussed in Chapter 8).

The use of animals in research is a controversial topic. Psychologists mainly use rodents and pigeons when conducting research. However, some experiments require the use of other animals, mainly primates. An experiment using any animal is subject to the strict ethical guidelines outlined in the Animal Welfare Act, the National Institute of Health's *Guide for the Care and Use of Laboratory Animals*, the National Institute of Mental Health's *Methods and Welfare Considerations in Behavioral Research with Animals*, the American Psychological Association's *Principles on Animal Use*, as well as numerous other state and federal animal usage laws.

Multiple-Choice Questions

1. Professor Jackson is conducting an experiment on the effects of chalk dust on memory retention. Two groups are given the same memory test. Participants in group A are exposed to chalk dust for 30 minutes a day, while those in group B are not exposed to chalk dust at all. Identify the dependent variable in Professor Jackson's study.
   (A) Exposure to chalk dust
   (B) Memory retention
   (C) Ability to form mnemonics
   (D) The length of time subjects were exposed to chalk dust
   (E) The amount of time between exposures

2. If a study is considered statistically significant, we can assume that
   (A) the study has both independent and dependent variables
   (B) the study is conducted in a controlled environment
   (C) all participants were debriefed after the experiment was completed
   (D) neither the experimenter nor the participants knew which groups participants were assigned to
   (E) there is a relatively small chance the results were caused by random variables

3. Researchers concluded that subjects who were given a sugar pill experienced the same results as those who took actual medication. This is known as the
   (A) confirmation bias
   (B) placebo effect
   (C) double-blind effect
   (D) hindsight bias
   (E) participation bias

4. Recent research found a correlation between the time one spends listening to heavy metal music and the number of books one reads. The correlation coefficient between these two variables was –.83. What does this correlation mean?
   (A) The more a person listens to heavy metal, the more books he or she reads.
   (B) The number of hours spent listening to heavy metal has no effect on the number of books a person reads.
   (C) The less a person listens to heavy metal, the more books he or she reads.
   (D) As the age of the subject increases, the number of books he or she reads decreases.
   (E) As the age of the subject decreases, the number of books he or she reads decreases.

5. Professor Gladhand is interested in studying the effects of caffeine on the aggression levels of rats. Which of the following research methods would be most useful in reaching a cause-and-effect conclusion?
   (A) Case study method
   (B) Experimental method
   (C) Naturalistic observation method
   (D) Survey method
   (E) Selective breeding method

6. Dr. Sanborn is interested in studying people who have sustained brain damage after ingesting banana peels. Over the past five years, he has studied only one patient. Which of the following research methods is Dr. Sanborn most likely using?
   (A) Naturalistic observation
   (B) Experimental
   (C) Survey
   (D) Case study
   (E) Twin studies

7. Which of the following is an example of a positive correlation?
   (A) As the number of hours a person sleeps increases, her violent behavior decreases.
   (B) As the number of dogs a person owns decreases, her violent behavior increases.
   (C) The less sleep a person gets, the lower her grade-point average.
   (D) The more a person watches television, the less she reads.
   (E) The number of reptiles a person owns has no effect on the number of emails she sends.

8. Dr. Cho is concerned that his body language might influence the outcome of his experiment. Which of the following methods should Dr. Cho use to ensure that he will not impact the results of the study?
   (A) Sampling size
   (B) Double-blind study
   (C) Single-blind study
   (D) Case study method
   (E) Survey method

9. Dr. Mallard conducted research that required 50 participants. The first 25 people that arrived on the day of the experiment were assigned to the experimental group, and the remaining 25 were assigned to the control group. Such a method of assignment may influence the results of his experiment. Instead, Dr. Mallard should have used which method of assignment?
   (A) Random sampling
   (B) Random placement
   (C) Random assignment
   (D) Random selection
   (E) Random blindness

10. In an experiment studying the effects of alcohol on memory, subjects' tolerance levels relating to alcohol consumption would be considered
    (A) the dependent variable
    (B) the independent variable
    (C) a confounding variable
    (D) random assignment
    (E) participant bias

11. Which of the following correlation coefficients would be considered to have the greatest relationship strength?
    (A) +.78
    (B) +.33
    (C) −.56
    (D) −.84
    (E) −.14

12. Descriptive statistics
    (A) allow the researcher to make generalizations to the wider population
    (B) are a numerical set of data used to describe an experiment
    (C) are used only in rare instances
    (D) allow the researcher to control for confounding variables
    (E) ensure that neither the subject nor the researcher influences the outcome

13. Professor Leonard is interested in studying the effects of caffeine on attention. One group of students is administered 100 mg of caffeine prior to a two-hour lecture on the migrating practices of North American geese. The other group receives no caffeine prior to hearing the lecture. In this study, what is the dependent variable?
   (A) The number of times Professor Leonard looks at his watch
   (B) The money students received for taking part in the study
   (C) Subjects' tolerance levels for caffeine
   (D) The ability of students to pay attention to the lecture
   (E) The amount of caffeine administered

14. The three measures of central tendency are
   (A) mean, medium, majority
   (B) majority, median, mode
   (C) mean, variability, reliability
   (D) mean, median, mode
   (E) validity, predictability, reliability

15. Professor Washburn noticed that her class's scores on their first test were between 89 and 14. Professor Washburn is describing her class's
   (A) range
   (B) reliability
   (C) sample size
   (D) standard deviation
   (E) correlation coefficient

Free-Response Questions

1. Professor Llama believes that watching cooking shows on television increases a person's cooking ability. Design the research method that would be used to test Professor Llama's theory. Be sure to include each of the following:
   a. Identify which research method Professor Llama should use
   b. Correctly identify the independent and dependent variables
   c. List one potential confounding variable

2. Identify three different types of research methods commonly used in psychological research. Identify the advantages and disadvantages of each method of research.

Answers

Multiple-Choice Questions

1. Answer: B. The dependent variable is the measurable outcome of the study. The experiment is testing whether chalk dust increases memory retention; therefore, memory retention is

the dependent variable, whereas exposure to chalk dust is the independent variable (*Psychology*, 8th ed. p. 40/9th ed. p. 43).

2. Answer: E. When a study is considered statistically significant, it means that the influence of outside variables on the study is minimal, and has not impacted the findings (*Psychology*, 8th ed. p. 53/9th ed. p. 55).

3. Answer: B. The placebo effect occurs when participants administered a fake pill (placebo) show the same results as those given the actual medication. This is the result of the person believing that the medication is working, even though it is doing nothing (*Psychology*, 8th ed. p. 42/9th ed. p. 44).

4. Answer: C. A negative correlation means that one variable increases while the other variable decreases. As the number of hours spent listening to heavy metal increases, the number of books read decreases (*Psychology*, 8th ed. pp. 51–52/9th ed. p. 54).

5. Answer: B. The experimental method allows the researcher to manipulate variables to determine cause and effect (*Psychology*, 8th ed. pp. 40–41/9th ed. pp. 42–43).

6. Answer: D. A case study is used when a rare event or situation has occurred. Because this research is considering a rare event, its results cannot be applied to the population at large (*Psychology*, 8th ed. pp. 35–37/9th ed. pp. 38–39).

7. Answer: C. A positive correlation indicates that both variables move in the same direction. Even though both variables (sleep and GPA) decrease, they are still moving in the same direction (*Psychology*, 8th ed. pp. 51–52/9th ed. p. 54).

8. Answer: B. In a double-blind study neither the researcher nor the participants know who has been assigned to the control and experimental groups (*Psychology*, 8th ed. p. 43/9th ed. p. 45).

9. Answer: C. Random assignment (randomizing) allows all subjects the same opportunity of being placed in either research group, and helps control for assignment that may skew the results (*Psychology*, 8th ed. p. 45/9th ed. p. 44).

10. Answer: C. A confounding variable is any factor that cannot be controlled by the researcher. In this study, a subject's tolerance level for alcohol may influence the outcome of the study (*Psychology*, 8th ed. p. 41/9th ed. pp. 43–44).

11. Answer: D. As correlation coefficients get closer to +1.00 or −1.00, the relationship between the variables strengthens (*Psychology*, 8th ed. p. 51/9th ed. p. 54).

12. Answer: B. Descriptive statistics numerically describe the data. This allows researchers to quantify their research and does not

involve generalizing to the population at large (*Psychology*, 8th ed. p. 52/9th ed. p. 51).

13. Answer: D. The dependent variable (attention) is the measurable outcome. The independent variable (caffeine) is the variable that is manipulated by the researcher (*Psychology*, 8th ed. p. 40/9th ed. p. 43).

14. Answer: D. The three measures of central tendency are mean, median, and mode (*Psychology*, 8th ed. pp. 49–50/9th ed. p. 52).

15. Answer: A. Range refers to the numerical difference between scores arranged from highest to lowest (*Psychology*, 8th ed. p. 51/9th ed. p. 53).

FREE-RESPONSE ANSWERS

1.
- Professor Llama should use the experimental research method when conducting his experiment.
- The independent variable in this study would be watching a cooking show.
- The dependent variable in this study would be the subjects' cooking ability.
- Some potential confounding variables for this study are:
  - previous experience cooking
  - motivation to cook
  - quality of the cooking show

2. Commonly used research methods are:
- Experimental research
  - Advantages
    - Allows the researcher to manipulate variables in a controlled environment
    - Indicates a cause and an effect relationship
  - Disadvantages
    - Cannot control for all confounding variables that may influence the results of the study
    - Difficult to apply to the real world (outside the lab setting)
- Naturalistic observation
  - Advantages
    - The researcher can observe subjects in their natural environments.
  - Disadvantages
    - The researcher may have to infer information based on his or her observations.
    - The researcher cannot control the environment or outside factors that may influence the outcome.
- Correlation research
  - Advantages
    - Demonstrates the relationship between two variables or factors
    - Can be represented graphically using a scatterplot

- Disadvantages
  - Does not prove causation
  - Correlation is not causation
- Survey
  - Advantages
    - Easy to administer to numerous people
  - Disadvantages
    - Cannot control for possible participation bias
- Case study
  - Advantages
    - Studies a rarely occurring case in depth
    - Allows for an in-depth view into a person or situation
  - Disadvantages
    - Can be time-consuming
    - Results cannot be generalized to entire population

BIOLOGICAL PSYCHOLOGY

Everything we as humans do is ultimately the result of our brains and the neural/cellular communication that takes place inside them. To understand how the brain processes information, biological psychologists study it and the physical or neurochemical changes that occur as the result of communication, learning, or maturation. On the simplest level, our everyday actions, the emotions we feel, and the memories we retain are the result of interactions among neurons within our brains.

BASIC STRUCTURE OF A NEURON

There are two basic types of cells in the nervous system: neurons and glial cells; each has its own distinct function in relation to the processes of the brain. **Neurons**, *cells that process incoming signals and respond by sending out signals of their own,* are the basic building blocks of the brain's anatomy. **Glial cells**, *cells that aid in the transferring of a signal and help keep the basic structure of the nervous system intact,* are necessary for neurons to function.

All neurons have an outer membrane that helps protect information kept within the cell body. The outer regions of a neuron contain **dendrites**, *branch-like structures that receive information from adjacent neurons.* Dendrites process incoming chemicals and propel information to the **nucleus**, *the centerpiece of a neuron that contains the information (DNA) that determines how a neuron will function.* The nucleus is surrounded by the **soma**, *the cell body of the nucleus that produces neurotransmitter substances and helps protect the vital information contained in the nucleus.* Just outside the soma is the **axon hillock**, *a gatekeeper-like structure that determines whether information will proceed down the neuron.* The axon hillock is responsible for sending an impulse down the **axon**, *the neural fiber that transmits or*

62

sends information from the soma to the other end of the neuron. In the most basic terms, an axon is a tube that carries information from one place to another.

The axon is encased by **myelin**, *a fatty tissue substance that protects information stored inside the axon.* Myelin also aids in the transmission of information. If the myelin begins to break down, the electrical impulses within the axon will leak out, thus prohibiting the information from being fully transmitted down the axon. The depletion of myelin has been linked to multiple sclerosis (MS). The spaces in between the myelin along the axon are called **nodes of Ranvier,** *gaps between sections of myelin that speed up the process of transmission.*

Once the information reaches the **axon terminal/buttons,** *the ending part of the neuron that releases information,* it is sent via release channels into the **synapse/synaptic cleft,** *the space between the axon terminal of one neuron and the dendrites of an adjacent neuron.* When the information, also known as **neurotransmitters,** *chemicals that transfer information from one neuron to another,* is released into the synapse/synaptic cleft, it searches out the appropriate **receptor site,** *an area on the dendrite that accepts neurotransmitters.* Neurotransmitters that do not quickly bind to the appropriate receptor sites are forced to return to the axon terminal via reuptake centers, where they wait until another signal allows them to reenter the synapse. It is the receptor site on the dendrite that binds the neurotransmitter substance to its appropriate place. Some medications or drugs work by mimicking the appropriate neurotransmitter, causing the cell to fire as if the appropriate and correct neurotransmitter were bound to the correct site. This false neurotransmitter signals the nervous system to stop producing the real neurotransmitter because it is tricked into believing that the appropriate and correct amount of the neurotransmitter is being produced naturally. In addition, some medications or drugs work by blocking the reuptake centers. Medications such as antidepressants increase the amount of the targeted neurotransmitter within the synapse after transmission has occurred. This increased amount allows for more neurotransmitters to be present during the next transmission, ensuring that all the receptor sites are filled and functioning properly.

AP Tip

Past multiple-choice questions have asked students to identify which area of the neuron is responsible for which function. Specifically, questions have focused on the dendrite, axon terminal, and myelin.

Nuts and Bolts

One way to remember what each part of a neuron does is to think of driving to a location, switching cars along the way. You first get into your car (nucleus), which is parked in your garage (soma). You pull out of the garage and back down your driveway. The point at which the driveway meets the road is similar to the axon hillock. Once on the road, you begin to travel to your destination. The road itself is the axon, which is protected by a curb on each side, similar to myelin, which helps protect the axon. As you travel to your destination, you encounter hills and valleys (nodes of Ranvier), which help slow you down or propel you toward your goal to speed up the process of arriving at your final destination. As you come to your initial destination, you pull into a parking spot (axon terminal), which is the end of the driving portion of your trip. You exit your vehicle through the car door (release channel) and step outside to the area between the car you arrived in and the new car you will be traveling in (synapse/synaptic cleft). If you have the correct key to enter the awaiting car, you will be allowed to enter the new car through its door (receptor site). Once inside the new vehicle (dendrite), you relay your destination to the driver of the new car (nucleus). The new car (nucleus) then repeats a similar process as above to transport you to either another car or your final destination.

Diagram of a Neuron

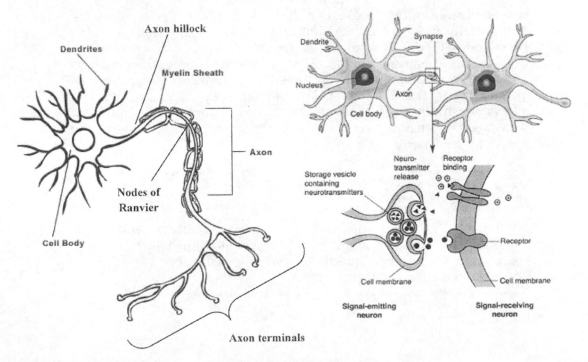

(taken from http://www.nida.nih.gov/JSP/MOD3/images/NEURON2.gif and http://www.niaaa.nih.gov/Resources/ GraphicsGallery/Neuroscience/synapse.htm)

TYPES OF NEURONS

Neurons are responsible for the communication of information. The type of information is dependent upon which type of neuron is activated. **Afferent (sensory) neurons**, *neurons that transmit information from the spinal cord to the brain*, help our brains register sensory information. **Efferent (motor) neurons** *are neurons that transmit information from the brain to muscles and glands*. For example, if you were to place your hand on a hot stove, sensory information about the stove's surface would be transmitted from your hand to the brain via afferent (sensory) neurons. Once the brain processed this information, it would send a signal from the brain through the spinal cord to the appropriate muscles that would then cause you to remove your hand from the stove. These two types of neurons are crucial for the occurrence of the reaction-action response.

Nuts and Bolts

 An easy way to remember the functions of afferent and efferent neurons is to remember Sensory Afferent, Motor Efferent (S.A.M.E.).

NEURAL COMMUNICATION

The communication of information from one neuron to the next is controlled by an impulse. Neural impulses are conducted within the neuron in exactly the same manner every time stimulation is experienced. Neural transmission is considered an electrochemical process, meaning that chemical messages are propelled because of the electrical changes that take place within the neuron. In order for a neuron to fire, or release information that will be carried down the axon to the axon terminal, several processes must occur. To simplify this process, note the terminology and precise order of events in the firing of a neuron:

POLARIZATION
Negatively charged chloride (Cl-) ions exist within the axon, resulting in a negative charge.

RESTING POTENTIAL
Negatively charged ions wait for stimulation within the axon. The neuron is said to be inactive and is waiting for another action potential.

DEPOLARIZATION
When stimulated, the channels along the axon allow positively charged sodium (NA+) and potassium (K+) ions to enter. This causes subsequent sodium (NA+) and potassium (K+) channels to open, thus propelling the electrochemical process down the axon.

ACTION POTENTIAL

A change in the balance of the overall charge of the neuron causes the electrochemical signal to travel (it is fired) along the axon.

THRESHOLD

A point of excitation on the neuron that must be reached for an action potential to occur.

ALL-OR-NONE (NOTHING) PRINCIPLE

Once the threshold is reached, the neuron will fire at full strength. If the threshold is not reached, the neuron will not fire.

REFRACTORY PERIOD

The period after a neuron fires, at which time it is less susceptible to stimulation from other neurons. The neuron must recharge itself electrically until it reaches polarization. Once this occurs, the neuron is ready to fire again.

AP Tip

Be familiar with the process of neural transmission—specifically, the all-or-none (nothing) principle, and know which ions enter and exit during polarization and depolarization.

NEUROTRANSMITTERS

Inside the buttons or knobs at the end of the axon terminals are sacs or vesicles that contain substances known as **neurotransmitters**, *natural chemicals produced by the body that transfer signals from one neuron to another.* Neurotransmitters are involved in everything from bodily movements to emotions and can be either inhibitory (discouraging the firing of the receiving neuron) or excitatory (encouraging the firing of the receiving neuron). The following is a list of common neurotransmitters, their functions, and the resulting effect of an excess or a deficiency.

Neurotransmitter	Function	Excess	Deficiency
Acetylcholine	Memory, mood, voluntary muscle movement	Convulsions or excess shaking	Alzheimer's disease, paralysis
Dopamine	Feelings of euphoria (reward), movement	Schizophrenia	Parkinson's disease

Neurotransmitter	Function	Excess	Deficiency
Serotonin	Mood, appetite, impulsiveness	Tremors, headaches	Depression, eating disorders, alcoholism, aggression
GABA	Mood, sleep, movement	Lethargy	Anxiety disorders, Huntington's disease
Norepinephrine	Alertness, sleep, learning	Fear, anxiety	Depression
Glutamate	Memory	Brain damage due to overstimulation	Neurological disorders

Nuts and Bolts

 Remember that Alzheimer's disease is caused by a lack of acetylcholine: both begin with the letter A. Dopamine is the body's "pleasure chemical," and lack of it results in Parkinson's disease. Lack of serotonin is associated with depression, (Remember that when Sara is not around people are sad.) A deficiency of GABA causes a person to be afraid to gab (talk) with people.

AP Tip

Past multiple-choice questions have asked students about specific neurotransmitter substances, such as serotonin, dopamine, and acetylcholine, and the resulting effects of an excess or a deficiency.

THE NERVOUS SYSTEMS

The nervous system is divided into two main branches: the central nervous system (CNS) and the peripheral nervous system (PNS). The CNS is composed of the brain and the spinal cord. Note that both of these components are surrounded by bones. The PNS is composed of the somatic (or skeletal) nervous system and the autonomic nervous system (ANS). Note that these two components are not surrounded by bones and that they play a crucial role in the transferring of sensory and motor information. The ANS is composed of the sympathetic and parasympathetic nervous systems. The former is responsible for the fight/flight response and expends energy, while the latter is responsible for the restoration of spent energy. In other words, the sympathetic nervous system arouses, whereas the parasympathetic calms.

Organization of the Nervous Systems

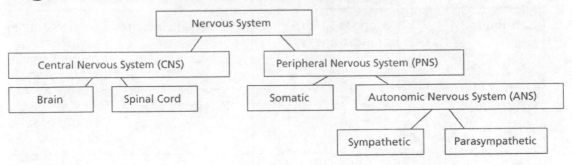

NERVOUS SYSTEM

Central Nervous System (CNS)—Responsible for processing and distributing information throughout the body

Brain—Responsible for cognitive functioning

Spinal Cord—Responsible for transmitting information throughout the body

Peripheral Nervous System (PNS)—Responsible for voluntary movement and regulation of vital processes

Somatic Nervous System—Responsible for voluntary movement

Autonomic Nervous System (ANS)—Regulation of vital human functioning (breathing, digestion, heartbeat, etc.)

Sympathetic Nervous System—Spends reserved energy

Parasympathetic Nervous System—Restores and repairs spent energy

THE BRAIN

All living animals share a common feature: a brain. The human brain weighs approximately three pounds and is the most complex organ of the human body. Each brain is divided into two halves, or hemispheres, with each side playing a crucial role in the overall functioning of the body. Research by Michael Gazzaniga has shown that the brain displays **lateralization**, *the tendency for one hemisphere to excel in the performance of certain tasks.* Gazzaniga reached this conclusion based on his research with split-brain patients. Split-brain patients are those who have had their **corpus callosum**, *the neural tissue/fiber that connects the two halves of the brain,* severed due to severe epilepsy that could not be controlled by medication. Research on such patients has helped shed light on the specialization of each hemisphere.

The right hemisphere controls most of the left-side functions of the human body. For example, if you suffer brain damage to the area associated with the movement of your arm in the right hemisphere, you may be unable to raise your left arm. Research suggests that in addition to being responsible for the left side of your body, the right hemisphere is in charge of visual-spatial tasks, the ability to recognize faces, creativity, and musical ability.

Conversely, the left hemisphere controls most of the right-side functions of the body. If you suffer brain damage to the area associated with the movement of your arm in the left hemisphere, you may be unable to move your right arm. Research suggests that the left hemisphere is also responsible for language and grammar, logical analysis and problem solving, and mathematical computations.

THE CEREBRAL CORTEX

Human brains are divided into four distinct lobes: frontal, parietal, temporal, and occipital. Each lobe expresses a series of important functions that, when integrated, allow us to function properly. Each lobe contains **association areas**, *areas of the brain that receive and combine information from multiple sources allowing for the performance of complicated tasks,* and **functional areas**, *areas of the brain that are specialized in the production of certain tasks.*

THE LOBES AND THEIR FUNCTIONS

FRONTAL LOBE

The frontal lobe is responsible for controlling inhibitions, short-term memory, reasoning, and planning for the future.

Damage to this area of the brain may result in the person being impulsive or profane, experiencing difficulty making decisions, and having trouble planning for future events.

Nuts and Bolts

 One way to remember the function and location of the frontal lobe is to think that when you do something stupid or dumb, you might thump the front of your forehead with the palm of your hand.

PARIETAL LOBE

The parietal lobe is responsible for receiving and combining tactile (touch) stimuli from all over the body to allow the formation of a single concept.

Damage to this area of the brain may result in an inability to integrate sensations normally.

Nuts and Bolts

 One way to remember the function and location of the parietal lobe is to think of a person patting the top of your head, saying "good job." You feel the sensation because that person is hitting your parietal lobe.

OCCIPITAL LOBE

The occipital lobe is responsible for processing visual stimuli, as well as maintaining balance.

Damage to this area of the brain may result in an inability to perceive movement, identify colors, and read or write words.

Nuts and Bolts

One way to remember the function and location of the occipital lobe is to think of a cartoon character who is hit in the back of the head and sees stars. Or you can simply remember that you do have eyes in the back of your head.

TEMPORAL LOBE

The temporal lobe is responsible for processing auditory stimuli.

Damage to this area of the brain may result in an inability to understand spoken words and possible difficulty in the formation of memories.

Nuts and Bolts

One way to recall the function and location of the temporal lobe is to remember that you hear the <u>tempo</u> of music through your ears.

Diagram of cerebral cortex and associated areas

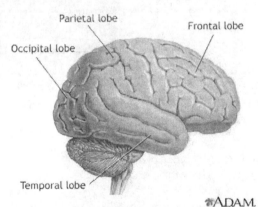

Taken from http://www.nlm.nih.gov/medlineplus/ency/imagepages/9549.htm

---

AP Tip

Past multiple-choice questions have asked students to identify the functions of the lobes of the brain.

ASSOCIATION AREAS IN THE LEFT HEMISPHERE

Wernicke's area: Responsible for transforming spoken words into thoughts

Damage (stroke, tumor, etc.) to this area can result in Wernicke's aphasia, an inability to understand speech. Those who suffer from this disorder may speak in long incoherent sentences because they are unable to understand the words they are speaking.

Broca's area: Responsible for transferring thoughts into audible spoken words

Damage (stroke, tumor, etc.) to this area of the brain can result in Broca's aphasia, which is an inability to speak coherently. Those who suffer from this disorder have a difficult time expressing their thoughts in spoken words.

Nuts and Bolts

 One way to remember that Broca's area is responsible for turning thoughts into words is to remember that "boca" means mouth in Spanish. Another way is to remember that if you have Broca's aphasia, your mouth is broken and you cannot talk. Broca's is to speech production as Wernicke's is to comprehension.

AP Tip

Past multiple-choice questions have centered on identifying the respective functions of Broca's and Wernicke's areas.

FUNCTIONAL AREAS OF THE CEREBRAL CORTEX

Motor cortex: Responsible for voluntary movements of the body; located in the back of the frontal lobe.

Damage to this area of the brain can result in an inability to voluntarily move parts of the body.

Nuts and Bolts

 One way to remember where the motor cortex is located is to remember that the <u>motor</u> is in the <u>front</u> of a car.

Somatosensory cortex: Responsible for receiving sensory information; located at the front of the parietal lobe and adjacent to the motor cortex.

Damage to this area of the brain can result in the loss of sensation from stimuli.

INSIDE THE BRAIN

The brain itself is divided into three parts: the hindbrain, the midbrain, and the forebrain. The hindbrain is considered the most primitive part of the brain, and is responsible for our basic life functioning (heartbeat, digestion, arousal, and balance/coordination). The midbrain transmits signals from the hindbrain to the forebrain and helps process information relating to our senses. The forebrain, the last part of the brain to form, is the most complex part. It includes the brain structures that help regulate emotions, hunger levels, formation of long-term memories, growth hormones, and sense of smell. A list of brain structures and their functions is below.

Location of Brain Structure	Brain Structure	Function	How to remember
Hindbrain	Medulla Oblongata	Automatically controls basic life support functions (respiration, digestion, heartbeat, and blood pressure)	You "gata" have the medulla to survive.
	Pons	Relays information between the cerebellum and the cerebrum (brain)	The pons ponders what information to send to the brain and the cerebellum.
	Reticular Formation (or Reticular Activating System)	Regulates alertness and arousal levels; damaging this area results in a coma	The reticular formation regulates our alertness.
	Cerebellum	Aids in balance and coordination of movement	Sound s like "Sarah balances."
	Brain stem	Lower part of the brain that connects to the spinal cord to send and receive information	Think of the stem of a piece of broccoli; it connects the stalk to the rest of the broccoli.
Midbrain	Striatum	Controls smooth body movements	Think of a tightrope walker, who must walk a straight line.

Location of Brain Structure	Brain Structure	Function	How to remember
Forebrain	Thalamus	Serves as a switchboard that relays information to the appropriate area of the brain for processing; does not process the sense of smell	Fifty years ago, an operator would connect the phone call to the house a person was trying to call. This is what the thalamus does.
	Hypothalamus	Regulates hunger (food), thirst, the fight or flight response, sex drive, and body temperature; maintains homeostasis (internal balance)	Remember the four f's: fight, flight, food, fornication, and temperature.
	Amygdala	Associated with fear and aggression	Don't get Amy mad!
	Hippocampus	Controls the formation of new explicit memories; has the largest concentration of acetylcholine (remember Alzheimer's disease is caused by an absence of acetylcholine)	Elephants have good memories— well, so do hippos!
	Olfactory bulb	Structure that transmits smell from the nose to the brain	Remember, old factories smell!
	Pituitary gland	Known as the "master gland," responsible for the production and distribution of hormones throughout the body	The pit of a cherry contains the information that allows the cherry to grow.

The limbic system, which is composed of the hippocampus, hypothalamus, thalamus, and amygdala, is an area of the brain that is associated with emotion, behavior, and long-term memory formation. This area of the brain is also known as the "pleasure system/center," and plays a vital role in dispersing the neurotransmitter dopamine.

HOW PSYCHOLOGISTS LOOK INTO THE BRAIN

Throughout history, scientists have been interested in studying the brain. As technology has increased so to has their ability to look deep inside the organ that has baffled them. Psychologists study the brain using a variety of techniques, each of which has advantages and disadvantages. The following are some of the more widely used techniques: electroencephalograph (EEG), computed tomography (CT or CAT) scans, magnetic resonance imaging (MRI), functional magnetic resonance imaging (fMRI), positive emissions tomography (PET) scans, and transcranial magnetic stimulation (TMS).

The first method of studying the brain relied on EEGs. An EEG uses electrodes that are placed on the scalp to measure the brain's electrical activity. Psychologists may use an EEG to measure the various brain waves emitted by the cerebral cortex. One area of research that relies on EEG recordings is the study of sleep; researchers use EEG to learn which stage of sleep a person is currently in. An advantage in using this technology is that it can quickly measure changes in brain activity. Although the use of EEG was a breakthrough for science, it is not without flaws, including poor spatial resolution. In addition, EEGs do not have the ability to measure activity deep within the brain.

A second technique used to study the brain is a computed tomography (CT or CAT) scan. A CT/CAT scan produces a two-dimensional image based on X-rays taken around a single axis. The image produced gives an inside view of the brain. One advantage of this technology is that it allows psychologists, as well as those in the medical profession, to view possible abnormalities that may exist—abnormalities that were undetectable by EEG. A disadvantage of the CT/CAT scan is that it does not allow the researcher to view the mental processes of the brain—essential to cognitive and experimental psychologists.

A third approach used to study the brain is magnetic resonance imaging (MRI), which provides a more detailed view of the soft tissue found in the brain. An MRI uses a large magnetic field to reconstruct the image within the body/brain. One advantage of the MRI technique is that it does not use X-rays, which are used in a CT/CAT scan to produce an image. In addition, a magnetic resonance image provides greater contrast within an image, allowing for discrimination between normal and abnormal tissue. However, one disadvantage of MRI is that it exposes the body to a strong magnetic field and cannot be used on people who have metal objects (pins or dental braces) in their body.

A fourth method used to study the brain is functional magnetic resonance imaging (fMRI), which measures neural activity within the brain. The resulting image shows the area of the brain associated with cognitive functioning, as measured by blood flow. This brain-imaging technique is used most often by cognitive and experimental psychologists to test cognitive processing. While the fMRI shows specific neural activity, it does not accurately show the working of **neural networks**, *the connection and functioning of neurons*, which are the basis of thinking.

A fifth technique used to study the brain is the positive emission tomography (PET) scan. PET scans use radioactive liquid to measure metabolic and glucose processing. The image produced by a PET scan is a three-dimensional view of the human body's or brain's metabolic processing of glucose. Scientists use this image to show the areas of the brain that are active during cognitive functions. Although the image does not show how neural networks process information, it does give a snapshot image of which areas of the brain are in use during cognition. In addition to the possible risks associated with injecting radioactive material into the bloodstream, PET scans do not provide the level of detail of MRIs, nor do they show real-time brain activity, as an EEG does.

A sixth and final technique used to study the brain is transcranial magnetic stimulation (TMS). TMS briefly excites neural activity, which may cause those neurons to temporarily become inactive due to overstimulation. Cognitive psychologists use this approach when trying to understand which area of the brain is responsible for cognitive functioning. Overstimulation to any area will result in the cessation (stopping) of neural activity in that region. If a person undergoing TMS is unable to complete a given task, psychologists can reasonably assume that the area of the brain being stimulated is vital to that task. Disadvantages associated with TMS range from brief pain or discomfort at the region of the scalp exposed to the stimulation, to the possible onset of a seizure (most notably in people who suffer from epilepsy).

Another way to differentiate among these techniques is to categorize them as either structural or functional brain-imaging devices. Structural devices—the CT/CAT scan and the MRI—are better at detecting structural abnormalities in the brain due to lesions, strokes, tumors, or aneurysms (burst blood vessels). Functional devices—the EEG, PET, fMRI, and TMS—measure brain activity.

ENDOCRINE SYSTEM

The endocrine system is responsible for the release of hormones throughout the body. **Hormones**, *chemical signals carried through the bloodstream*, are responsible for metabolism, height, muscle growth, and the onset of puberty. The endocrine system contains ductless glands, meaning that information is restricted within the bloodstream. The endocrine system works in an opposite way from the exocrine system, which includes duct glands, such as tear ducts, saliva, and sweat glands.

MAJOR GLANDS, THEIR HORMONES, AND THEIR FUNCTIONS

Name of gland	Location	Hormone produced	Function of hormone and gland
Hypothalamus	Forebrain/ Limbic System	None	Known as the "master of the master gland." Controls the pituitary gland.
Pituitary	Forebrain/ Limbic System	Growth hormones (regulates a person's height) Endorphins (natural pain killer produced by body) Prolactin (stimulates production of breast milk)	Known as the "master gland," it regulates the production and distribution of all glands and hormones throughout the body.
Pineal	Forebrain/ Limbic System	Melatonin (regulates sleep)	As melatonin levels rise, a person becomes more tired. Hormone levels should increase as darkness (nighttime) sets in.
Thyroid	Neck; u-shaped, wraps around Adam's apple	Thyroxin (controls basal metabolic rate or BMR)	Metabolizes food to produce energy.
Adrenal	Above kidneys	Adrenalin (boosts supply of oxygen to brain and muscles) Cortisol (released in response to stress, acts as a stress fighter) Dopamine (acts as both a neurotransmitter and a hormone, depending on where it is released; increases blood pressure)	Used for alertness levels, regulating stress, and preparing body for the fight or flight response.
Reproductive	Located in lower trunk/torso	Testosterone (increases size of muscles, growth of secondary sex characteristics, increased bone density) Estrogen (growth of secondary sex characteristics, reduces muscle mass, increases height)	Found in males in the testes. Responsible for production of sperm and male sex hormones. Found in females in the uterus. Responsible for female sex characteristics.

CASE STUDIES TO UNDERSTAND COGNITIVE FUNCTIONING

Ways of understanding the functions of the brain are not limited to technology. Psychologists have also been able to learn about the functioning of the brain through case studies that are the result of brain injury or the removal of neural tissue. One of the most famous such studies is that of Phineas Gage, a railroad worker who suffered severe damage to his frontal lobe. While using a tamping iron to pack gunpowder in a hole in the ground, Gage inadvertently caused the gun powder to explode, resulting in the tamping iron shooting straight through his frontal lobe, causing **ablation**, *the removal of tissue*, in that area of the brain. After being thrown to the ground, Gage regained his footing and stood up. Prior to the accident Gage had been a respected railroad foreman/manager. After the accident, Gage was unable to make decisions, acted impulsively, and was profane; his friends noted that "Gage was no longer Gage." In a sense, Gage's personality had completely changed. Psychologists who have studied the remains of Gage's skull and those of others who have suffered traumatic brain injury to the frontal lobe have concluded that that area of the brain is responsible for our inhibitions, ability to plan for future events, and regulation of emotions.

Psychologists have also studied animals and people with brain lesions. A **lesion**, *tissue damage resulting from disease,* in the brain has been shown to alter proper cognitive functioning. Studies indicate that lesions in young animals and human beings may ultimately have little or no effect on the cognitive functioning of the individual, thanks to the **plasticity**, *changes that occur in the brain due to environmental factors,* of the human brain.

Multiple-Choice Questions

1. The area of the brain essential to the formation of long-term explicit memories is
   (A) the pineal gland
   (B) the hypothalamus
   (C) the thalamus
   (D) the hippocampus
   (E) the pituitary gland

2. While running a marathon, Emily experienced an increase in the body's natural painkiller. Which of the following chemicals has been associated with the alleviation of pain?
   (A) Serotonin
   (B) GABA
   (C) Melatonin
   (D) Endorphins
   (E) Acetylcholine

3. A person who has lesions on his brain is having difficulty verbalizing complete or coherent sentences. This person most likely suffered damage to what part of the brain?
   (A) Broca's area
   (B) Wernicke's area
   (C) Motor cortex
   (D) Auditory cortex
   (E) Somatosensory cortex

4. The fact that a neuron either fires at full strength or does not fire at all is the result of which of the following?
   (A) Depolarization
   (B) All-or-nothing principle
   (C) Level of excitation
   (D) Refractory period
   (E) Axon hillock processing

5. Dr. Dolan is interested in studying short-term memory and the role of the prefrontal cortex in related tasks. Which of the following techniques would he most likely use to determine whether the prefrontal cortex is involved in short-term memory?
   (A) Positive emissions tomography (PET) scan
   (B) Electroencephalograph (EEG)
   (C) Magnetic resonance imaging (MRI) scan
   (D) Computed tomography (CT or CAT) scan
   (E) Transcranial magnetic stimulation (TMS)

6. Underproduction of _____ has been associated with Alzheimer's disease, whereas underproduction of _____ has been associated with Parkinson's disease.
    (A) dopamine; acetylcholine
    (B) serotonin; GABA
    (C) acetylcholine; dopamine
    (D) norepinephrine; dopamine
    (E) acetylcholine; serotonin

7. Acetylcholine appears to plays a vital role in the formation of long-term memories. It is reasonable to conclude that which area of the brain is most likely affected by Alzheimer's disease?
    (A) Amygdala
    (B) Hypothalamus
    (C) Hippocampus
    (D) Corpus callosum
    (E) Thalamus

8. Olds and Milner (1954) concluded that which area of the brain is responsible for producing the neurotransmitter dopamine and has thus been given the distinction of being the brain's "pleasure center"?
    (A) The limbic system
    (B) The auditory cortex
    (C) Broca's area
    (D) Wernicke's area
    (E) The reticular activating system

9. After having his corpus callosum severed, Juan would most likely experience which of the following problems?
    (A) An inability to form complete and coherent sentences
    (B) An inability to plan for future events
    (C) An inability to distinguish where a sound is coming from
    (D) An inability to control smooth bodily movements
    (E) An inability to correctly identify an object while holding it in one hand

10. An excess of which neurotransmitter has been associated with schizophrenia, while a deficiency of the same neurotransmitter has been associated with Parkinson's disease?
    (A) Serotonin
    (B) Melatonin
    (C) Dopamine
    (D) GABA
    (E) Acetylcholine

11. The deterioration of myelin, causing leakage of electrical activity within the axon, has been associated with which neurological disorder?
    (A) Parkinson's disease
    (B) Alzheimer's disease
    (C) Muscular dystrophy
    (D) Multiple sclerosis
    (E) Huntington's disease

12. Which of the following results in the activation of the sympathetic nervous system?
    (A) Your palms are dry.
    (B) Your mouth is wet with saliva.
    (C) Your digestive system is processing food.
    (D) Your heartbeat is elevated.
    (E) Your respiration rate is lowered.

13. Which of the following is an example of the functioning of the somatic nervous system?
    (A) Dana just finished lunch, and her digestive system is working to process the food.
    (B) Feelings of embarrassment caused Alex's face to turn red.
    (C) While he was running, Steve's heart rate increased.
    (D) Aleshia began to perspire when she thought about her upcoming test.
    (E) Karly picked up her pencil after it had fallen to the floor.

14. Brittney's ability to maintain balance during a dance routine is due to the functioning of which areas of the brain?
    (A) Temporal and frontal lobes
    (B) Frontal and occipital lobes
    (C) Cerebellum and temporal lobe
    (D) Occipital and temporal lobes
    (E) Cerebellum and occipital lobe

15. Tim is fifteen years old and seven feet tall. His parents are both about five-and-a-half-feet tall. Tim's height is most likely due to an
    (A) overactive pineal gland
    (B) underactive pituitary gland
    (C) overactive pituitary gland
    (D) underactive thyroid gland
    (E) overactive thyroid gland

Free-Response Questions

1. Describe the effects of brain damage on each of the following regions of the brain.
    a. Frontal lobe
    b. Temporal lobe
    c. Occipital lobe
    d. Parietal lobe

2. Neurotransmitters play a vital role in behavior. Discuss the functions of three neurotransmitters and the resulting effects of an excess and a deficiency.

Answers

MULTIPLE-CHOICE QUESTIONS

1. Answer: D. The hippocampus has been associated with the formation of long-term explicit memories. Studies have shown that people who have damaged this area of the brain experience difficulty in transferring short-term memories into long-term memories, a process that is known as memory consolidation (*Psychology*, 8th ed. p. 100/9th ed. pp. 82–83).

2. Answer: D. Endorphins are the body's natural painkiller and are produced during times of physical exertion (*Psychology*, 8th ed. p. 98/9th ed. pp. 101–102).

3. Answer: A. Broca's area is responsible for turning thoughts into coherent words and sentences. Damage to this area will result in the person's not being able to form complete or coherent words or sentences (*Psychology*, 8th ed. p. 86/9th ed. p. 90).

4. Answer: B. The all-or-nothing principle says that either a neuron fires or it does not; there is no half-firing of a neuron. This firing occurs when the threshold has been reached, causing the action potential to propel the electrical charge down the axon to the adjacent neuron (*Psychology*, 8th ed. pp. 62–65/9th ed. p. 67).

5. Answer: E. Transcranial magnetic stimulation excites neurons in the applied area of the brain. Overstimulation of these neurons causes them to temporarily stop functioning. The prefrontal cortex region of the brain is associated with short-term memory. Thus, overstimulating neurons in this region will decrease activity, making short-term memory tasks difficult (*Psychology*, 8th ed. pp. 71–73/9th ed. pp. 74, 76).

6. Answer: C. Alzheimer's disease has been associated with the lack of acetylcholine. Parkinson's disease has been associated with the lack of dopamine (*Psychology*, 8th ed. pp. 96–97/9th ed. pp. 99–100).

7. Answer: C. The hippocampus plays a vital role in the formation of long-term explicit memories. Alzheimer's patients suffer from a deficiency of acetylcholine and have difficulty forming long-term memories; therefore, researchers conclude that the hippocampus is vital in the formation of long-term memories (*Psychology*, 8th ed. p. 96/9th ed. pp. 82–83).

8. Answer: A. The limbic system is considered to be the "pleasure center" of the brain and produces the neurotransmitter dopamine (*Psychology*, 8th ed. p. 79/9th ed. p. 82).

9. Answer: E. The corpus callosum allows information to be communicated between the right and left hemispheres of the brain. If Juan held something in his left hand, he would be unable to correctly state the name of the object. Information received by his left hand would be processed in the right hemisphere, but Broca's and Wernicke's areas are located in the left hemisphere, so labeling the object would be a difficult task for John (*Psychology*, 8th ed. pp. 87–90/9th ed. pp. 91–92).

10. Answer: C. An excess of the neurotransmitter dopamine has been associated with schizophrenia, while a deficiency in it has been associated with Parkinson's disease (*Psychology*, 8th ed. pp. 97–99/9th ed. p. 100).

11. Answer: D. Multiple sclerosis (MS) is associated with the depletion of the myelin, which insulates the axon, within the central nervous system (*Psychology*, 8th ed. p. 63/9th ed. pp. 67–68).

12. Answer: D. The sympathetic nervous system is responsible for spending stored energy. When your heart rate is elevated, the sympathetic nervous system is functioning properly (*Psychology*, 8th ed. p. 68/9th ed. p. 72).

13. Answer: E. The somatic nervous system is responsible for voluntary muscle movement (*Psychology*, 8th ed. p. 67/9th ed. pp. 71–72).

14. Answer: E. The cerebellum is associated with balance and coordination. The occipital lobe is responsible for the processing of visual stimuli that help maintain balance (*Psychology*, 8th ed. pp. 78, 83/9th ed. pp. 80–81, 87).

15. Answer: C. The pituitary gland, also known as the master gland, is responsible for the secretion of growth hormones. An overactive pituitary gland will result in excessive secretion of growth hormones (*Psychology*, 8th ed. p. 100/9th ed. p. 103).

FREE-RESPONSE QUESTIONS

1. a. Damage to the frontal lobe would result in difficulties with problem solving, planning for future events, proper motor functioning, impulsiveness, and short-term memory.
   b. Damage to the temporal lobe would result in difficulty recognizing language (Wernicke's aphasia), processing of auditory stimuli, and possible memory impairment.
   c. Damage to the occipital lobe would result in difficulty processing visual stimuli, the production of hallucinations and visual illusions, and an inability to process movement of an object.

    d. Damage to the parietal lobe would result in difficulty processing information associated with touch perception, and possibly hand-eye coordination.

2. Acetylcholine is responsible for the formation of long-term memories and voluntary muscle movement, and it plays a role in mood. An excess of acetylcholine would result in muscle spasms or violent convulsions. An acetylcholine deficiency is associated with Alzheimer's disease or paralysis.

    Dopamine is known as the reward neurotransmitter and is responsible for feelings of euphoria. An excess of dopamine has been associated with schizophrenia. A deficiency of dopamine has been associated with Parkinson's disease.

    Serotonin is associated with mood, hunger, sleep, and aggression. An excess of serotonin may result in headaches or tremors. A deficiency of serotonin has been associated with depression, impulsiveness, aggression, and alcoholism.

    GABA is associated with mood, sleep, and movement. It is an inhibitory neurotransmitter. Consequently, an excess of GABA is associated with lethargy (the dampening of neural activity). A GABA deficiency has been linked to the racing thoughts associated with anxiety disorders and to Huntington's disease.

    Norepinephrine is associated with alertness, sleep, learning, and mood. An excess of norepinephrine has been associated with anxiety disorders and fearfulness. A norepinephrine deficiency has been linked to depression.

    Glutamate is vital in memory functioning. An excess of glutamate may result in overstimulation, which may lead to the destruction of the neuron. A deficiency of glutamate may result in memory problems, as well as various neurological disorders.

3

DEVELOPMENTAL PSYCHOLOGY

Developmental psychology is *the study of human development and the changes that occur within a person's life span.* Two major influences on human development are nature (genetics) and nurture (interactions with one's environment). The biggest question developmental psychologists ask is: Which has a greater impact on human development—nature or nurture? Science has yet to provide a definitive answer, but most psychologists agree that human development is a combination of the two.

Early philosophers, including John Locke in the 1690s, believed that humans are born with a blank slate (*tabula rasa*), meaning that we come into the world pure, and it is our interaction and experiences with our environment, particularly in early childhood, that ultimately shape who we become. Years later, French philosopher Jean-Jacques Rousseau argued the opposite viewpoint. Rousseau proposed that development in children occurs naturally, and that any interference by parents or others may harm that natural development.

Many psychologists would argue that Arnold Gesell was the first to systematically investigate the development of children. In the early 1900s, Gesell used naturalistic observation (watching subjects in their natural environments) to reach his conclusions. He noted that babies progressed through stages in a predetermined order. Gesell used the term **maturation**, *the growth of an organism that occurs on its own based on a predetermined timetable and without the aid of the environment,* to describe this progression.

John B. Watson, the founder of American behaviorism, proposed during this time that the environment (nurture) is solely responsible for any and all development. However, it was Swiss psychologist Jean Piaget who first considered the interaction of nature (maturation) and nurture (environment) in human cognitive development.

84

DIMENSIONS OF EARLY PHYSICAL DEVELOPMENT

The beginning of human development occurs when a **zygote**, *a new cell created by the fertilization of the ovum by the sperm*, is formed. The following are the stages of prenatal development:
- Germinal stage: zygote begins to divide into more cells
- Embryonic stage: basic life support systems (heart, nervous system, stomach, esophagus, ovaries or testes) begin to form
- Fetal stage: roughly the last seven months of prenatal development

PRENATAL RISKS

During prenatal development, the placenta, a protective and nutrient-filled organ, allows the fetus to mature properly by filtering out harmful substances. However, the placenta is not impermeable. Certain agents can and do penetrate it, and some of them can have dire consequences for the developing fetus. The term **teratogen** refers to *any agent that will harm the development of the fetus*. Below is a list of some teratogens, as well as their known effects on development:
- Alcohol: Impaired cognitive functioning; child is more likely to become alcohol dependent later in life
  - Fetal Alcohol Syndrome (FAS): mental impairments or retardation, facial abnormalities (thin lips, pointed chin, small eyes, smaller then normal head size)
- Smoking: Underweight, premature birth, irritability, attention difficulties, possible nicotine addiction/withdrawal
- Cocaine: Underweight, premature birth, impairment in cognitive and motor development, addiction/withdrawal

THE NEW BABY

Babies are born with many **reflexes**, *involuntary unlearned motor skills*, which are demonstrated without any outside influences. These include the following:
- **Grasping/palmar:** Placing any object in the palm of the baby's hand will cause the baby to grab hold of that object tightly.
- **Rooting:** Lightly touching/rubbing the cheek will cause the baby to turn toward that side in preparation for nursing. The baby is vigorously "rooting" for the mother's nipple (source of nourishment).
- **Sucking:** Inserting an object into the baby's mouth will cause the baby to begin the act of obtaining food. This typically follows the rooting process and involves the drawing of milk from the mother's nipple.
- **Babinski:** Lightly moving a finger upward on the baby's foot causes the toes to fan outward.

- **Swallowing:** Placing liquid in a baby's mouth will elicit this reflex.
- **Stepping:** Baby will step when held upright (this fades after first two months and returns when baby is physiologically capable of walking, around eight months).
- **Moro:** When startled or dropped, the baby will exhibit this reflex by flinging the arms outward and then inward across chest (as if it is groping for support); this reflex will disappear completely after a few months and is considered part of an earlier stage of human evolutionary development.

TEMPERAMENT

When babies are born, they have few ways to communicate their needs to others, due to the fact that their brains are not yet fully developed. Psychologists who study the way babies communicate often refer to their **temperament**, *a natural tendency to express emotions and needs in a particular way*. The way a baby expresses his or her needs is in large part due to heredity (nature). However, as each child grows, the environment can and will affect overall temperament and eventually personality.

DEVELOPMENTAL THEORIES OF PIAGET

Psychologist Jean Piaget (1896–1980) is considered one of the most important figures in the field of child development. His work focused on understanding how a child learns to think, and he devised numerous demonstrations to explain the sequence of child development.

JEAN PIAGET'S TERMINOLOGY

Before discussing Piaget's theory on child development, it is important to discuss his terminology. According to Piaget, each child develops a **schema**, *a mental representation or map of the environment or world based on experiences*. A child will form a schema about his or her environment. In this schema, there are individual schemes, such as a throwing scheme or a biting scheme. These are simply pieces of a much larger schema.

Two words that are often confused are **assimilation** and **accommodation**.

Assimilation: *An attempt to integrate new information into an existing schema*
- Brody, who is eleven months old, is given a balloon, which he then proceeds to bang on with his hands.
- This example shows that Brody is using an existing scheme—that round objects can be hit—to make sense of the new toy.

Accommodation: *The modification of an existing schema into a new one*
- Jillian, who is eighteen months old, is given a balloon, which she then begins to bang on with her hands. She then lets go of the balloon and it floats toward the ceiling. She learns that an object that is round and out of reach is called a balloon. Jillian then points to the chandelier and says "balloon." Her father corrects her and

says, "That's a light." Jillian has to make an accommodation to her existing balloon schema.

◾ This example shows that Jillian is using an already existing schema (that all round objects close to the ceiling are balloons) to make sense of this new information. Mentally, Jillian will have formed a new schema to accommodate and make sense of this new information.

JEAN PIAGET'S STAGE THEORY

Jean Piaget believed that children develop cognitively in a series of stages, each one built on the one prior to it. Because of that progression, Piaget believed that a child must move in an orderly manner through the stages.

◾ Sensorimotor (0 to two years)
  ◾ **Object permanence,** *the belief that an object exists despite its being out of sight*
  ◾ The child understands that if an object is covered up or out of sight, the object still exists. Prior to the child's obtaining object permanence, if an object is out of sight, it fails to exist; out of sight is out of mind.
  ◾ According to Piaget, understanding that object permanence exists, even though it is out of sight, is crucial for all future cognitive development.
  ◾ Joe, who has mastered object permanence, understands that even though his toy is covered up by a cloth it still exists; thus, he removes the cloth to find his toy.
◾ Preoperational (three years to seven years)
  ◾ **Egocentrism,** *understanding the world through the child's own perspective; the inability to see the world through another's perspective (note: this is not synonymous with selfishness)*
    ◾ Only apparent for first few years of this stage; research shows that by around age five the child should no longer be egocentric
    ◾ Jamie receives a new toy for her birthday. While on the phone talking to her grandfather, she holds the toy up for her grandfather to see. Jamie does not understand that her grandfather cannot see the toy the way she can.
  ◾ **Conservation,** *understanding that despite an apparent change in size/shape/length, the substance remains constant*
    ◾ This understanding occurs toward the end of the preoperational stage.
    ◾ When asked to choose which plate of hot dogs he wants, four-year-old Sam chooses the plate with the hot dog cut into six smaller pieces rather than the plate with the hot dog cut into three larger pieces. Each plate holds the same amount of food, but Sam believes that the plate with six pieces has more on it because he has yet to grasp the principle of conservation.
  ◾ **Animism,** *the belief that inanimate objects share human characteristics, such as feelings*

- Tori was sad because she thought the trees were waving goodbye to her as she and her mother drove past.
- **Artificialism,** *the belief that events of nature are man-made*
  - Jeff thought the thunder was the sound of people bowling in the sky.
- Concrete operational (seven to eleven years)
  - **Seriation,** *the process of putting objects into a series (smallest to largest) or putting objects that share similar characteristics (such as color or size) into the same category*
    - Julia can sort all the blocks with circles on them into one pile and all the blocks with squares on them into a separate pile.
  - **Reversibility,** *understanding that concepts can be reversed and remain the same*
    - Timmy understands that $8 + 4 = 12$ and that $12 - 4 = 8$.
    - Sally understands that she and her two sisters share the same mother, and that her mother has a total of three children.
- Formal operational (twelve and up)
  - The child begins to think abstractly and hypothetically, weighing several options at once.
  - The child can understand the consequences of various decisions he or she or others might make.
- Adolescent egocentrism
  - **Personal fable,** *an individual's belief that he or she is invincible and will not be harmed in any instance; he or she also believes that his or her ideas and opinions are unique*
  - The term "personal fable" was first coined by David Elkind, not Jean Piaget. However, because personal fable is displayed during adolescence, Piaget's formal operational stage, it is important to note it here.
  - Joe drives fast and cuts in and out of traffic because he thinks nothing will happen to him and that he will not get into an accident.
  - **Imaginary audience,** *the belief that everybody is looking at one, who is on a stage for others to watch*
  - The term "imaginary audience" was also coined by David Elkind. However, because it is displayed during adolescence, Piaget's formal operational stage, it is noted here.
  - Tammy needs two hours to get ready to go grocery shopping with her mother on Sunday morning.

Nuts and Bolts

 One way of differentiating between the concrete operational stage and the formal operational stage is that in the concrete stage, children can only think about concrete information in front of them, whereas formal operational stage children can think about events in the future and things that do not exist in the real world. This could explain why a seventh grader, still in the concrete operational stage, may not be concerned about failing a class and the consequences of doing so on his graduating.

AP Tip

Past AP questions have focused on identifying which stage (sensorimotor, preoperational, concrete operational, formal operational) a child is in when a particular behavior took place.

STRENGTHS AND WEAKNESSES OF PIAGET'S STAGE THEORY

Jean Piaget was the first psychologist to suggest that children cognitively develop in a series of stages. Over the years, researchers have scrutinized Piaget's theories and identified several strengths and weaknesses in them.

STRENGTHS
- Piaget identified changes that occurred cognitively.
- According to Piaget, the child was an active learner in the environment.
- Piaget pioneered research in child development.

WEAKNESSES
- Cognitive changes that take place during each stage appear to not be as rigid as Piaget hypothesized.
- Some children can understand higher-stage concepts before progressing to the next stage. Piaget thought that children MUST fulfill each stage before moving to the next stage, but recent research has proved this not to be true.
- Cognitive development does not appear to be as culturally universal as Piaget hypothesized.

ENVIRONMENTAL INFLUENCES ON CHILD DEVELOPMENT

Another prominent figure in the field of child development is Lev Vygotsky, who proposed that one's cognitive functioning is influenced by one's culture. It is this interaction that produces a culturally specific way of thinking (cognition). In addition, according to Vygotsky, a child can learn more difficult tasks at an earlier age than was proposed by Piaget if he or she has the aid of someone older. Vygotsky proposed a theory known as the **zone of proximal development**, *the number of tasks a child can complete with or without the aid of someone older.*

Aside from cultural differences, there are numerous other environmental conditions that can influence cognitive development. A child raised in an environment offering relatively few stimuli (sights, sounds, interactions) is at serious risk for cognitive impairment or delay. Other factors that can contribute to cognitive delays are poor nutrition, neglect, low socioeconomic status (SES, the overall income level of a child's care providers), and low intellectual abilities of the care providers. Conversely, a child raised in a stimulating environment with proper nutrition, and whose care providers are of normal to high cognitive functioning, is more likely to develop properly.

ATTACHMENT

In the first years of life, a baby grows increasingly attached to those around him or her. **Attachment**, *a strong bond between the primary caregiver(s) and the baby,* is a closely studied area of child development. Psychologists argue that the attachment an infant has early in life can set the stage for his or her personality later on. However, what contributes to this attachment?

HARRY HARLOW

Harry Harlow conducted an important study about attachment. The belief at the time (1930s – 1950s) was that infants were attached to their mothers because the mothers provided their offspring with food, thus reducing the hunger drive in the infant. Harlow sought to prove that attachment was about more than just food. In his now-famous study, Harlow isolated infant monkeys from their mothers (at birth) and placed them in a separate cage with two surrogate mothers. One surrogate was composed only of wires, but held a bottle from which the monkeys could drink. The other surrogate mother was made of soft terrycloth, but provided no food. Harlow noted that the monkeys spent far less time with the wire surrogate than they did with the cloth monkey. They initially went to the former for nourishment, but once sated spent a majority of the remaining time with the latter. To Harlow, this proved that there was more to attachment than a simple relief of hunger. The reason for the attachment to the terrycloth mother was that it provided **contact comfort**, *the touch of another, a sense of security.* This contact comfort proved to be more powerful than the drive of hunger.

However, even though the monkeys received contact comfort from the terrycloth mother, this was still no substitute for their real mothers. When placed in an environment with other monkeys, the terrycloth-raised monkeys acted as though in extreme distress, rocking back and forth and ignoring the other monkeys. As adults, the terrycloth-raised monkeys avoided other adult monkeys and acted in a violent manner when approached. As mothers, the terrycloth-raised monkeys were neglectful; some even attacked their offspring. The results of Harlow's study indicate the importance of infant–adult bonding. Without constant contact from the caregiver, an infant may display the same serious effects as the terrycloth-raised monkeys.

Konrad Lorenz

Another important psychologist in the field of attachment studies is Konrad Lorenz. Lorenz was interested in discovering how attachment comes about. In an experiment with goslings (baby geese), he demonstrated that there was a **critical period**, *a time frame during which a stimulus must be experienced in order for a certain stage of development to be achieved.* According to Lorenz, during this time frame the subjects (geese) formed an attachment to him. Lorenz explained that his goslings must have thought of him as their mother due to **imprinting**, *the eliciting of behavior due to exposure of a certain stimulus,* which took place during the critical period. Some argued that the same imprinting that occurred in Lorenz's goslings occurs in humans. There are several critical periods throughout human development, such as that for language. If the window of opportunity passes, the subject may have missed the crucial time period for language development to occur.

AP Tip

Free-response questions on past tests have asked students to understand the concept of a critical period and to identify the potential effects of missing a particular critical period (e.g., attachment and language).

Attachment in Infants

A discussion of attachment is not complete without mention of psychologist Mary Ainsworth. Ainsworth's "strange situation" experiment introduced an infant to new people or objects. While the new person or object was in the room, the caregiver would exit the room, leaving the child behind for a short time. Ainsworth was particularly interested in the reaction of the child when the caregiver returned. This, according to Ainsworth, was the way to gauge a child's attachment style. The following are Ainsworth's three attachment styles developed from her experiments:

- Secure attachment
  - Child seeks comfort from the caregiver when he or she returns.
- Insecure attachments (two forms)
  - Anxious/avoidant attachment
    - Child ignores the caregiver when the caregiver returns.
  - Anxious/Ambivalent attachment
    - Child is happy to see the caregiver when he or she returns, but then pushes the caregiver away.

According to Ainsworth, the attachment style displayed in childhood has a life-long impact as development continues.

Psychosocial Development

Erik Erikson also believed that we develop in stages. Unlike Piaget, who emphasized the learner's active role in development, Erikson thought that at each stage of life we encounter a crisis. How each crisis is resolved has long-lasting implications on how we view the world as we develop. It is important to note that Erikson believed in the importance of early parental influence on personality (similar to Freud), but he also believed that the environment itself affected this development, thus giving rise to his psychosocial theory of development. Erikson said that if an individual does not successfully resolve a particular crisis, it may make the following crisis/crises that much more challenging to resolve. Erikson's eight stages of development are outlined below, along with examples.

Stage & Age	Crises	Example
One (0–12 months)	Trust versus mistrust	Infant trusts that his or her needs (food, shelter, etc.) will be met. If they are not, the infant learns to mistrust the world.
Two (1–2 years)	Autonomy versus shame and doubt	Child learns to control his or her environment as well as his or her biological functioning (going to the bathroom). If child is made to feel too much shame, he/she may lack self-confidence.
Three (3–5 years)	Initiative versus guilt	Child is given more responsibility and independence and learns he or she can take charge. If the child is not allowed to try new tasks on his or her own, he or she may develop low self-esteem and feel guilty for acting independently.
Four (6–puberty)	Industry versus inferiority	Child wants to be productive and if given the chance will be eager to learn. If productivity is limited, child may develop a feeling of inferiority.
Five (Adolescence)	Identity versus role confusion	Adolescents try to figure out exactly who they are and how they fit into society. They may change their social peer group often as they attempt to resolve this crisis. If the adolescents are unable to find their place in society, they may have difficulties identifying with a social group and experience role confusion.
Six (Early adulthood)	Intimacy versus isolation	Young adults look for a stable relationship they can commit themselves to. If they cannot find that relationship, they may become self-absorbed (i.e., seek isolation).

Stage & Age	Crises	Example
Seven (Middle age)	Generativity versus stagnation	Middle-aged adults attempt to give back to society, especially to members of the next generation. This may take the form of coaching a Little League team or raising a family. If they feel their generosity is unwelcome, they may become uninterested and inactive (i.e., stagnant).
Eight(Old age)	Integrity versus despair	Older adults reflect on their lives. Knowing life has been meaningful and worthwhile leads them to develop a sense of integrity. However, if they feel they have not accomplished all they wanted to and dwell on what they were unable to complete, they may experience despair.

PARENTING STYLES

Diana Baumrind developed a list of three distinct parenting styles commonly seen in European and European-American homes. According to Baumrind, these parenting styles are **authoritarian, permissive, and authoritative**.

▪ Authoritarian
  ▪ Strict and relatively unsympathetic
  ▪ Believe that what they say goes: "Because I said so!"
  ▪ Child learns not to question authority
▪ Permissive – aka laissez-faire
  ▪ Allows child to do as he or she pleases
  ▪ Sets few, if any, boundaries
  ▪ Allows the child to fend for him- or herself
▪ Authoritative – synonymous with democratic
  ▪ Compromising
  ▪ Compassionate
  ▪ Allows independence, but with limits
  ▪ Input from children is solicited when setting rules and consequences for violating said rules

Parenting styles not only affect the development of the child but also have a long-lasting impact on how the child will raise children of his or her own. According to Baumrind, authoritative parents produce well-adjusted children who get good grades in school and are cooperative and respectful of others. Authoritarian and permissive parenting produces socially inept children who may become aggressive, uncooperative, unfriendly, and disrespectful to others. It must be noted that much of Baumrind's data is based on correlation, and thus cannot be proven right or wrong.

Nuts and Bolts

One way to remember the difference between each of the parenting styles is to keep in mind that authoritarian parents are strict and rigid, like barbarians. Permissive parents do not require permission. Authoritative parents are most supportive. Another quick way to remember these styles is to use the acronym APA.

ENVIRONMENTAL INFLUENCES ON SOCIALIZATION

The socialization process is an important part of development. During this process, the child learns what behaviors are appropriate and inappropriate. Which individuals influence the child in this process varies as he or she ages.

SOCIAL SKILLS

As children age, they are exposed to a variety of influences and interactions that help build the skills essential for adult life. Many important social skills, such as cooperation, are learned at an early age. **Cooperation**, *the ability to share with others,* is learned through daily routines, mainly in interactions with other children, also known as play. Play teaches the growing child life-long strategies that are useful in adult society. Another crucial social skill learned at an early age is **empathy**, *the ability to relate to and understand others emotionally.* A third important social skill is **self-regulation**, *the ability to understand how to control one's emotions and their corresponding behaviors.*

GENDER ROLES

Understanding the roles of each gender is important in a society that emphasizes male-female differences. Many of the gender roles that children of each sex display are the result of the intersection of nature and nurture. Social learning theory emphasizes the influence of outside factors in the establishment of gender roles. Children learn from an early age—through the media (television, print media) or social interaction with the opposite sex—exactly what is expected of each gender.

ADOLESCENCE

It is important to understand that the term "adolescence" is largely a Western cultural phenomenon. The adolescent time period typically starts with **puberty**, *the physical change of the body as it prepares for the ability to sexually reproduce,* and lasts until approximately the end of the teenage years or early twenties. During this time, **primary sex characteristics**, *essential reproductive organs,* and **secondary sex characteristics**, *the development of nonessential reproductive characteristics (such as body hair and the deepening of the voice in* *males)*, begin to develop. In addition to the physical changes that take place, adolescents begin to search for their own identities, trying to discover who they are and where they fit in society at large. During this period of exploration, it is not uncommon for adolescents to frequently change peer groups, trying to find the group they best identify with.

For many teens, adolescence is a turbulent time; discovering their identities, experiencing an influx of new hormones and emotions, and feeling increased pressure from their peers can produce much confusion in teens as they search for themselves.

LAWRENCE KOHLBERG'S MORAL REASONING

In his well-known "Heinz dilemma," Kohlberg asked children of all ages to respond to a difficult moral dilemma. In it, a man named Heinz is contemplating stealing a drug that could possibly save the life of his dying wife. As he asked children to respond to Heinz's situation, Kohlberg, who followed the cognitive school of thought, constructed three levels of moral reasoning. According to Kohlberg, the level of moral reasoning was based on each child's particular level of cognitive functioning—as a child ages, so does his or her level of cognitive functioning. Below are Kohlberg's three levels of cognitive functioning: preconventional, conventional, and postconventional.

Level 1: Preconventional, based on avoiding punishment or personal gain
   Stage 1: Obedience orientation
   - Obey rules for fear of punishment
     - Don't cheat on that test because you will get detention.
   Stage 2: Personal gain (hedonistic) orientation
   - Do what is best for yourself
     - Cheat on the test because you need an A to get twenty dollars.

Level 2: Conventional, based on the approval of others and society
   Stage 3: Good boy, nice girl orientation
   - Act in a way that is socially acceptable
     - Don't cheat because "good" people don't cheat
   Stage 4: Law and order orientation
   - Understand that society needs laws and order to uphold a civilized society
     - If you cheat and get caught, you should be prepared to face the consequences.

Level 3: Postconventional, based on higher morals; there are exceptions to everything
   Stage 5: Contractual legalistic
   - People in a civilized society understand that individuals enter into a social contract with each other, ultimately deciding what is good for all.
     - Allow someone to cheat off your exam because you know his or her parents are going through a divorce and that person has not had time to study.

Stage 6: Universal ethical orientation
 ▪ There are certain universal ethical principals that all people believe in.
   ▪ Cheating could be justified because much of the material on the test was never covered in class, and the test was given simply out of spite rather than as an assessment.

CRITICISM OF KOHLBERG

Research has shown that levels one and two appear to be universal, but that level three appears to be culturally specific. In addition, Kohlberg has been criticized for not including women in his study.

AP Tip

Be prepared to examine a behavior and identify the level of moral development (preconventional, conventional, postconventional) in which the behavior would take place.

PHYSICAL, SOCIAL, AND COGNITIVE DIMENSIONS IN ADULT DEVELOPMENT

As people age they go through numerous physical, cognitive, and social changes, listed below. The changes that occur at each stage of life are important for successful aging.

EARLY ADULT YEARS (APPROXIMATELY 20S–30S)
 ▪ Physical changes
   ▪ Increase in physical abilities
   ▪ Muscle mass stays the same or increases
   ▪ Typically in top physical shape (20s)
 ▪ Cognitive changes
   ▪ Increase in cognitive abilities (vocabulary, knowledge, understanding)
 ▪ Social changes
   ▪ Search for life partner begins
   ▪ Balance between work and marriage
   ▪ May create a family and have children
     ▪ Satisfaction with marriage may decrease during this time
     ▪ Peer relationships may diminish due to increased family obligations

MIDDLE ADULT YEARS (APPROXIMATELY 40S–50S)
 ▪ Physical changes
   ▪ Decline in senses (hearing, vision, smell), muscle mass, sexual functioning
 ▪ Cognitive changes
   ▪ Increase in cognitive abilities (vocabulary, knowledge, understanding)

- Social changes
  - Midlife transition
    - People reevaluate what they have done and where they are going
  - Midlife crisis (Michael Levinson)
    - An understanding that half of life is over and anger at this realization; some try to "reclaim" their youth
    - Example: getting a tattoo and going to dance clubs
  - Middlescence (Gail Sheehy)
    - A second adolescence
    - Example: buying a sports car because it is finally affordable

LATE ADULT YEARS (APPROXIMATELY 60S–BEYOND)
- Physical changes
  - Decrease in senses (hearing, vision, smell), muscle mass, sexual functioning, digestive functioning, height
- Cognitive changes
  - Decreased fluid intelligence, ability to think quickly, assess situations, complete tasks quickly, and parallel process information
    - Memory that appears to fade is typically related to episodic (event-based) memories, which is consistent with fluid intelligence
    - Important to note that staying mentally active (doing crossword puzzles, creating crafts, participating in arts) appears to slow down the loss of fluid intelligence
  - Increased crystallized intelligence, general/overall knowledge
- Social changes
  - Begin to lose friendships (usually due to death)
  - Find current relationships more satisfying and meaningful

TWO THEORIES ON AGING: NATURE VERSUS NURTURE

The way a person ages continues to be a controversial subject. Some believe that our lives and bodies are preprogrammed, while others argue that our interaction with the elements in our environments dictates our longevity. Identifying the correct aging process is a difficult task, mainly because of the various confounding variables that exist.

1. Programmed Senescence: Nature
   - The body is biologically preprogrammed as to when it will die; this program is expressed in our genes
     - Some support for this theory exists in the longevity gene. People found to possess this gene appear to live much longer than those who are void of such a gene.

2. Wear-and-tear theory (active living approach): Nurture
   - When we are young, our bodies repair themselves quickly; one example is the brain's ability to adapt to damage that

may occur when a person is young. As we age, our body loses its ability to repair itself due to environmental situations we encounter throughout life, ultimately leading to death.

DEATH AND DYING

According to Elisabeth Kübler-Ross, M.D., a dying person progresses through five stages: denial, anger, bargaining, depression, and acceptance. Many have praised Kübler-Ross for her insight into the dying process, while others have questioned the five stages. For example, a person who suddenly becomes ill may not have adequate time to progress through all five. Another source of disagreement for some psychologists is whether the stages are also felt by family members of the dying person. Some people argue that not every individual progresses in this order, while others believe that these are not stages, per se, but rather emotions that some people experience, and thus may not apply to all of those who are dying.

Stage	Explanation	Example
Denial	Person does not believe he is dying and may seek numerous opinions from medical professionals.	Jerry seeks a second and third opinion about his diagnosis.
Anger	Person does not understand why he is dying, and may express anger to others.	Jerry becomes angry at his wife because she is not ill.
Bargaining	Person may begin to bargain, saying he will improve some aspect of his life if he is allowed to live.	Jerry says that he will be a better father if he is allowed to live.
Depression	Person may want to be alone, realizing that death is approaching.	Jerry sits alone at the park each day.
Acceptance	Person understands that death is a natural process and accepts his fate.	Jerry realizes that he is dying and that it is a normal part of life.

Nuts and Bolts

 A good way to remember the order of the stages of death and dying/grief is to think of the acronym D.A.B.D.A.

AP Tip

Make sure you are able to identify which stage of death/dying/grieving a person is in when demonstrating a certain behavior.

Multiple-Choice Questions

1. Vinnie is five months old and enjoys playing peek-a-boo mainly because, as Vinnie understands it, the human face is there, then it disappears, then it reappears. According to Piaget, what stage is Vinnie currently in?
   (A) Preconventional
   (B) Concrete operational
   (C) Sensorimotor
   (D) Preoperational
   (E) Formal operational

2. Tim is fourteen years old and believes that everyone is as concerned with his looks as he is. What is Tim experiencing?
   (A) Personal fable
   (B) Imaginary audience
   (C) Conservation
   (D) Identity confusion
   (E) Thought disorder

3. Keiko drops out of her high school drama club and joins the rugby club instead in an effort to meet new people. According to Erikson's psychosocial theory of development, Keiko is currently experiencing
   (A) trust versus mistrust
   (B) initiative versus guilt
   (C) secure attachment versus insecure attachment
   (D) identity versus role confusion
   (E) industry versus inferiority

4. Harry Harlow felt that for infant monkeys
   (A) the need for contact comfort is less important than the reduction of the hunger drive
   (B) the need for social interaction is clearly overestimated
   (C) the need for contact comfort is more important than the reduction of the hunger drive
   (D) infant monkeys raised in a rich, stimulating environment are more likely to be securely attached
   (E) there is a critical period during which imprinting must take place

5. Lightly touching an infant's cheek will result in the movement of the infant's mouth to whichever side of his face was touched. This is known as what type of reflex?
   (A) Babinski
   (B) Moro
   (C) Palmar
   (D) Sucking
   (E) Rooting

6. Students at Bayside High School are amazed by all the knowledge Dr. Jones possesses. Having taken psychology, you know that the professor's extensive knowledge can likely be attributed to a high level of
   (A) fluid intelligence
   (B) crystallized intelligence
   (C) self-efficacy
   (D) wisdom
   (E) creativity

7. Maturation refers to
   (A) environmental influences that can potentially put the baby at risk for developing a disorder
   (B) development that occurs naturally, and without the influence of the environment
   (C) development that occurs because of the influence of the environment
   (D) the adaptation of new objects in an already existing schema
   (E) the implementation of a new schema to make sense of new information

8. Which of the following correctly represents Elisabeth Kübler-Ross's theory of death and grief?
   (A) Denial, anger, fear, bargaining, acceptance
   (B) Fear, anger, bargaining, denial, acceptance
   (C) Denial, anger, curiosity, bargaining, acceptance
   (D) Denial, anger, bargaining, depression, acceptance
   (E) Anger, bargaining, grief, anger, acceptance

9. Brody is contemplating whether to cheat on his upcoming psychology examination. He knows that he needs to get an A on the test. However, he also recognizes that if he gets caught cheating, he will have to accept any punishment he receives. Brody then decides that getting an A on the exam outweighs the risk of getting caught. According to Kohlberg, Brody is currently at what level of morality?
   (A) Preconventional
   (B) Operational
   (C) Post-conventional
   (D) Concrete
   (E) Conventional

10. The term used to define any agent that may interfere with development in a human fetus is called
   (A) maturation
   (B) a teratogen
   (C) egocentrism
   (D) the critical period
   (E) a personal fable

11. According to Baumrind, the type of parenting that would most likely produce a cooperative, caring, and empathetic child is
   (A) permissive
   (B) avoidant
   (C) egocentric
   (D) authoritarian
   (E) authoritative

12. According to Erikson, the first crisis encountered in human development is
   (A) trust versus mistrust
   (B) identity versus role confusion
   (C) shame versus doubt
   (D) generativity versus stagnation
   (E) intimacy versus isolation

13. Fluid intelligence _____ with age, while crystallized intelligence _____ with age.
   (A) remains the same; remains the same
   (B) increases; increases
   (C) decreases; decreases
   (D) decreases; increases
   (E) increases; decreases

14. Tommy, a toddler, is sitting in a room with his mother when a stranger enters, causing Tommy to cling tightly to his mother. His mother reassures Tommy that everything is all right and that he can play with the stranger. According to Mary Ainsworth, Tommy is displaying
    (A) insecure attachment
    (B) ambivalent/resistant attachment
    (C) obstinate attachment
    (D) secure attachment
    (E) unasserted attachment

15. When asked why the sky is blue, Erin responds, "Because blue is my favorite color!" According to Piaget, Erin is displaying
    (A) animism
    (B) egocentrism
    (C) artificialism
    (D) personal fable
    (E) industry versus inferiority

Free-Response Questions

1. Discuss how each of the following viewed human development.
   (a) Jean Piaget
   (b) Lawrence Kohlberg
   (c) Erik Erikson
   (d) Lev Vygotsky

2. Jim is a sixteen-year-old who is contemplating dropping out of high school. Jim says, "Nobody understands me and everyone stares at me all the time! Plus, I have really big ideas, and my band is going to make it as soon as people actually appreciate something unique and truly culture-changing." Explain how each of the following influences Jim.
   (a) Formal operational stage
   (b) Personal fable
   (c) Imaginary audience
   (d) Identity versus role confusion

Answers

MULTIPLE-CHOICE QUESTIONS

1. Answer: C. Piaget's earliest stage is sensorimotor. During this stage, the child improves in his or her sensory and motor skills, but is limited cognitively because he or she does not understand the principle of object permanence until about twelve months of age (*Psychology*, 8th ed. pp. 466–467/9th ed. pp. 474–475).

2. Answer: B. Adolescents reenter a phase of egocentrism that is similar to the egocentrism experienced in Piaget's

preoperational stage (*Psychology*, 8th ed. p. 495/9th ed. pp. 501–502).

3. Answer: D. According to Erikson, adolescents search to find who they are and where they fit in society. Adolescence is a difficult time because people at that age are substantially influenced by their peers (*Psychology*, 8th ed. p. 485/9th ed. pp. 490–491).

4. Answer: C. Harlow's research was conducted with monkeys, but subsequent studies have shown that humans raised in isolated or neglectful environments display the same behaviors as Harlow's test subjects raised alone. Harlow believed that the need for attachment is stronger than the need for food (*Psychology*, 8th ed. pp. 481–482/9th ed. pp. 486–487).

5. Answer: E. Rooting allows the infant to turn toward a possible food source (nipple/breast). This reflex appears to be innate and not learned (*Psychology*, 8th ed. p. 463/9th ed. p. 471).

6. Answer: B. Crystallized intelligence is knowledge that one accumulates throughout a lifetime. Fluid intelligence is one's ability to quickly process information. As a person ages, his or her fluid intelligence decreases while crystallized intelligence increases (*Psychology*, 8th ed. p. 505/9th ed. pp. 510–511).

7. Answer: B. Maturation is the development of an individual independent of environmental influences (*Psychology*, 8th ed. p. 458/9th ed. p. 466).

8. Answer: D. Kübler-Ross outlined the five stages of dying/grief: denial, anger, bargaining, depression, acceptance. Note that the friends and family members of the dying may also experience these stages (*this material does not appear in either textbook edition*).

9. Answer: E. Kohlberg's middle level of moral development (conventional) is centered around the desire to maintain law and order (*Psychology*, 8th ed. p. 499/9th ed. p. 506).

10. Answer: B. Any substance that may interfere with the development of the fetus is called a teratogen. Teratogens affect cognitive and physical development as the individual continues his or her lifelong development (*Psychology*, 8th ed. pp. 460–461/9th ed. p. 469).

11. Answer: E. Parenting styles affect the development of the human. According to Baumrind, they also have long-reaching effects in future relationships. Studies indicate that authoritative (or democratic) parenting leads to more cooperative, socially well-adjusted children (*Psychology*, 8th ed. pp. 485–486/9th ed. p. 491).

12. Answer: A. Erikson believed that human development was a result of the interaction between a person and his or her environment. His early stages focus on the parent-child

relationship and how that influences the child as he or she develops. A sense of basic trust in one's primary caregiver will help an individual successfully resolve other crises (*Psychology*, 8th ed. p. 485/9th ed. p. 490).

13. Answer: D. Fluid intelligence refers to one's cognitive quickness, thinking, and problem solving. Crystallized intelligence is the knowledge one accumulates over the course of a lifetime. As a person ages, his or her fluid intelligence decreases while his or her crystallized intelligence increases (*Psychology*, 8th ed. p. 505/9th ed. pp. 510–511).

14. Answer: D. The three attachment styles proposed by Mary Ainsworth show the attachment of the child and the parent. This type of attachment, according to Ainsworth, has long-lasting positive effects when it comes to later relationship building (*Psychology*, 8th ed. p. 482/9th ed. pp. 487–488).

15. Answer: B. Piaget said that children in the preoperational stage of cognitive development believe that the world revolves around them, so they have a difficult time taking another person's point of view (*Psychology*, 8th ed. p. 471/9th ed. pp. 475–476).

FREE-RESPONSE QUESTIONS

1. (a) Jean Piaget believed that human cognitive development occurred in stages and that each stage was predicated on the previous one. Piaget also believed that the stages occurred in a predictable and universal order.
   (b) Lawrence Kohlberg focused on moral development. Each level of development was influenced by the age, and thus the cognitive abilities, of the individual.
   (c) Erik Erikson believed that development was based on a series of psychosocial crises. The way in which each crisis was resolved would influence the behavior of the individual later in life.
   (d) Lev Vygotsky believed that development was based on one's culture and that the tasks a child can accomplish varied within the zone of proximal development.

2. Jean Piaget would say that Jim is currently in the formal operational stage and is experiencing adolescent egocentrism. Specifically, Jim is experiencing personal fable when he says that "nobody understands" him. Another aspect of adolescent egocentrism is that Jim is experiencing an imaginary audience. This is evident when he says, "everyone is staring at me all the time." Piaget would say that in time Jim will understand that his ideas are in line with what other adolescents believe.

   Erik Erikson would say that Jim is currently experiencing the psychosocial crisis known as identity versus role confusion. Jim does not know who he is and is trying to find his own identity. According to Erikson, if Jim is able to resolve this conflict, he will be able to find his place in society. Erikson would say this is a normal crisis that many adolescents face.

COGNITION

Cognition refers to the mental processes that enable an organism to think, comprehend, and communicate. Cognitive skills allow organisms to adapt to environmental changes and needs, increasing the likelihood for survival. As cognitive skills improve, the processes of thinking, language, and memory also increase.

THE BASIC FUNCTION OF THOUGHT

What makes us human? Some psychologists argue that one defining characteristic of human beings is their ability to think. Yet how can something not overtly observable be the very thing that makes us human? For cognitive psychologists this process of mental activity, or circle of thought, is essential in that it allows us to interpret sensory information, form an opinion and consider options, arrive at a decision, and, finally, act appropriately. This circle of thought is completed each time we are faced with a situation that requires action. Cognitive psychologists are interested in studying how **thinking**, *the cerebral management of information received from our senses and transferred into concepts that are used to solve problems and ultimately reach decisions*, affects our daily lives. Understanding exactly which tools we use to make decisions involves an analysis of the thought process.

MEASURING INFORMATION PROCESSING

When psychologists discuss the idea of measuring the thought process they are essentially talking about measuring mental chronometry, which relies on **reaction time**, *the elapsed time between the presentation of a stimulus and the behavioral response*. Measuring the reaction time allows cognitive psychologists the opportunity to infer how long it takes to cognitively process information. However, measuring reaction time is influenced by four factors: complexity, expectancy, stimulus-response compatibility, and speed-accuracy tradeoff.

A task's complexity or level of difficulty influences the reaction time exhibited by a person. More complex tasks require a longer thought process, which means a slower reaction time. If you pass the same person in the hall every day, the time it takes you to recognize this person will grow shorter. However, if you are walking down the hall and see someone new, you will need longer to process that information because the complexity of the situation has increased. The more familiar you are with a situation, the less complex it is, and the easier it is to process.

If we anticipate that something will occur, we are able to process the information more rapidly. For example, if you are expecting a loud noise—say the sound of fireworks—you will be able to react more quickly than if you were surprised. The expectancy of an event is a crucial factor in how quickly the human brain processes information. Unexpected events take longer to process, which leads to an increase in reaction time.

If stimulus-response compatibility is high, we tend to react in an appropriate manner during times of stress. For example, if you are washing your hands and the water begins to get too hot, you would most likely automatically reach for the faucet and turn it in the opposite direction, reducing the amount of hot water you were being exposed to. Here, stimulus-response compatibility is high: you knew exactly what to do when the situation presented itself, and reaction time was thus minimal. However, when stimulus-response compatibility is low, reaction time will be increased. For example, most car accidents are the result of low stimulus-response compatibility. Given that most car accidents are unexpected, and often include extremely stressful moments just prior to their happening, the brain is unable to process this information quickly; thus people often "freeze" up and do not react appropriately.

Lastly, if a person tries to respond too quickly, errors will likely occur. However, if response time increases, the chance that errors will be committed decreases. This is the speed-accuracy tradeoff. Focusing on the speed of the reaction decreases the accuracy. For example, if you are playing *Jeopardy!* and you are eager to be the first person to "buzz in" to answer a question, you might "jump the gun" and press the buzzer too quickly. Although your speed (reaction time) was increased, you may have "buzzed in" to a question to which you did not in fact know the answer, thus decreasing the accuracy of your answer.

THE BRAIN AND REACTION TIME

The areas of the brain responsible for processing new situations and tasks that require a great deal of cognition are localized in the frontal lobes. Remember, the frontal lobes are important for short-term memory. However, once the situation or task becomes familiar, we no longer rely on our frontal lobes to process this information. Rather, we rely on the hippocampal region, which is responsible for the formation of long-term explicit memories.

Nuts and Bolts

 Think of your hippocampus as an "autopilot" in that it allows you to complete tasks without much thought. If you have to "think" about a situation or task, then your frontal lobes are more active, thus increasing the chance that you won't perform the needed task or behavior accurately.

AP Tip

Free-response questions integrate multiple chapters, so be prepared to answer how the brain is involved in memory and cognition.

MENTAL REPRESENTATIONS: THE INGREDIENTS OF THOUGHT

When cognitive psychologists discuss thought they are referring to the specific components of thought. Breaking down the components of thought—as shown in the following table—allows psychologists to understand how each person's thought process works.

Component of thought		Definition	Example
Concept		A category that encompasses information that shares similar features or characteristics	a dog
Component of a concept	Prototype	The best example that incorporates all essential features of a concept; this differs from person to person and is based on experience	You were asked to think of a dog and you immediately thought of a poodle because you own a poodle.
	Formal concepts	A concept that is defined by a set of rules	Any geometrical shape that has defined rules to dictate its shape. A rectangle has four equal sides.
	Natural concepts	A concept formed through everyday experiences	Your concept of a "dog" is based on your experiences with dogs.
Schema		A mental framework that helps organize information based on experiences	You believe that dogs are nice, and therefore are willing to pet a dog if you see one.

Component of thought	Definition	Example
Script	A personal view on how an event will be played out, based on experience	If you meet a new dog, you have a plot in mind of what behaviors will need to be performed before the dog will allow you to pet it.
Mental model	A mental representation of a situation, event, or object based on experience	If all the dogs you had ever met growled, then when you saw a new dog, you would automatically assume that it would growl as well, based on your experience.
Cognitive maps	A mental representation of an environment	If a friend told you that she saw a dog at the park you frequently visit, you would be able to form a mental representation of where she was describing in the park.

AP Tip

Past multiple-choice questions have asked students to define concepts, prototypes, and schemas.

THINKING STRATEGIES

Cognitive psychologists refer to thinking strategies when they discuss the ways in which a person has reached a decision. Thinking strategies allow us to reach conclusions and solutions to problems. This thinking is known as **reasoning**, *a cognitive process used to reach a decision*. When faced with a new situation, you rely on strategies you have previously used. Psychologists refer to two types of reasoning, formal and informal, both of which offer strategies to formulate decisions and justify conclusions.

FORMAL REASONING

Formal reasoning (deductive reasoning) *is used to justify a conclusion based on the truth of the premise*. This type of reasoning is often used to help formulate a decision. For example, all dogs have tails; Fido is a dog; therefore, Fido must have a tail. The conclusion is deduced to be true, because the premises are true. An **algorithm**, *a systematic procedure used to guarantee a correct solution to a problem*, is also considered to be a type of formal reasoning. Although algorithms do guarantee that the correct conclusions will be reached, they are time consuming.

Nuts and Bolts

 One way to remember the definition of an algorithm is to think about going to a grocery store to buy eggs. If you were to use an algorithm to find the eggs, you would walk up and down each aisle, looking at every product on every shelf until you found the eggs. This would be time consuming, but you would be guaranteed to find the eggs.

INFORMAL REASONING

Informal reasoning (inductive reasoning), *is used to form a conclusion based on the believability or accessibility of information.* Psychologists often use this type of reasoning when conducting an experiment. For example, if you saw four dogs during a walk in a park, and all four dogs had tails, then you might conclude that all dogs must have tails. If you encountered a dog that did not have a tail, you might induce that it was not a dog, because your experiences with dogs had never included one with no tail.

Another example of informal reasoning is a **heuristic,** *a rule of thumb or cognitive shortcut used for problem solving.* Unlike algorithms, which use a defined set of rules, heuristics allow quick decision making. However, quick decisions are not always correct, and can lead to inaccurate judgments. The three most commonly used heuristics are availability, representativeness, and anchoring and adjustment. **Availability heuristics,** *rules of thumb that rely on the most easily accessible information known to the person to assist in problem solving,* are used each day, especially when it is necessary to quickly reach a conclusion.

Nuts and Bolts

 When asked which country has a higher population, Canada or Australia, many people rely on accessible information to formulate a conclusion. Therefore, if the only thing you know about Canada is that it is cold, you might conclude that fewer people live there than in Australia, which is not as cold. However, you might be surprised to learn that Canada has approximately 10 million more residents than Australia. Because you used only information that was most easily accessible to you to form your judgment, you did not account for the size of each country, which might have affected your answer.

Representativeness heuristics, *rules of thumb that rely on how well a situation matches a generalization or prototype we have about an established concept,* are used to help make quick decisions. Although they do allow for judgments to be reached quickly, they can also lead to errors, such as stereotyping or misrepresentation of a certain segment of the population. For example, you've just met Josh, a quiet and shy person. Is Josh a librarian or a boxer? If you believe that Josh is most likely a librarian, you have reached your conclusion by using a representativeness heuristic. People tend to make judgments based on how well a particular description fits the more general population.

AP Tip

Past free-response questions have required proper identification of which heuristic is being used and have asked students to provide an example based on a given question.

Anchoring and adjustment heuristics, *rules of thumb that rely on a starting or reference point to begin with and then adjust to accommodate information*, allow us to make snap judgments based on a beginning frame of reference. We then make adjustments to accommodate any new information that may come along. For example, many high school students share the same political beliefs (anchor) as their parents. However, as those students learn more information independently, their initial beliefs (anchor) may change slightly to incorporate this newly acquired information (adjustment).

PROBLEM SOLVING

Cognitive psychologists are interested in studying how human beings solve problems, as well as in any obstacles that might hinder the process. How we approach a given problem is based largely on prior exposure to similar problems. However, not all problems are similar to previous ones, and often we must approach a new problem in a new way. Common problem-solving techniques include means-end analysis, analogies, incubation, and insight.

MEANS-END ANALYSIS

The **means-end analysis**, a problem-solving technique that relies on the identification of a final goal and the prerequisite steps needed to achieve that goal, is a widely used problem-solving technique. When faced with a problem, the individual identifies the ultimate goal, and then determines what subgoals or behaviors are needed to achieve the final goal. After every subgoal is reached, the individual will reevaluate each subsequent step needed to achieve the final goal. For example, if your ultimate goal is to achieve a 5 on the AP Psychology Exam, you will have to outline the subgoals that you need to meet before taking the exam. First you will have to allocate sufficient time each day for studying, then you will have to progress through each chapter of the textbook, making sure you understand each one along the way. If, for some reason, you do not understand a particular concept, you may have to revise your plan of scoring a 5 on the exam. If you are able to achieve each subgoal, then your final goal will likely be achieved.

ANALOGIES

Another problem-solving technique is the use of **analogies**, *finding similarities between a current problem and prior problems*. Analogies are useful when trying to solve a current problem. Looking at previous problems and how they were solved allows an individual to apply a technique that may have been successful in the past to help solve a current problem. Although analogies can facilitate problem solving, they may also serve to obstruct problem solving by limiting the individual to techniques that may not apply to current problems. If you failed a recent psychology test, for example, you might think back to another test that you passed and try to apply the same studying techniques you used there.

INCUBATION

A third problem-solving technique is **incubation**, *stepping back from a problem to allow the problem to work itself out.* If you have ever had difficulty finding the solution to a problem, it is often helpful to simply walk away, or stop thinking about the problem. Stepping back often allows you to sort out the problem and find the best solution. It also allows you to view it from a fresh perspective.

INSIGHT

A fourth problem-solving strategy involves **insight**, *the sudden realization of a solution to a problem.* During incubation the solution to the current problem may become obvious. The moment that this solution is realized is said to be insight, which is also known as the "eureka effect" or the "aha phenomenon." This problem-solving technique is useful when you are faced with a problem that appears to have no solution.

OBSTACLES TO PROBLEM SOLVING

Cognitive psychologists are also interested in the different obstacles that can hinder problem solving. These can include mental set, functional fixedness, and confirmation bias.

MENTAL SET

One obstacle to problem solving involves the use of a **mental set**, *the tendency to approach new problems with strategies that may have worked in the past.* Mental sets can limit our ability to "think outside the box" because we can be locked into previously useful strategies.

Nuts and Bolts

 Many students miss questions on a test that are written in the negative, with wording such as "which of the following DOES NOT . . ." because all previous questions required the correct answer, while ignoring the wrong answers. One way to break a mental set is to read the question slowly.

FUNCTIONAL FIXEDNESS

Another obstacle to problem solving is **functional fixedness**, *the inability to see an object as being used for other than its intended purpose.* Functional fixedness can impair problem solving if you don't think that an object can be used any other way other than its intended use. Because of this stubbornness, some people will not be able to solve a problem that might otherwise have been easily solved. For example, if you need to tighten a screw but don't have a screwdriver, you may think you're out of luck. However, if you have a dime or another coin in your pocket you can use it as a screwdriver. If you do this, you have overcome the functional fixedness associated with coins.

> ## AP Tip
>
> Past multiple-choice questions have asked students about mental sets or functional fixedness. Be ready to explain how these are an obstacle to problem solving; be sure to know the different obstacles to problem solving.

CONFIRMATION BIAS

A third obstacle to problem solving is **confirmation bias**, *the tendency to accept information that supports our beliefs while ignoring information that counters our beliefs.* Confirmation bias is a problem-solving obstacle that is familiar to just about everyone. When given information that is different from your personal beliefs you may simply ignore it, while choosing to accept information that confirms your beliefs. For example, if you believe that the human race is the sole cause of global warming then you will ignore all opinions to the contrary.

> ## Nuts and Bolts
>
> A way to remember the definition of confirmation bias is that people do not generally like to be given information that is counter to their beliefs, and therefore may ignore the information presented. They prefer information that confirms their beliefs.

DECISION MAKING

The process of decision making is of great interest to cognitive psychologists. Decision making involves evaluating the options presented to see if there is a favorable outcome, and then ultimately going forth with a decision. Evaluating options involves comparing the attributes each possible decision may have. Each option has a factor known as **utility**, *a measurement of satisfaction received by choosing that option.* When making a decision we want to maximize the utility (satisfaction) and minimize the potential dissatisfaction. Despite efforts to increase utility, some decisions will inherently have flaws. One potential flaw in the decision-making process is known as the **gambler's fallacy**, *the belief that the probability of a random sequence is influenced by a preceding behavior.* This fallacy can lead to faulty decision making, because the person believes that if he or she performs a certain behavior, the chances of obtaining the desired outcome are increased. Decisions made because of the gambler's fallacy typically result in an unwanted outcome.

Nuts and Bolts

To help remember gambler's fallacy, think about stories you have heard about athletes believing that if they perform a certain behavior they will improve their chances of winning. You can also think of gambler's fallacy as essentially a superstitious behavior that a person believes will influence the outcome in a favorable manner.

Another influence in the decision-making process is known as **the framing effect**, *influencing the decision by altering the words used in describing the decision.* The way a question is worded, or framed, can influence a person's decision. An example of the framing effect would be if a person were asked to decide which kind of ice cream he wanted, option A, which is labeled 97 percent fat free, or option B, which is labeled 3 percent fat, he would most likely chose option A. The decision to choose option A is based on the wording on the label: 97 percent fat free is more attractive than 3 percent fat.

Nuts and Bolts

Surveys often take advantage of the framing effect by using carefully chosen words. These words can, and often do, influence survey outcomes.

AP Tip

Past free-response questions have asked students to identify how the framing effect could alter the outcome of a decision. Multiple-choice questions have asked students to identify obstacles that influence decision making.

LANGUAGE AND ITS ELEMENTS

It is often said that the ability to communicate our thoughts is uniquely human. However, some believe that the ability to communicate is not uniquely human. While it is true that animals can communicate with each other, psychologists do not consider that form of communication true language. True language, psychologists say, must have three characteristics: **syntax and semantics**, *the rules regarding the* *structure of grammar and its meaning,* **infinite creativity,** *the ability to generate an infinite number of sentences,* and **displacement,** *the ability to communicate events in the future or in the past.* When all three of these criteria are met, language is said to exist. The ability to communicate *thoughts* is uniquely human.

True language is composed of elements. Below is a list of these elements and the relation of each to language.

Element of Language	Definition	Example
Phonemes	The smallest basic unit of sound that can influence the production of speech	The word "bat" contains three phonemes: "b," "a," "t"
Morphemes	The smallest unit of meaning in language	The word "opened" has two syllables, which are morphemes. In addition, the "-ed" is also a morpheme because it changes the meaning of the word "open." Consequently, there are three morphemes in the word "opened."
Syntax	The rules associated with the organization of a sentence.	In English, a verb is always preceded by a noun. The proper order of an English sentence is subject, verb, object.
Semantics	Rules that establish the meaning of a sentence.	The words "to," "too," and "two" can be confusing and therefore you must rely on semantics to establish proper meaning. Where do you want <u>to</u> go? I want to go <u>too.</u> Can we have <u>two</u> ice cream cones, please?

Nuts and Bolts

 A good way to distinguish between a phoneme and a morpheme is to remember that there is **MORE** to a <u>more</u>pheme than to a phoneme.

AP Tip

Be prepared to identify the different elements of language.

UNDERSTANDING SPEECH

How do we understand the words we hear? Psychologists have identified Werrnicke's area as that part of the brain that is responsible for turning audible words into thoughts. Human vision also appears to play a role in helping to decode what we hear. The **McGurk effect**, *a combination of hearing and vision that allows us to understand speech*, has shown the important role vision plays in our understanding of what we are hearing. Words can often be misinterpreted when we lack visual stimuli; sometimes the words we hear may not be the words that were actually said.

DEVELOPMENT OF LANGUAGE

Is language something we are born with, or is it something we acquire through experience and maturation? Children are able to understand language long before they are able to produce audible language. The acquisition of spoken language is a long process, with the most significant milestones reached during the first three years of life. The table below outlines the process of language during those first three years.

Year of life	Language displayed	Example
First	Babbling stage	"Gagaga" "babababa"—these are the child's initial attempts to communicate.
	One-word stage/ overextension of words	One word is used to mean multiple objects or a more complex meaning. For example, the word "da" may mean "what's that" or "look over there."
Second	Two-word stage/telegraphic speech	Between 18 months of age and two years the child increases his vocabulary and begins to string words together in a manner that resembles a telegraph. For example, a child may say, "Want juice," meaning he would like something to drink.
	Three-word stage	The use of three-word sentences that are typically composed of a subject, a verb, and an object.
	Overregularization	The misapplication of the rules of grammar. For example, a child may say, "I sitted down" or "I goed there."
Third	"Wh" words	Beginning usage of words such as "who," "what," "where," and "why"

Acquisition of Language

How do children learn language? Numerous theories surround this perennial mystery. Some psychologists believe that language is the result of imitation, while others believe that language is the result of an inborn communication device within the brain. Regardless, psychologists agree that there exists a window of opportunity, or critical period, for the acquisition and development of language.

Behavioral Theory of Language Acquisition

According to behaviorists including B.F. Skinner, language is developed by reinforcement and imitation. A child learns the words he or she hears and is rewarded for saying them. For example, a parent says "mama" to the child with the hopes of having the child repeat the word. When the child imitates the word, the parent responds by praising the child. According to behaviorists, this positive reinforcement then serves to increase the behavior, in this case, saying "mama." Although positive reinforcement does play a role in the frequency of speaking, it fails to account for the inaccurate words often produced by children. For example, a three-year-old child may say "I goed to the store." While it is likely that the child has heard the sentence "I went to the store," he or she has probably not heard "goed." This expression of words not otherwise heard cannot be accounted for by such a strict behaviorist perspective.

Biological Theory of Language Acquisition

The fact that children throughout the world acquire language at approximately the same rate lends credibility to the notion that acquisition is at least partially innate. Noam Chomsky has proposed that humans possess **universal grammar**, *innate knowledge in all humans for the basic structure of grammar*. Exposure to language triggers this innate knowledge and language can then develop. Limited or no exposure to language will result in that person's being unable to develop language properly. This theory is also supported by the critical period theory of language, which states that there is a timeframe, usually up to age twelve, for the proper development of language. If, during this critical period, a child is not exposed to language, the ability to produce language will be lost. Further support of Chomsky's view on language as innate comes from studies on specific language impairment (SLI). Specific language impairment is a developmental language disorder in which language is impaired, despite otherwise normal cognitive development.

Nuts and Bolts

 There are numerous terms for describing something you are born with, including inborn, innate, hereditary, inherited, predisposed, natural, and nativist.

CULTURE, LANGUAGE, AND THOUGHT

Does where you live dictate how you think? According to psychologist Benjamin Whorf, the answer is yes. Whorf developed the theory of linguistic determinism to explain that not all cultures share the same words. In some cultures a given word may not exist, and therefore a member of that culture may not cognitively process the same information. Linguistic determinism states that culture dictates language, and language dictates thought and ultimately perception. Whorf cited the Inuits as an example of how language influences thought. Some believe that the Inuits have more than 100 words that mean "snow," although the exact number is unknown. Regardless, the basic idea behind Whorf's hypothesis (that language influences thought) holds. It has been hypothesized that the reason the Inuits have so many words for snow is because snow was such a significant part of the landscape of their region. In contrast, the spoken language of U.S. English has numerous words for time (second, minute, hour, day, year, era, and so forth), mainly because of the importance our culture places on time.

Critics of the Whorfian view of language and thought claim that this connection is false, citing the fact that we may often have trouble finding the words that correctly identify what we are talking about. Although a strict interpretation of the Whorfian view of language and thought does not appear to be correct, neither does the idea that language has no influence whatsoever over thought. The correct assumption lies in the middle, meaning that language does play some role in thought, just not to the extent Whorf believed.

MEMORY

Memory refers to *the mental processes needed to acquire, retain, and retrieve information.* Memory does not result from a single process, but from three distinct processes: the encoding, storage, and retrieval of information. **Encoding** *includes the process of acquiring and entering information into memory.* **Storage** *involves maintaining the encoded information over a period of time so it can be retrieved later.* **Retrieval** *refers to the process of accessing the stored information.*

Nuts and Bolts

 Think of the process of memory as similar to creating a document on a computer. Encoding is the act of typing the material into a word processing document. Storage is like saving the document. Retrieval could be compared to reopening the document on the computer.

AP Tip

Be prepared to identify the three steps necessary to process, store, and retrieve memories.

MODELS OF MEMORY

The **parallel distributed processing (PDP) model** *is a model in which new information is integrated with existing memories, resulting in a change in a person's overall knowledge base.* These newly integrated memories expand and improve the person's cognitive ability and enable him or her to have a better understanding of the environment. This integration is possible through the formation and connections of neural networks that occur between units of information. Each unit of information is connected with another piece of information. These neural networks are made stronger as each bit of information is associated—or experienced at the same time—with another type of information. When connections are strengthened, parallel processing is possible. Parallel processing enables multiple networks in the brain to process different kinds of sensory information simultaneously. For example, you can look at a car and read a description of it at the same time that a salesperson is describing the features of the car, all while you are remembering what a friend recently told you about that model.

The **information processing model** (Atkinson and Shiffrin) *is a model in which memory must be processed through three stages: sensory memory, short-term memory, and long-term memory.* Each stage is distinct, with the amount of information that can be stored, how long the information can be stored, and how the stored information is used varying.

AP Tip

Be prepared to identify the three stages of the information processing model.

STORING MEMORIES

Information must be stored in the human brain in order for a person to access it. There are several memory systems that accomplish this.

SENSORY MEMORY

George Sperling was among the first researchers to study sensory memory. Sperling presented subjects with a series of twelve letters arranged in four rows, with three letters in each row. He showed subjects the letters on a screen for just a brief moment. He then asked the participants to recall all the letters they could remember. Subjects, on average, were only able to recall four to five letters, even though they all reported seeing all of the letters. Through this experiment Sperling concluded that human visual sensory memory is brief—just long enough to pay attention to a few specific details.

Researchers have found that people have a distinct sensory memory for each sense. Visual memory and auditory memory have been studied the most. **Visual sensory memory**, *also referred to as iconic memory, is retained for less than a second.* **Auditory memory**, *also referred to as echoic memory, tends to be retained for a few seconds.* These extra few seconds allow speech to be heard as continuous words, and a melody to be heard as a series of notes.

Nuts and Bolts

 To remember that iconic sensory memory represents visual memory, think about the pronunciation of the word "iconic:" "eye-conic." On the other hand, an "echo" is heard, which is a good way to remember that echoic sensory memory represents auditory memory.

The benefit of storing sensory memory so briefly is that a person is then able to analyze a large variety of sensory information simultaneously.

AP Tip

Be prepared to answer a question about which type of sensory memory tends to be retained longer.

SHORT-TERM MEMORY

Short-term memory *receives information from sensory memory and then uses information stored in long-term memory to understand and associate the new information.* Working memory is part of short-term memory. **Working memory** *refers to the information that a person is actively "working with" in short-term memory.* For example, you are actively "working" with the material in this chapter by trying to comprehend and apply the content. The duration of short-term memory is about twenty to thirty seconds. **Maintenance rehearsal**, *repeating a unit of information over and over, makes it possible to keep the information in short-term memory for a longer period of time.*

In addition to having time constraints, short-term memory's capacity is also limited. Through his research, George Miller discovered that short-term memory is limited to a *"magic number seven plus or minus two."* This means that the average capacity of short-term memory is limited to seven units of information plus or minus two units. When a person's short-term memory reaches or exceeds seven items, some of those items will be "bumped" out of short-term memory. Maintenance rehearsal, as mentioned earlier, helps keep units of information in short-term memory longer, while chunking allows more information to be processed in short-term memory. **Chunking** *refers to the process of grouping individual units of information into meaningful chunks.* Grouping information into chunks expands the capacity of short-term memory into seven chunks of information instead of seven bits of information. Even though they are seven digits, phone numbers are actually learned as two chunks. The dash in between the first three and the last four digits makes it possible to learn the number as two chunks of information rather than as seven separate units of information. Think about the way you say your phone number. You probably say the first three digits together and then pause before saying the last four.

AP Tip

Be prepared to identify short-term memory as "working memory" and to explain the duration and capacity of short-term memory.

LONG-TERM MEMORY

Long-term memory *is the "warehouse" that stores a limitless amount of information over a period of time.* Certain memories stored in long-term memory can span a person's entire life. For example, long-term memories could range from what you ate for lunch yesterday to as far back as where you sat in your kindergarten classroom.

Nuts and Bolts

 Think of long-term memory as an attic. People store objects in their attics from as recently as last week to as long ago as when they first moved into the house. Most people are amazed at what they find when they go up in their attics. A typical response on finding something is, "I didn't know I still had this." The same is true of long-term memory. People are often amazed by what they can remember.

ENCODING INFORMATION INTO LONG-TERM MEMORY

Encoding is the process of transferring information from short-term to long-term memory. In short-term memory, information is kept active through **maintenance rehearsal,** *or the recitation of information over and over.* In order for this information to become stored in long-term memory, a more meaningful rehearsal has to occur. This is referred to as elaborative rehearsal. **Elaborative rehearsal** *is the application of personal meaning and understanding to help ensure that the information is encoded into long-term memory as demonstrated* *through higher-order thinking skills, which include application and evaluation.* When you personalize the material—when you provide personal significance to the material being studied— you are forming a relationship with it. This relationship helps to encode information into long-term memory. For example, you may have learned that William James is the father of American psychology. If you only memorized this concept, you might later forget what James is known for. That's because memorization keeps information active only for a brief period of time in short-term memory—possibly long enough to quickly answer a quiz question. If instead you use elaborative rehearsal by forming an association that ties William James to a concept you already know, that will increase the likelihood that William James will be encoded into your long-term memory. For example, you might associate James's last name with the American colony Jamestown: William James the first American psychologist/Jamestown the first American colony.

AP Tip

You should understand the difference between maintenance rehearsal and elaborative rehearsal and be prepared to identify in which stage of memory each type of rehearsal is used.

TYPES OF LONG-TERM MEMORY

There are different types of long-term memories. Memories that describe general, everyday information are called explicit memories; memories that involve "how to" information—for example, how to ride a bike or tie a shoe, are called implicit memories.

Explicit memories are also referred to as *declarative memories and require conscious thinking to recall information.*

Nuts and Bolts

Your explicit memories require "explicit" answers that must be "declared" through your consciously thinking about them.

Explicit memories are divided into episodic information and semantic information. **Episodic information** *includes personal memories*—for example, the date of your birthday, or your home address. **Semantic information** *involves general knowledge about your environment,* for example, how many tires are on a car, or the capital of the state you reside in.

Nuts and Bolts

Episodes in a TV series are comprised of "personal" stories describing characters. In other words, a TV series is actually a series of personalized episodes comparable to the episodic information that describes who you are.

Implicit memories are also referred to as *nondeclarative memories and do not require conscious thinking to recall.* Implicit memories contain **procedural information**, like *skills*. An example of procedural information would be the "procedure" of how to tie your shoes. For example, if someone were to ask you right after you tied your shoes how you did it you might respond, "I don't know, I just did." The reason you don't really know is that it is a procedure that does not require conscious thought. You could probably tie your shoes while thinking about what you have to get done later in the day. A second type of implicit memory includes one's predispositions and information acquired through conditioning. For example, a conditioned fear of white rats (as in Watson's Little Albert study) would be an implicit memory. The fear is automatic and is retrieved without conscious thought.

AP Tip

A free-response question might ask students to identify a specific example as either explicit or implicit memory. Be prepared to identify which type of memory is consciously or unconsciously recalled.

ORGANIZING LONG-TERM MEMORY

Information in long-term memory is organized into a hierarchical model based on similarities and associations. When new information is encoded into long-term memory it is grouped with similar information. This process improves later retrieval of the information. For example, when you see a new car that you find appealing, the image is "filed" into an already formed category of cars stored in long-term memory. By seeing another car that you also like you are quickly and simply able to recall the image of the first car for comparison. In other words, one image of a car triggers an image of a similar one. Organizing long-term memories based on similarities is like using a filing system. A person may organize phone, electric, and auto bills in separate files. When a new phone bill arrives, he will then file the information in the established phone file. This not only organizes new information with similar established information, but later helps him when he needs to find the information quickly.

The **semantic network model** *suggests that memories are stored through associations.* For example, the memory of a fire truck is associated with the color red, which then may be associated with a stop sign, which then could be associated with the stop sign at the end of a certain street. These associations could go on and on, resulting in several memories being retrieved through the recall of one memory. This is an example of **priming**, *a process that refers to activating and associating the strands of memories positioned in the semantic network.* Priming often occurs unconsciously. For example, if you saw a picture of your fourth-grade teacher, it might unconsciously trigger, or prime, memories you associate with fourth grade—where you sat in the classroom, the students who sat near your desk, projects that you worked on, and so forth.

AP Tip

You might be asked to write an essay about how long-term memories are organized.

RETRIEVING LONG-TERM MEMORY

Once information is stored in long-term memory it is only useful if it can be retrieved. Retrieval is the process of getting information out of long-term memory and bringing it into conscious awareness. This can be accomplished through retrieval cues. **Retrieval cues** *are clues, or hints, that help trigger a long-term memory.*

Nuts and Bolts

 Think of a long-term memory as a balloon. The string on the balloon is like a retrieval cue. In other words, the string helps you retrieve the balloon from the ceiling. A retrieval cue helps retrieve a long-term memory.

Retrieval cue failure *occurs when a retrieval cue is not adequate to trigger a long-term memory.* For example, when a friend is trying to help you remember something from a month ago and you don't understand what she is asking, you may respond by saying, "I don't know what you are talking about." When the friend restates her response by adding more information you may then respond by saying, "Oh, I remember—that was funny [sad, weird, etc.]." You were having retrieval cue failure, but your friend helped you recover the memory by adding improved retrieval hints.

The above situation is also an example of the **tip-of-the-tongue phenomenon**, *which occurs when information is stored in long-term memory but the retrieval cues fail to trigger the memory.* During a test, students may ask their teacher to explain a question. When the teacher restates the question, students often respond by saying, "Oh, I understand now." This expression shows that students had the information in long-term memory, but that the question was not triggering the memory, causing retrieval cue failure.

Serial position effect *occurs when people often have an easier time retrieving information that is located at the beginning (primacy effect)* *and the end of a list (recency effect), but are more likely to forget items in the middle.*

Nuts and Bolts

The serial position effect holds that the middle items of a list are most easily forgotten. When studying the order of events, such as stages of development, for example, pay particular attention to the stages that occur in the middle, as you are more likely to forget these. For example, students often get the order of Freud's psychosexual stages mixed up. When studying the oral, anal, phallic, latency, and genital stages, pay particular attention to the order of the anal, phallic, and latency stages.

AP Tip

You may be asked to identify tip-of-the-tongue as a retrieval failure.

METHODS OF RETRIEVING INFORMATION

Several different methods can be used to retrieve information. Students often inquire about the format of a test because it tells them both how they should prepare and the expected difficulty of the test. The following chart applies these methods for retrieving information to the various types of tests typically found in a high school class.

Type of Test	Retrieval	Format
Multiple-choice/matching	List of answers serve as retrieval cues.	Recognition of information.
Fill-in-the-blank	Questions help to cue information.	Cued recall
Essay	Free recall—no clues or hints to help trigger information in long-term memory.	Recall

---

Nuts and Bolts

If you're like most students, you would prefer to take a multiple-choice test rather than an essay test because the multiple-choice answers provide retrieval cues to the information learned. Essay tests tend to be more challenging because you have to recall the information without the aid of retrieval cues.

FACTORS THAT AFFECT RETRIEVAL

The **encoding specificity principle** *states that retrieval is more effective when retrieval conditions are similar to those that were in effect when the information was encoded, or learned.* The term **context-dependent memories** *refers to retrieving information in the same setting in which the information was encoded.* This occurs because the setting is also encoded, and it later becomes a retrieval cue. For example, when you are getting ready for school, you may realize that you are out of toothpaste. You remind yourself to stop on the way home from school and pick some up. During the day you become preoccupied with the tasks of school and forget about the toothpaste, until you get all the way home and go into the bathroom. You remembered because the bathroom, where you first realized that you were out of toothpaste, was where you encoded the information to long-term memory.

The **mood congruence effect** *refers to emotions and moods that can also help retrieve memories.* When a person is in a happy mood, that person tends to think of happy memories. For example, arguments between boyfriends and girlfriends tend to deteriorate because of the mood congruence effect. When a boyfriend and girlfriend start arguing their mood becomes negative. This then triggers other negative memories, resulting in an escalation in the argument. It is difficult to think of a happy memory when you're in a bad mood.

State-dependent memories *involve a person's internal state that can also serve as a retrieval cue.* For example, if Joe learns new information while under the influence of alcohol, he will probably remember the information when he is again under the influence of alcohol.

The significance and personal meaning of an event can help retrieve more vivid memories, called **flashbulb memories**. For example, many people have reported remembering exactly what they were doing when they first heard about the events of September 11.

Nuts and Bolts

 Think of a flashbulb memory as an actual picture taken by a camera. The picture is detailed and includes objects in the background that were not the focus of the picture. Flashbulb memories capture not only the significance of the event, but also background information, like a song being played at the time or other people who were in the area.

AP Tip

In a free-response question, you might be asked to write about which factors affect the encoding process and how they could contribute to forgetting.

CONSTRUCTING MEMORIES

Parallel distributed processing models (PDP) *suggest that semantic and episodic memories become integrated with existing information.* As mentioned earlier, this newly learned information alters a person's general knowledge of the environment. This allows him or her to make more connections between what he or she already knows and information he or she has just acquired. In Psychology 101, students learn that William James is the father of American psychology. In AP Psychology, students also learn that William James wrote Principles of Psychology. The parallel processing model explains that now every time an AP student hears about William James he or she will recall not only that James is the father of American psychology, but also that he wrote Principles of Psychology. In other words, the information learned in AP Psychology was added to the established information learned in Psychology 101.

Schemas are another way that memories are organized. **Schemas** *are established mental representations of people, objects, and events.* For example, when your teacher reviews the purpose of experiments, the mere mention of experiments may trigger the terms "dependent and independent variables" and "control and experimental groups." This occurs because your mental representation of experiments includes these terms. When your teacher adds that confounding variables can also occur in an experiment you will encode and add confounding variables into your established schema of experiments.

Schemas can also contribute to memory distortions. Schemas make it hard to incorporate new information that contradicts established information represented by a schema.

For example, think of your established schema of a kitchen. When imagining what other people have in their kitchens, you are first likely to think of items found in your own kitchen. In other words, you add items from your kitchen schema to the description of other people's kitchens, even if those items are not necessarily present.

Elizabeth Loftus conducted research to find out if presenting misleading information could alter people's memories. In her experiment, people were shown the scene of a car accident and then asked a series of questions pertaining to how the accident occurred. In one question wording was changed to determine whether people would report differing accounts of how fast the cars were going when they collided. By changing the word that described the contact between the two cars, subjects reported different speeds. For example, when "bumped" and "smashed" were used, subjects who read "smashed" reported faster speeds than people who read "bumped." Loftus was able to demonstrate that how you ask a person to recall an event could affect his or her memory of that event. She referred to this as the **misinformation effect**. By providing misleading information, a memory could be distorted to incorporate the misleading information into the already established memory. Sometimes, by presenting misleading information, people can "trick" someone into thinking that they had done something they in fact had not. For example, if you were confident that last night you got home at 10:00 and your brother disagreed and insisted that you arrived at home at 11:00, you eventually might question the conviction of your memory.

> ## AP Tip
>
> Be prepared to explain how schemas could lead to memory distortion.

FORGETTING

Herman Ebbinghaus was one of the first researchers to investigate the elements of forgetting. Using himself as a subject, he tried to memorize nonsense syllables that did not resemble his past memories. After repeating and learning the list of nonsense syllables, Ebbinghaus tested his memory during periods ranging from twenty minutes to thirty-one days. He plotted his data in what is now called the Ebbinghaus forgetting curve. He discovered that much of what is learned is quickly forgotten. How quickly varied, depending on how effectively the information was encoded, how it was remembered, and how much it was rehearsed. He also discovered that over time the amount of information that was forgotten leveled off. In other words, information that is not quickly forgotten tends to remain in long-term memory over a substantial period of time.

> ## AP Tip
>
> A free-response question might ask you how Herman Ebbinghaus explained why people forget information.

FACTORS THAT AFFECT FORGETTING

Encoding failure occurs when information was never encoded into long-term memory.

On a test you may encounter a question that seems unfamiliar; you have no idea what the question is asking. This could be an indication that you never learned the material covered in the question. That is different from thinking you know what the answer is but just can't remember it, which indicates that at some point you learned the material but are now experiencing retrieval failure.

Interference theory *suggests that memories can interfere with each other, causing information to be forgotten.* Two types of interference are proactive and retroactive.

Interference	Definition	Example
Retroactive interference	A new memory interferes with your remembering an old memory.	Learning your new locker combination prevents you from remembering your old locker combination.
Proactive interference	An older memory interferes with your remembering a new memory.	You keep on dialing your old cell phone number, which prevents you from learning your new cell phone number.

AP Tip

Past test questions have asked students to differentiate between retroactive and proactive interference. Be prepared to identify a situation for each type of interference.

MOTIVATED FORGETTING

Motivated forgetting happens when a person intentionally suppresses information. The person may believe the memory to be traumatic or bothersome. **Suppression** *is used to consciously forget information.* For example, your boyfriend or girlfriend breaks up with you, and you choose not to think about it. However, even though you are not thinking about the break-up, it is difficult to simply forget that it happened. Sigmund Freud believed that when information is traumatic and hurtful, the person who received it represses that information. **Repression** *is the unconscious forgetting of information.* According to Freud, even though memories are not consciously remembered, these memories can still influence a person unconsciously. There is much debate about the role of repression (see the discussion in the chapter on personality).

THE DECAY THEORY

The **decay theory** *suggests that people forget memories that they are not actively using.* When a new memory is formed it creates a memory trace, which makes a distinct change in the chemistry of the brain. When the memory is not continuously retrieved, the once-established memory trace starts to diminish, causing the memory to decay and be forgotten. There has been much debate about the relevance of the decay theory. Some researchers have suggested that memories can remain throughout a person's lifetime regardless of whether they have been actively retrieved. This has been demonstrated by using new types of retrieval cues that are able to trigger memories that were thought to have decayed. For example, if you haven't dialed the phone number from your childhood home for a number of years, you probably don't remember it. This would be considered an example of the decay theory. However, if you were at a garage sale and saw the same style phone you had growing up, the sight of it might retrieve your old phone number into your memory. This would demonstrate that your old phone number did not vanish from your long-term memory; it simply needed a stronger retrieval cue.

BIOLOGICAL BASIS FOR MEMORY

Karl Lashley researched how the brain plays a role in forming memories. In particular, Lashley wanted to find the specific area of the brain responsible for memory. Through his research on rats, he was able to conclude that memory is not localized in one section of the brain, but instead is spread over many different areas. He demonstrated this by removing certain parts of the rat's cerebral cortex, the higher-order thinking elements of the brain. He found that no matter how much of the cerebral cortex he removed, the rat was still able to run through a maze that it had previously learned.

Donald Hebb, Lashley's student, discovered that each memory connects a group of neurons in the brain. He referred to these connections as a cell assembly and stated that through certain associations of sensory stimulation, the cell assembly could be strengthened, allowing that memory to be easily retrieved at a later time.

Neurons also play a role in forming new memories. Communication between neurons takes place when a neurotransmitter crosses the synapse between the axon of one neuron and the dendrites of another. When a message is repeatedly sent across a synapse, the receiving neuron's dendrites become larger, enabling better and faster communication. In addition, researchers have discovered that when neurons constantly fire at the same time, they stimulate a third neuron. Through this constant firing, the third neuron will become even more sensitive to stimulation, enabling the formation and later retrieval of memories. This is referred to as **long-term potentiation**. In the hippocampus, these changes are facilitated by the neurotransmitters glutamate and acetylcholine. People with Alzheimer's disease have shown an acetylcholine deficiency.

AP Tip

Be able to identify which neurotransmitters are involved in the process of memory, and how memory occurs.

AMNESIA

Amnesia *is severe memory loss*. Two types of amnesia are retrograde and anterograde. **Retrograde amnesia** *is the inability to remember events from the past, specifically episodic memories*. This could occur as the result of an injury to the brain. People with head injuries often have difficulty recalling events that preceded the head injury. Studying retroactive amnesia has shown that before information can become permanent in long-term memory, a certain amount of time is necessary to encode the information. This time allotment is referred to as memory consolidation. If a head injury occurs before memories are consolidated to long-term memory, then the memory will not become permanent. For example, if you are looking at a paper and someone grabs it away from you before you have time to process what was on it, you may not be able to recall the information. This happens because you did not have time to consolidate the information to long-term memory.

Anterograde amnesia *is the inability to form new memories.* This could occur through damage to the hippocampus and was demonstrated through research on a subject known as H.M. (only the initials H.M. were used because the subject wanted to remain anonymous). H.M. experienced severe seizures, and in an attempt to reduce the severity of the seizures, doctors removed his medial temporal lobe and hippocampus. The surgery did reduce the number of seizures H.M. experienced, but without the hippocampus, H.M. was not able to form new memories. Through continued research with H.M., doctors realized that even though he was not able to generate new memories, H.M. was still able to learn new procedures or skills. This showed that the hippocampus is not as vital for implicit memories as it is for explicit memories. It also made clear that different areas of the brain are responsible for different types of memories.

AP Tip

Be prepared to explain the difference between retrograde and anterograde amnesia.

BRAIN STRUCTURE AND MEMORY

Karl Lashley was able to show that memory does not take place in one specific area of the brain, but rather, in several areas. The hippocampus, cerebellum, amygdala, medial temporal lobe, and prefrontal cortex all play a role in the formation of memories.

Brain Structure	Function
Hippocampus	Encodes new explicit memories to long-term memory (Note: It is the pathway through which all new explicit memories must go; it is not necessarily where new memories are stored)
Cerebellum	Stores memories that involve movement and coordination used in implicit memories
Amygdala	Encodes the emotional elements of a memory
Medial Temporal Lobe	Encodes new explicit memories to long-term memory
Prefrontal Cortex	Processes memories involving a sequence of events; does not actually process the events—just the sequence that has taken place

> ### AP Tip
>
> Be able to identify the different areas of the brain associated with memory.

IMPROVING MEMORY

Improving memory has been shown to be vital for learning and remembering information. As you prepare for the AP Psychology exam, you are trying to develop improved methods to remember the material. Mnemonics may be an alternative you want to try. **Mnemonics** *are memory aids that help organize information.* **Acronym**s *are an example of a mnemonic device.* Many people were taught the acronym HOMES to remember the great lakes: Huron, Ontario, Michigan, Erie, and Superior. In the chapter on personality, you learned the acronym OCEAN to help you remember the Big Five Traits of Personality: Openness, Conscientiousness, Extraversion, Agreeableness, and Neuroticism.

   Method of loci *is another mnemonic device used to remember information.* Associating an item with the actual place the item is found can help you remember an entire list of items. If you don't want to use a grocery list, you might rely on the method of loci to remember what you need to buy at the store. For example, to remember freezer items you might picture the freezer and the items that are normally located there.

> ### AP Tip
>
> An essay question might ask you to explain how mnemonic devices improve memory. Be prepared to give examples.

Multiple-Choice Questions

1. When asked to give an example of what a bird is, Tom replied, "Do you mean a robin?" For Tom, a robin is an example of a(n):
    (A) algorithm
    (B) mental set
    (C) concept
    (D) prototype
    (E) script

2. Which of the following best describes the use of availability heuristics?
   (A) Jack believes that all secretaries are women.
   (B) Sam is completing a mathematical problem step by step.
   (C) Andrea fails to turn in an assignment, thinking it is due tomorrow.
   (D) Steve believes that more injuries occur in hockey than in baseball.
   (E) Angelica thinks that bulldogs are the best example of a dog.

3. Jillian is struggling with a challenging physics problem she can't seem to solve. Which problem-solving strategy would she benefit from?
   (A) Functional fixedness
   (B) A representativeness heuristic
   (C) An availability heuristic
   (D) Insight
   (E) Incubation

4. One-year-old Hayden points to a horse and says "duggie." Hayden is displaying
   (A) overregularization
   (B) telegraphic speech
   (C) overextension
   (D) incubation
   (E) babbling

5. According to psychologists, what distinguishes true language from the language produced by lower animals?
   (A) Syntax and semantics, morphemes, phonemes
   (B) Plasticity, syntax and semantics, infinite creativity
   (C) Syntax and semantics, finite creativity, displacement
   (D) Syntax and semantics, infinite creativity, counterproduction
   (E) Syntax and semantics, infinite creativity, displacement

6. Mr. Flanders asks Sean to deliver a message to Mrs. Rogers. Sean has never been to Mrs. Rogers's room, but is told that it is two classrooms to the right of Mr. Smith's room. Because Sean had Mr. Smith last year for psychology, he knows where Mrs. Rogers's classroom is. Sean has used what component of thought to help him?
   (A) Cognitive map
   (B) Script
   (C) Functional fixedness
   (D) Mental set
   (E) Algorithm

7. Many students often miss multiple-choice questions that state, "Which of the following does NOT" apply to a given question. Their failure to notice a differently worded question such as this is an example of which obstacle to problem solving?
   (A) Functional fixedness
   (B) Mental set
   (C) Algorithm
   (D) Confirmation bias
   (E) Incubation

8. Clarisse goes to the store to purchase chips for her upcoming graduation party. Which problem-solving strategy would ensure that Clarisse finds the aisle containing the chips?
   (A) Representativeness heuristic
   (B) Availability heuristic
   (C) Mental set
   (D) Incubation
   (E) Algorithm

9. Which of the following demonstrates the principle of confirmation bias?
   (A) After learning that her friend was depressed, Julie says, "Of course she was depressed. She never wanted to do anything."
   (B) Joe is passionate about environmental conservation, and refuses to listen to or read any data that contradicts his views.
   (C) Carly hears that the new English teacher loves to read books and attend plays. She then assumes that the teacher is female.
   (D) Erica is trying to solve a physics problem, but cannot think of which equation to use to do so, and instead begins her math homework.
   (E) Samantha wants to eat a can of soup but does not have a can opener, so she uses a knife to cut a hole in the soup can.

10. The process of acquiring information and entering it into memory is referred to as
    (A) storage
    (B) encoding
    (C) retrieval
    (D) gathering
    (E) stimulating

11. Mary is able to remember her mother's birth date. Remembering that date is an example of which type of memory?
    (A) Procedural memory
    (B) Semantic memory
    (C) Episodic memory
    (D) Nondeclarative memory
    (E) Flashbulb memory

12. Rosita was having a hard time remembering the material she learned in class and that she knew was going to be on a test. As she walked into her classroom on the day of the test she immediately started to remember the forgotten content. This sudden occurrence could be explained by
    (A) recency effect
    (B) context-dependent memory
    (C) primary effect
    (D) retrieval failure
    (E) semantic association

13. Steve can only remember his old locker combination; he keeps forgetting his new combination. Steve is experiencing
    (A) blocking interference
    (B) retroactive interference
    (C) proactive interference
    (D) repression interference
    (E) suppression interference

14. Ray hurt his head in a car accident and has been experiencing problems recalling past events. Ray's doctors told his parents that Ray may be suffering from
    (A) anterograde amnesia
    (B) misinformation effect
    (C) incomplete schemas
    (D) retrieval failure
    (E) retrograde amnesia

15. What psychologist believed that the forgetting of information will occur rapidly at first and will then level off, with the remaining information being retained for a long period of time?
    (A) Herman Ebbinghaus
    (B) Donald Hebb
    (C) Karl Lashley
    (D) Sigmund Freud
    (E) Elizabeth Loftus

Free-Response Questions

1. The process of memory is said to be influenced by numerous factors. Explain how each of the following contributes to recall.
    (a) Serial position effect
    (b) Representativeness heuristics
    (c) Framing effect
    (d) Elaborative rehearsal

2. Jerry is preparing for a geography test on the names of the states and their capitals.
    (a) Explain how each of the following would impact Jerry's taking the test. Be sure to define each term before citing an example that applies to the question.
        i.   Context dependent memory
        ii. Cognitive map
    (b) How might the following strategies aid Jerry in remembering the locations of the states, their names and the name of each state's capital?
        i.   Method of Loci
        ii. Incubation

Answers

MULTIPLE-CHOICE QUESTIONS

1. Answer: D. A prototype is a person's best example of a concept. The prototype for any one thing will be different for every person, because it is that person's best example *(Psychology,* 8th ed. p. 286/9th ed. p. 291).

2. Answer: D. When using an availability heuristic, you are using a rule-of-thumb strategy to reach a conclusion. By thinking that hockey players suffer more injuries than do baseball players, Steve is using whatever information is easily accessible *(Psychology,* 8th ed. p. 294/9th ed. p. 299).

3. Answer: E. Incubation occurs when a person steps back from the current problem and performs a different task as a way to take his or her mind off the problem. If Jillian steps back and allows time for the problem to work itself out, this would give her a break from a mental set, or from functional fixedness *(this material does not appear in either the textbook edition).*

4. Answer: C. Overextension occurs when a single word is used to express a more complex meaning *(Psychology,* 8th ed. p. 314/9th ed. p. 319).

5. Answer: E. Syntax and semantics are the rules regarding the structure of grammar and its meaning; infinite creativity, the ability to generate numerous sentences that convey meaning; and displacement, the ability to discuss the past or plan for future events. These are the three characteristics of true language *(this material does not appear in the either textbook edition).*

6. Answer: A. A cognitive map is a mental model of a location *(Psychology,* 8th ed. p. 289/9th ed. p. 295).

7. Answer: B. Mental sets interfere with the ability to problem solve because they rely on previous experiences to formulate a conclusion. In the case of a student missing a question that includes the phrase "Which of the following does NOT," he or she may fail to notice the "NOT" because all of the previous questions had asked the student for the correct answer *(Psychology,* 8th ed. p. 299/9th ed. pp. 304–305).

8. Answer: E. Although algorithms can take longer to arrive at the correct solution, they are guaranteed to produce the correct solution. Using a heuristic, Clare might not find the chip aisle right away, and might waste unnecessary time locating it *(Psychology,* 8th ed. p. 290/9th ed. p. 295).

9. Answer: B. Confirmation bias occurs when a person accepts information that confirms his or her belief, but rejects information that contradicts that belief. By ignoring

information that is the opposite of what a person believes, problem solving becomes more difficult *(Psychology,* 8th ed. pp. 300–301/9th ed. p. 297).

10. Answer: B. Encoding is the process of acquiring information that can later be stored in the memory *(Psychology,* 8th ed. p. 238/9th ed. p. 242).

11. Answer: C. Episodic memories are a type of explicit memory that describe information that is meaningful to the person *(Psychology,* 8th ed. p. 239/9th ed. p. 243).

12. Answer: B. The context effect suggests that retrieval is enhanced when retrieved in a setting or context that is similar to that in which it was encoded, or learned *(Psychology,* 8th ed. p. 253/9th ed. p. 257).

13. Answer: C. Proactive interference is the inability to recall new memories because of the interference caused by older memories *(Psychology,* 8th ed. p. 263/9th ed. pp. 265–266).

14. Answer: E. Retrograde amnesia is the inability to recall past memories, often as the result of a traumatic head injury *(Psychology,* 8th ed. p. 270/9th ed. p. 274).

15. Answer: A. Herman Ebbinghaus studied the effects of forgetting, noting that most information is forgotten quickly. The remaining information is then forgotten at a more even pace, with most of that remaining information being retained for a long duration *(Psychology,* 8th ed. pp. 261–262/9th ed. pp. 264–265).

FREE-RESPONSE QUESTIONS

1. (a) The serial position effect refers to the difficulty of recalling information presented in the middle of a list, while information provided at the beginning (primacy effect) and at the end of the list (recency effect) is more easily remembered. Therefore, it will be more difficult to remember words that are presented in the middle of a list than it will be to remember those that are given at the beginning or the end, for example.

   (b) Representativeness heuristics are shortcuts (a rule of thumb) that allow a person to arrive at a conclusion more quickly than if he or she had gone through a step-by-step process (algorithm). The crucial component of representative heuristics is the fact that they rely on stereotypes, or assumptions, to help formulate a conclusion. Therefore, if the list of words being memorized shares a common characteristic of another, more general word, using a representativeness heuristic would allow a person to conclude the word is the more general term, even if that word was never given. For example, if you are given the following words: eye, haystack, thimble, thread, point, sharp, pain, and then asked to recall the list, you might erroneously add the word "needle" even though it was not included. All the words given represent the concept of a needle; thus, using representativeness heuristics we might conclude that the word "needle" was part of the list.

(c) The framing effect involves the wording of a sentence to influence a person's response to a question. The way a question is worded can influence the person's memory. For example, if you witnessed a car accident and a detective asked you, "How fast were the cars going when they smashed into each other?" you would be likely to say the cars were traveling at a higher rate of speed than they were, simply because the word "smashed" implies that two objects were traveling at a high rate of speed before impact.

(d) Elaborative rehearsal involves associating newly learned information with previously learned information. Linking the new information with older, more concrete information will improve memory retention.

2. (a) i. Context-dependent memories are those memories that rely on the environment and are more easily recalled if placed in the same environment. According to the principles of context-dependent memory, Jerry should sit in the same desk he was in while learning the locations and names of the states and their capitals.

ii. A cognitive map is a mental representation of a location or its surroundings. By constructing a cognitive map of the location of the states, their names, and their capitals, Jerry will have an easier time recalling them. For example, if Jerry remembers where the large states (California, Florida, Texas, New York, and Illinois) are, it will be easier for him to remember those states that surround them.

(b) i. The method of loci is a strategy for improving memory that relies on a mental map of a familiar location and placing items in order within this mental map. Jerry could place a cutout of each state in a different area of his room. By attaching their names and capitals to a particular object in that area of his room and mentally walking through his room, Jerry would be able to see both which states are in which regions of the country, as well as the capital of each state, based on the objects that were within his mental map of an area of his room.

ii. Incubation is removing oneself from a situation when problem solving becomes impeded. If Jerry is stuck on one particular region of the map, he would benefit from working on another region. While working on another region he might recall state names and capitals through their similarity to others.

5

MOTIVATION, EMOTION, AND STRESS

Motivation is *what drives people to do the things they do, the internal and external factors that direct behavior.* Motivation is often related to the level of effort and persistence shown toward the completion of an activity, and each person's motivation is particular to him or her. For example, some people work just to put food on the table, while others work for the inner satisfaction and sense of accomplishment it brings.

THEORIES OF MOTIVATION

Motives can be grouped into several different categories. Certain theories of motivation suggest that biological needs, or internal factors, are what motivate an organism, while others hold that external factors play more of a crucial role.

The **instinct theory** *explains motivation through instinctual behavior.* An **instinct** *is an unlearned, innate, and automatic response to a specific stimulus.* For example, geese fly south in response to colder weather. The instinct theory was influenced by the evolutionary perspective and the work of Charles Darwin, who believed that organisms are motivated to perform certain behaviors to enhance their survival or the survival of their species. Geese enhance their survival by flying south—where they can find food—for the winter. The instinct theory has been criticized for providing labels and descriptions of behavior instead of explaining why and how behaviors occur.

Homeostasis *is the premise that the body oversees and maintains its internal physiological systems at a constant, stable level.* When internal conditions fall or rise above a desired level, your brain detects this change and alerts the body to return to the normal optimal range. For

138

example, body temperature is monitored and maintained through homeostasis. When a person's temperature rises above 98.6 degrees, homeostasis detects this increase and notifies the body to modify. In response, the body initiates sweating to help cool itself.

A **need** is *a biological requirement essential to proper bodily functioning.* A **drive**, *such as thirst, hunger, or pain, is a psychological state of tension, or arousal, that directs an organism to take action to reduce the drive.* Biological needs and drives are monitored and maintained through homeostasis. When needs are not met, drives are produced. According to Clark Hull, the **drive reduction theory** *suggests that motivation is based on the desire to reduce internal tension within the body that is caused by biological needs not being met as indicated through homeostasis.* For example, when you are dehydrated, it is through homeostasis that your brain is alerted that the fluid levels in your body are low. As a result, a <u>need</u> for water is created. This, in turn, produces a <u>drive</u> (thirst) that causes (motivation) you to get a drink of water, restoring homeostasis to a stable level and reducing the drive (drive-reduction).

Nuts and Bolts

 Think of homeostasis as the functioning of a thermostat in your home. A thermostat monitors and maintains a constant predetermined temperature. When the air becomes too hot, the thermostat activates the air conditioner to cool the air to a temperature preselected by the occupant. When the air becomes too cold, the thermostat activates the furnace to warm the air to the set temperature. Homeostasis likewise alerts the body when certain physiological systems become unbalanced.

Drive-reduction theories cannot account for all types of motivation. Not everything people do is motivated by a biological need. People who continue to buy lottery tickets even though they never win are not purchasing the tickets to reduce an internal tension caused by a biological need. In addition, people may drink or eat even if they are not hungry or thirsty. For example, an individual may eat because everybody else is eating or because that's his or her response to stress.

AP Tip

A past multiple-choice question asked students to give an example of the drive-reduction theory. Be prepared to explain how homeostasis is involved in the drive-reduction theory.

OPTIMUM AROUSAL THEORY

People are motivated out of curiosity to try new experiences. Curiosity causes an increase in arousal. **Arousal** is *the result of several heightened physiological states.* People who are highly aroused experience a rapid heartbeat, intensified breathing, and muscle strain. The **optimum arousal theory** *suggests that people try to maintain an ideal level of arousal through various behavioral activities.* Motivation is directed at maintaining an optimum, stable level of arousal. After experiencing a boring day at school (low arousal), some people might be more motivated to partake in an exciting activity (high arousal) that night. On the other hand, someone who has had a very intense, stressful day (high arousal) might be more motivated to take it easy and stay home to watch a movie (low arousal). In other words, a person's desired level of arousal directs motivation toward or away from certain activities. A person who has a higher level of arousal may participate in activities that are risky, like smoking or drinking. People with lower levels of arousal may stay away from riskier activities.

People tend to perform well in activities in which there is a moderate level of arousal and are more likely to make mistakes when arousal is either too high or too low. For example, at the start of a football game, a player with extremely high arousal might not be concentrating and inadvertently jump offsides before the ball has even been kicked, thus incurring a penalty.

According to the **Yerkes-Dodson law**, *difficult or challenging tasks cause arousal to be lower, and easy tasks cause arousal to be higher.* Fluctuations in arousal could impair a person's ability to function. People perform best when arousal is maintained, or moderate.

INCENTIVE MOTIVATION

Incentive theories *suggest that external stimuli "push" people to positive incentives and "pull" people away from negative incentives.* For example, the external stimulus of paid overtime may "push" a person to work longer hours. On the other hand, the external stimulus of having a paycheck reduced for showing up late may "pull" a person to get to work on time.

Incentive theories are based on the principles of physiological, cognitive, and social factors. A food incentive is more appealing to someone who is hungry than it is to someone who has just finished a large meal. For example, using a treat as an incentive to train a dog would be more appealing and productive if the dog were hungry. Cognitive factors contribute to the wanting and liking of an incentive. Wanting an incentive is based on the value a person places on it. The more an incentive is "wanted," the more the incentive will push, or motivate behavior. Liking an incentive is based on the immediate pleasure it brings. Someone might "want" a new car but is then initially disappointed when it does not meet her immediate expectations or satisfaction. Social influences may define which incentives are good and which are bad. For example, the opinions of others may affect a person's "wanting" and "liking" certain incentives. A friend's suggestion that a certain car is "the best" may add to the individual's "wanting" that car.

Not all motivational aspects can be explained by incentives. For example, some people help others without the expectation of a reward or incentive—they do so just for the sake of being helpful.

HUMANISTIC THEORIES OF MOTIVATION

The humanistic theory suggests that people seek to build a positive self-concept and are motivated to fulfill their potential. Even though most humanistic psychologists believe that the motivation to achieve one's potential is innate (inborn), many also recognize that the environment is an important contributor. Without a supportive and positive environment, achievement of one's potential would be significantly hindered.

Abraham Maslow developed the **hierarchy of needs** *to explain how a person achieves his or her potential.* According to Maslow, at each level in the hierarchy, the individual has needs that must be satisfied before he or she can address the next level. For example, safety needs, including a sense of security and stability, must be met before the individual can address the needs of the next level, belongingness and love. Maslow suggested that as people move up the hierarchy of needs, addressing each level and satisfying the required needs, it becomes possible to achieve self-actualization. According to Maslow, **self-actualization** is *the striving and realization of one's talent and potential.* If a previous level is not satisfied in the hierarchy of needs, then self-actualization is not possible. If the environment does not offer supportive relationships and resources, then a person cannot achieve his or her innate potential. Listed below is the order of succession, from bottom (level 1, physiological needs) to top (level 5, self-actualization), of Maslow's hierarchy of needs.

5. <u>Self-actualization:</u> achievement of one's potential

4. <u>Esteem needs</u>: feelings of worth and accomplishment

3. <u>Belongingness and love needs</u>: supportive friendships and intimate relationships

2. <u>Safety needs</u>: security and stability

1. <u>Physiological needs</u>: food and water

Nuts and Bolts

 Think of the succession of the hierarchy of needs as high steps to a top floor. One must step on each step (level) to reach the top (self-actualization). If you don't address each level, then the chances of reaching self-actualization are in doubt; if you don't step on each step, you won't reach the top floor—the steps are too big to allow you to skip any.

AP Tip

Be prepared to identify which level is the highest in Maslow's hierarchy of needs. Be prepared to explain how a person achieves self-actualization.

HUNGER

Human beings get hungry and need to eat, do so, and then get full, which is the point at which they cannot eat anymore. Researchers have investigated which signals from the body and brain cause a person to become hungry, as well as which signals indicate satiety, or no longer wanting to eat. Signals from the stomach are an obvious starting point. A person who is hungry detects "hunger pangs" as his stomach contracts, and will then sense feelings of satiation when his stomach expands. However, these stomach signals do not offer enough evidence for a complete explanation as to why people get hungry and satiated. For example, people who have had their stomachs removed as part of a treatment for cancer still report feelings of hunger and still eat normal amounts of food.

The most important signals that start and stop hunger come from the blood. The brain monitors both the amount of nutrients absorbed in the blood sent from the digestive system and the level of hormones released into the blood in response to the nutrients in the bloodstream.

As food moves from the stomach to the bloodstream, a hormone called **CCK** (cholecystokinin) is released; *this hormone is detected by the brain, where it acts as a neurotransmitter signifying short-term satiation*. In other words, CCK is responsible for indicating fullness during a meal.

Nuts and Bolts

A good way to remember that CCK is responsible for short-term satiation is to associate the "short," or small number of letters in CCK with the "short-term" feeling of fullness.

Leptin is *another hormone that indicates satiation.* Leptin is released into the bloodstream as the fat supplies increase; it then notifies the brain to stop eating. When leptin levels are high, a person feels satiated; when leptin levels are low, feelings of hunger increase.

Nuts and Bolts

When people eat a "fatty" meal they tend to feel full for a longer period of time. After people eat a meal low in fat they report feelings of hunger sooner. A "fatty" meal causes more leptin to be released into the bloodstream, causing the sensation of fullness for a longer period of time. In other words, CCK is responsible for short-term satiation; leptin is responsible for longer-lasting feelings of satiation.

The brain also monitors glucose levels to determine hunger or satiation. **Glucose** is *sugar that the body uses for energy.* When glucose levels drop, the individual experiences hunger. Insulin has an effect on the amount of glucose in the body. **Insulin** is *a hormone that is used to convert glucose to energy.* When insulin levels rise, glucose levels decrease, causing the sensation of hunger.

Nuts and Bolts

You have probably seen the commercial from a candy bar company that claims the candy bar will satisfy your hunger. The main ingredient in a candy bar is sugar. When sugar levels drop and you experience hunger, a candy bar simply raises the amount of sugar in your body, thereby decreasing hunger.

AP Tip

Be prepared to identify which factors contribute to hunger and which to feelings of satiety. Be ready to explain which factors initiate and stop hunger.

THE BRAIN'S ROLE IN HUNGER

The hypothalamus was the first area of the brain to be seen as the control center for hunger. Later research showed that specific areas of the hypothalamus play opposing roles in starting and stopping hunger. Researchers believed that the **ventromedial hypothalamus** *stopped hunger* and the **lateral hypothalamus** *initiated hunger*. Research also showed that damage to the ventromedial hypothalamus would cause a rat to eat until it became obese. In addition, later research showed that damage to the lateral hypothalamus would cause an animal to stop eating altogether. The lateral hypothalamus produces **orexin**, *a hormone that triggers hunger*.

However, it turned out that this explanation was too simple—that one area of the hypothalamus started and another stopped hunger. Further research found that the damage to a rat's ventromedial hypothalamus did not cause the rat to continue to eat until it exploded; rather, the rat became more particular in what it ate. Similar findings were demonstrated when damage occurred in the lateral hypothalamus. Not only was food intake reduced, but other behaviors and drives controlled by the hypothalamus were likewise affected. In other words, this finding demonstrated that the hypothalamus is responsible for more than just hunger. A better understanding and explanation is that a person, using more sophisticated areas of the brain, consciously makes a choice when to eat and when to stop eating.

AP Tip

A past multiple-choice question asked students to differentiate between the lateral and ventromedial areas of the hypothalamus. Be prepared to explain the role of the hypothalamus in hunger.

BODY WEIGHT

Throughout the course of a day, about one-third of a human being's energy is spent maintaining a lifestyle: walking to class, studying, and driving home. The other two-thirds is used for vital functions such as breathing, heart rate, and brain activity. The **basal metabolic rate (BMR)** *regulates the expenditure of energy used to maintain our body's vital functions*. Many factors affect the functioning of the BMR. For example, as a person ages, his or her BMR slows down. If a person continues to eat the same amount of food he or she did when younger, that person is going to notice a weight gain. Women have a slower BMR than men, and heavier people tend to have a high BMR rate. Genetics have also been shown to play a part in one's BMR.

Many people don't understand how the BMR works, thinking that if they eat less food they will lose weight. After a couple of weeks, they may be surprised to discover that their weight has not decreased. They didn't understand that lowering their caloric intake also slows their BMR. When the BMR slows, fewer calories are burned off; as a result, weight is not reduced. Good diet advice suggests it is helpful to eat several small meals throughout the day. The reason this is good advice is because it causes the BMR to continue to work and burn off calories. When an individual stops eating regularly, the BMR slows down, resulting in the burning off of fewer calories. Conversely, when an individual eats at more regular intervals, the BMR speeds up, resulting in the burning off of more calories.

> ## AP Tip
>
> Be prepared to explain which factors affect the BMR.

SET-POINT THEORY

As mentioned earlier, homeostasis monitors and maintains internal body conditions, including body weight. A person's ideal weight, called the **set point**, *is maintained through increases or decreases in the BMR.* For example, if a person's set point is 160 pounds, then the BMR will respond to caloric intake over and under that weight. If that person eats more than the amount of calories that will keep him at the set point, the BMR will increase, adjusting the amount of calories to maintain a weight of 160. If a person consumes fewer calories, the BMR will slow down to conserve the amount of calories necessary to keep the weight at 160.

The number and size of a person's fat cells also play a role in gaining and losing weight. If a person is not careful about the types of food consumed, then the size of his or her fat cells will increase. These enlarged fat cells contribute to weight gain. If a person continues to consume fattening foods, then not only will his or her size increase, but so will the number of fat cells. The set point will then increase in response to the greater number of fat cells. The increase in a person's set point will cause the BMR to function differently to account for the gained weight. Once the number of fat cells increases, there is no way to decrease it.

OBESITY

BMI (body mass index) *is the measure of a person's weight in proportion to his or her height.* A normal BMI is 18.5 to 25. Obese people are those who are severely overweight; they have a BMI greater than 30. A person who has a BMI between 25 and 29.9 is classified as overweight. (The BMI should be interpreted with caution. It doesn't take into account muscle mass or bone density. A muscular individual may have a BMI that indicates he or she is overweight, when in fact he or she is not.) Many factors can contribute to obesity, including genetics, a higher number of fat cells, lack of physical activity, a stronger response to food cues, and where one lives. For example, in Western cultures obesity rates are high due to the availability of highly fatty foods. Most restaurants offer "very large" versions of meals, which not only means larger portions, but also more fat. Researchers have concluded that obese people should seek information and advice from a dietician before staring a diet. People often make an extreme cut in the amount of calories they consume, not knowing that they are thereby slowing the BMR.

AP Tip

Be prepared to explain the factors that contribute to obesity. Be ready to explain the disadvantages of the BMI, and how fat cells contribute to obesity.

EATING DISORDERS

In the United States, there is a lot of pressure—especially for teenage girls—to look a certain way. This pressure comes from the media, friends, and even family. As mentioned earlier, dieting is a complex process that requires examining a number of factors. Frequently, people don't take the time to research safe and effective methods for dieting. Misinformation about weight loss can lead to an eating disorder.

Anorexia nervosa *is an eating disorder characterized by a dramatic drop in calories consumed and an obsession with exercise.* This disorder primarily affects young women. Anorexics develop an intense fear of becoming overweight, to the point that although they may be dramatically thin, they still see themselves as overweight. This perceptual inconsistency can ultimately lead to death. The causes of anorexia are vague. Some researchers have speculated that there could be a genetic predisposition or a biochemical imbalance. The pursuit of perfectionism, combined with cultural and media expectations promoting thinness, may lead to obsessions of thinness and physical attractiveness.

Bulimia nervosa *is another type of eating disorder and is characterized by periods of binging—eating large amounts of food—and purging—getting rid of consumed food by intentional vomiting or use of laxatives.* Bulimics are more likely to be female and have problems with their eating habits. The "binge-purge" characteristics can lead to throat damage and tooth decay, caused by the acidity in vomit, and sometimes death. Group therapy and antidepressant medications can help bulimics develop better eating practices.

AP Tip

Be prepared to explain how eating disorders develop, as well as the differences between anorexia and bulimia.

ACHIEVEMENT AND MOTIVATION

The desire for achievement also directs and affects motivation. **Competence motivation (need motivation)** *is shown by people who are driven to master a task or achieve a personal goal.* **Achievement motivation** *occurs when people try to outdo, or beat, other people demonstrate.*

Nuts and Bolts

The reasons why you study for the AP psychology exam could be an indicator of the type of motivation you have. If you are studying for the exam because you want to prove to yourself that you can pass it, that behavior is an indication of competence motivation. However, if you are studying because you want to have the highest score in the class, that is an indication of achievement motivation.

Henry Murray was one of the first psychologists to measure achievement motivation. He did so through the use of thematic apperception tests (TATs), which consist of a series of ambiguous pictures. Subjects were asked to make up a story about each picture. Murray then interpreted each story by indicating achievement themes present throughout it. These tests have been correlated to the level of achievement a person needs to succeed in his or her school, work, and personal lives.

Albert Bandura believed that self-efficacy beliefs play an important role in determining personal achievement. A **self-efficacy belief**, according to Bandura, *is the level of confidence one has when facing the challenges and demands of a situation.* If a person has positive self-efficacy beliefs, then she has a higher chance of achievement and success.

Nuts and Bolts

Self-efficacy beliefs are an important factor in passing the AP psychology exam. If you are confident that you can pass the exam, then you will have a better chance of achieving your goal. If you think you are going to fail, then often attitude dictates results.

AP Tip

A past multiple-choice question has asked students to differentiate between competence and achievement motivation.

MOTIVATION AT WORK

Industrial-organizational psychologists *apply psychological concepts to optimize the workplace as an effective and productive environment.* **Personnel psychology** is *a field of industrial-organizational psychology; personnel psychologists try to match the right job with the right employee,* often by administering personality questionnaires to help employers properly place employees. Such questionnaires often indicate an employee's intentions and desired achievement. Some people are motivated through either **intrinsic motivation**, *a desire to achieve internal satisfaction, personal* *accomplishment*, or **extrinsic motivation**, *a desire to achieve an external factor, such as a pay raise.* When an employer can properly place an employee, the chances of that employee working at or toward his or her maximum potential increases.

Organizational psychology, *another field of industrial-organizational psychology, addresses worker satisfaction and productivity.* Psychologists in this field seek to develop favorable working conditions that will increase worker performance. This may include bonus schedules, profit sharing, flex-time, or other incentives that make workers feel like a part of the company. If an employee believes that his or her work is meaningful and important to the company, then he or she will work toward a higher level of achievement.

AP Tip

Be prepared to explain how industrial-organizational psychology can improve the workplace.

INTRODUCTION TO EMOTIONS

Emotions are related to motivation. People are more motivated to perform activities that produce positive emotions (happiness), and less motivated to take part in activities that produce negative emotions (anger or fear). **Emotions** *are based on cognitive appraisal, physiological reactions, which are innate and learned, and expressive behaviors.* Researchers have found that there are basic emotions, such as happiness and anger, as well as more complex emotions, which are a blend of several emotions at the same time. People often experience complex emotions when interpreting situations and events. For example, students may be a mix of nervous, excited, and sad about graduating from high school. During a graduation ceremony, some students may be seen laughing, then crying, then smiling, then crying again in a matter of a few minutes.

Emotions are different from moods. Emotions tend to last a brief amount of time, whereas moods generally last longer, perhaps throughout the course of a day. Emotions usually alter a person's thought process. For example, a positive emotion improves attention for acquiring information. In addition, positive emotions can bring about more positive behavior.

Nuts and Bolts

 When you're in a good mood you are likely to participate more in class and act nicer to others. However, when you are experiencing negative emotions you probably have a tendency to not focus on the subject matter, and you may respond negatively to other people's comments.

People differ in their level of intensity and expression of emotions. For example, you know right away when some people are happy, while with others you may have to inquire. As a result of the previously mentioned factors, emotion results from the subjective interpretation of stimuli, which can cause different responses of physical arousal and expression.

AP Tip

An essay question may ask you to explain how motivation affects emotion. Be prepared to define motivation and emotion and provide examples.

BIOLOGICAL ASPECTS OF EMOTION

The central nervous system and the autonomic nervous system play critical roles in the generation and interpretation of emotions. People experience certain types of emotions through the activation of the sympathetic nervous system, a division of the autonomic nervous system, which arouses the body. For example, when an individual is threatened by a harmful stimulus or situation, his or her heart rate accelerates, breathing becomes shallow and muscles tighten. These reactions are described as the **fight-or-flight response,** *as the body prepares and responds to what are perceived as threatening stimuli.* The "fight" component produces anger, and the "flight" component produces fear. Love and excitement also activate the sympathetic nervous system, producing responses similar to fear and anger. However, some emotions, such as contentment, produce lower levels of arousal not generated through the activation of the sympathetic nervous system.

Nuts and Bolts

 To remember how the autonomic nervous system affects emotions, think of situations in which your heart raced—perhaps in anticipation of bad or good news. For example, when you receive your AP exam score in the mail, your heart rate will probably accelerate before you even open the letter.

Different physiological responses have been linked to different patterns detected throughout the body. For example, anger tends to elevate skin temperature, whereas fear lowers it.

Nuts and Bolts

 Have you ever heard someone say of an angry person, "He's getting hot under the collar"? In fact, that might be true, as body temperature rises in response to anger. The expression "She got cold feet" could also be factual, because fear lowers body temperature.

Emotions cause different areas of the brain to become active. Activity in the limbic system, primarily the **amygdala**, *is critical in learning emotions, recognizing emotional expression, and interpreting emotional stimuli.* The **pyramidal motor system**, *which includes the motor cortex, is responsible for voluntarily forming facial expressions that represent certain emotions.* The **extrapyramidal motor system** *governs natural, or involuntary, facial expressions. For example, when a person is truly happy, he or she automatically and naturally smiles.* The **cerebral cortex** *also plays a role in the expression of emotions.* Specifically, the **right hemisphere** *is associated with the experience and expression of emotion.* People who have suffered damage to the brain's right hemisphere show understanding of a comical event but lack the ability to express humor.

AP Tip

A free-response question might ask you to identify the parts of the brain responsible for emotion. Be prepared to identify each part with an example.

THEORIES OF EMOTION

Several theories have attempted to explain how we experience emotion. Most researchers conclude that emotions result from the interaction of physiological, behavioral, and cognitive processes. However, different researchers stress different processes in determining emotional experience.

Theory	Researcher(s)	Definition	Example
James-Lange Theory of emotion	William James Carl Lange	Emotion is the result of the interpretation of bodily fluctuations. Criticism: If emotions are the result of changes in the body, then somebody with a spinal cord injury would not experience emotion. This is not true. Also, how would a person differentiate between being excited or angry when both accelerate the heart and body?	Sally was almost in a car accident. Sally's heart started racing and THEN she experienced fear as a result of her heart beating faster.

Theory	Researcher(s)	Definition	Example
Cannon-Bard Theory of emotion	Walter Cannon Phillip Bard	Emotions are the result of the thalamus receiving sensory information about emotional stimuli and relaying the information simultaneously to the autonomic nervous system and the cerebral cortex.	Sally was almost in a car accident. Sally experienced fear (cerebral cortex) at the SAME TIME that her heart started to race (autonomic nervous system.)
Two-factor theory of emotion (cognitive-arousal theory of emotion) (Schachter-Singer theory of emotion)	Stanley Schachter Jerome Singer	Emotion is the result of the interaction of two separate factors: physiological arousal and a cognitive label that explains why there is physiological arousal. Criticism: Some people may cognitively misinterpret changes that occur in their bodies. For example, a person who has just experienced a traumatic event may feel the need to express his or her feelings toward another person as the event occurs or just after it.	Jim experiences anxiety as he opens his report card. His heart starts to race as he thinks that he might have failed a few classes.
Cognitive-mediational theory of emotion	Richard Lazarus	Emotions are the result of the cognitive appraisal of a situation and how a person decides it will affect his or her well-being.	Suzy notices a man approaching her on a dark street. Suzy starts to become scared, but then she realizes (appraises) that it is just her brother and her heart rate decreases at the same time that she stops feeling afraid.

EMOTIONAL EXPRESSION

The expressional part of the emotional process contributes to the behavioral component. People express emotions through nonverbal cues, such as body posture, hand gestures, and facial expressions. Carroll Izard believed that facial expressions, especially for pain, are present at birth. He said that smiling begins at around three to four weeks and sadness and anger are facially visible around two months, and that at about six to seven months the facial expression indicating fear emerges. Researchers have suggested that these facial expressions are learned through modeling, but infants who were born both deaf and blind are still able to express themselves facially.

Paul Ekman and others have determined that facial expressions for basic emotions such as happiness seem to be similar across many cultures, although people differ in their intensity of displaying emotions. When you go to the theater and watch a funny movie, you probably notice that some people laugh louder than others, while some may not laugh at all. Societal and cultural norms, called display rules, can restrict the expressiveness of emotion.

Nuts and Bolts

In the United States, it is not considered the "norm" for a man to cry in public or for a woman to start yelling obscenities at an official during a football game.

INTRODUCTION TO STRESS

At some point, everyone experiences some kind of stress. **Stress** is characterized by *a negative emotional state in response to circumstances or situations that exceed a person's ability to control them.* People vary in what they interpret as stressful, and in how much stress is considered too much. People's reactions to stress are determined by their interpretation of the circumstances that contribute to the stressful situation, which resources are available for coping with the stressful situation, and how much stress can be dealt with during a particular time period. Individuals also tend to feel the effects of stress at certain times. For example, if you are taking several AP exams during a two-week span in May, then you may feel "stressed out." However, if you take one exam at a time, rely on teachers and friends for support, and believe that you can get through this stressful time period, then you may be able to reduce its negative effects.

Health psychologists study the effects of stress on the human body. They look at how a person's psychological interpretation of an event influences his or her health, and how to prevent stress-related illnesses by applying productive methods for thinking and acting during stressful times. As a result, health psychologists suggest that the interaction of biological, psychological, and social factors contribute to a person's health and illness. These interactions are described through the **biopsychosocial model** for identifying and preventing illness.

AP Tip

Be prepared to explain how health psychologists contribute to the study and reduction of stress.

TYPES OF STRESSORS

Stressors are *circumstances, events, and situations that contribute to stress*. There are a variety of stressors, and while some occur on a daily basis, others occur only infrequently.

Daily hassles are *minor inconveniences that occur throughout the day*. For example, having to get up for school, getting stuck in traffic, or getting up for work or school are all considered daily hassles. People who experience multiple daily hassles tend to become highly stressed. Richard Lazarus suggested that each person's interpretation of daily hassles and the occurrence, or timing, of each hassle plays an important role in how he or she will cope with these minor inconveniences.

Life changes, *events and situations that cause a person's lifestyle to dramatically change,* do not occur as often as daily hassles. Thinking and behavior are affected by a life change because the individual has to adapt to new circumstances brought on by the change. According to the Social Readjustment Rating Scale, the death of a spouse is considered the most difficult life change. For an adolescent, the death of a parent is considered the most stressful.

CAUSES OF STRESS

Causes of stress include conflicts, frustration, and pressure. People experience stress when they have to make tough choices, lose their purse or wallet, or feel obligated to perform or conform at a certain level.

People experience a conflict when they are indecisive about the alternatives. **Approach-approach conflict** *occurs when a person has to make a decision between two appealing choices.* For example, students experience approach-approach conflict when they have to choose between two courses they would like to take because they only have room for one in their schedule.

Avoidance-avoidance conflict *occurs when a person has to make a decision between two unappealing choices.* A student who is not particularly strong in science may experience avoidance-avoidance conflict when choosing a required science course. He or she doesn't really want to take chemistry or physics, but must do so to graduate.

Approach-avoidance conflict *is interpreted as the most stressful type of conflict.* In this type of conflict a choice has both appealing and unappealing features. Students are sometimes indecisive about taking an AP course. They find the chance to earn college credits appealing, but at the same time, they find the extra requirements to complete the course unappealing.

Multiple approach-avoidance conflicts *occur when two choices have both positive and negative points.* An example of a multiple approach-avoidance conflict for many students is the choice of going away to college or staying at home and commuting. Going away to school would help the student develop independence, but he or she would have to leave his or her friends. Commuting and staying would save the student money, but he or she would not be able to live on campus.

Frustration is another cause of stress. People experience **frustration** *when their pursuit of a goal is blocked.* Failures and losses account for two types of frustration. For example, the man who can't find his car keys experiences frustration because he can't get to work on time. In other words, losing his keys becomes frustrating because the man's goal of getting to work on time is affected.

People perceive pressure as very stressful. **Pressure** *is made up of the extra demands placed on a person to perform a certain way.* When people feel under pressure, performance is affected. Some people rise to the occasion in pressure-filled situations, while others perform worse. Coaches have to be careful when placing extra demands on their athletes. In other words, they have to recognize who can and cannot handle the added pressure.

AP Tip

Be prepared to identify different types of stressors. Also be prepared to identify the various types of conflicts.

STRESS AND THE BODY

Stress can affect the body both indirectly and directly. Stress can indirectly affect the body by interfering with sleep schedules, leading a person to eat poorly, increasing unfavorable behavior such as drinking alcohol and smoking, and causing disruptions in cognitive processes. Stress can directly affect the body by weakening the immune system, producing muscle tension and headaches, and speeding up the progression of diseases.

Stress directly affects the endocrine system. It can cause changes in the body as shown through the fight-or-flight response to perceiving an immediate threat. Walter Cannon was one of the first psychologists to research the effects of the fight-or-flight response on the body. He found that this response activates the nervous and endocrine systems. The process works as follows:

1. The hypothalamus and lower-brain structures activate the sympathetic nervous system.

2. The sympathetic nervous system activates the adrenal medulla.

3. The adrenal medulla releases hormones called catecholamines, which include adrenaline and noradrenaline.

4. Catecholamines circulating throughout the bloodstream cause increases in heart rate, blood pressure, respiration (breathing), and blood flow to the muscles; digestion slows down and pupils dilate.

Hans Selye was another researcher who studied the effects of prolonged stress. He referred to the toll stress has on the body through the **general adaptation syndrome (GAS),** *which identifies physical changes that occur through continued exposure to stress.* He described this process as a series of three stages.

Stage	Description
Alarm Stage	Intense body arousal occurs as the threat of a stressor is interpreted. This intense arousal, as Walter Cannon stated, causes the release of catecholamines, which alarm the body.
Resistive Stage	This stage is characterized by the body's trying to adjust to the intense arousal triggered in the alarm stage.
Exhaustive Stage	If the stressor continues to arouse the body, the body becomes exhausted, which can lead to illness, mental exhaustion, and, in extreme cases, death.

Nuts and Bolts

 A good way to remember the three stages of Hans Selye's general adaptation syndrome response to stress is to think of the following statement: "**ARE** you stressed?" **A**–alarm, **R**–resistance, **E**–exhaustion.

Selye also discovered a second endocrine pathway that occurs during prolonged stress.

1. The hypothalamus triggers the pituitary gland.

2. The pituitary gland triggers the release of the adrenocorticotropic hormone (ACTH).

3. ACTH triggers the adrenal cortex to release the stress hormones known as corticosteroids.

4. Corticosteroids increase the release of stored energy and reduce the response of the immune system. That state can lead to illness if allowed to continue unchecked.

THE EFFECT OF STRESS ON THE IMMUNE SYSTEM

As mentioned earlier, stress can reduce the effectiveness of the immune system. The human immune system protects the body by attacking harmful bacteria and viruses with lymphocytes, white blood cells created in the bone marrow. Early researchers believed that the immune system was isolated from the nervous and endocrine system, resulting in the notion that psychological processes could not affect the functioning of the immune system. Robert Adler and Nicholas Cohen demonstrated that the immune system could, in fact, be affected through the psychological process of classical conditioning. In their research with rats, they showed that pairing flavored water (neutral stimulus) with a drug (unconditioned stimulus) that caused the immune system to become suppressed (unconditioned response) would eventually cause the flavored water alone (conditioned stimulus) to suppress the immune system (conditioned response). Adler and Cohen's research led to the development of a field, **psychoneuroimmunology**, *which looked at the connections of the psychological, nervous, and immune systems.*

Researchers Ronald Glaser and Janice Kiecolt-Glaser discovered that even ordinary stressors such as being stuck in traffic, preparing for exams, or an argument could weaken the immune system.

Nuts and Bolts

During final exams, many students develop colds, coughs, and other illnesses. The stress of taking an exam reduces the effectiveness of the immune system, leading to illness.

BEATING STRESS AND PROMOTING WELLNESS

Researchers have identified several productive factors that could contribute to a healthy lifestyle and a reduction in stress.

Method	Definition	Example
Perceived control	The more sense of control a person has over a situation or circumstances, the less stress that person will encounter.	Surgery Jill is nervous about her surgery because she knows that once she is under the anesthetic, she will not be in control.
Optimistic versus pessimistic explanatory styles	Optimistic people tend to explain negative events through specific explanations and consideration of external factors. Pessimistic people explain negative events with personal vindication and self-defeating attitudes.	Losing a baseball game: Optimist: "I didn't play my best today because I didn't get enough sleep last night—plus we did play a great team." Pessimist: "I stink at baseball, and I'm never going to get better."
Type A behavior versus Type B behavior	Meyer Friedman and Ray Rosenman researched the effects of Type A behavior in contrast to Type B. Type A people are impatient and competitive and display anger and irritation frequently. As a result, they have a greater chance of developing heart disease and chronic illnesses. Type B behavior is characterized by a calm, relaxed response style.	Stressful working conditions: Type A yells, "Why is nothing done? We need to finish this instant. If anyone doesn't finish his or her work, then he or she is fired!" Type B calmly states, "Everyone is working very hard, but let's take a step back and address what still needs to be done."
Social support	Advice and resources provided by knowledgeable and productive friends and family.	Problem at school: Pete is having problems at school. He recognizes that he can go to his older brother for advice because his brother has graduated.

AP Tip

Be able to identify how certain factors can reduce stress. Also be ready to explain the difference between Type A and Type B behavior in relation to stress.

COPING STRATEGIES

Coping refers to the adjustments and changes made to handle stressful situations or circumstances. There are two types of coping strategies: problem-focused coping and emotion-focused coping.

Strategy	Definition	Example
Problem-focused coping	Addressing the problem by changing the factors associated with the problem.	Jimmy gets nervous when he sees a certain group of guys. As a result, Jimmy walks a different way to school to avoid seeing those guys.
Emotion-focused coping	Changing certain emotions that are triggered by a stressor.	As Jimmy approaches a group of guys who have caused him stress, he reminds himself to be calm and not let them bother him.

THE ROLE OF CULTURE ON STRESS

People of all cultures experience stress, but not all cultures deal with stress the same way. Individualistic cultures, as in the United States, tend to handle stress alone. They are less likely to go to others for support and more prone to blame themselves for their situation. Individualistic cultures also emphasize problem-focused coping strategies for handling stress. On the other hand, collectivist cultures, such as those in Asia, tend to seek out social support by turning to others when facing stressors. They also tend to use emotion-focused coping strategies to handle stressful situations.

An individual who moves into a different culture can experience stress. **Acculturative stress** *occurs through the pressure of trying to adapt to a new culture.* People experience stress as they try to hold onto their cultural practices and viewpoints in a new surrounding that might not embrace certain practices and viewpoints.

AP Tip

Be prepared to explain the difference between problem- and emotion-focused coping. Which cultures use problem- and emotion-focused coping strategies?

Multiple-Choice Questions

1. Internal and external factors that direct an organism's behavior towards a desired outcome is referred to as
   (A) emotion
   (B) homeostasis
   (C) motivation
   (D) arousal
   (E) behavior

2. Jimmy got up in the middle of night for a drink of water. Which theory of motivation best explains why Jimmy got out of bed?
   (A) Instinct theory
   (B) Optimum arousal theory
   (C) James-Lange theory
   (D) Drive-reduction theory
   (E) Self-actualizing theory

3. Jenny wants to leave a party because it is boring. Which theory of motivation would explain Jenny's reason for leaving the party?
   (A) Instinct theory
   (B) Optimum arousal theory
   (C) Drive-reduction theory
   (D) Cannon-Bard theory
   (E) James-Lange theory

4. Joe was motivated to work flex-time at his job because if he worked an extra hour Monday through Thursday he could leave at noon on Friday. Which motivational theory would best explain the rationale for Joe's wanting to work a flex-time schedule?
   (A) Drive-reduction theory
   (B) James-Lange theory
   (C) Instinct theory
   (D) Incentive theory
   (E) Yerkes-Dodson law

5. CCK is a signal for satiety of _____ hunger, and leptin is a signal for satiety of _____ hunger.
   (A) long-term; short-term
   (B) short-term; long-term
   (C) long-term; long-term
   (D) short-term; short-term
   (E) none of the above

6. _____ monitors the internal states of the body.
   (A) Drive
   (B) Parallel processing
   (C) Homeostasis
   (D) Hemoglobin
   (E) Activity-synthesis

7. _____ hypothalamus initiates hunger, and
_____ hypothalamus stops hunger.
(A) Lateral; lateral
(B) Ventromedial; lateral
(C) Ventromedial; ventromedial
(D) Lateral; ventromedial
(E) Amygdala; ventromedial

8. Suzy has started to consume less and less food. She also spends three to four hours at the gym working out each day. The mention of food upsets her, and she won't listen to anybody who suggests that she is not eating enough. Suzy may be suffering from
(A) anorexia nervosa
(B) bulimia nervosa
(C) the misinformation effect
(D) serial processing
(E) the egocentrism effect

9. According to Abraham Maslow, _____ is /are at the top of the hierarchy of needs.
(A) love and belongingness needs
(B) safety needs
(C) physiological needs
(D) esteem needs
(E) self-actualization

10. The _____, a part of the limbic system, is important in perceiving emotion.
(A) hippocampus
(B) amygdala
(C) hypothalamus
(D) pons
(E) cerebellum

11. When Julie heard a noise outside her window, her heart started to beat faster, and as a result she became scared. Which theory of emotion could best explain Julie's response of fear?
(A) Cannon-Bard theory of emotion
(B) James-Lange theory of emotion
(C) Two-factor theory of emotion
(D) Cognitive-mediational theory of emotion
(E) Facial-feedback hypothesis

12. Which theory suggests that emotion is the result of applying a cognitive label to explain a physiological reaction?
(A) Cannon-Bard theory of emotion
(B) James-Lange theory of emotion
(C) Two-factor theory of emotion
(D) Cognitive-mediational theory of emotion
(E) Facial-feedback hypothesis

13. _____ psychology is a field of psychology that studies the effects of stress on the human body and shows how to handle stress by promoting a positive lifestyle.
(A) Cognitive
(B) Behavioral
(C) Industrial-organizational
(D) Health
(E) Social

14. In the fight-or-flight response, the adrenal medulla releases _____, a hormone that alerts the body by elevating heart rate and respiration while tightening muscles.
(A) catecholamines
(B) corticosteroids
(C) melatonin
(D) insulin
(E) leptin

15. Tracy doesn't like to talk in front of large groups, so she convinces a co-worker to make her scheduled presentation. Which type of coping strategy did Tracy use?
(A) Emotion-focused coping
(B) Problem-focused coping
(C) Avoidance coping
(D) Perceptual inconsistency coping
(E) Self-help coping

Free-Response Questions

1. Jenny has decided to lose weight. She doesn't know how to diet and therefore has to find information that explains effective dieting strategies. Jenny specifically wants to know how the basal metabolic rate (BMR) functions and how it could help her lose weight. Define the BMR and explain how the following factors could affect it.
   ▪ Age
   ▪ Gender
   ▪ Food
   ▪ Exercise
   ▪ Body type

2. Describe how the following factors could affect a person's level of stress. Provide definitions and examples that support your answer.
   ▪ Social support
   ▪ Type A vs. Type B behavior
   ▪ Perceived control
   ▪ Optimistic vs. Pessimistic explanatory styles

Answers

MULTIPLE-CHOICE QUESTIONS

1. Answer: C. Motivation refers to the internal and external factors that affect an organism's behavior (*Psychology*, 8th ed. p. 404/9th ed. p. 413).

2. Answer: D. The drive-reduction theory of motivation says that organisms are driven to satisfy biological needs that are not being met (*Psychology*, 8th ed. p. 408/9th ed. p. 417).

3. Answer: B. The optimum arousal theory states that people are motivated to maintain a certain amount of arousal (*Psychology*, 8th ed. p. 409/9th ed. p. 418).

4. Answer: D. Incentive theory suggests that people are pushed or motivated by appealing stimuli, such as being able to leave work early on a Friday (*Psychology*, 8th ed. pp. 410–411/9th ed. pp. 418–420).

5. Answer: B. CCK sends signals that signify short-term satiation, as during a meal, and leptin sends signals that signify the amount of fat in the bloodstream, which contributes to long-term satiation (*Psychology*, 8th ed. pp. 412–413/9th ed. pp. 421–422).

6. Answer: C. Homeostasis monitors the internal states of the body, producing tension when levels become too high or too low (*Psychology*, 8th ed. p. 408/9th ed. p. 417).

7. Answer: D. The lateral hypothalamus initiates hunger and the ventromedial hypothalamus stops it (*Psychology*, 8th ed. p. 413/9th ed. p. 422).

8. Answer: A. Anorexia nervosa is an eating disorder characterized by lack of caloric intake, vigorous exercise, and a fear of gaining weight (*Psychology*, 8th ed. p. 418/9th ed. p. 427).

9. Answer: E. Self-actualization, according to Abraham Maslow, is on top of the hierarchy of needs and signifies mastery and working at potential (*Psychology*, 8th ed. p. 433/9th ed. pp. 441–443).

10. Answer: B. The amygdala is located in the limbic system and is responsible for expressing and perceiving emotion (*Psychology*, 8th ed. pp. 438–439/9th ed. pp. 446–447).

11. Answer: B. The James-Lange theory of emotion states that emotions are the result of physiological changes in the body (*Psychology*, 8th ed. pp. 441–442/9th ed. pp. 449–451).

12. Answer: C. The two-factory theory of emotion states that emotion is the result of providing a cognitive label as an

explanation for changes in physiological responses (*Psychology*, 8th ed. pp. 446–447/9th ed. pp. 453–455).

13. Answer: D. Health psychology studies the effects of stress by providing information that helps people learn what stress is and how it affects the body (*Psychology*, 8th ed. p. 517/9th ed. p. 523).

14. Answer: A. Catecholamines are released into the bloodstream by the adrenal medulla, where they work to elevate the heart and breathing rates and increase muscle tension, thus preparing the body for fight-or-flight (*Psychology*, 8th ed. p. 523/9th ed. p. 528).

15. Answer: B. Problem-focused coping addresses the problem, or the cause of the problem, and seeks a more favorable solution (*Psychology*, 8th ed. p. 530–531/9th ed. p. 536).

FREE-RESPONSE QUESTIONS

1. The BMR regulates the amount of energy needed to maintain a person's body weight. The BMR slows down with age. The older a person becomes, the more slowly the BMR will perform. Women tend to have slower BMRs than men. Not eating enough food slows the BMR down. People should eat smaller meals, which keeps the BMR functioning properly, whereas not eating at all merely slows it down. Exercise helps to stimulate the BMR. For example, walking throughout the day helps speed up the BMR. A person who is overweight will have a higher BMR due to the fact that his or her body has to worker harder to accommodate the extra weight.

2. Social support involves gaining knowledge about how to deal with stressful situations from knowledgeable people—for example, turning to a friend or family member who has expertise on what one is experiencing.

    Type A behavior is characterized by impatience, aggressiveness, and competitiveness. A Type A person loses his or her temper quickly and responds negatively to stressful situations. Type B behavior is characterized by relaxed, calm responsiveness. A Type B person examines what is causing him or her stress and searches for an effective way to handle it.

    Perceived control is dictated by the amount of control one has in a situation. People who don't have control in situations experience more stress.

    Optimistic explanatory style looks for external causes of stress and tries to develop a more productive outlook. For example, an optimistic person may realize that some stressful situations are beyond his or her capabilities to change. Pessimistic people tend to blame themselves for their misfortunes and look at the negative side of events and circumstances. A pessimistic person may believe that he or she is the reason why nothing is going right, and that there is nothing he or she can do to better the situation.

6

SENSATION AND PERCEPTION

Sensation *is the detection of a physical stimulus in the environment.* Physical stimuli include light, sound, odors, heat, taste, and pain or pressure. **Perception** *refers to the interpretation of a sensation.* Perception is what causes people to have different interpretations about what they sense, or detect, in the environment. For example, all people use olfactory receptor cells to detect smell; however, two people may have different opinions, or perceptions, of a given smell.

PROCESS OF SENSATION

1. The sensation process starts with an **accessory structure**, *the part of a sense organ such as the lens of an eye or the outer ear that is responsible for collecting and modifying energy from the environment.*

2. The next step involves **sensory receptors**, *specialized cells that respond to certain energy fluctuations in the environment.* When certain fluctuations exceed the receptor's threshold, an action potential is fired, causing neurotransmitters to be released to neighboring cells. Sensory receptors are similar to neurons; however, they do not have dendrites and axons.

3. As sensory receptors detect certain types of energy, the process of transduction begins. **Transduction** *occurs when physical energy is converted into neural code, making it possible for the brain to interpret the energy.* Transduction would not occur if it were not for sensory receptors.

4. Information from the sensory receptors is transmitted via sensory nerves to the central nervous system.

5. All of the sensory information, except for smell, is then sent to the **thalamus,** *where information is analyzed and relayed to the appropriate area in the cerebral cortex.*

6. The **sensory cortex,** *located in the cerebral cortex,* processes the sensory information.

AP Tip

Be prepared to describe how transduction affects the process of sensation and perception.

FACTORS THAT AFFECT SENSATION

Energy from the environment can only be detected if it is strong enough to trigger an action potential within a cell. The **absolute threshold** *is the smallest amount of stimulus energy necessary for sensation to take place 50 percent of the time.* Stimuli that are not strong enough to exceed the absolute threshold are referred to as subliminal stimuli, and are not perceived.

The **signal detection theory** *examines factors that affect the process of sensation.* This theory is based on a mathematical formula that determines when people will report the detection of a stimulus that is right around a threshold level. Whether a person detects a stimulus depends on that individual's sensitivity and response criterion. **Sensitivity** *refers to the ability to detect a stimulus,* and is affected by the strength of the stimulus. Detection decreases if the stimulus is not strong enough. **Response criterion** *refers to a person's willingness to respond to a stimulus,* and is affected by his or her motivation. For example, if a student is not motivated to pay attention during a lecture, then he or she probably won't understand what the lecturer is discussing. The end result, according to advocates of the signal detection theory, is that there can be no absolute threshold, because each individual's levels of motivation and attentiveness are always changing.

The **difference threshold**, also called the *just noticeable difference (JND), is the smallest detectable "difference" between two stimuli.* For example, in order for a person to detect the difference between two musical notes, there has to be enough of a difference between the notes to be distinguishable. If a person can't tell the difference between the two notes, then there isn't enough variation. **Weber's law** suggests that *a difference threshold depends on the strength of the new stimulus in relation to the original stimulus.* For example, if a person who weighs 200 pounds and a person who weighs 400 pounds both lose 20 pounds, the person who originally weighed 200 pounds will notice the loss more.

Sensory adaptation also affects the process of sensation. **Sensory adaptation** *occurs as sensory receptors lose their sensitivity in response to an unchanging stimulus.* For example, a person who jumps into a cold pool may complain immediately how cold the water is, but then may comment a few minutes later how nice the water feels. Did the temperature of the water dramatically change? No. Sensory adaptation made it possible for the swimmer to find the temperature of the water enjoyable. This is the result of the person's sensory receptors losing sensitivity, or adapting, to an unchanging stimulus, the water.

Nuts and Bolts

 Another example of sensory adaptation, to which many of us can relate, would be when you first start your car in the morning and you are startled at how loudly the music is playing on the radio. The volume of the music did not bother you on the drive home the previous night because you had time to <u>adapt</u> to the volume of the music as you drove. The next morning when you first start your car you have not yet had time to adapt to the volume.

AP Tip

Be prepared to explain the role of thresholds with detection of a stimulus. Also be able to explain the association between difference thresholds and Weber's law.

THE VISUAL SYSTEM

Light is a form of energy referred to as electromagnetic radiation. Much of electromagnetic radiation, which includes radio waves, x-rays, television signals, and radar, is not visible to the human eye.

HOW WE ARE ABLE TO SEE

There are several parts within the eye that are responsible for the detection and conversion of visible light.

1. The visual process begins when light passes through the **cornea,** *a clear, protective membrane that covers the eye.*

2. Light then passes through the pupil. The **pupil** *is the opening in the eye that allows light to enter.* The **iris** *is a muscle that determines the amount of light that enters through the pupil.* The iris is the colored portion of the eye that constricts and expands, changing the size of the pupil. For example, when a person detects a bright light, the iris constricts the diameter of the pupil so the intensity of the light doesn't damage the eye. If it is dark out and visual information is not easily detected, the iris expands the diameter of the pupil, allowing more light to enter.

3. The **lens,** *located directly behind the pupil, bends the light wave, focusing it on the retina.* **Accommodation** *refers to the process of how the lens focuses in and out on images.* A problem in the accommodation process could result in nearsightedness or farsightedness. Nearsightedness occurs when the individual

cannot focus on faraway images, and farsightedness occurs when the individual cannot focus on objects at close range.

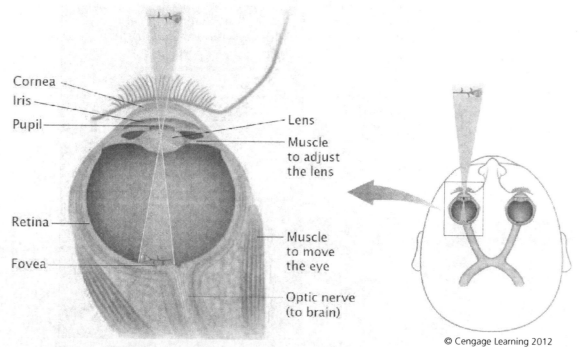

Cornea
Iris
Pupil
Lens
Muscle to adjust the lens
Retina
Fovea
Muscle to move the eye
Optic nerve (to brain)

© Cengage Learning 2012

4. The **retina** *is a light-sensitive membrane located in the back of the* eye and is where transduction occurs. The retina contains **photoreceptors**, *which are the sensory receptors responsible for converting light energy into neural code.* Photoreceptors are divided into rods and cones.

- **Rods** *are more activate in dimly lighted conditions.* However, rods adapt very slowly compared to cones, which could explain why it takes longer to detect objects in the dark. There are many more rods than cones in the retina.

- **Cones** *are more activate in bright-light conditions and help in the detection of fine details and color.* The greatest concentration of cones is in the **fovea**, *which is the area of the retina where visual acuity is sharpest.* For example, when you are trying to detect fine details you have to stare straight at the object to activate the cones, located in the center of the retina. You wouldn't try to discern fine details by holding the object to the side of your face.

Nuts and Bolts

 Remember to associate **cones** with **color**.

5. In order for information detected by rods and cones to reach the brain, it must pass through bipolar cells. **Bipolar cells** *are*

specialized neurons that connect rods and cones to ganglion cells, which eventually carry the information to the brain.

6. Information from the bipolar cells is then passed to the ganglion cells. **Ganglion cells** *are specialized neurons that receive and process information from the receptor cells before the information is sent to the brain.*

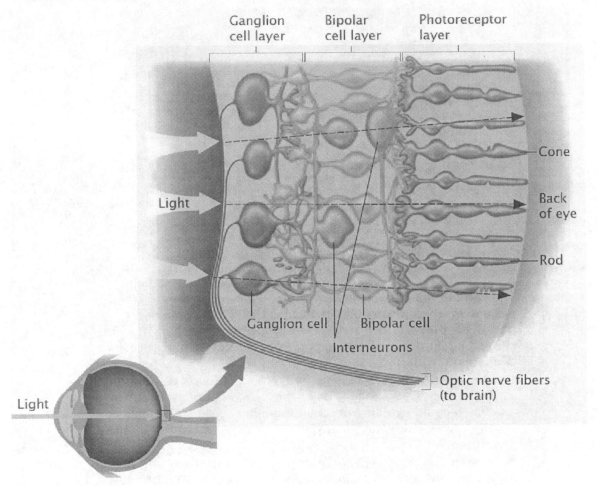

7. The axons of the ganglion cells form the **optic nerve**, *which carries visual information to the brain.* The **optic disk** *is an area that contains no rods and cones.* It is at the optic disk that the optic nerve leaves the eye. A **blind spot** *occurs where the optic nerve leaves the retina, producing a void in the visual field.* The blind spot is unnoticed because the other eye compensates for it.

8. **Optic chiasm** *refers to the point where the nerves from each eye meet in the brain and then cross to the opposite side of the brain.* Information detected by the right half of each eye is transmitted to the brain's left hemisphere, and information from the left half of each eye is transmitted to the brain's right hemisphere.

9. From the optic chiasm, information is sent to the thalamus, where it is then relayed to the **primary visual cortex**, *which processes the visual information.* **Feature detectors** *are neurons in the*

primary visual cortex, specialized to respond to different aspects of an image such as size, shape, and angle. Feature detectors are able to process multiple aspects of an image through parallel processing. **Parallel processing** *refers to how the brain processes multiple sources of information simultaneously.*

Nuts and Bolts

A good way to associate feature detectors with visual processing is to remember that a movie can be called a motion feature presentation. Remember you **watch** with your eyes a motion feature presentation.

AP Tip

Be prepared to identify the parts of the eye and the role each plays in vision.

COLOR VISION

How we perceive color depends on three characteristics of light waves: hue, saturation, and purity. **Hue** *refers to the color that people psychologically experience.* Hue is determined by the wavelength—specifically, the distance from the peak of one wave to the peak of the next. Short wavelength distances produce bluish colors. Long wavelength distances produce reddish colors. Medium wavelength distances produce orange, green, and yellow colors.

Nuts and Bolts

To remember that shorter wavelengths produce bluish colors think of the cartoon characters the Smurfs. Remember, not only are Smurfs **blue**, they are also **short**. To remember that long wavelengths display a reddish color think of the character Clifford the dog. Clifford is a **long**, **red** dog.

Saturation *refers to the purity of the color.* Purity depends on the complexity of the light wave. For example, red, which is comprised of a single wave, is more pure, or saturated, than pink, which is the combination of red and white light. **Brightness** *refers to the intensity of the light wave, which is determined by the amplitude, or height, of a wave.* Great amplitude, which would resemble a tall wave, would be a very bright color. Low amplitude, a low wave, would show a dull color.

AP Tip

You may be asked to identify the parts of a light wave.

COLOR MIXING

Colors are based on the dominant wavelength present. How colors are mixed determines which color people will perceive. Subtractive and additive are two types of color mixing. **Subtractive color mixing** *occurs by mixing different paint colors; through this process wavelengths are subtracted, or absorbed.* Color is determined by which wavelengths are absorbed and which are reflected. A stop sign is red because it absorbs certain wavelengths, but reflects the wavelength that produces red. White doesn't absorb any wavelengths, but actually reflects all the wavelengths. For example, when you look through a prism, notice that you see a variety of colors. This happens because none of the wavelengths are being absorbed. In contrast, black is the result of all the wavelengths being absorbed. **Additive color mixing** *involves adding more light wavelengths.* By adding new light wavelengths, different colors can be produced. Combing red, green, and blue light produces white.

THEORIES OF COLOR VISION

Thomas Young and Hermann von Helmholtz discovered that if they mixed only three specific wavelengths, they could produce a variety of colors. This led them to believe that the eye has three types of receptors, each responsive to different wavelengths. The **trichromatic theory of color vision**, also called Young-Helmholz theory, *stated that there are three types of cones, each sensitive to a specific wavelength: red-sensitive cone, long wavelengths; green-sensitive cone, medium wavelengths; blue-sensitive cone, short wavelengths.* A color other than blue, green, or red triggers a combination of the cones, which then produces other colors. For example, purple is the result of triggering both a blue-sensitive and a red-sensitive cone. Color blindness can be explained by the trichromatic theory. People who have red-green color blindness cannot discriminate between red and green colors. These people have blue-sensitive cones, but lack either red or green cones, or possibly both.

Ewald Hering proposed the **opponent-process theory of color vision,** *which states that the color-sensitive components of the eye are grouped into three pairs: red-green, blue-yellow, and black-white.* Each member inhibits, or opposes, the other. When red is activated, green is inhibited, or "off." Seldom does someone describe an image as reddish-green. The same understanding can also be applied to the blue-yellow and black-white pairs. According to Hering, different colors are produced through combinations of the pairs being activated at the same time. For example, purple is the result of the red and blue elements being "on" while the green and yellow elements are "off."

Nuts and Bolts

Think of the opponent-process theory as two people playing basketball. When one player has the ball, the other player, the defender, does not. When red (the player with the ball) is activated, green (the player who does not have the ball) is not activated.

The opponent-process theory and sensory adaptation can explain the occurrence of an **afterimage**, *when an image is perceived even though the stimulus has been removed.* For example, if you were to stare at a yellow dot for a minute or so and then look away, you would see the afterimage of a dot, but actually you would see a blue dot. Over time, if you stared at a yellow dot your sensory receptors would start to diminish in sensitivity (sensory adaptation) to the constant stimulation of the yellow dot. This would cause the other opponent member, blue, to turn "on," resulting in yellow turning "off" or becoming inhibited (opponent-process theory).

AP Tip

Be prepared to explain and differentiate between the trichromatic and opponent-process theories of color vision.

HEARING

Hearing is referred to as audition. Sound is continuous changes that occur in the pressure of air, water, or other substances referred to as mediums. Such changes in pressure cause sound waves to be produced. Sound waves can travel great distances and move through various mediums, including water and air. For example, a person who is underwater could hear another person yell his or her name, or a person at one end of a football field could hear somebody shout from the other end. On the moon, where no medium exists, sound does not exist.

Sound waves have certain properties. Loudness depends on the amplitude, or intensity, of each sound wave. Amplitude is shown by the height of the wave and is measured in decibels. A tall wave correlates to a loud sound with a high decibel measurement. Normal conversation is about 60 decibels. Loudness is similar to brightness in vision, which is also measured through amplitude. **Pitch**, *another property of a sound wave, refers to the highness or lowness of sound, which is determined by the frequency.* **Frequency** *is the number of complete waves that pass though a medium every second.* **Hertz** *is the measurement of frequency.* Waves that are very close together, or have a short distance between peaks, have a high frequency and therefore a high pitch. **Timbre** *refers to the purity of the sound wave.* Most sound waves are not comprised of a single frequency, but of many different frequencies. Timbre is determined by the complexity, or multiplicity, of the different frequencies.

AP Tip

Be prepared to identify the parts of a sound wave, and also to compare them to the properties of a light wave.

PARTS OF THE EAR

There are three parts of the ear that make it possible to detect and perceive sound waves. The outer ear channels the sound, the middle ear amplifies the sound, and the inner ear transduces the sound wave into neural messages.

Location	Parts	Function
Outer ear	Pinna: the visible outer part of the ear; locates the sound wave Auditory canal: channels the sound wave to the eardrum Eardrum: a membrane that vibrates in response to incoming sound waves (eardrum vibrations match frequency of sound wave)	Collects and channels sound waves
Middle ear (mechanical part of the ear)	Made up of three tiny bones: hammer (malleus), anvil (incus), and stirrup (stapes) Each bone causes the next bone to vibrate, resulting in increased amplitude.	Amplifies sound onto the oval window, which separates the middle ear from the inner ear
Inner ear	Cochlea: fluid-filled tube, resembles a snail Basilar membrane: lines the cochlea and contains hair cells (also called cilia), the sensory receptors for audition The auditory nerve then carries the message to the thalamus, which then sends it to the auditory cortex.	Vibrations from the oval window cause the fluid in the cochlea to move, causing basilar membrane vibrations, which cause the hair cells to move. Transduction takes places as the hair cells move back and forth, causing cells in the auditory nerve to become stimulated. The auditory nerve then carries the message to the thalamus, which then sends it to the auditory cortex.

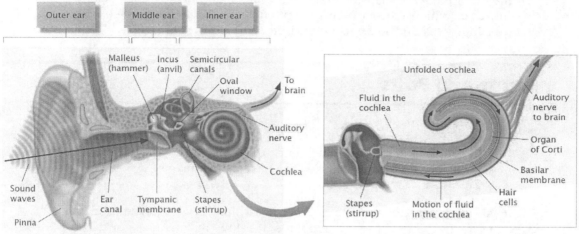

© Cengage Learning 2012

Nuts and Bolts

 A good way to remember that the middle ear is comprised of the three tiny bones—hammer, anvil, and stirrup—is to think of the following statement, "The middle ear **HAS** three tiny bones. **H**ammer, **A**nvil, **S**tirrup."

AP Tip

A multiple-choice question might ask how each part of the ear contributes to audition.

THEORIES OF AUDITION

The basilar membrane is the key structure responsible for distinguishing pitch, which is determined by frequency. The frequency-matching and place theories explain how people are able to discriminate among different pitches.

According to the **frequency-matching theory**, sometimes referred to as the volley principle, *the vibrations of the basilar membrane are determined by the frequency of the vibrations.* A high frequency will cause large vibrations on the basilar membrane, whereas a low frequency causes small vibrations. The vibrations on the basilar membrane affect the hair cells, generating a neural message to travel via the auditory nerve to the brain. The greater the vibrations and the more movement among the hair cells, the faster the message will travel up the auditory nerve. However, neurons can only fire about a thousand times per second; this makes it hard for the frequency theory to account for frequencies that cause neurons to fire faster than their capabilities. Therefore, the frequency theory can only account for low frequencies.

The **place theory**, also called the traveling wave theory, *suggests pitch depends on where vibrations stimulate the basilar membrane.*

Higher frequencies trigger hair cells on one end of the basilar membrane, which causes a certain pitch, whereas lower frequencies trigger hair cells on the opposite end, causing a different pitch.

Nuts and Bolts

 Compare the place theory to playing a guitar. The note played depends on where the player places his or her finger on the neck or fret of the guitar. According to the place theory, pitch is the result of where a vibration strikes the basilar membrane.

In short, both theories are correct in explaining the perception of pitch. The frequency theory accounts for low frequencies, and the place theory is used to explain high frequencies.

AP Tip

Be prepared to differentiate between the place and frequency explanations for pitch perception.

HEARING LOSS

Overexposure to certain stimuli can cause hearing damage. Conduction and sensorineural are two examples of hearing loss. **Conduction hearing loss** *occurs when either the eardrum is punctured or there is damage to any of the three tiny bones located in the middle ear.* **Sensorineural hearing loss**, or nerve deafness, *occurs when there is damage to the hair cells located in the inner ear or auditory nerve.* Damage to the hair cells is almost always permanent. This damage may be caused by the aging process, by heredity, or by overexposure to certain sounds. Hearing aids may help to trigger the hair cells, but cochlear implants have proven a better alternative. Such implants help in converting sounds into electrical signals that could trigger the auditory nerve to carry a message to the auditory cortex.

SMELL

The sense of smell is referred to as olfaction and, along with taste, is identified as a chemical sense.

The sensation of smell comes from molecules that enter the nose. The nasal passage, within the nose, is lined with millions of olfactory receptor cells, which are responsible for the detection of air molecules. Once a receptor cell is stimulated, a neural message passes through its axon, which combines with other olfactory axons to form olfactory nerves. **Olfactory nerves** *then carry information to the olfactory bulb.* The **olfactory bulb**, *located at the end of the olfactory cortex, is responsible for processing the sensation of smell.* From the olfactory bulb, information is then sent via olfactory tracts to the temporal lobe, where recognition of the smell occurs, and also the limbic system, where emotional significance is associated with the smell.

Nuts and Bolts

To remember what the olfactory system is used for, remember that old factories smell.

Sensory adaptation for most senses occurs over an extended period of time, but because the olfactory neurons go directly to the brain (remember that smell is the only sense that does not first send information to the thalamus), sensory adaptation for smell does not take as long. In other words, most people will adapt to smells quicker than they will to cold temperatures, bright lights, or loud sounds.

TASTE

Taste, like smell, is a chemical sense and is referred to as gustation. **Taste buds** *are sensory receptors that are activated when substances enter the mouth.* As a person eats food or drinks liquids, saliva breaks it down, which makes it possible for taste buds to detect the substance of the food and the liquid. There are five types of taste buds: sweet, salty, sour, bitter, and umami. Babies are genetically predisposed to drink a mother's breast milk because they are receptive to the sweet and salty taste. Umami was recently identified and is receptive to protein-rich foods, or "meaty" foods.

Each taste bud has about 50 to 100 receptor cells, which are sensitive to and activated by particular substances. Taste buds are located in groups on the tongue called papillae, and are also scattered throughout the mouth. When a taste bud is activated, neural messages are sent to the thalamus. Taste buds regenerate about every two weeks, but as a person ages, his or her taste buds don't regenerate as quickly. A person who smokes cigarettes or drinks alcohol heavily will have even fewer taste buds.

Nuts and Bolts

To associate taste with gustation, remember, "That tastes disgustation!"

SENSORY INTERACTION

Taste and smell are examples of sensory interaction. **Sensory interaction** *occurs when one sense influences another.* For example, when a person has a cold and a stuffy nose, he or she may complain that food doesn't taste right. Likewise, if someone associates a bad smell with a food, then his or her perception of that food's flavor could be affected.

Nuts and Bolts

An example of sensory interaction occurs when people smell something good and then smack their lips. It's almost as if they can taste the smell.

AP Tip

One multiple-choice question might ask which senses interact. Also, be prepared to identify the receptors for olfaction and gustation.

THE BODY SENSES

The body or somatic senses includes skin senses, which detect touch, temperature, and pain. The skin is the largest sense organ in the body and is comprised of sensory neurons scattered unevenly throughout it. The lips, fingertips, and face have the greatest number of sensory neurons, meaning increased sensitivity in those areas. The back, legs, and arms have the fewest. A person with a small cut on his lip experiences more discomfort than he would if he had a cut on his back. **Pacinian corpuscles**, *located beneath the skin, detect touch and pressure.* In response to pressure and touch, the Pacinian corpuscles become compressed, in a manner comparable to a spring's being compressed, which then sends a neural message to the brain. Sensory adaptation occurs from constant pressure, which makes it possible for human beings to tolerate wearing clothes, glasses, or a hat.

TEMPERATURE

In addition to receptors that detect pressure, there are receptors that detect temperature variations. Certain stimulus temperatures stimulate either warm or cold receptors. The sensation of hot results from the combined stimulation of warm and cold receptors. For example, people sometimes describe having frostbite as a "burning" sensation.

PAIN

Pain is the unpleasant feelings and discomfort experienced when a person is exposed to an aversive stimulus. Most people would like to live without pain, but it's necessary for survival. Pain signals help alert people to pull away, or stop doing something that could cause injury. Pain can also occur internally. For example, if someone were to accidentally swallow a small, sharp object, pain signals would be sent to the brain, making the person aware that something was wrong.

Ronald Melzack and Patrick Wall developed the **gate-control theory**, *which suggests that pain is determined by the opening and closing of neurological gates in the spinal cord.* When the "gates" are closed the individual doesn't experience pain; when they are open, sensory neurons detect and send pain messages to the brain. Sensory neurons are different from other neurons in that they do not have dendrites, but free nerve endings that extend from the spinal cord to the skin and muscles. When the free nerve endings are stimulated they release **substance P**, *a neurotransmitter that activates other neurons to open the "gate," resulting in the perception of pain.* This information is then sent to the thalamus, which relays the information to the somatosensory cortex, the frontal lobes, and the limbic system. The limbic system provides the emotional elements associated with pain.

Psychological factors such as not focusing on the painful stimulus or trying to remain positive can also affect the sensation of pain. These factors can inhibit the release of endorphins, a neurotransmitter that reduces pain by blocking substance P in the spinal cord.

Nuts and Bolts

 Endorphins are released in response to pain. When you receive a massage, notice at the beginning that it may hurt a little. This occurs because substance P is being released, causing the gates to open and you to experience pain. But as the massage continues, notice that it starts to feel good. This occurs because endorphins are released, inhibiting substance P.

AP Tip

An essay question might ask you to describe how people experience pain and what factors contribute to increased or decreased pain perception.

BODY MOVEMENT AND BALANCE

The **kinesthetic sense** *monitors and coordinates movement among body parts through information sent from sensory neurons called* **proprioceptors**, *which are located in joints, muscles, and the inner ear and communicate information to the brain concerning tension and movement in the body.*

The **vestibular sense** *monitors balance in response to movement detected by the proprioceptors.* The vestibular sense receives information from the semicircular canals and the vestibular sacs, located in the ear. The semicircular canals and vestibular sacs are filled with fluid and lined with hair cells that respond to movement and changes in the body. A person who is dizzy will often hold his or her head or stare at a fixed object, without realizing that he or she is trying to level the fluid in the inner ear.

Nuts and Bolts

Have you ever used a level while constructing something or hanging a picture? A level has a bubble in liquid; the object is level when the bubble is exactly in the middle of the liquid. Think of the vestibular sac and semicircular canal as a level. When the fluid in these structures is level, you are physically balanced. When the fluid is not level, as when the water bubble is not between the lines, you feel dizzy.

PERCEPTION

Psychologists refer to **perception** as *the awareness, integration, and organization of sensory stimuli.* When studying perception, psychologists aim to understand how a person perceives the world and events around them. While no one fully understands how we label and organize sensory stimuli, psychologists have made some remarkable discoveries.

PERCEPTUAL ORGANIZATION

When you look at an object, what do you see? Do you start by looking at the top, the middle, or the bottom of the item? Do you use prior knowledge to make sense of the object, or do you look at each individual element and then come to understand what the object is? The way in which we view an object is the result of two primary kinds of organization: bottom-up processing and top-down processing. **Bottom-up processing** *is the organization of information, without the use of prior knowledge, beginning with individual elements that are structured together to form a whole.* In bottom-up processing each individual element is given in great detail, and it is not until the individual elements are connected that the whole object is recognized. Opposite this approach is **top-down processing**, *the organization of information that uses prior knowledge to form the whole.* In top-down processing, the final whole is already known, mainly due to prior information, and then the individual elements are observed.

Nuts and Bolts

Think of bottom-up processing as putting a puzzle together upside down. You don't have any idea what the puzzle will look like until you are finished. In contrast, if you were putting a puzzle together while looking at a picture on the box, you would be using top-down processing (you use the prior knowledge of the assembled puzzle to put it together).

GESTALT LAWS

How we organize sensory stimuli into meaningful experiences is the interest of Gestalt psychologists. *Gestalt*, which translates from German as "organization" or "whole figure," is a field of psychology in which the whole is believed to be greater than the sum of its parts. Gestalt psychology can trace its beginnings to the works of Max Wertheimer, Kurt Koffka, and Wolfgang Köhler, who said that human perception is based on the integration of individual elements into a whole.

Gestalt psychologists have identified certain "laws" or principles regarding perceptual organization, listed below.

Gestalt Law		Definition	Example
Figure-ground		The ability to distinguish between the figure as the foreground and the ground as the background.	Can you see the vase and the two faces? The above is known as the vase-face (Boring image)
Grouping	Proximity	The tendency to perceive objects that are close together as belonging together.	Are there nine x's or three groups of three x's? XXX XXX XXX
	Similarity	The tendency to group similar objects together to make one whole.	How are these letters grouped? OOOOOOXOOOOO OOOOOXOOOOOO OOOOXOOOOOOO OOOXOOOOOOOO
	Continuity	The tendency to see an object as continuing despite an obvious break.	Does each line stop, or does it continue? X
	Closure	The tendency to fill in the missing spaces to complete the object and see it as a whole.	Is this really a circle?

Gestalt Law		Definition	Example
	Common fate	The tendency to see objects that move in the same direction as together.	If group A moved down and group B moved up, you would perceive the circles in group A as moving together and the circles in group B as moving together. Group A ◯ ◯ ◯ Group B ◯ ◯

Nuts and Bolts

 One way to remember the figure-ground effect is that you can see your teacher as he stands in front of a chalk- or whiteboard. You see the figure in the foreground and the ground in the background. It is also important to know the names of some of the "famous" figure-ground pictures such as the vase-face (Boring image).

AP Tip

Past multiple-choice questions asked students to identify which Gestalt law or principle was being displayed, either by looking at a picture or by name.

PERCEPTION OF LOCATION, DISTANCE, AND MOTION

Being able to judge where or how far away an object is in relation to where you are standing is an important concept in perception. Without this ability to perceive you might be hit by the object. We are able to judge the location and distance of an object with our vision. Each eye sends cues to the brain and allows us to form a spatial relation of that object. The cues that are received by one eye are known as **monocular cues**, *information perceived from one eye that plays a crucial role in the ability to detect depth perception.* Monocular cues are primarily responsible for depth perception. Below is a list of perceptual information we receive from monocular cues.

Type of Cue	Perceptual Information	Definition	Example
Monocular	Relative size or area	The size/area of an object is judged to be relative to the size/area of objects that surround the original object. The closer an object, the larger it appears to be.	The white circles are the same sizes. However, because of the surrounding circles, our perception of their size/area is skewed.
	Interposition	The object that is farther away is partially hidden by the object that is closer.	
	Texture gradient	Lesser clarity is perceived as being farther away.	
	Motion parallax	Objects that are farther away appear to move in the same direction at the same rate; closer objects move at a rapid speed in the opposite direction.	Looking at the landscape while a car is in motion, trees closer to the car move quickly in the opposite direction, but the airplane in the sky appears to moving in the same direction at a slow pace.

For accurate depth perception we rely on cues from both eyes. **Binocular cues,** *images that are perceived by both eyes and allow for accurate detection of depth perception,* integrate the perception of information by both eyes. **Binocular (retinal) disparity** is *information that is processed by each eye and fused to form one image.* Because our eyes are close together they must turn inward in order to create a clear image for each retina. This process is known as **convergence,** *turning inward of each eye to focus on an up-close object.* As objects move closer to our noses, our eyes converge and take on a "cross-eyed" appearance.

PERCEPTUAL CONSTANCIES

Perceptual constancies involve the ability to see an object as maintaining its original shape, color, brightness, or size without having to reinterpret it each time a change occurs. **Shape constancy** is *the perception that the shape of an object remains the same despite a change in the angle from which it is viewed.* For example, a closed door appears flat; however, while it is being opened, the size of the door appears to change. Because of shape constancy we can understand that the door itself does not actually change size. **Color constancy** is *the perception that the color of an object remains the same despite a change in the lighting.* For example, you are able to see that a green apple remains the same color green even when the lighting in the room changes. **Brightness constancy** is *the perception that the brightness of an object remains the same despite a change in the brightness of the background.* For example, you understand that even though a red circle looks brighter on a white background than it does on a black background, it is the same shade of red. **Size constancy** is *the perception that the size of an object remains the same despite the fact that size changes based on distance.* For example, if you were looking at a person across the room, you would be able to put your hand in front of your eyes and essentially cover up the person. However, the person did not change size; rather, the distance between you and the person is greater than the distance between your eyes and your hand.

Nuts and Bolts

 Remember that constancy means that an object remains constant despite an apparent change.

PERCEPTION OF MOVEMENT

The perception of movement is an area of interest to psychologists. The human brain is able to correct for the time delay that is experienced as information travels from the retina to the optic nerve and finally to the visual cortex. To correct this delay the brain simply fills in the missing pieces, based largely on experience. If you have seen a particular object move before, your brain essentially acts as if it were on autopilot. A problem may arise when you lack the experience of having seen a certain image move.

Three ways our brain interprets apparent motion, even though no actual motion has occurred, are the autokinetic effect, stroboscopic motion, and the phi phenomenon. The **autokinetic effect** is *the perception of movement of a stationary point of light in a totally darkened room.* If you are in a room that is completely darkened except for a single point of light, and you fixate your gaze on that point of light, it will appear to move. The reason for this apparent movement is because the stationary point of light is being projected on a featureless background, and your eyes have no point of reference against which to judge it.

Nuts and Bolts

 Another way to remember the autokinetic effect is to recall that "auto" means automatic, and "kinetic" means movement.

Stroboscopic motion is *the perception of movement due to the rapid presentation of changing stationary images.* If you have ever seen a movie, you have experienced stroboscopic motion. Movies are the rapid presentation of stationary images. The fact that the movie appears to move smoothly is due to this rapid succession of stationary images. **Phi phenomenon** is *apparent movement due to the sequential presentation of stationary images.* If an image of a circle is presented on the left side of a screen for a brief moment, and then a circle is presented on the right side of the screen, many people would say that the image had moved from left to right. However, there was no movement, only the appearance of movement created by the presentation and then quick removal of the circle on the left, followed by the presentation and quick removal of the circle on the right.

Nuts and Bolts

 One way to remember the phi phenomenon is to think of a baseball scoreboard that displays fireworks after a homerun is hit. The perception of the fireworks exploding is simply the lights turning on and off in a sequential pattern.

AP Tip

Past multiple-choice questions have asked students to identify the autokinetic effect and the phi phenomenon.

EXPERIENCE AND PERCEPTION

Perception depends on experience. The experiences we have with certain objects and images influence what we perceive. In a classic study conducted by Eleanor Gibson and Richard Walk (1960), infants were used to determine whether depth perception is innate or learned. Infants were placed on a checkerboard fabric-covered table. The table consisted of a shallow side and a deep end, which had Plexiglas laid across it to create the illusion of a drop-off. This experiment is referred to as the "visual cliff experiment" because of the fabricated illusion of a cliff. The infant was placed on the shallow side while his or her mother waited across the table at the deep-end side. The mother was instructed to encourage the infant to come to her. However, the study infants did not journey across the deep end to their mothers. Gibson and Walk theorized that the infants must have the ability to perceive depth. Critics claim that depth perception is not innate, and that the infants must have had prior experiences with the perception of depth. Whichever theory is correct, it can be hypothesized that experience plays a role in the perception of depth.

ATTENTION

Attention, *the ability to focus psychological resources on a task or object while ignoring other tasks or objects*, is crucial for both physical and mental performance. Human beings are able to selectively focus attention on a particular stimulus while disregarding other stimuli. This process is known as selective attention. For example, you are able to voluntarily focus your attention on your teacher despite the fact that there are other stimuli in the room, such as the hum of the lights or the temperature of the room. However, if someone knocks at the classroom door your attention will involuntarily shift to the knock. Once the door is answered and the person enters the room to deliver a piece of paper and then leaves you are able to voluntarily refocus your attention on your teacher. Focusing on your teacher's words may cause you to miss less important information, such as the person next to you stretching his or her arms. The fact that you missed this activity is due to **inattentional blindness**, *the inability to see objects due to distraction*. Our brains cannot possibly focus our attention on everything all at once, so they select what to focus on and what to ignore. While listening intently to your teacher continuing the lecture, you are also writing down the information that is being presented. **Multitasking** is *the ability to focus your attention on two distinctly different tasks*. However, the ability to multitask is limited, and if we are asked to focus on too many different tasks, performance will likely suffer. Another concept that involves attention is known as the **cocktail party effect**, *the ability to focus on one task while simultaneously focusing on another*. For example, if you are having a conversation with one person and you hear your name being mentioned by another person in a conversation in a different part of the room, you are able to process that information as well as continue your current conversation.

Multiple-Choice Questions

1. Sensation refers to the
   (A) detection of stimulus energy from the environment
   (B) conversion of stimulus energy into neural code
   (C) organization and interpretation of stimulus energy
   (D) adaptation to an unchanging stimulus, resulting in diminished sensitivity
   (E) relaying of information that occurs in the brain

2. When Sue first went outside she found the cold unbearable. She complained how cold it was, but after a while the temperature did not seem to bother her. Which sensational process allowed Sue to tolerate the cold?
   (A) Transduction
   (B) Selective attention
   (C) Sensory adaptation
   (D) Accommodation
   (E) Perceptual set

3. The height of a sound wave determines the
   (A) pitch
   (B) frequency
   (C) timbre
   (D) loudness
   (E) transduction

4. _____ are the receptor cells for audition and _____ are the receptor cells for vision.
   (A) Olfactory cells; rods and cones
   (B) Taste buds; rods and cones
   (C) Rods and cones; hair cells
   (D) Hair cells; rods and cones
   (E) Proprioceptors; rods and cones

5. The optic chiasm is
   (A) responsible for color vision
   (B) where the optic nerve leaves the eye, causing a blind spot
   (C) where the optic nerves cross over to report information to opposite sides of the brain
   (D) where information from rods and cones is passed to the ganglion cells
   (E) responsible for detecting fine details

6. All sensory information is sent to the thalamus EXCEPT
   (A) taste
   (B) vision
   (C) audition
   (D) touch
   (E) smell

7. John complains that when he gets out of bed that he feels dizzy. He also says his ears hurt. Why is John commenting that his ears hurt?
   (A) The inner ear, specifically the semicircular canals and vestibular sacs, provide information for the vestibular sense, which monitors balance.
   (B) The inner ear, specifically the hammer, anvil, and stirrup, provide information for the vestibular sense, which monitors balance.
   (C) The middle ear, specifically the semicircular canals and vestibular sacs, provide information to the vestibular sense, which monitors balance.
   (D) The outer ear, specifically the semicircular canals and vestibular sacs, provide information to the kinesthetic sense, which monitors balance.
   (E) The middle ear, specifically the semicircular canals and vestibular sacs, provide information to the kinesthetic sense, which monitors balance.

8. According to the Gestalt principle of proximity,
   (A) objects that display the same features are grouped together
   (B) objects that are close together are interpreted as belonging together
   (C) monocular cues allow the size of an object to remain constant
   (D) binocular cues allow the color of an object to remain constant
   (E) objects that are farther away look as if they are moving more slowly than do closer objects

9. Study subjects were placed in darkened room and told to focus on a single stationary point of light on the wall. After a few minutes subjects reported that the point of light was moving. This apparent movement is known as
   (A) the phi phenomenon
   (B) the Gestalt law of proximity
   (C) stroboscopic motion
   (D) the autokinetic effect
   (E) perceptual constancy

10. Devin understands that when a door is opening it does not lose its original shape. This is known as
    (A) perceptual ability
    (B) inattentional blindness
    (C) shape constancy
    (D) shape proximity
    (E) shape closure

11. Armando was tearing up old papers when he realized that he had accidently torn up the homework that was due the next day. Because Armando knew what his homework was he was able to put the pieces back together with relative ease. Armando used which organizational strategy to reconstruct his homework?
    (A) Bottom-up processing
    (B) Top-down processing
    (C) Similarity processing
    (D) Perceptual blindness
    (E) The cocktail-party effect

12. Which of the following would be most difficult for a person who only had one eye?
    (A) Inserting a toothpick into a horizontal straw
    (B) Watching a movie at a theatre
    (C) Correctly identifying the color of a car
    (D) Organizing objects into similar patterns or colors
    (E) Understanding that a line continues despite a break in it

13. The ability to talk on the phone and type on the computer at the same time is the result of
    (A) bottom-up processing
    (B) perceptual processing
    (C) selective attention
    (D) closure
    (E) convergence

14. Laticia is listening to her teacher conduct a lesson on the parts and functions of the brain. Laticia can distinguish her teacher from the board because of which Gestalt principle?
    (A) Proximity
    (B) Closure
    (C) Similarity
    (D) Continuity
    (E) Figure-ground

15. Awareness, integration, and organization of information into meaningful information is known as
    (A) sensation
    (B) perception
    (C) illusions
    (D) false perception
    (E) convergence

Free-Response Questions

1. Marcus is attending his school's winter pep rally. As he looks around, he notices that all the students are sitting by grade level and all are wearing their class colors. He is also aware of the music being played on the sound system, as well as the cheers from the crowd and the cheerleaders spelling out the school letters. Define each of the following and explain how each contributes to what Marcus is experiencing.
    ▪ Proximity
    ▪ Closure
    ▪ Similarity
    ▪ Figure-ground
    ▪ Selective attention

2. Explain how each of the following factors could affect the process of sensation. Simply stated definitions will not be scored.
    - ▓ sensory adaptation
    - ▓ sensitivity
    - ▓ response criterion
    - ▓ absolute threshold
    - ▓ Weber's law

Answers

MULTIPLE-CHOICE QUESTIONS

1. Answer: A. Sensation involves the detection of energy provided by something that stimulates sensory receptors (*Psychology,* 8th ed. p. 107/9th ed. p. 109).

2. Answer: C. Sensory adaptation occurs in response to an unchanging stimulus, causing diminished sensitivity among sensory receptors (*Psychology,* 8th ed. p. 109/9th ed. pp. 110–111).

3. Answer: D. Loudness is shown through the height of a sound wave. This is referred to as the amplitude of the sound wave. The greater the height, the louder the sound (*Psychology,* 8th ed. p. 111/9th ed. pp. 114–115).

4. Answer: D. Hair cells, also called cilia, are the receptor cells that respond to sound waves, making audition possible. Rods and cones, located in the retina, are activated in response to light waves, making the visual process possible (*Psychology,* 8th ed. pp. 113, 121/9th ed. pp. 115, 123).

5. Answer: C. The optic chiasm is the location in the brain where the optical nerves touch and cross over, reporting information to the opposite sides of the brain. The left eye's information is sent to and processed in the right side of the brain and vice versa for the right eye (*Psychology,* 8th ed. p. 124/9th ed. p. 126).

6. Answer: E. Smell is the only sense that doesn't send information to the thalamus. Instead, olfactory information goes to the olfactory bulb before being sent to the appropriate areas of the brain (*Psychology,* 8th ed. p. 134/9th ed. p. 137).

7. Answer: A. Information is provided by the inner ear's semicircular canals and vestibular sacs, which assist the vestibular sense in monitoring balance in relation to movement (*Psychology,* 8th ed. p. 146/9th ed. p. 150).

8. Answer: B. The Gestalt law of proximity states that objects that are close together are seen as belonging together (*Psychology,* 8th ed. p. 164/9th ed. p. 168).

9. Answer: D. According to the autokinetic effect, a stationary point of light in a darkened room will appear to move. The reason behind this apparent movement is that there is no other point of reference for the eyes to focus on *(this material does not appear in either textbook edition)*.

10. Answer: C. Shape constancy is the ability to understand that despite an apparent change, the shape of an object does not change. Knowing that a door is the same shape whether it is opened or closed means that its size remains constant *(Psychology,* 8th ed. p. 164/9th ed. p. 175).

11. Answer: B. Having prior knowledge of the outcome allows for the organization of the pieces into the whole *(Psychology,* 8th ed. pp. 176–177/9th ed. p. 177).

12. Answer: A. Binocular cues, information received from each eye, are needed for judging the correct depth of objects *(Psychology,* 8th ed. pp. 168–169/9th ed. p. 170).

13. Answer: C. Selective attention allows a person to process different stimuli at the same time. The ability to focus on one stimulus while ignoring another is the result of selective attention *(Psychology,* 8th ed. p. 182/9th ed. p. 184).

14. Answer: E. The ability to distinguish a figure from its background and vice versa is the Gestalt principle of figure-ground *(Psychology,* 8th ed. p. 163/9th ed. p. 167).

15. Answer: B. Integration and organization of sensory input into meaningful information is known as perception *(Psychology,* 8th ed. p. 153/9th ed. p. 157).

FREE-RESPONSE QUESTIONS

1. Proximity is defined as the perception that two objects that are close together belong to each other. Therefore, the students sitting together according to grade levels will be grouped together.

   Closure is the ability to perceive a whole despite missing pieces that are filled in by the brain. The cheerleaders who are spelling out the school letters are actually individual people who are organized in a manner that allows a person to perceive them collectively as a letter.

   Similarity means that objects that appear the same will be grouped together. Students sitting together by grade level and wearing similarly colored shirts will be seen as a whole, or grouped together.

   Figure-ground is the ability to distinguish the figure from the background. Mark can distinguish his friend in another grade level even though his friend is sitting amidst other people in his own grade.

   Selective attention is the ability to distinguish particular stimuli even though there are other stimuli that may distract from it. Mark is able to hear both the music and his classmates cheering. He can decide which stimuli to pay attention to.

2. Sensory adaptation occurs from constant stimulation to an unchanging stimulus, resulting in diminished sensitivity. This diminished sensitivity would affect the detection of the stimulus.

    Sensitivity indicates whether a stimulus can be detected. If a person doesn't have certain sensory receptors then sensation is not possible.

    Response criterion refers to the willingness to respond to a stimulus. If a person is not motivated to pay attention to a stimulus then sensation will not take place.

    Absolute threshold indicates the minimum level of stimulation necessary for detection. If a stimulus is too weak, the sensation will not occur.

    Weber's law states that in order to detect a difference between two stimuli, a constant proportion of difference is necessary. If one stimulus does not increase in relation to another stimulus, then that stimulus will not be detected.

7

STATES OF CONSCIOUSNESS

Conscious awareness includes *all of the mental processes a person is aware of at any given moment.* For example, when you are aware of your teacher's voice, or the smell of perfume from the person sitting in front of you, or the notes you are jotting down on your paper, then these are all examples of conscious awareness. But not all mental activities occur in conscious awareness. For example, the brain monitors body temperature at a nonconscious level. There are also other levels of awareness that could affect the conscious awareness. This includes the preconscious and the unconscious levels. The content of the **preconscious level** *resides just below the level of consciousness, which makes it easy to access.* For example, if a student next to you asks what you did after school yesterday, even if you were not presently thinking about what you did yesterday, it would not be hard to recall, and thus affect your present conscious awareness. The content of the **unconscious level** *is absent from conscious awareness, but still could influence a person's thoughts and actions.* Sigmund Freud, as discussed in Chapter 10, believed the unconscious to be comprised of wishes, inner conflicts, and memories that we are unaware of but that still affect our behavior. He believed that even though people are unaware of the unconscious, it can enter conscious and preconscious awareness through symbolic points.

EXPLORING THE LEVELS OF CONSCIOUSNESS

Philosophers were the first to be interested in the role of consciousness. This arose through their mind-body debate, which questioned the relationship between the conscious mind and the physical brain. **Dualism** is *the belief that the mind and the body are separate.* This approach at one time was popular, but is rarely accepted by modern psychologists. In contrast, **materialism** suggests that *the mind and the body are one and the same.* Support for this approach has been validated when damage to the brain causes a disruption in consciousness.

Sigmund Freud drew attention to the effects of consciousness through his interest in the role of the unconscious. Freud believed that some mental processes occur without conscious awareness. Even though many of Freud's viewpoints have been refuted, his work helped pave the way for the later study of consciousness.

STATE OF CONSCIOUSNESS

One's state of consciousness is the mental awareness of a particular stimulus at any given moment.

Nuts and Bolts

 If you are sitting in class and your teacher asks you to solve the next problem, then for the next few moments your state of consciousness is going to involve solving the problem.

Attention and levels of arousal affect the state of consciousness. William James believed consciousness is like a stream that always changes but keeps on flowing. In other words, many things can flow down the stream, but they are all flowing at the same time. A person who is typing on a computer may be unaware of music being played in the next room. Even though he or she is unaware of the music, its sound still enters his or her conscious awareness. The individual is unaware of the music being played because he or she is not focusing on the music but rather on the material being typed.

AP Tip

A possible multiple-choice question could ask who suggested that consciousness could be compared to a stream.

CIRCADIAN RHYTHMS

Throughout each day, human beings experience fluctuations in our physiological and psychological processes. For example, you might feel alert at certain times of the day but groggy at others. **Circadian rhythms** are *repeating fluctuations, such as sleeping and waking, that occur over a period of twenty-four hours.* An "internal clock" located in the hypothalamus, the suprachiasmatic nucleus, monitors circadian rhythms. The suprachiasmatic nucleus receives information from ganglion cells located in the retina that send information based on whether it is light or dark out. In response, neurons in the suprachiasmatic nucleus trigger the release of a hormone called melatonin, which is produced in the pineal gland. When the ganglion cells detect darkness and melatonin is released, the individual experiences tiredness. When it starts to become light outside, melatonin decreases, helping the individual wake up. This "internal clock" makes it possible to maintain circadian rhythms regardless of external cues.

Nuts and Bolts

 A good way to remember the role of the suprachiasmatic nucleus and the release of the hormone melatonin is to think of the nucleus as the eye in the hypothalamus because it monitors light and darkness. Also think of melatonin as "mellowing" you out. When melatonin is released you "mellow" and get tired

Environmental factors can disrupt circadian rhythms. For example, if a person were to travel across different time zones from California to New York, he or she would experience what is known as "jet lag." That is because initially the time in New York does not mesh with that person's internal clock (circadian rhythm). Taking melatonin supplements can lessen the symptoms of jet lag; such supplements are also a common treatment for insomnia.

AP Tip

Be ready to identify which hormone causes a person to become drowsy when released. Also be able to identify which gland releases this hormone.

STAGES OF SLEEP

Researchers follow the different stages of sleep with a device called an electroencephalograph (EEG), which monitors changes in brain waves. A person who is awake and attentive shows brain activity through beta waves. A person who is awake but inattentive would show alpha waves. Theta waves follow alpha waves and indicate even slower brain waves. Finally, delta waves show low brain activity and are associated with deep sleep. As a person sleeps, he or she experiences four NREM (non-rapid eye movement) stages of sleep as well as periods of REM (rapid eye movement) sleep. Different levels of brain activity characterize each stage of sleep.

Nuts and Bolts

 A good way to remember that beta waves signal that a person is awake and attentive is to think of this: You "BETAer" be wide awake when taking the AP psychology exam! Also, remember that the first two letters of **de**lta waves match the first two letters of **de**ep sleep.

Sleep Stage	Brain Waves	Characteristics
NREM Stage 1	Alpha and theta waves	Lasts only a few minutes Person can quickly gain consciousness Experiences hypnagogic hallucinations—vivid sensory experiences. The most common hypnagogic hallucination is the sensation of falling, which is accompanied by a myoclonic jerk—an involuntary muscle spasm throughout the body that often awakes the person.
NREM Stage 2	Theta and start of delta waves	Start of true sleep Sleep spindles in EEG patterns—sudden bursts of brain activity
NREM Stage 3	Delta brain waves	Considered NREM Stage 3 when 20 percent of brain activity shows delta waves Referred to as slow-wave sleep (or S-sleep)
NREM Stage 4	Delta brain waves	Considered NREM Stage 4 when delta waves exceed 50 percent of brain activity Person does not experience sensory stimulation—hard to wake up Referred to as slow-wave sleep (or S-sleep)
REM sleep	Beta brain waves	Brain activity becomes more active, resembling that of an awakened state; approximately 85 percent of dreams occur during this stage Muscle activity is suppressed (referred to as "muscle atonia") Physiological arousal is high—heart rate, blood pressure Eyes move rapidly back and forth beneath eyelids—Rapid Eye Movement (also called paradoxical sleep)

SEQUENCE OF SLEEP STAGES

Most people experience four to six cycles of NREM and REM sleep every night:

- Begins with NREM Stage 1; lasts a few minutes
- Followed by about 20 minutes in NREM Stage 2
- Roughly the next 40 minutes are spent in NREM Stages 3 and 4
- Once a person is relaxed and deeply asleep in NREM Stage 4, the sequence reverses
- The person then goes back through NREM Stage 3 and into NREM Stage 2
- After NREM Stage 2, the person enters REM sleep, which usually lasts for about 5 to 15 minutes

As sleep continues, the periods of REM sleep get longer and slow-wave NREM Stages 3 and 4 become shorter. The last few sleep cycles are primarily NREM Stage 2 and REM sleep lasting up to 40 minutes. Over the course of a person's lifetime, NREM Stages 3 and 4 gradually decrease. In fact, by late adulthood, most individuals average only about 20 minutes in these stages as compared to the young child, who spends two or more hours in NREM Stages 3 and 4.

AP Tip

Be prepared to explain which stages of sleep become longer and, in contrast, which become shorter throughout the night as a person sleeps.

FUNCTIONS OF SLEEP

Studies of sleep deprivation have provided evidence that sleep is necessary for adequate physiological and psychological functioning. A person who does not get enough sleep experiences fatigue and irritability and has problems focusing on tasks, especially when those tasks are considered boring or repetitive. For example, fatal car accidents are most common between midnight and the early morning hours. Also, when a person does not get enough REM sleep, REM rebound will occur. A person experiencing **REM rebound** *will go right into REM sleep instead of through the normal sequence of sleep.*

SLEEP THEORIES

The **restorative theory of sleep** *suggests that sleep is necessary for the body to repair itself.* REM sleep allows the brain to improve the functioning of neurons, which are essential to understanding newly learned material and forming congruent memories. This is because the amygdala (emotion) and hippocampus (forming new, explicit memories) are active during REM sleep. REM sleep also allows time for nerve cells to create and make connections to other cells. This may also explain why infants, whose brains are still developing, spend so much time in REM sleep. For example, REM sleep helps in the restoration of norepinephrine, a neurotransmitter necessary for alertness. Because norepinephrine is continuously released throughout the day, the brain's neurons lose sensitivity to it. During

REM sleep, however, norepinephrine is not active, allowing it to return to adequate functioning. NREM sleep is necessary for the body to physiologically recover, which may explain why human beings spend the first part of sleep in NREM stages and why NREM sleep represents a larger portion of the sleep cycle earlier in the night.

Nuts and Bolts

 A good way to remember the restorative theory of sleep is to think about why people tell you to get a good night's sleep. A good night's sleep before the AP exam is a good idea, for example, because it will help your brain restore itself to optimal functioning. Coaches tell athletes to get a good night's sleep before a big game so their bodies will be fresh.

The **adaptive theory of sleep** *states that sleep is a behavior that promotes the survival of a species (i.e., it is adaptive).* This theory is based on evolutionary principles and suggests that humans and animals sleep when it is dangerous to be awake. For example, bears hibernate when conditions in their environment become too hostile. The **behavioral theory of sleep** *suggests that we sleep because there is no more stimulation.* Think how children resist going to bed when there are stimulating activities, such as watching television, to keep them awake.

AP Tip

A possible essay question might ask you to explain why sleep is necessary and how it affects the brain and body. Be prepared to give specific examples and cite theories.

SLEEP DISORDERS

Most people experience sleep problems at some point in their lives. The most common problem is insomnia, the inability to fall or stay asleep. Insomnia may occur because of a tough day, a fight with a friend, or the anticipation of a hectic day. When a person experiences the symptoms of insomnia for longer than a month, help may be needed. This could include a prescription for sleeping pills or techniques to show the insomniac how to relax and cope with stressful situations. Other common sleep disorders are listed in the chart below.

Sleep Disorder	Characterizations
Narcolepsy	Falling suddenly and without warning into REM sleep at any time of day or in inappropriate situations/locations
Sleep apnea	Temporary cessation of breathing during sleep
Somnambulism (sleep walking)	Occurs in NREM sleep Stage 4
Nocturnal enuresis (bedwetting)	Occurs in NREM sleep Stage 4
Night terrors	Occur in NREM sleep Stage 4—can be frightening; high physiological arousal; usually there is no recollection of events (primarily occurs in children)
Nightmares	Occur in REM sleep
REM sleep behavior disorder	Acting out dreams; connected with damage to lower brain centers (brain stem), common in older men
Sleep bruxism	Grinding teeth during sleep

DREAM THEORIES

Dreams are described as a story-like sequence of events, images, or sensations; they occur most vividly in REM sleep. People often wonder why they have certain dreams, and some have reported that they can directly affect their dreams. This is referred to as lucid dreaming, and during it, the individual has control over a dream's storyline. Other people who are awakened during REM sleep have difficulty recalling their dreams. Evidence has shown that during REM sleep, the frontal lobe areas are inactive, which makes it hard to form new memories. In addition, the neurotransmitters—dopamine, norepinephrine, and serotonin—are reduced during sleep. These neurotransmitters are needed for forming new memories. Researchers have also noted that any mental or physical activity during sleep is hard to remember. For example, people have reported that they do not remember getting up or going to get a drink of water.

Sigmund Freud was interested in the content of people's dreams. He believed that some thoughts, feelings, and wishes are repressed into the unconscious. He thought that, through dream analysis, he could tap into a person's subconscious and reveal meaning. In his book *Interpretation of Dreams*, he said that dreams were the "royal road to the knowledge of the unconscious mind." Freud also said that each dream was comprised of two parts: manifest content and latent content. The **manifest content** consisted of *the remembered meaning of the dream*; the **latent content** was *the symbolized part of the dream*. It was the symbols of the latent content that Freud thought represented the deep-seated wishes of the unconscious. Unfortunately, there is no way to prove Freud's dream theory.

Nuts and Bolts

 A good way to remember that the manifest content is the remembered meaning of the dream is to think of the statement, "**Man (ifest)**, I had a crazy dream last night."

AP Tip

Be prepared to distinguish between manifest and latent content in Freud's dream theory.

The **activation-synthesis theory of dreaming** *supports the idea that signals within the brain activate other areas of the brain, including the amygdala and hippocampus.* As the brain synthesizes these signals, it attempts to provide meaning. This could include synthesizing fragments of memories to provide meaning, which might explain why many dreams do not make sense.

HYPNOSIS

Hypnosis is *an altered state of consciousness that could produce increased responsiveness to suggestion that could in turn lead to changes in behavior and thinking.* People may seek the help of a hypnotist when they want to stop smoking or lose weight, for example. Hypnosis gets mixed reviews, however. Children tend to have a greater likelihood of being able to be hypnotized than adults. In many cases it boils down to the subject's willingness and positive belief about being hypnotized.

EXPLAINING HYPNOSIS

Hypnosis is based on the social interaction between a hypnotized person and the suggestions of a hypnotist. Hypnosis can affect the subject's perception, memory, and behavior. The statements made by a hypnotist are referred to as the **posthypnotic suggestions**, *suggestions that may be carried out after the person has been hypnotized.* Often people who are hypnotized have **posthypnotic amnesia**, meaning they *cannot recall what took place during the hypnotic session.*

Through his research, psychologist Ernest Hilgard determined that during hypnosis people experience a splitting of consciousness called "dissociation." **Hilgard's neodissociation theory of hypnosis** suggested that *a person experiences distinct multiple streams of consciousness.* The first stream of consciousness is tuned to the hypnotist's suggestions, while the second is so distinct from consciousness that it is unattainable to the subject. He accidentally stumbled upon this second stream, which he referred to as the **hidden observer**. While Hilgard was conducting experiments on hypnosis he hypnotized a student not to hear any sounds. Another student, viewing the experiment, asked if the subject would respond to a voice command. Hilgard instructed the hypnotized subject to raise his right index finger, and to Hilgard's surprise he did. When the subject awoke from hypnosis he had no recall of what he had done. Hilgard concluded that one stream of consciousness was tuned to hypnotic suggestions, not hearing loud noises, while a dissociated stream of consciousness continued to process information—the request that he raise his index finger—that was unattainable to the person being hypnotized, which he referred to as the hidden observer.

Role and belief expectancy theory suggest that hypnosis is not an altered state of consciousness, but an expected role one should play under hypnosis. Psychologist Nicholas Spanos believed hypnosis could be explained through terms covered in social psychology. He said that if hypnosis is based on the social interaction between a person being hypnotized and the hypnotist, the person being hypnotized is only responding to the social demands of hypnosis and the hypnotist. A hypnotized person is motivated to act a certain way that is associated with the demands and roles of what is expected of him during hypnosis. In other words, the person being hypnotized is conforming to the demands of the hypnotist and his own expectations of what should occur during hypnosis. Spanos supported his claim by showing that highly motivated people not under hypnosis respond the same way as someone who has been hypnotized.

AP Tip

Be prepared to identify contrasting views of hypnosis.

PSYCHOACTIVE DRUGS

Psychopharmacology is *an area of psychology that studies the effects of psychoactive drugs on the brain and nervous systems.* In order for a drug to have an effect on the brain, it must pass the **blood-brain barrier**, which *helps prevent certain substances from entering brain tissue.* However, if a drug is able to pass through this barrier, then it will affect the thinking and behavior of the person taking it. Once past the blood-brain barrier a drug can either *mimic/excite* (**agonist**) or *block/inhibit* (**antagonist**) the role of a neurotransmitter. Some drugs are also capable of slowing the reuptake of excess neurotransmitters in the synapse. (There is more information about this in the chapter on biological psychology.)

EFFECTS OF DRUGS

People take drugs for known reasons, often without anticipating their unwanted side effects. **Substance abuse** occurs *when a pattern of drug use interferes with personal and social meaning and functioning.* What used to be important to a person does not seem as significant compared to the option of taking the drug. People often realize they have a problem when they continually choose to consume the drug. **Psychological dependency** is *when a person chooses to take a drug despite knowing the ramifications it could cause in other areas of his or her life.* For example, a person may choose to get high rather than take an important midterm exam. **Physical dependency**, also referred to as addiction, *results in the body's dependence on the drug to function.* If the body does not get the amount it desires, the person experiences **withdrawal symptoms,** which *include unpleasant headaches, shaking, and intense cravings for the drug.* To prevent withdrawal symptoms, a certain amount of that drug must be taken. The amount needed will be affected by the person's **tolerance level**. That is, when someone routinely takes a drug, his or her body builds up a greater need for the drug, causing his or her tolerance level to increase—which could result in withdrawal symptoms if that tolerance level is not met or exceeded regularly.

AP Tip

Be prepared to explain how withdrawal symptoms and tolerance contribute to drug abuse.

TYPES OF DRUGS

Drugs are designed to have different effects on the brain and body. In turn, people have different reasons and expectations for taking certain drugs. These reasons and expectations are based on what they may know about a drug or what they have observed in other people who have taken the drug. Drugs are classified as depressants, stimulants, opiates, and hallucinogens.

Drug Classification	Physical Effects on the Brain and Body	Examples	Psychological Effects
Depressants	Slow down activity in central nervous system Increase number of GABA neurotransmitters, which inhibit brain activity	Alcohol Barbiturates Sleeping pills Tranquilizers GHB: "club drug" produces loss of inhibition, increased sex drive, relaxation	Mild euphoria Talkativeness Friendliness Reduces inhibitions and self-control Causes aggressiveness and violence Impairs judgment

Drug Classification	Physical Effects on the Brain and Body	Examples	Psychological Effects
Stimulants	Speed up the activity of the nervous system Increase the release of neurotransmitters norepinephrine (arousal) and dopamine (pleasure)	Amphetamines Cocaine Caffeine Nicotine Ecstasy	Increase mental alertness Reduce fatigue Produce stimulant-induced psychosis-schizophrenia-like symptoms, hallucinations
Opiates	Cause sleepiness and relieve pain Agonist for endorphins	Opium Morphine Heroin	Intense rush or euphoria Feelings of contentment Severe withdrawal symptoms
Hallucinogens	Also called psychedelics Similar to the neurotransmitter serotonin, which regulates moods and perceptions	LSD Ketamine Mescaline Marijuana	Create loss of contact from reality Alter emotion, perception, thought; Produce hallucinations: hearing, seeing things that are not real

AP Tip

Past multiple-choice questions have asked test takers to identify the effects of depressants, stimulants, opiates, and hallucinogens on the brain and body.

Multiple-Choice Questions

1. Susanne is paying close attention to her teacher as he lectures about the history of psychology. Which level of awareness describes Susanne's attentiveness?
   (A) Conscious awareness
   (B) Preconscious awareness
   (C) Nonconscious awareness
   (D) Subliminal awareness
   (E) Nocturnal awareness

2. Carlos's friend asks Carlos what he ate for dinner last night. Carlos hesitates a few moments and then is able to remember. Which level of awareness describes his ability to remember last night's dinner?
   (A) Conscious awareness
   (B) Preconscious awareness
   (C) Nonconscious awareness
   (D) Subliminal awareness
   (E) Nocturnal awareness

3. Jen is excited to be taking the AP psychology exam. She is fully alert and ready to handle the task at hand. Which waves of brain activity is Jen displaying?
   (A) Delta
   (B) Theta
   (C) Beta
   (D) Alpha
   (E) Circadian

4. As Tracy sits in class she grows tired. She is having a hard time paying attention to the teacher and often loses her place in her book. Tracy is experiencing which type of brain waves?
   (A) Delta
   (B) Theta
   (C) Beta
   (D) Alpha
   (E) Circadian

5. REM sleep is characterized by
   (A) delta brain activity and muscle atonia
   (B) cessation of breathing and heavy snoring
   (C) muscle atonia and high levels of beta activity in the brain
   (D) vivid sensory imagery
   (E) myoclonic jerks displayed by the body

6. As an individual sleeps throughout the night, which two stages of sleep become longer?
   (A) NREM 1 and NREM 2
   (B) NREM 1 and NREM 3
   (C) REM and NREM 2
   (D) REM and NREM 3
   (E) NREM 3 and NREM 4

7. Jon traveled from Nashville to Los Angeles yesterday. He has had a hard time adapting to the time change. Last night he found it hard to fall asleep and during the day he has had a hard time staying awake. The time change has affected Jon's
   (A) circadian rhythms
   (B) memory consolidation
   (C) adrenal cortex
   (D) biopsychological timing
   (E) ultradian rhythms

8. What hormone, released by the pineal gland, causes a person to become drowsy and tired?
   (A) Adrenaline
   (B) Corticosteroid
   (C) Catecholamines
   (D) Melatonin
   (E) Testosterone

9. The restorative theory of sleep suggests that _____ sleep helps the brain to restore and _____ helps the body to recover.
   (A) NREM; REM sleep
   (B) REM; NREM sleep
   (C) REM; REM sleep
   (D) NREM; NREM sleep
   (E) NREM Stage 3; NREM Stage 4

10. Jim has reported that he can control his dreams and affect the content of his dreams. This is referred to as
    (A) wishful thinking
    (B) NREM sleep
    (C) lucid dreaming
    (D) hallucinogenic dreaming
    (E) the Muller-Lyer illusion

11. Nate has had problems quitting smoking in the past. A friend suggested he see a hypnotist. Nate was a bit reluctant but agreed. After the hypnotic session, the hypnotist told Nate that he would no longer have the urge to smoke. This is referred to as
    (A) posthypnotic suggestion
    (B) posthypnotic amnesia
    (C) suggestion of the mind
    (D) posthypnotic fugue
    (E) social conformity

12. The role theory of hypnosis states that
    (A) a hypnotist produces a "hidden observer" unresponsive to commands
    (B) people fall into a deep sleep
    (C) altered states of consciousness are produced
    (D) a dissociation is produced and causes multiple streams of consciousness
    (E) hypnotized people are acting in accordance with the socially accepted behavior of what is supposed to be shown during hypnosis

13. Which of the following is characterized by an altered state of consciousness in which the power of suggestion is able to affect behavior?
    (A) Shock therapy
    (B) Operant conditioning
    (C) Token economy
    (D) Systematic desensitization
    (E) Hypnosis

14. Ever since Deb quit smoking, she has experienced terrible headaches, nausea, and a tremendous craving for nicotine. Deb is experiencing what kind of symptoms?
    (A) Toxic
    (B) Withdrawal
    (C) Hormonal
    (D) Synaptic
    (E) Distortion

15. Depressants depress activity in the central nervous system by causing neural communication to slow down. Which of the following is an example of a depressant?
    (A) Heroin
    (B) Cocaine
    (C) LSD
    (D) Alcohol
    (E) Caffeine

Free-Response Questions

1. Nan has been asked to return to her elementary school to help make a presentation on the dangers of drugs. She will describe how drug abuse can occur, citing physical and psychological dependency. She also has been asked to explain how tolerance is established and how the body responds when the drug stops being taken.

   What would you expect Nan to share with the elementary students? Be sure to provide examples—simply citing definitions means no score.

2. Explain how the following psychoactive drugs affect the body's physiological systems. Provide at least two examples for each of the psychoactive drugs listed.
   (a) stimulants
   (b)depressants
   (c) opiates
   (d) hallucinogens

Answers

Multiple-Choice Questions

1. Answer: A. Conscious awareness describes mental activities a person is aware of at a given moment (*Psychology,* 8th ed. p. 328/9th ed. pp. 333–334).

2. Answer: B. Preconscious awareness resides just below conscious awareness, which makes it easy to retrieve the content into conscious awareness (*Psychology*, 8th ed. p. 329/9th ed. p. 334).

3. Answer: C. Beta waves show brain activity, indicating that a person is awake and attentive (*Psychology*, 8th ed. p. 337/9th ed. p. 341).

4. Answer: D. Alpha brain waves indicates that the person is awake but drowsy and inattentive (*Psychology*, 8th ed. p. 336/9th ed. p. 340).

5. Answer: C. REM sleep is characterized by beta brain activity and full relaxation in the body and muscles (*Psychology*, 8th ed. p. 337/9th ed. p. 340).

6. Answer: C. A person progresses through NREM Stages 1–4 and then reverses from NREM 4 to 3 and then 2. After NREM Stage 2, REM sleep takes over. As the night goes on, more time is spent in REM sleep and in NREM Stage 2 (*Psychology*, 8th ed. pp. 337–338/9th ed. pp. 341–342).

7. Answer: A. Jon is experiencing jet lag, and it has affected his circadian rhythms, which cycle periods of wakefulness and tiredness (*Psychology*, 8th ed. pp. 341–342/9th ed. pp. 343–344).

8. Answer: D. Melatonin is released by the pineal gland in response to darkness monitored by the suprachiasmatic nucleus (*Psychology*, 8th ed. p. 342/9th ed. p. 344).

9. Answer: B. REM sleep is necessary for the brain to revitalize neural communication, and NREM sleep is necessary for the body to rebuild muscle (*Psychology*, 8th ed. p. 344/9th ed. pp. 344–346).

10. Answer: C. Lucid dreaming occurs when a person feels that he or she can control the content of his or her dreams (*Psychology*, 8th ed. p. 345/9th ed. p. 349).

11. Answer: A. The posthypnotic suggestion refers to the hypnotist's instruction that is to be carried out by the subject after the hypnotic session (*Psychology*, 8th ed. p. 347/9th ed. p. 351).

12. Answer: E. The role theory of hypnosis suggests that people who undergo hypnosis are conforming to the demands of the expected roles associated with the process of hypnosis (*Psychology*, 8th ed. p. 348/9th ed. p. 352).

13. Answer: E. Hypnosis uses techniques to help subjects relax, enabling suggestion to cause changes in behavior (*Psychology*, 8th ed. p. 346/9th ed. p. 351).

14. Answer: B. Withdrawal symptoms are physiological changes that result from the body's not being able to get a drug on which it has depended (*Psychology*, 8th ed. p. 352/9th ed. p. 356).

15. Answer: D. Alcohol is an example of a depressant. It depresses, or slows down, the central nervous system (*Psychology*, 8th ed. p. 353/9th ed. pp. 358–359).

FREE-RESPONSE QUESTIONS

1. Answer: Drug abuse occurs when consumption of a drug disrupts thought processes, behavior, and social responsibilities. Psychological dependency occurs when the consumption of a drug takes precedent over meaningful activities. Tolerance occurs as a person uses a drug and then, over time, discovers that more of the drug is needed to deliver the same effect. This results in physical dependency, or addiction, as the person's body builds up a need for that drug. If he or she stops using the drug, the result will initially be withdrawal symptoms. This could include headaches, body aches, and a preoccupation with taking the drug.

2. (a) Stimulants overactivate the central nervous system, resulting in increased brain activity and mental alertness, as well as aroused behavior. Nicotine, caffeine, cocaine, and amphetamines are examples of stimulants.

   (b) Depressants slow down the central nervous system, resulting in a slower response time, which can impair mental and motor functions. Alcohol, barbiturates, and tranquilizers are examples of depressants.

   (c) Opiates affect the body by relieving pain. Opiates mimic endorphins, a neurotransmitter responsible for pain and pleasure sensations. Morphine and heroin are examples of opiates.

   (d) Hallucinogens distort sensation and perception. Examples include LSD and marijuana.

LEARNING

The study of **learning**, *a relatively permanent change in behavior based on prior experiences*, and of how human beings learn has been the subject of numerous psychological theories and experiments. Behaviorists believe that learning is measured by observable behavior, whereas cognitivists view it as a mental process. Despite the subtle differences between the two, the foundation that learning is based on prior experience remains constant. In earlier times, many thought psychology should focus only on observable behavior, leaving no room for the integration of the mind. For strict behaviorists such as B. F. Skinner and John B. Watson, the mind could not be seen and therefore should not be studied. However, other psychologists, such as Edward Tolman and Robert Rescorla, believed that it is the mental representations in our mind that influence learning.

CLASSICAL CONDITIONING

While researching the digestive systems of dogs in the late 1800s, Ivan Pavlov discovered that the dogs in his study began to salivate when his assistant made a clanging noise on the dogs' food trays while replenishing their food. Puzzled by this phenomenon, Pavlov began to speculate why this unlearned response, salivation, was occurring without the actual presence of the food or meat powder. He conducted a series of experiments and discovered that his dogs were associating the clanging of the food bowls with the delivery of food. According to Pavlov, this learning demonstrated by the dogs was the result of **classical conditioning**, *the repeated pairing of an unconditioned stimulus with a neutral stimulus to produce the same behavior*. In order to best explain the concepts of classical conditioning, we must first discuss some commonly used terminology:

- **Unconditioned stimulus (UCS/US)** – An event that produces, or elicits, an automatic or unlearned response

- **Unconditioned response (UCR/UR)** – An automatic or unlearned response/reaction that is preceded, or elicited, by an unconditioned stimulus
- **Neutral stimulus (NS)** – A stimulus that does not elicit a response prior to learning
- **Conditioned stimulus (CS)** – An original neutral stimulus that has been paired repeatedly with the unconditioned stimulus to produce, or elicit, a conditioned response
- **Conditioned response (CR)** – A response/reaction elicited by the conditioned stimulus

PAVLOV'S EXPERIMENT

During the initial phase of the experiment, Pavlov and his associates placed food or meat powder (unconditioned stimulus or UCS / unconditioned stimulus or US) on the tongue of one of the dogs. The food or meat powder (USC/US) automatically produced saliva (unconditioned response or UCR /unconditioned response or UR) in the dog's mouth; the production of saliva is a **reflex**, *an involuntary response elicited from a stimulus*. The unconditioned stimulus (UCS) always produces an unconditioned response (UCR) prior to learning. During the second phase of the experiment Pavlov introduced a musical tone, which served as the neutral stimulus (NS). A tone (NS) was then presented with the food or meat powder (UCS/US). After repeated pairings, the tone no longer served as the neutral stimulus (NS), but changed to the conditioned stimulus (CS). When the conditioned stimulus (the tone) was presented to the dog, he responded by salivating (CR). Keeping the conditioned stimulus (CS)-conditioned response (CR) connection does require that the unconditioned stimulus (UCS) be presented periodically. To ensure that the bell/tone/object was associated with the salivation (CR), Pavlov would present the meat powder (UCS) with the bell/tone/object (CS) periodically.

Diagram of Pavlov's Experiment

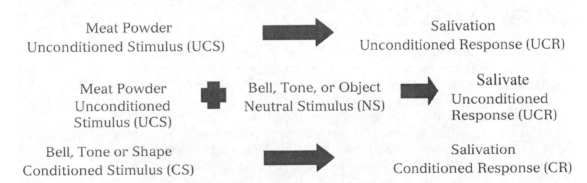

© 2012 Cengage Learning. All Rights Reserved. May not be copied, scanned, or duplicated, in whole or in part, except for use as permitted in a license distributed with a certain product or service or otherwise on a password-protected website for classroom use.

Nuts and Bolts

Remember that the unconditioned response (UCR) and the conditioned response (CR) are similar, if not the same. The goal of classical conditioning is to pair the neutral stimulus (NS) with the unconditioned stimulus (UCS/US) to allow the formation of the conditioned stimulus (CS). Another way to correctly identify the unconditioned stimulus and the unconditioned response is to remember that unconditioned means <u>unlearned</u>.

AP Tip

Past multiple-choice questions have asked students to identify the NS, UCS, UCR, CS, and CR. Prior free-response questions have asked students to identify how a behavior is formed using the classical conditioning model.

FACTORS IN CLASSICAL CONDITIONING

Within classical conditioning are numerous other factors that may influence the conditioning process. Concepts such as generalization, discrimination, second- or higher-order conditioning, extinction, reconditioning and spontaneous recovery all have their origins in Pavlov's research.

GENERALIZATION

In Pavlov's experiment, the dogs were conditioned to salivate to a tone or object. After the association was established, Pavlov noticed that the dogs were also salivating to similar tones or objects. The dogs displayed a common behavior known as **generalization**, *the tendency for a conditioned response (behavior) to be elicited by similar stimuli.* For example, a dog has been conditioned to salivate at the sight of a circle. When the dog also salivates at the sight of an ellipse, a somewhat similar shape, behaviorists refer to this process as generalization.

DISCRIMINATION

Differentiating between two stimuli is advantageous to an organism: the ability to recognize friend or foe could mean the difference between life and death. Pavlov understood the profound effects of this and began conditioning his dogs to salivate only to a particular tone. After successful conditioning trials, Pavlov was able to train his dogs to salivate only when that original tone was presented. Behaviorists refer to this as **discrimination**, *the ability to distinguish between the conditioned stimulus (CS) and similar stimuli that are not associated with the unconditioned stimulus.*

SECOND-ORDER (HIGHER-ORDER) CONDITIONING

Once the CR has been associated with the CS, it is possible to condition other neutral stimuli. With **second- or higher-order conditioning**, *a new neutral stimulus (NS) is repeatedly paired with the conditioned stimulus in order to elicit the same conditioned response.* Pavlov demonstrated this by pairing a tone (CS) that elicited salivation (CR) with a light (NS). After repeated trials the light became a conditioned stimulus that elicited the salivation (CR). This showed that a conditioned stimulus (CS) could also be used as an unconditioned stimulus (UCS) to form a new conditioned stimulus (CS) that elicited the conditioned response (CR).

Nuts and Bolts

 A real-life example of second-order (higher-order) conditioning would be if you changed the ring tone on your cell phone. You would know that you were getting a call when you heard the new ring because you knew that hearing the old ring tone meant that you were getting a phone call. The earlier ring tone signaled a behavior (answering the phone); your new ring tone signals the same behavior (answering the phone).

EXTINCTION

When a conditioned stimulus (CS) no longer elicits the conditioned response (CR), it is said to experience extinction. Therefore, **extinction** is *when the conditioned stimuli no longer elicits the conditioned response after repeated presentation of the CS without the UCS.* In extinction experiments, Pavlov stopped presenting the meat powder (UCS) with the tone (CS). After a series of trials, the dogs no longer salivated (CR) when presented with the conditioned stimulus (CS). Pavlov had successfully broken the conditioned stimulus (CS)-conditioned response (CR) connection.

RECONDITIONING AND SPONTANEOUS RECOVERY

Extinction successfully disrupts the (CS)-(CR) association. However, this connection is simply inhibited rather than lost forever. If the (UCS) is once again presented with the (CS), the previously acquired (CS)–(CR) association will return. This is known as **reconditioning**, *a quick relearning of a previously extinct (CS)–(CR) association.* Even if the (UCS) is not paired with the (CS), the association is not entirely extinct. If the (UCS) is once again paired with the (CS), the association between the (CS)–(CR) will return. This abrupt return of the (CS)–(CR) is known as **spontaneous recovery**, *the recovery of a previously extinguished response after a passage of time.*

Nuts and Bolts

 Think of spontaneous recovery as a behavior that suddenly returns after it has disappeared for a while. For example, if you are listening to the radio and hear a song that reminds you of a dance you attended during middle school, the feelings and memories that you have about that dance and your life at that time may return.

A PRACTICAL EXAMPLE OF CLASSICAL CONDITIONING

No two things are alike. A cell-phone ring is different from a landline ring. Knowing the difference between the two is important, especially when you are waiting for a phone call. The ability to distinguish between the two is a form of learning—being able to correctly identify which phone is ringing means you have been able to separate (discriminate) between the two. However, if you are at a gathering and a cell phone rings, many people respond in a similar way (generalization), checking to see if it was their phone that was ringing. Knowing whether it was your own or another person's cell phone is the result of conditioning. If you no longer own a cell phone, then you will not check to see if it is your phone that is ringing (extinction). However, if you purchase a new cell phone, you will once again check to see if it is your phone that is ringing when you hear a phone ring (spontaneous recovery).

LITTLE ALBERT

In 1920 an experiment took place that launched American behaviorism. John B. Watson wanted to apply Ivan Pavlov's principles of conditioned reflexes to humans. Watson believed that if psychology was to be accepted as a true science, psychologists should only study observable (overt) behavior. He also believed that nurture (environment) alone dictated human development. To prove his belief, John B. Watson and his assistant Rosalie Rayner set out to condition the emotion of fear in a human infant. This highly questionable study (questionable because Watson conditioned fear in an infant without prior consent) could not be replicated in the modern era because of laws and ethics. However, the lessons learned from this experiment proved that Pavlov's principles could be applied to humans.

Nuts and Bolts

 Remember that UCS stands for unconditioned stimulus, UCR stands for unconditioned response, NS stands for neutral stimulus, CS stands for conditioned stimulus, and CR stands for conditioned response.

In the initial trials of his experiment, Watson exposed the nine-month-old infant (Albert) to numerous stimuli (a white rat, a rabbit, a dog, cotton balls, burning paper) designed to test Albert's emotional responses. When initially exposed to the white rat (neutral stimulus), little Albert displayed no signs of fear. In subsequent trials, when Albert was exposed to the white rat (NS) along with a loud noise (UCS), the loud noise startled him and caused him to display a typical infant response to fear: crying (UCR). After repeated pairing of the loud noise (UCS) with the white rat (NS), the white rat eventually became Albert's conditioned stimulus (CS), which now produced the conditioned response (CR), crying. Watson had successfully shown that he could condition an infant to cry at the sight of a white rat.

Diagram of Watson's Experiment

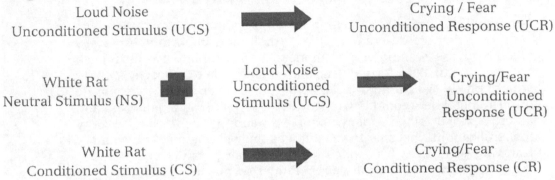

After establishing that the white rat (CS) elicited the crying behavior (CR), Watson further applied Pavlov's principles of classical conditioning. Watson began trials of second-order (higher-order) conditioning by pairing the white rat (CR) with other neutral stimuli (NS), such as a white rabbit and a white mask. After successful trials, Albert began to generalize his fear to similar stimuli that shared the common characteristic of being white and fluffy. Despite the controversy surrounding the study, Watson's experiment effectively showed that Pavlov's classical conditioning principles could be applied to humans as well. It should be noted that modern researchers are expected to remove any undesirable consequences of an experiment. Watson and Rayner clearly violated this ethical guideline by not extinguishing any of Little Albert's conditioned fears.

AP Tip

Be sure you can identify the NS, UCS, UCR, CS, and CR in Watson's Little Albert study.

APPLICATIONS OF CLASSICAL CONDITIONING

Classical conditioning is an important part of learning. It is how we learn that a particular stimulus comes to serve as a signal for behavior. For example, you know that when your cell phone rings, someone is calling to speak to you, and you answer the phone. It is classical conditioning that has allowed you to make this connection. Classical conditioning has numerous practical applications, from treating phobias to controlling predatory animals through conditioned taste aversion.

TREATING PHOBIAS

One way to reduce a phobia is to apply a technique known as **flooding**, *continuously exposing an individual to the fear-evoking conditioned stimulus to eliminate the conditioned response (fear).* For example, if a person is afraid of balloons, the psychologist would surround him or her with balloons. Constant exposure to the fear-evoking stimulus in a manner that would not harm that person causes the conditioned stimulus (CS)–conditioned response (CR) association to become extinct. This technique, although at first unpleasant for the individual, is effective in extinguishing phobias. A less aversive treatment option for phobias is the **systematic desensitization** method. The basic technique consists of *exposing the patient to a series of approximations to the anxiety-producing stimulus under relaxed conditions until finally the anxiety reaction is extinguished.* For example, for the person afraid of balloons, a psychologist would establish a hierarchy of the fear-evoking stimuli. The person would be gradually exposed to the fear, while learning to relax during each exposure. Upon successful completion of systematic desensitization, the previous phobia would become extinct. Yet another use of classical conditioning when treating phobias is **counterconditioning**, *pairing the fear-evoking stimulus with a pleasant stimulus to reverse the effects of the phobia.* For example, for the person with a balloon phobia, a psychologist would pair a pleasant stimulus, such as that person's favorite food, with the fear-evoking stimulus in hopes of countering the negative effects of the balloon. This approach is useful, but may result in higher-order conditioning, thus making the person afraid of the previously enjoyed stimulus (in this example, the favorite food).

Each of these three techniques has been proven effective in reducing phobias while using classical conditioning principles.

CONDITIONED TASTE AVERSION

A fascinating application of classical conditioning that many people can relate to is **conditioned taste aversion**, *when exposure to a noxious substance causes sickness and results in the individual associating the food with the sickness, making him or her avoid that food in future.* Think of a food that you have eaten that made you ill. Was the illness the result of the food, or was it caused by other factors? Despite what may have actually caused the illness, you are likely to attribute this feeling of illness to the particular food you ate. Unlike most forms of classical conditioning that require the unconditioned stimulus (UCS) and the conditioned stimulus (CS) to be paired closely together and repeated multiple times, taste aversion does not require the food and illness to be contiguous, nor does it require multiple trials.

Conditioned taste aversion has been used by livestock owners who were plagued by predatory animals destroying their cattle. By pairing a noxious stimulus (a stimulus that results in making an animal feel ill) with their cattle, ranchers were able to ward off further attacks by predatory animals on their livestock. In this case, the unconditioned stimulus (UCS) was the unpleasant/tainted food; the unconditioned response (UCR) was feeling ill. The neutral stimulus (NS) was the cattle/livestock. By pairing the noxious stimulus (UCS) with the neutral stimulus (NS), the predatory animals began to associate illness (CR) with the cattle (CS) and no longer preyed on the livestock.

Evolutionary psychologists would probably attribute conditioned taste aversion to the notion that, in order for a species to survive, the species must quickly learn what foods cause illness. This understanding will increase the chances that the species will stay away from further consumption of the illness-evoking stimulus, thus increasing its chances for survival. As noted, applications of classical conditioning are useful not only in treating phobias but also for the survival of a species.

INSTRUMENTAL AND OPERANT CONDITIONING

Not all learning theorists agree that classical conditioning can explain the complexity of human and animal learning. Edward Thorndike believed that the subject in his experiments was instrumental in manipulating the environment in order to receive a reward. Thorndike's experiments required a cat be placed in what he termed a "puzzle box," with several strings and levers. In order for the cat to escape from the box and obtain the reward, the cat needed to perform tasks that ranged from simple to complex. It was the cat who had to correctly figure out what behavior would allow it to escape from the box and acquire the food waiting on the other side. According to Thorndike, behaviors that resulted in escape and the acquisition of food would be forever "stamped in" and displayed in future similar situations. Behaviors that did not allow the cat to escape or receive food would be "stamped out" and would not be displayed in future trials. This theory is known as the **law of effect**: *behaviors that resulted in rewards are stamped in (strengthened), while behaviors that did not result in rewards are stamped out (weakened).* This theory would be further explained by behaviorist B. F. Skinner.

OPERANT CONDITIONING

B. F. Skinner believed that while classical conditioning explained behaviors that occur because of reflexes, operant conditioning required the subject to operate on, or manipulate, its environment. How a subject interacts with its environment is based primarily on the reinforcement or punishment the subject receives.

Skinner believed that a **punishment**—*a stimulus that, when made contingent on a behavior, decreases the strength of the exhibited behavior*—acts as a deterrent to behavior. Conversely, a **reinforcer**—*a stimulus that, when made contingent on a behavior, increases the strength of the exhibited behavior*—is necessary for the continuation of a behavior. According to Skinner, there are two reinforcers that allow learning to take place: **primary reinforcers**, *any reinforcing stimuli that satisfy a biological need (food, water, sex, warmth, and so forth),* and **secondary (conditioned) reinforcers**, *any previously neutral stimuli that have gained reinforcement value after being associated with another reinforcer (grades, money, praise).*

Nuts and Bolts

 Remember that a primary reinforcer satisfies biological necessities (food, water, sex, warmth, and so on) that are needed for survival. Secondary reinforcers (good grades, money, praise, and so forth) are not necessary for survival, but are nice to have because they have been associated with a biological need.

REINFORCEMENT TYPES ("SKINNER SQUARES")

How is it that one behavior continues to be exhibited while another behavior ceases to exist? Skinner believed that all behavior can be explained in one of four ways: positive reinforcement, negative reinforcement, positive punishment, and negative punishment (omission). In order to understand the "Skinner squares," it is important to understand the terminology:

- Positive = the addition of a stimulus
- Negative = the removal of a stimulus
- Appetitive = a desirable/liked stimulus
- Aversive = an undesirable/disliked stimulus
- Increase in behavior = the exhibited behavior continues
- Decrease in behavior = the exhibited behavior declines

APPETITIVE	AVERSIVE
Positive Reinforcement Presenting an appetitive stimulus Behavior increases ⬆ Example: Every time Jimmy gets an A on his report card, his parents give him $20.	Positive Punishment Presenting an aversive stimulus Behavior decreases ⬇ Example: Every time Jimmy talks in class, he gets detention.
Negative Punishment (Omission) Removing an appetitive stimulus Behavior decreases ⬇ Example: Every time Jimmy stays out past his curfew, his parents take away his car.	Negative Reinforcement Removing an aversive stimulus Behavior increases ⬆ Example: Every time Jimmy has a headache, he takes an aspirin.

Nuts and Bolts

When thinking about behavior and whether it increases or decreases, remember that increasing means that the behavior you are doing continues, whereas a decrease means it stops. Do not confuse an increase in behavior with behaving better or a decrease in behavior as behaving worse.

AP Tip

Past multiple-choice questions have centered on identifying what type of reinforcement is being provided. It is possible there will be a question asking you to identify which of the following displays negative reinforcement, for this is a concept that may confuse people. Remember that all reinforcers, whether negative or positive, will encourage the repetition of a behavior.

DISCRIMINATIVE STIMULUS AND STIMULUS GENERALIZATION

Being able to understand when reinforcement is available and when it is not is an important aspect of both classical and operant conditioning. **Discriminative stimulus (stimulus discrimination),** *is a stimulus that signals to the subject that reinforcement is available*, and the behavior needed to obtain this reinforcement can now be performed. Opposing discriminative stimulus is **stimulus generalization**, *a behavioral response performed to similar stimuli that signaled the availability of the reinforcement*. Responding to similar stimuli can be useful during the initial phase of training.

Nuts and Bolts

One way to remember discriminative stimulus is to think of it as a stop light at an intersection. When the light is red, you do not proceed through the intersection. However, once the light turns green, you are allowed to go. This is a form of discriminative stimulus: it discriminates by telling you when you are and are not allowed to proceed.

FORMING OPERANT BEHAVIORS

In operant conditioning the formation of a specific behavior may require multiple trials. During these trials, it is important to understand the principles of **shaping (via successive approximations),** *creating a new behavior based on a sequence of rewarding behaviors that come closer and closer to the ultimate behavioral goal*. For example, if you want to get your friend to jump on one foot and turn in circles, it would be necessary to reward her first for jumping, then for jumping on one foot, and finally for reaching the final goal (jumping on one foot and turning in circles).

Shaping the desired behavior depends on when the reinforcement is presented. The strength of the behavior is also dependent on the timing of the reinforcement. The more immediate the reinforcement, the stronger the effect it will have on initially learning the behavior. Delaying the reinforcement will weaken the stimulus-response association. For example, if you are teaching your dog to sit, the association with the command "sit" will be stronger if you present the reinforcement (a treat) immediately after the behavior is performed.

STRENGTHENING OPERANT BEHAVIOR

Two important reinforcement schedules are continuous reinforcement and partial reinforcement. **Continuous reinforcement** is *reinforcement that occurs after every desired behavior is exhibited.* An example of continuous reinforcement is rewarding a dog with a treat every time it follows your command to sit. While continuous reinforcement is necessary for the initial learning, a problem with this schedule of reinforcement is that the subject may expect the reinforcement each time and, if reinforcement is not provided, the stimulus-response connection may become quickly extinct. To properly ensure the stimulus-response connection is made, a schedule of partial reinforcement should be implemented. **Partial reinforcement (intermittent reinforcement schedule)** *is when reinforcement for the desired behavior is given occasionally.* The use of a partial reinforcement schedule elicits a greater number of the desired responses in the long term because it is unknown when the reinforcement will take place. There are four basic types of partial reinforcement (intermittent reinforcement) schedules. Note that *ratio* schedules of reinforcement are based on behaviors performed whereas *interval* schedules of reinforcement are based on time elapsed.

- **Fixed-Ratio (FR)**
  - *Reinforcement is provided after a set number of the correct responses are performed.*
    - A gumball machine provides a piece of gum each time a quarter is put in the machine.
- **Variable-Ratio (VR)**
  - *Reinforcement is provided after a varying number of correct behaviors.*
    - A slot machine at a casino rewards the player after a varying number of pulls.
- **Fixed-Interval (FI)**
  - *Reinforcement is provided for the first desired response after a set amount of time has elapsed.*
    - Your favorite television show comes on every Monday at 8:00 p.m.
- **Variable-Interval (VI)**
  - *Reinforcement is provided after the first desired response after a varying amount of time has elapsed.*
    - Your favorite television show will come on after the football game ends.

REMOVING OPERANT BEHAVIOR

Extinction may also occur in operant conditioning. For extinction to take place, the reinforcement must be absent from the desired behavior. Not reinforcing the desired behavior will eventually lead to that behavior's becoming extinct. However, if the reinforcement is presented again with the previously extinct behavior, spontaneous recovery of the behavior will return.

AP Tip

Past multiple-choice questions have centered on identifying which schedule of reinforcement is being illustrated. Free-response questions have also focused on reinforcement schedules in relation to time.

APPLICATIONS OF OPERANT CONDITIONING

The principles of operant conditioning are evident in our daily lives. Parents, teachers, coaches, bosses, doctors, and wardens all use the principles set forth by B. F. Skinner every day. In each of these environments, operant conditioning is displayed in the form of **behavior modification**, *a change in a previous behavior to a newly desired behavior,* and a token economy. Operant conditioning principles are used daily to modify a child's behavior in a classroom. To effectively modify a student's behavior in a classroom, the teacher may simply ignore the inappropriate behavior or reward the appropriate behavior. Ignoring the behavior and not providing the attention the student desires is a form of negative punishment (omission). Removing the appetitive stimulus, the attention the student receives from the teacher or classmates, will cause the inappropriate behavior to become extinct. In addition, rewarding appropriate behavior is a form of positive reinforcement, and will increase the desirable behavior.

Another practical application of operant conditioning is known as a **token economy**, *an environment that reinforces desirable behavior by rewarding the behavior with secondary reinforcers that can be exchanged for other reinforcers.* This form of behavioral modification is seen in elementary schools, psychiatric hospitals, and prisons. For example, many classrooms in elementary schools reward students for displaying desirable behaviors (e.g., raising their hands to answer a question) by giving them gold stars next to their names on a board in the front of the classroom. After a given number of stars has been obtained (a fixed-ratio schedule), students are rewarded with a new pencil. This form of behavior modification is useful in promoting desirable behavior.

COGNITIVE LEARNING

Cognitive psychologists believe that the mental interpretation or representation of an event is necessary for learning to take place. Research on the importance of cognition on learning has been demonstrated by research on learned helplessness, cognitive mapping, and observational learning.

LEARNED HELPLESSNESS

Martin Seligman proposed the idea of **learned helplessness**, *failure to continue exerting effort for an outcome because all previous attempts have failed.* This theory explains that if a person or animal perceives they have no control over the outcome of a situation, they will abandon all efforts in trying to change the situation. Learned helplessness explains why some students stop trying in school. They believe that no matter how much effort they exert it will have little to no effect on the outcome. For example, Linda has tried numerous studying techniques to help her pass the AP psychology test. Because Linda has not seen any favorable results from trying the different techniques, she feels that she will never pass an AP psychology test and stops studying for the class altogether. In this example, Linda's mental interpretation or thinking that she lacks control over the outcome of an event brings about a feeling of hopelessness, which in turn leads to her no longer trying.

LATENT LEARNING AND COGNITIVE MAPPING

Edward Tolman conducted research on the cognitive learning of mice when placed in a maze. He proposed that learning takes place cognitively, and thus is not necessarily immediately observable. **Cognitive maps**, *mental representations people rely on to understand complex patterns,* are used by all of us each day. Many people are amazed at the ability of taxi drivers to successfully navigate their way around a city without the use of a traditional map. Yet they do use a map—a mental map. An experienced taxi driver is able to drive to the desired location based on experience and a mental representation of the city he or she is navigating. When the taxi driver first learned the layout of the city, he or she most likely used a map or rode along with another experienced taxi driver. When the time came to demonstrate his or her knowledge of the city streets, the new taxi driver would most likely be able to do so with great accuracy. **Latent learning**, *learning that may not be displayed until a later time,* is not always immediately observable and may lie hidden until a circumstance arises that requires this prior learning to be displayed.

Nuts and Bolts

One way to remember cognitive maps and latent learning is to think back to the first time you traveled to your high school. Chances are you were not driving yourself. However, you were able to learn the route to school simply by being a passenger in the car. When it came time for you to drive yourself to school you were able to get there with no problems (latent learning) because you had a mental map of how to do so.

OBSERVATIONAL LEARNING

Watching what another person does can affect your own behavior. Albert Bandura conducted an experiment on the effects of **observational learning**, *acquiring knowledge by watching others perform a task*. Bandura's study, known as the Bobo doll experiment (because of the use of a children's toy that when pushed over returns immediately to the upright position) is considered one of the more influential studies in psychology. The purpose of the study was to examine what effects the violence displayed in the media might have on children's behavior. Bandura's study concluded that children who watched a recorded adult actor behave violently toward the Bobo doll **modeled**, *imitated or copied the behavior that was directly observed*, the same aggressive behavior when they were allowed to interact with the Bobo doll. Children who watched the adult actor play "nice" with the Bobo doll displayed the same behavior when put in the room with the toy. This study demonstrated the impact that witnessing violent or aggressive acts on television can have on a child's behavior.

Bandura's research on the effects of media violence on children is not without criticism. Some argue that there are confounding variables in his study: previous exposure to violent behavior or possible previous exposure to the Bobo doll toy.

AP Tip

Past free-response questions have asked students to identify the effects of media violence, specifically the effects that may lead to aggression.

Multiple-Choice Questions

1. In operant conditioning, removal of an aversive stimulus causes the behavior to
   (A) decrease
   (B) increase
   (C) stay the same
   (D) increase, then decrease
   (E) decrease, then increase

2. In the Little Albert experiment conducted by John B. Watson, the white rat, prior to conditioning, served as what?
   (A) Neutral stimulus (NS)
   (B) Unconditioned stimulus (UCS)
   (C) Unconditioned response (UCR)
   (D) Conditioned stimulus (CS)
   (E) Conditioned response (CR)

3. Jake is training his dog to sit on command. Jake gives his dog a treat every time the dog sits. Which type of reinforcement schedule is Jake displaying?
   (A) Partial reinforcement
   (B) Continuous reinforcement
   (C) Fixed-interval reinforcement
   (D) Variable-interval reinforcement
   (E) Variable-ratio reinforcement

4. Lian has an intense phobia of birds. Her psychologist believes that in order to alleviate her phobia, Lian must be placed in a room where she is surrounded by birds. Lian's therapist believes in the effectiveness of what type of phobia-reduction technique?
   (A) Systematic desensitization
   (B) Counterconditioning
   (C) Flooding
   (D) Second-order conditioning
   (E) Stimulus generalization

5. Students in Mr. Winn's class receive a gold star each time they answer a question correctly. After a student receives ten gold stars, he or she earns a pencil. Mr. Winn is using an operant conditioning technique known as
   (A) counterconditioning
   (B) flooding
   (C) aversive conditioning
   (D) token economy
   (E) observational learning

6. Julie works at a shoe factory and is paid based on the number of shoes she produces in a day. This is an example of which type of schedule of reinforcement?
   (A) Fixed-interval
   (B) Fixed-ratio
   (C) Variable-interval
   (D) Variable-ratio
   (E) Sequential reinforcement

7. Jillian was out past curfew on Saturday. As a result, her parents took away her driving privileges. Jillian no longer stays out past curfew. According to Skinner, which type of punishment did Jillian experience?
   (A) Negative punishment (omission)
   (B) Positive punishment
   (C) Negative reinforcement
   (D) Positive reinforcement
   (E) Continuous reinforcement

8. Which of the following is considered a primary reinforcer?
   (A) Receiving $20 for every A on a report card
   (B) Receiving praise for a job well done
   (C) Inventing a new product
   (D) Drinking a glass of water
   (E) Discovering a buried treasure

9. When Zach was eight years old, he ate a piece of shrimp that caused him to become ill. Now Zach is seventeen and becomes nauseous whenever he smells shrimp. Zach has experienced what principle of classical conditioning?
   (A) Negative reinforcement
   (B) Systematic desensitization
   (C) Higher-order conditioning
   (D) Latent learning
   (E) Conditioned taste aversion

10. In operant conditioning, a _____ is any stimulus that increases behavior; a _____ is any stimulus that decreases behavior.
    (A) punishment; reinforcement
    (B) punishment; punishment
    (C) reinforcement; reinforcement
    (D) reinforcement; punishment
    (E) higher-order punishment; conditioned stimulus

11. Every time Rachel's parents leave her with Lisa, the babysitter, Rachel cries. Lisa came to Rachel's third birthday party, which caused Rachel to cry. According to the principles of classical conditioning, what is the conditioned stimulus?
    (A) Rachel's parents' leaving
    (B) Rachel crying
    (C) Rachel seeing Lisa at her house
    (D) Lisa leaving Rachel's house
    (E) People singing at Rachel's birthday party

12. A rat receives a food pellet after a certain desired behavior is performed after an elapsed time of 45 seconds. Which of the following correctly identifies which schedule of reinforcement the rat has been placed on?
    (A) Fixed-interval
    (B) Fixed-ratio
    (C) Variable-interval
    (D) Variable-ratio
    (E) Continuous reinforcement

13. According to the principles of observational learning, what is seven-year-old Robert most likely to do after watching a violent television program?
    (A) Behave in a way that is opposite the behaviors on the television program
    (B) Behave in a way that is different from the behaviors on the television program
    (C) When experiencing a situation similar to what he saw on the television program, he will imitate what he saw
    (D) See the reaction of others and then decide how to behave
    (E) Behave in the same manner he would have if he had not seen the television program

14. If you want to train your dog to roll over, it is best to initially put her on which schedule of reinforcement?
    (A) Continuous reinforcement
    (B) Contiguous reinforcement
    (C) Partial reinforcement
    (D) Fixed-interval reinforcement
    (E) Variable-interval reinforcement

15. While giving your friend directions to a local fast-food restaurant, you close your eyes and recall all the landmarks that he will pass on the way. This is an example of
    (A) a cognitive map
    (B) latent learning
    (C) an overt behavior
    (D) discriminative process
    (E) a variable-ratio reinforcement

Free-Response Questions

1. Discuss how the research conducted by each of the following theorists may explain the acquisition of a spider phobia.
   (a) John B. Watson
   (b) B. F. Skinner
   (c) Albert Bandura

2. When Luis was three years old, he was a passenger in a canoe that flipped over, trapping him underneath. This experience has resulted in Luis's fear of canoes. Describe how a therapist might use each of the following behavioral techniques to help Luis overcome his phobia. Providing a definition alone is not sufficient; you must give an example that demonstrates your understanding of each behavioral technique.
   (a) Flooding
   (b) Systematic desensitization
   (c) Counterconditioning
   (d) Positive reinforcement
   (e) Observational learning

Answers

MULTIPLE-CHOICE QUESTIONS

1. Answer: B. Removal of an unpleasant or undesired stimulus will result in that behavior continuing in the future. This is referred to as negative reinforcement (*Psychology*, 8th ed. p. 207/9th ed. p. 209).

2. Answer: A. Prior to conditioning, the white rat served as the neutral stimulus. It was only after classical conditioning was established that the white rat came to serve as the conditioned

stimulus (this material does not appear in the 8th ed./ *Psychology,* 9th ed. pp. 200–201).

3. Answer: B. Providing reinforcement each time the desired behavior occurs is known as a continuous reinforcement schedule (*Psychology,* 8th ed. p. 211/9th ed. p. 214).

4. Answer: C. Surrounding a person with his or her phobia does increase initial anxiety, but after a while the person realizes the illogical reasoning behind the phobia (*Psychology,* 8th ed. pp. 655–656/9th ed. p. 664).

5. Answer: D. A token economy is an application of operant conditioning principles, in that tokens are rewarded to those displaying proper behavior. These tokens can then be exchanged for a more substantial reward (*Psychology,* 8th ed. p. 657/9th ed. p. 662).

6. Answer: B. In a fixed-ratio schedule, a behavior is rewarded after a predetermined or set number of behaviors occurs. In this case, Julie is paid for the number of shoes she produces, regardless of how much time it takes to complete her work (*Psychology,* 8th ed. p. 212/9th ed. p. 214).

7. Answer: A. Negative punishment involves removing an appetitive (pleasurable) stimulus, resulting in a decrease in the behavior (*Psychology,* 8th ed. pp. 215–216/9th ed. pp. 217–218).

8. Answer: D. Primary reinforcers satisfy biological needs (food, water, sex, warmth, and so on). Secondary reinforcers (praise, money) are pleasing because they have been associated with a primary reinforcer, but they do not satisfy a biological need (*Psychology,* 8th ed. pp. 210–211/9th ed. p. 213).

9. Answer: E. Conditioned taste aversion is when the association between an illness and a stimulus has been made. Becoming ill after one ingests a particular food can cause the person to associate illness with the food. This association can last for many years (*Psychology,* 8th ed. p. 202/9th ed. p. 205).

10. Answer: D. Reinforcers increase behaviors, whereas punishments decrease behaviors (*Psychology,* 8th ed. pp. 207, 215/9th ed. p. 209).

11. Answer: C. The conditioned stimulus is a previously neutral stimulus that has been paired with the unconditioned stimulus repeatedly. Once the association is made, the neutral stimulus becomes the conditioned stimulus and elicits a conditioned response (*Psychology,* 8th ed. p. 198/9th ed. p. 202).

12. Answer: A. A fixed-interval schedule of reinforcement provides a reinforcing stimulus after a set period of time has elapsed, even if the desired behavior has yet to be performed (*Psychology,* 8th ed. p. 212/9th ed. p. 214).

13. Answer: C. According to Albert Bandura's research on the effects of television violence and modeling behavior, a person imitates the behaviors he or she witnesses on television (*Psychology*, 8th ed. p. 226/9th ed. pp. 227–229).

14. Answer: A. Schedules of continuous reinforcement work best when initially shaping a behavior because you are trying to establish that a behavior will elicit a reinforcement (*Psychology*, 8th ed. p. 211/9th ed. p. 214).

15. Answer: A. Cognitive maps are mental representations of an environment. In using landmarks, you will use your cognitive map to recall directions to the restaurant (*Psychology*, 8th ed. pp. 223–224/9th ed. pp. 225–226).

FREE-RESPONSE QUESTIONS

1. (a) John B. Watson would argue that a phobia of spiders would be the result of classical conditioning. The unconditioned stimulus (USC), such as being bitten by a spider, would produce an unconditioned response (UCR) of screaming or feeling pain. The neutral stimulus (NS) is the spider. Because the spider bit a person, it now becomes the conditioned stimulus (CS), which produces fear (CR).

   (b) B. F. Skinner would argue that a phobia of spiders is the result of operant conditioning. Screaming and showing fear of a spider elicits attention from others. Therefore, by continuing to scream or show fear in the presence of a spider, the behavior will continue. In addition, Skinner may argue that in removing the aversive stimulus (fear or discomfort) every time a spider is removed from the situation, the fear would increase.

   (c) Albert Bandura would argue that a phobia is the result of observational learning. The person would model what he or she has seen others do when encountering a spider (or insect), and would therefore display that behavior if put in a similar situation.

2. (a) Flooding occurs when a person is put in a situation where he or she is surrounded by the fear-evoking stimulus. For example, as treatment, Joe could be placed in a canoe in the middle of a lake.

   (b) Systematic desensitization is when a fear-evoking hierarchy is created and relaxation techniques are supposed to be acted on during each step of the hierarchy. For example, Joe could be first taught some relaxation techniques. Then, while starting at the bottom of the hierarchy (a picture of a canoe), he could work his way up while applying relaxation techniques throughout.

   (c) Counterconditioning is when an appetitive (pleasant) stimulus is paired with a fear-evoking stimulus to reverse the effects of the latter. For example, if Joe likes cookies, the therapist might place cookies in the canoe and allow Joe to eat them, but only while he is in the canoe.

(d) Positive reinforcement occurs when an appetitive (pleasant) stimulus is used to increase behavior. For example, each time Joe gets into the canoe, he is rewarded with an appetitive (pleasant) stimulus, cookies.

(e) Observational learning occurs when a person imitates the actions of another. For example, Joe's therapist could show Joe how to sit properly and safely in a canoe. This would convey to Joe that it is safe to sit in a canoe. Joe would then imitate the actions of his therapist.

9

TESTING AND INDIVIDUAL DIFFERENCES

What is intelligence? What makes one person seemingly more intelligent than another? Is intelligence what you know, or how well you perform in school? Psychologists often disagree on how to define intelligence; some believe that intelligence can take numerous forms, while others believe in a single intelligence. For the most popular views of intelligence, the definition lies somewhere in between. A simplified definition of **intelligence** *is the cognitive abilities (thinking, reasoning, and problem solving) of a person based on his or her experiences.*

THEORIES OF INTELLIGENCE

Psychologists have devised varying techniques in an attempt to decipher the mystery surrounding intelligence. Many psychologists believe that in order to define intelligence, they must be able to measure it. Sir Francis Galton (1822–1911) is often mentioned as the father of **psychometrics**, *the measurement of knowledge and ability by using defined tests.* Galton believed that intelligence was based on genetics. Therefore, if your parents were intelligent, you would most likely be intelligent as well. Galton studied the history of a select number of people and their relatives; this study led him to conclude that intelligence is the result of heredity. Galton's work inspired a movement referred to as "eugenics" (well-born), which embraced this core tenet (that intelligence is inherited, or the result of nature). His research laid the groundwork for studying intelligence, but it was not without its critics. The main criticism of Galton's work centers on the fact that he studied only males. While this appears to be sexist in nature, one must take into consideration the time period in which Galton was working.

In the early twentieth century, Charles Spearman used **factor analysis**, *a statistical method used to show the relationship between variables*, to study intelligence; he was the first psychologist to do so. Spearman intended to provide data that supported his theory. He believed that there was a single intelligence, which he called general knowledge, or *g*. According to Spearman, if a person was intelligent in one area, then he or she was intelligent in other areas as well. Spearman also noted that within the *g* there exist specific intelligences, or *s*. These specific intelligences combine to form the *g*. Each person possesses specific knowledge about a subject, and those who display a high *g* also display high specific factors.

Nuts and Bolts

One way to remember the meaning of Spearman's *g* is to think of someone you know who does well in school. Typically an "A" student receives good grades in all of his or her classes, and thus would have a high overall intelligence, or *g*.

L.L. Thurston believed that Charles Spearman had oversimplified intelligence, and that one type of intelligence was not enough. Instead, Thurston believed that each person has a number of **primary mental abilities (PMAs)**, *sets of independent abilities that each person possesses in varying degrees*. According to Thurston, there are seven primary mental abilities (PMAs), and they are a better representation of a person's abilities than Spearman's *g*. Spearman agreed that there were specific factors, *s*, that influence cognitive ability, but thought the overall *g* was most important when defining a person's intelligence.

Psychologist J. P. Guilford agreed with Thurston that intelligence could not be summed up in one *g*, but believed that seven primary mental abilities (PMAs) oversimplified human beings. Guilford also used factor analysis and proposed that there were more than 180 different intellectual abilities, far surpassing the seven proposed by Thurston. According to Guilford, each of these factors is responsible for a person's cognitive abilities, or overall intelligence. Although 180 factors may seem excessive, Guilford challenged the mainstream idea that intelligence was limited to a set number of factors.

One of the more popular theories of intelligences comes from psychologist Robert Sternberg, who hypothesized that there were three different types of intelligences: analytical, creative, and practical. His theory is known as the **triarchic theory of intelligence**, the idea that *intelligence is composed of three different domains*. According to Sternberg, **analytical intelligence** is *a person's accumulated knowledge gained through education*, or book smarts. **Creative intelligence** is *the ability to generate novel (new) ideas and solutions*. People who possess creative intelligence are those who create new products, such as a work of art or a new product. The third type of intelligence is **practical intelligence**, *the ability to interact with one's environment*, also known as street smarts.

Another psychologist who believed that intelligence tests do not show a person's true cognitive abilities was Howard Gardner. According to Gardner, human beings possess numerous strengths and weaknesses, which he called multiple intelligences (MI). Gardner's multiple intelligences include:

- Linguistic intelligence: the ability to learn and use language in its fullest capacity
- Logical-mathematical intelligence: the ability to use logic associated with math and science
- Musical intelligence: the ability to compose and play musical instruments
- Bodily-kinesthetic intelligence: the ability to use one's body and physical abilities to accomplish tasks
- Spatial intelligence: the ability to use spatial relations when solving problems
- Interpersonal intelligence: the ability to understand the motives and emotions of others
- Intrapersonal intelligence: the ability to understand and control one's emotions
- Naturalistic intelligence: the ability to categorize and understand the environment

Gardner based his theory on studies of people with traumatic brain injuries. According to Gardner, a person who suffers damage to a particular region of the brain does not necessarily lose all cognitive functioning. For example, a person who suffers a stroke affecting the left hemisphere, specifically in Broca's area, does not lose his ability to tie his shoes, paint a picture, or dance. Recall from the biological bases unit, however, that this person would lose the ability to clearly articulate his thoughts, because Broca's area is responsible for speech production. According to Gardner, this was evidence that proved the existence of multiple intelligences.

Nuts and Bolts

 One criticism of Gardner's theory of multiple intelligences is that they are too broad, and that some intelligences are simply skills that can be modified and enhanced.

The most recent theory of intelligence, known as emotional intelligence, was proposed by Salovey and Mayer, and popularized by Daniel Goleman. **Emotional intelligence** is *the ability to perceive and manage the emotions of oneself and others.* Goleman believes that this is the most important type of intelligence, and those who are emotionally intelligent are those who are most likely to succeed in life.

INFLUENCES ON INTELLIGENCE

Where does intelligence come from? Is it something you are born with, as proposed by Galton, or does it develop from your experiences? Those who believe that intelligence is inherited, or the result of nature, say it is determined before you are even born. One way to prove this theory is by conducting kinship studies, which examine the intelligence of those who are biologically related. Research on the influence of genetics on intelligence focuses on the intelligence between identical twins. Identical twins raised in a similar environment appear to have a strong correlation, meaning that their intelligence scores are nearly identical. Twins raised in different environments also show a strong correlation coefficient. In addition, those who were adopted show a moderate correlation with their birth parent(s). Siblings raised in similar environments also show a moderate correlation pertaining to their intelligence scores. However, it is important to remember that correlation does not mean causation, and psychologists cannot say with certainty that intelligence is genetically determined.

Those who believe that intelligence is the result of environmental factors argue that even though identical twins raised together show a strong correlation, one cannot conclude it was genetics alone that dictated the similarity. Being raised in the same environment could mean that each twin was exposed to the same environmental conditions, which would explain similarities in intelligence. Psychologists who believe that environmental (nurture) factors dictate intelligence often study individuals who were adopted. Some studies have found a moderate correlation between an individual's intelligence and the intelligence of the adoptive parents, boosting support for the influence of environmental factors on intelligence.

One of the most frequently cited studies on intelligence is the Seattle Longitudinal Study (SLS), which looked at how adult cognitive abilities change over a span of 40 years. The SLS used a cross-sectional design to track the cognitive functioning of thousands of adults. The findings of the study suggest that unless the brain is affected by diseases such as Alzheimer's, the decline of cognitive functioning in adults is minimal. This study might lend support to the nature argument, which holds that intelligence is fixed from birth.

TESTING INTELLIGENCE

While psychologists disagree on what intelligence is and how it can be measured, thousands of intelligence tests are administered every year, each one claiming to be the true measure of intelligence. Depending on the situation, an intelligence test can be administered on an individual or a group basis.

INDIVIDUALIZED TESTING

The process of testing intelligence has changed since the first modern intelligence test was created in 1904 by Alfred Binet. Binet's test was developed to assist the French government in identifying special needs students. According to Binet, a person's level of intelligence could be determined using a simple mathematical formula: mental age (MA) divided by chronological age (CA). The mental age of an individual was based on the number of test questions he or she answered correctly; the resulting number—mental age divided by chronological age—signified that child's intelligence. Binet's test was not without its critics, the biggest one being that although chronological age always increases, mental age may not, thus creating a problem in that the older a person gets, the lower his or her intelligence score would be.

In 1912, German psychologist Wilhelm Stern proposed multiplying the score derived from the MA/CA calculation by 100. This new formula would be known as the Intelligence Quotient (IQ). If a child's MA and CA were the same, the resulting IQ would be 100. A score of 100 would be considered average, and a child who scored above 100 would be said to have above-average intelligence. Psychologist Lewis Terman, at Stanford University, was responsible for translating Binet's work into English—hence the name Stanford-Binet Intelligence Scale (SBIS). The SBIS was the most widely used intelligence test until David Wechsler created his own in 1939.

Wechsler developed ways to measure intelligence in both children and adults: the Wechsler Intelligence Scale for Children (WISC) and the Wechsler Adult Intelligence Scale (WAIS). Wechsler set out to fix the numerous criticisms of the SBIS by creating a test that consisted of two separate scales, verbal and performance. The verbal scale consists of seven subtests that measure a person's verbal abilities, such as memory, word definitions, and mathematical problem solving. The performance scale is divided into seven subtests and requires a person to manipulate special relations between objects, such as assembling pictures, arranging pictures to form a story, and completing mazes. The resulting score from each of the two main scales is then calculated into a final IQ score. Instead of using the SBIS formula to calculate IQ, Wechsler compared one individual's score to the scores obtained by people of the same age. The resulting score is known as the deviation IQ. According to Wechsler, the average IQ score obtained by 50 percent of individuals falls between 90 and 110. The chart below shows an approximate distribution of IQ scores.

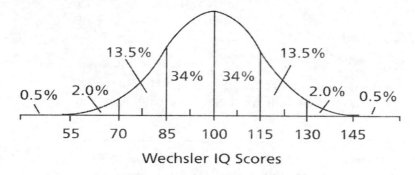

Wechsler IQ Scores

Information from
http://allpsych.com/researchmethods/images/deviationIQ.gif

Nuts and Bolts

It's important to remember that 50 percent of the individuals who take the WAIS or WISC score between 90 and 110, with 100 being the middle. It is also important to remember that the standard deviation used in an IQ test is 15. So if a person is two standard deviations above the norm, his or her IQ score would be 130.

APTITUDE AND ACHIEVEMENT TESTING

Group tests are administered to assess either an individual's readiness to perform at a certain level or an individual's knowledge of a particular subject. Group tests can be divided into two categories: aptitude and achievement. **Aptitude tests**, *designed to measure a person's performance potential,* are commonly given to students who plan to attend college. Examples include the SAT (once known as the Scholastic Aptitude Test), the American College Testing Assessment (ACT), and the Graduate Record Examination (GRE). Each of these aptitude tests is used as a predictor of how well a student will do in college or graduate school. Although the tests are not 100 percent accurate in their ability to predict success, they have been proven to be a good predictor on future performance capabilities. **Achievement tests**, *designed to measure a person's knowledge of a particular area,* are used in assessing how much a person knows about a given subject matter. Examples of achievement tests include the Advanced Placement (AP) examination, the National Assessment of Educational Progress (NAEP), and various state-administered exams. Each of these tests is designed to test the student's academic knowledge in relation to others taking the same exam.

ADVANTAGES AND DISADVANTAGES OF INDIVIDUAL AND GROUP TESTING

While individualized and group tests are useful for certain situations, they are not without their flaws. The following are the advantages and disadvantages of both types of tests.

Type of Test	Advantages	Disadvantages
Individualized	The test taker can dictate the flow of questions. There's greater rapport between test administrator and test taker.	This test is more expensive and more time consuming to administer. It can only test one person at a time.

Type of Test	Advantages	Disadvantages
Group	It's easy to administer to a large number of people. The scoring is more objective. It's relatively inexpensive to administer.	There's less rapport between test administrator and test taker. Responses are more restricted. Test fatigue can cause a lower score. The subject does not dictate the flow of questions.

MEASURING TESTS

Tests are designed to measure various things. Some gauge an individual's overall intelligence, while others measure knowledge on a given subject matter. Regardless of the test's purpose, there are certain criteria that must be met when determining whether the test is accomplishing its goal. The following are some of the terms commonly used to measure any test, whether IQ, aptitude, or achievement.

Terminology		Definition	Example
Reliability		The test's ability to yield consistent results after repeated testing.	Hans takes the WISC twice. His first score is a 105, while his second score is a 103.
Validity	Validity	How well a test measures what it was designed to measure.	The math test Brittany took Friday was on the material covered the week before in class.
	Content validity	The information included on the test measures what it was designed to measure.	In psychology, Aleshia took a test on intelligence that included questions asking her to specify who is credited with a particular intelligence theory.
	Criterion (predictive) validity	The ability of a test to predict how well a person will do in future.	Adam took the SAT, which has been shown to be a good predictor of how well he'll do during his first semester of college next year.
	Construct validity	How well the test is designed (constructed) to measure the specified theory.	A question on an intelligence test is in small print/text. Therefore Brock has a difficult time reading the question, thus possibly lowering his final score.
Standardized		The process of setting a common standard by comparing one's score to those attained by a pretested group.	Kendra attends Central High School, and Marcus attends North High School. Both students took the same AP psychology test last Tuesday.

> ## AP Tip
>
> Past multiple-choice questions have asked students to identify different terminology relating to tests. It is important to know these terms in relation to any type of test.

EVALUATING INTELLIGENCE TESTS

Many psychologists believe that intelligence tests do not accurately measure a person's intelligence, citing examples of bias in the wording of questions or the general content of a question itself. One example of bias would be if an intelligence test asked the participant to decide what is missing from a picture of a snowman. If a person lives in a region that doesn't get snow, he or she might never have built a snowman, or may not even have ever seen snow. This participant is at a disadvantage and may ultimately achieve a lower overall score than a person who lives in a region with snow. Another factor that may influence the results of an IQ test is socioeconomic status (SES). Critics of intelligence tests use the fact that the better-fed and better-educated sectors of the U.S. population score higher on IQ tests to support their conclusion that intelligence tests may be inherently biased. Their ultimate concern is that a lower SES may limit an individual's academic experiences, thus undermining performance on IQ tests. Other factors that may influence the results of an IQ test are related to environmental factors. Room temperature or noisiness can affect a person's ability to concentrate, thus influencing overall IQ score. Even though intelligence tests are subject to numerous biases, they remain in use today.

> ## AP Tip
>
> A past free-response question asked students to identify bias in IQ tests and propose ways to improve IQ scores.

DIVERSITY IN COGNITION

Despite the fact that there is no consensus on what is considered intelligence, the tests used to determine intelligence have yielded much insight into the diversity that exists in this field.

CREATIVITY

Creativity, *the ability to generate novel ideas or products,* is often thought to go hand-in-hand with intelligence. To examine the relationship between creativity and intelligence, psychologists use tests that measure **divergent thinking**, *the ability to generate multiple solutions to a given problem.* These tests attempt to measure what intelligence cannot: the ability to think outside the box when solving a problem. Those who excel in divergent thinking may score poorly on traditional intelligence tests, which measure **convergent thinking,** *narrowing down to a single best solution or answer to a problem.* Because traditional intelligence tests make use of convergent thinking, those who do not excel creatively will typically have higher IQs.

UNUSUAL COGNITIVE ABILITIES

Psychologists have long been puzzled by unusual cognitive abilities, such as in those who are gifted and in those who have mental retardation or autism.

People who excel at a rapid pace in school are said to be gifted. Gifted students are usually identified through the numerous standardized tests they must take throughout elementary school. Once labeled as gifted, many students are faced with pressure to live up to the expectations. However, does being labeled gifted automatically mean the student will succeed?

One of the most famous longitudinal studies on giftedness was conducted by Lewis Terman. Terman believed that having a superior IQ (above 135) meant that a person was going to be successful in life. To test his hypothesis, Terman recruited 1,500 children with superior IQs measured by age ten. His subjects named themselves "Terman's termites." Terman and his colleagues tracked these students and recorded their progress for the next 60 years. As it turned out, only 11 of the 1,500 subjects failed to graduate high school, and approximately 250 of them earned advanced degrees and above-average incomes. However, does being gifted automatically ensure that a person will succeed in life? You can draw that conclusion for yourself. Terman did not live to see the end result of this research, which is ongoing.

Other forms of unusual cognitions include people with below-average IQs. A person who has an IQ below 70 is considered mentally retarded. The following table shows the different levels of **mental retardation,** *significantly delayed or impaired learning of language or motor skills, and having an IQ below 70.*

Level of retardation	IQ score	Characteristics
Mild	50–70	Approximately 85 percent of all mentally retarded people fall within this category. May display few or no physical symptoms (typically found at higher end of spectrum). Academic learning is limited to approximately a sixth-grade level.
Moderate	35–49	Display signs of impaired motor and physical symptoms. Live with caretaker or in group home. Mental capacity of an individual is often limited to that of a child ages 4–7.

Level of retardation	IQ score	Characteristics
Severe	20–34	Require constant supervision and will not be able to care of themselves. Limited language abilities. Significantly impaired motor and physical functioning. Mental capacity is similar to that of a 3- to 4-year-old child.
Profound	Below 20	May be able to feed themselves with extensive training, but typically cannot. Language is limited to grunts. Significant impairment in physical or motor functioning; may never walk. Mental capacity is limited to that of a 3-year-old.

FACTORS ASSOCIATED WITH MENTAL RETARDATION

Three factors associated with mental retardation are Down syndrome, fetal alcohol syndrome (FAS), and fragile X syndrome. **Down syndrome**, also known as trisomy 21, *is a genetic disorder caused by the presence of an extra 21st chromosome resulting in mental retardation.* People with Down syndrome are typically mildly or moderately retarded. **Fetal alcohol syndrome** (see the chapter on human development for further explanation) *results in permanent physical and cognitive impairment and is the result of the mother's consuming alcohol during pregnancy.* **Fragile X syndrome** *is a genetic disorder that is caused by a mutated gene on the X chromosome.* Having fragile X syndrome does not guarantee severe cognitive impairment, but those who suffer from significant mutation of the X chromosome will undoubtedly face some level of cognitive impairment.

AUTISM SPECTRUM DISORDER

Autism spectrum disorder (ASD), *impairment in social communication and interaction, restricted or compulsive behavior,* is one of the fastest growing unusual cognitions. ASD consists of three main forms: autism, Asperger syndrome, and Pervasive Developmental Disorder-Not Otherwise Specified (PDD-NOS). Autism is considered the central feature of ASD. Children who suffer from autism are typically diagnosed between the ages of two and four. However, recent research has suggested that autism can be detected as early as four months of age. Individuals diagnosed with autism show impairment of social skills and functioning. Those who are diagnosed with Asperger syndrome appear to show no delay in language and communication skills. However, they typically display very narrow, yet highly attentive, preoccupations with subjects, to the point of obsession. Asperger syndrome sufferers typically show an above-average intelligence, yet may not be successful in school, mainly due to their obsessive preoccupations. Those who suffer from PDD-

NOS display some symptoms related to autism but not all, and therefore are not classified as autistic. While there is no definitive cause of ASD, there are numerous theories: it may be genetically inherited, the lack of mirror neurons in a person with ASD, the result of vaccinations, or simply the result of an increased understanding of ASD.

Nuts and Bolts

 It is important to know that autism is NOT mental retardation. To be classified as mentally retarded a person must have an IQ lower than 70, whereas autism is characterized by an impairment of social skills/functioning.

SAVANT SYNDROME

With **savant syndrome**, *a person has cognitive impairments in certain areas but has one or more abilities that are displayed on a genius level.* Savant syndrome is a disorder that is more likely seen in those with autism, although having autism does not guarantee that a person is a savant. The study of savant syndrome has aided psychologists in their efforts to answer the question of what makes one person more intelligent than another. Some psychologists who study intelligence, such as Howard Gardner, use savant syndrome to validate the existence of multiple intelligences.

Multiple-Choice Questions

1. Ava excels in her art class, but has tremendous difficulty in math and English. According to Robert Sternberg, Ava displays what type of intelligence?
   (A) Analytical
   (B) Practical
   (C) Creative
   (D) General
   (E) Emotional

2. The psychologist who developed the first modern intelligence test used to help the French government with the placement of special needs students was
   (A) Charles Spearman
   (B) Robert Sternberg
   (C) Howard Gardner
   (D) Lewis Terman
   (E) Alfred Binet

3. Anan is taking a final exam in his calculus class. All of the questions on the exam relate to material that was covered over the course of the year. Therefore, the test can be said to display high
   (A) criterion validity
   (B) standardization
   (C) reliability
   (D) content validity
   (E) test-retest reliability

4. Garrett scored a 28 the first time he took the college entrance exam. Six months later, he took it again and scored a 29. Because his scores were so close together the test would be considered
   (A) valid
   (B) normed
   (C) standardized
   (D) reliable
   (E) predictable

5. Together with 200 other high school students, Claude is taking a timed test that is said to predict how well a person will do in his or her first semester in college. Claude is most likely taking what type of intelligence test?
   (A) Individualized
   (B) Group
   (C) Motivational
   (D) Stamina
   (E) Interest

6. Which of the following best illustrates Spearman's concept of *g*?
   (A) Lisa does well in mathematics, but poorly in chemistry.
   (B) Fatima does not know the capital of her state but can compose music successfully.
   (C) Quon is an excellent baseball player who has received a scholarship to play in college.
   (D) Sarah has maintained straight A's throughout high school.
   (E) Kris is an excellent actor and singer.

7. Bailee recently took the Weschler Intelligence Scale for Children (WISC) and scored one standard deviation above the mean. Bailee would most likely have an IQ of
   (A) 115
   (B) 85
   (C) 130
   (D) 95
   (E) 100

8. Mr. Trevor believes that students with high IQs are more likely to succeed in life than are those with low IQs. Which psychologist would most likely agree with Mr. Trevor?
   (A) Daniel Goleman
   (B) Lewis Terman
   (C) Robert Sternberg
   (D) Noam Chomsky
   (E) Leon Festinger

9. Professor Yanders recently conducted a study that examined the IQs of 1000 different families. He concluded that if parents had high IQs, their children would also have high IQs. Professor Yanders believes in which view of intelligence?
   (A) Standard
   (B) Nature
   (C) Nurture
   (D) Longitudinal
   (E) Factoring

10. Jason received a low score on the Weschler Adult Intelligence Scale (WAIS) but is capable of navigating his way through a busy city without the assistance of a map. According to Robert Sternberg, Paul displays what type of intelligence?
    (A) Creativity
    (B) Analytical
    (C) Practical
    (D) Emotional
    (E) General

11. Which of the following best illustrates the concept of divergent thinking?
    (A) Hank is good at listening to other people and helping them with their problems.
    (B) Gloria is an excellent softball player who receives a scholarship to play in college.
    (C) Tony does extremely well in school, but has a difficult time making friends.
    (D) Richard knows the lyrics of every song he has ever heard.
    (E) Ali designs workplace accommodations for the physically impaired.

12. Which of the following is not considered an advantage of individualized intelligence tests?
    (A) They allow good rapport between the test taker and the person administering the test.
    (B) If a person is having a bad day the test can often be rescheduled to accommodate extenuating circumstances.
    (C) They are cheap and easy to administer to many people at once.
    (D) The test taker can help dictate the pace of the test.
    (E) If the test taker has a question, he or she can ask the test administrator for clarification.

13. Which of the following would score high on the emotional intelligence scale?
    (A) Jaelyn can complete crossword puzzles quickly.
    (B) Claude is good at interpreting the emotions of others.
    (C) Pauline is good at fixing mechanical machines.
    (D) Marcus knows how to make spaghetti.
    (E) Elle has invented a new device to help others learn to read.

14. Who was the first psychologist to propose that intelligence is the result of nature?
    (A) Robert Sternberg
    (B) Howard Gardner
    (C) Charles Spearman
    (D) Sir Francis Galton
    (E) Lewis Terman

15. Which of the following is a disadvantage of group intelligence tests?
    (A) They are relatively cheap to administer.
    (B) They can be administered to numerous people at the same time.
    (C) There is considerable rapport between the test taker and the test administrator.
    (D) Test fatigue may cause a low score.
    (E) The test is given in a controlled environment.

Free-Response Questions

1. Explain how each of the following psychologists views intelligence.
    ▨ Charles Spearman
    ▨ Robert Sternberg
    ▨ Howard Gardner
2. Intelligence has always been a controversial area of study.
    ▨ Contrast opposing views regarding intelligence.
    ▨ Explain why intelligence tests must be updated.
    ▨ Discuss validity and reliability in intelligence tests.

Answers

MULTIPLE-CHOICE QUESTIONS

1. Answer: C. According to Sternberg, a person who excels at creating new ideas and products has a high level of creative intelligence. Analytical intelligence is similar to book smarts, and a person who has a high level of this form of intelligence generally does well on standardized tests. A person who has a high level of practical intelligence displays street smarts, is aware of his or her surroundings, and is able to think quickly to process information (*Psychology*, 8th ed. pp. 389–391/9th ed. pp. 396–397).

2. Answer: E. Alfred Binet is credited with developing the first modern intelligence test, used to help identify special needs students in France (*Psychology*, 8th ed. p. 367/9th ed. p. 374).

3. Answer: D. Any test that includes questions that pertain to the subject matter studied is said to have content validity. It is valid

to ask an algebra question on an algebra test (*Psychology*, 8th ed. pp. 373–374/9th ed. p. 380).

4. Answer: D. Tests that yield the same results on different occasions are considered reliable. Since the scores did not vary much, it could be concluded that Garrett's results would be similar in subsequent tests (*Psychology*, 8th ed. pp. 372–373/9th ed. p. 379).

5. Answer: B. Group intelligence tests can be administered to a large number of people at the same time. They are the opposite of an individualized intelligence test, which is given in a one-on-one situation (*this material does not appear in either textbook edition*).

6. Answer: D. Spearman's concept of *g* states that those who excel in one area excel equally in other areas. The basic concept is that intelligent people are intelligent in all areas (*Psychology*, 8th ed. p. 387/9th ed. p. 394).

7. Answer: A. The average IQ for the WISC and WAIS tests are equal to 100, and one standard deviation is equal to 15 points. Therefore, one standard deviation above the mean would be 115, while one standard deviation below the norm would be 85 (*Psychology*, 8th ed. p. 371/9th ed. pp. 377–378).

8. Answer: B. Lewis Terman believed that students with above-average IQs would be more successful in life than those with average or below-average IQs. This led him to conduct a longitudinal study of 1,500 students with above-average IQs (this material does not appear in the 8th edition/ *Psychology*, 9th ed. pp. 404–405).

9. Answer: B. The nature view of intelligence states that IQ is the result of genetics or heredity, and therefore if the biological parents are intelligent, their children will also be intelligent (*Psychology*, 8th ed. pp. 377–378/9th ed. pp. 384–385).

10. Answer: C. According to Robert Sternberg, there are three types of intelligence: analytical (book/academic smarts), creative (the ability to generate new ideas), and practical (street smarts) (*Psychology*, 8th ed. pp. 389–391/9th ed. pp. 396–397).

11. Answer: E. Divergent thinking occurs when a person is able to think of multiple solutions to a problem. Convergent thinking happens when a person is able to think of one possible answer or outcome (*Psychology*, 8th ed. pp. 395–397/9th ed. p. 403).

12. Answer: C. Individualized intelligence tests are more expensive and time consuming than group intelligence tests (*this material does not appear in either textbook edition*).

13. Answer: B. Emotional intelligence is the ability to interpret the emotions of others and manage one's own emotions (this material does not appear in the 8th edition/ *Psychology*, 9th ed. p. 399).

14. Answer: D. Sir Francis Galton conducted the first kinship studies in trying to determine the origins of intelligence. He believed that intelligence is the result of genetics (*this material does not appear in either textbook edition*).

15. Answer: D. Group intelligence tests can be given to numerous people at once and are relatively inexpensive to administer. The testing environment is highly controlled, prohibiting any outside factors from interfering with the testing situation. However, the tests usually are rather long and are timed, which may cause test fatigue in an individual and thus lead to a lower overall score (*this material does not appear in either textbook edition*).

FREE-RESPONSE QUESTIONS

1. These psychologists viewed intelligence in the following ways:
   - Charles Spearman viewed intelligence as monarchic—meaning singular—in nature. He believed that a person's overall intelligence affects numerous areas. If a person is smart in one area, he or she will be smart in all areas. Spearman called his monarchic intelligence *g*, which stands for general intelligence.
   - Robert Sternberg developed the triarchic theory of intelligence. According to Sternberg, there are three forms of intelligence: analytic (book smarts), practical (street smarts), and creative.
   - Howard Gardner believes that intelligence comes in numerous, different forms. According to Gardner's multiple intelligence (MI) theory, there is no one intelligence.

2. Explaining two different and opposing theories of intelligence is sufficient to score a point on this question.
   - Intelligence tests must be updated for numerous reasons:
     - Technology has improved, which leads to an increase in intelligence.
     - Nutrition has improved, which leads to an increase in intelligence.
     - There needs to be a control for cultural biasness that may exist in the tests.
   - Validity is the measure of how well a test measures what it is intended to measure.
   - Reliability refers to a test's producing the same results after successive trials.

PERSONALITY

Personality is *the unique and consistent pattern of behavior, thinking, and feeling that makes up an individual.* Personality researchers have tried to provide answers that explain how personality develops and how people are similar and different. Personality research has generated widespread interest, from employers who seek to find the perfect employee to people wondering whether someone they have recently met is trustworthy.

SIGMUND FREUD'S PSYCHODYNAMIC APPROACH

Sigmund Freud believed that personality is influenced by the **unconscious**, which is comprised of *wishes, inner conflicts, and memories that we are unaware of but that still affect our behavior.* He believed that even though people are unaware of the unconscious, it can enter conscious and preconscious awareness through symbolic points. **Conscious awareness**, as discussed in Chapter 7, *includes all of the mental processes a person is aware of at any given moment.* **Preconscious awareness** is made up of *memories and information that are not presently in conscious awareness but can easily be recalled.*

Nuts and Bolts

 The role of the unconscious can be compared to an iceberg. The bulk of an iceberg is hidden below the surface, like the unconscious. The visible portion of the iceberg—conscious awareness—does not reflect the overall size of the iceberg.

THE DEVELOPMENT OF PERSONALITY: ID, EGO, AND SUPEREGO

Freud believed that personality is the result of psychological energy that produces three distinct components of personality: the id, the ego, and the superego.

The **id,** *which is present at birth, is the unconscious portion of personality. The id is primitive and is not affected by values, ethics, or morals. The id's psychological energy comes from two opposing instinctual drives called Eros and Thanatos.* The nature of **Eros** *is to preserve life by alerting an individual to hunger, thirst, and sexuality.* Freud believed that a person's sex drive provides a psychological energy he referred to as the **libido.** He thought that **Thanatos,** *or the death instinct, is responsible for aggressive and destructive behaviors.*

The id is governed by the **pleasure principle,** *which demands immediate gratification.* For example, an infant, operating solely by the id, cries repeatedly and loudly until a caregiver meets his or her demands and needs.

The second component of personality, the **ego,** *emerges from the psychological energy of the id.* The ego is partly conscious and represents the rational, decision-making part of the personality. The ego relies on the **reality principle**, which, when necessary, *delays the demands and the needs of the id until a more appropriate time.*

Nuts and Bolts

 Think of the ego as the boss of a company of unruly employees. The boss is the decision maker trying to run a successful business. When an employee wants to leave early, it is up to the boss (ego) to compromise with the employee (following the reality principle) to find a better time for him or her to leave, perhaps when the work is done—thus delaying gratification to a more appropriate time.

The final component of personality, the **superego,** *emerges at about age five or six and represents the internal voice of reason.* The superego is comparable to a person's conscience acting as a judge and jury. The individual who doesn't live up to the demands of the superego experiences guilt and anxiety.

Nuts and Bolts

 There may have been a time when you were about to do something inappropriate but stopped when you heard a "little voice" advising you not to. That "little voice" represents your superego.

TYPES OF EGO DEFENSE MECHANISMS

Freud believed that the urges of the id and the demands of the superego could cause conflicts, and that the role of the ego is to mediate such conflicts, which Freud called "intrapsychic." Intrapsychic conflict, he held, can lead to anxiety. In order to reduce this anxiety and protect itself against unpleasant impulses and circumstances, the ego relies on **defense mechanisms.**

Defense Mechanism	Definition	Example
Repression	The exclusion from conscious awareness of a painful, unpleasant, or undesirable memory or urge (Note: "suppression" is a conscious decision to forget about something or avoid thinking about it)	Someone who experienced child abuse represses those memories.
Rationalization	Providing excuses or explanations to justify thoughts or behaviors	A student blames the teacher for not allowing enough time to finish a test.
Projection	Ascribing or assigning one's own undesirable feelings or thoughts to others	You say to your friend, "You're such a liar!" when you feel guilty about recent lies you told.
Reaction formation	When a person behaves in a way that contradicts their actual thoughts	Jimmy has a crush on Jill, but instead of showing it he makes fun of her.
Sublimation	Attempting to turn unacceptable thoughts or actions into socially acceptable behaviors	Many aggressive people join football or hockey teams.
Displacement	Shifting anger and hostility to a less threatening target	Mason got into an argument with his teacher and slammed the door on the way out.
Compensation	Trying to make up for unconscious impulses or fears	Julie is very strict with her employees, trying to make up for her shortcomings as an effective boss.
Denial	Not being willing to accept the truth	People who are addicted to drugs don't want to admit it.
Regression	In times of stress, an individual's reverting to a behavior that is associated with an earlier stage of development	Evie cried in response to getting a speeding ticket.

STAGES THAT OCCUR THROUGH PERSONALITY DEVELOPMENT

Freud believed that personality develops through a series of five distinct psychosexual stages. Each stage is unconsciously associated with an area of pleasure (erogenous zone) in which the unconscious tries to achieve satisfaction. If the unconscious is not able to adequately satisfy the needs associated with a particular stage, then fixation could occur. **Fixation** *is a defense mechanism that occurs when the individual remains locked in an earlier developmental stage because his or her needs were either under- or over-gratified during that stage.* This can affect the individual in adulthood as he or she unconsciously tries to achieve pleasure through adult activities that were denied him or her in childhood.

FREUD'S PSYCHOSEXUAL STAGES

1. **Oral Stage (0 to one year old):**
   - Pleasure: associated with the mouth
   - Activities: putting objects such as pacifiers into the mouth; sucking, biting or chewing
   - Fixation: could result in adult oral activities such as chewing fingernails, smoking, overeating, chewing on straws, or being overly talkative or sarcastic

2. **Anal Stage (two years old):**
   - Pleasure: associated with anal area
   - Activity: proper toilet training: child learning control over bowels
   - Fixation: If toilet training is too harsh or not mastered, this could result in adult anal retentive characteristics such as obsessive neatness or anal expulsive characteristics such as extreme messiness

3. **Phallic Stage: (three to five years old)**
   - Pleasure: associated with genitals (one's own)
   - **Oedipus complex:** *occurs when the son displays incestuous feelings for his mother and resistance towards his father.* As a result of these feelings, the boy develops castration anxiety. This anxiety arises from the thought that the father will eventually punish the boy for his incestuous thoughts for his mother by castrating his penis.
   - **Electra complex:** On the other hand, the Electra complex: *occurs when the daughter questions why boys have penises and girls do not.* In turn, the girl develops penis envy and starts to display incestuous feelings towards her father and resistance towards the mother.
   - **Identification:** *Boys resolve and reduce the anxiety caused by the Oedipus complex and castration anxiety by forming an alliance with the father, who once was the enemy.* The boy uses the defense mechanism of identification, which involves imitating his father's attitudes and values. It is during this stage that the boy's superego starts to develop. Similar to boys, girls resolve the Electra complex and penis

envy by identifying with the mother, who in turn helps develop the girl's superego.

Nuts and Bolts

 A good way to remember the process of identification is to think about which parent disciplines the child during this age. Often a mother will refer the son to the father, saying, "I couldn't get through to your son. You try; he identifies with you."

---

4. **Latency Stage: (late childhood)**
   - Sexual impulses lie dormant with focus on same-sex friendships and the development of social and intellectual skills. Through redirecting energy into emotionally safe and socially acceptable activities (i.e., sublimation), the child forgets the highly stressful conflicts of the phallic stage.

5. **Genital Stage: (adolescence)**
   - Sexual impulses reemerge and emphasis is again placed on the genitals (individual's and others'). The focal activity during this stage is experimenting with loving, intimate relationships that are mutually gratifying.

AP Tip

You should be able to identify the sequence of the psychosexual stages.

THE NEO-FREUDIAN VIEW OF PERSONALITY

Neo-Freudians were followers of Freud who taught and delivered his theories and ideas. However, over time these neo-Freudians started to move away from some of Freud's ideas to develop their own theories of personality.

CARL JUNG

Carl Jung disagreed with Freud primarily on the role of the libido. He believed that the libido was not just a driving sexual interest, but a life force that brings about human growth and conflict resolution. He also did not agree with the distinct personality stages, but thought each person should be viewed as either an **introvert**, *someone who prefers privacy and ponders his or her own actions and thinking,* or an **extrovert**, *someone who receives energy through being active and part of the outside social world.* The variation of introversion and extraversion, in Jung's viewpoint, leads to personality similarities and differences. Jung also believed in a **collective unconscious**, *a collection of past experiences shared by all people that are inherited from ancestors and passed from generation to generation.* Jung believed that the collective unconscious contains **archetypes**, which are *generational symbols of perpetual themes and symbols.* For example, snakes are an archetype of evil, appearing in literature and art across time and place. Past experiences and archetypes unconsciously influence present decisions and behavior.

ALFRED ADLER

Adler believed that people have an innate desire to overcome inferiorities experienced in childhood. These inferiority complexes stem from our reliance on others (primarily parents) in caring for us when we're young. This leads to a desire to strive for superiority throughout life by compensating for childhood inferiorities. People try to achieve superiority in unique ways that account for personality similarities and differences.

Nuts and Bolts

A good way to remember Adler's inferiority complex is to think about how children often reject parental help. Children often prefer to do something wrong rather than ask for help. The child is trying to achieve superiority and prove that he or she can be in control.

KAREN HORNEY

Karen Horney, the first feminist personality researcher, attacked Freud's claim that women have penis envy. She did not agree that penis envy could cause females to become jealous and develop feelings of inferiority toward males. Instead, Horney felt that social restraints were responsible for women's feeling inferior to men. She added that men actually feel inferior to women because women have the ability to bear children, which she referred to as "womb envy." Horney also believed that conflicts within social relationships could lead to anxiety that would affect personality. She thought these conflicts could cause anxiety that would disrupt the functioning of personality. She added that people respond to such anxiety by displaying defensive personality styles. She identified these styles as moving toward, moving against, and moving away from these anxieties. Individuals with a strong desire for approval are described as moving toward. Those with a strong desire for control are described as moving against, while people who place importance on independence are described as moving away.

Nuts and Bolts

A good way to understand Horney's viewpoint of how social relationships affect personality is to think about a time you had a disagreement with a friend. After this disagreement you probably did not act like yourself. Did you feel a desire for approval from other people, or a need to be in control, or did you just want to be left alone?

AP Tip

Be ready to distinguish between each of the neo-Freudians' contributions to the theory of psychodynamic personality development.

EVALUATING THE PSYCHODYNAMIC APPROACH

Recent personality researchers have given limited support to the psychodynamic perspective. The main criticism cited is the difficulty of proving the existence and consequent influence of the unconscious. There is no empirical way to study the origins and the effects of the unconscious. In addition, case studies, Freud's main research method, are limited in providing applicable data and cannot be generalized to a larger population. Studying one individual does not correlate to an entire population because the case study may be atypical, only representing that one individual. Freud also based his theory on Western European thought and North American values, which makes it difficult to relate to other cultures.

However, the psychodynamic perspective brought about additional research in the development of personality, since in order to disprove Freud's theories, researchers had to search for theories that would offer differing explanations.

TRAIT THEORIES

Personality traits *are internal characteristics that are stable, consistent over time, and displayed through multiple situations.* Trait theories predict how people will act or think based on their specific traits. For example, a person who is described as caring is caring in the classroom as well as at home. In addition, no two people display the exact same list of traits.

Nuts and Bolts

 A good way to remember the role of a trait is to think about a personal ad. Someone creating such an ad often uses traits to describe who they are. For example, a person may describe him- or herself as thoughtful, affectionate, or hardworking. The problem with these descriptors is that they do not explain *why* that individual is thoughtful, affectionate, or hard-working.

TYPE VERSUS TRAITS

People often confuse personality traits with personality types. Traits provide a list, or number, of descriptors that are used to describe a person, whereas types address whether a person "fits" that particular type, or whether he or she has certain characteristics. For example, if a person is the *feeling type,* then that person displays affection, sympathy, and dependability. If a person is not the feeling type, then that person does not display those traits. The problem with using types to describe a person is that they are vague and general. Types are not as specific as traits.

Nuts and Bolts

 Sometimes you might wonder whether someone is the kind of person to perform a particular behavior. For example, if you wonder whether someone is the type to cheat, you would look at a number of traits: mistrustfulness, deceptiveness, or selfishness. Remember: just because someone is selfish does not necessarily mean that he or she is a cheater.

GORDON ALLPORT'S TRAIT THEORY

Gordon Allport, one of the first trait researchers, chose to identify traits based on their importance in describing personality. Through his research, he was able to identify more than 18,000 traits. He grouped these into central and secondary traits. Allport believed **central traits**, or **source traits**, are *easily recognized and have a strong influence on personality*, whereas **secondary traits**, or **surface traits**, are *more specific to certain situations and have less of an effect on personality*. For example, on the surface Jim is competitive (secondary trait), but deep down he is a nice person (central trait).

RAYMOND CATTELL

Raymond Cattell based his research on Gordon Allport's and used a questionnaire that asked people to rate themselves on a number of traits to show which best described them. He then used a technique called **factor analysis**, *a mathematical formula that explains how traits are related to one another*. He believed that central traits could give rise to a number of secondary traits. For example, if a person's central trait is caring, you could predict that that person would be dependable (secondary trait) in various situations. Through factor analysis, Cattell was able to identify sixteen basic personality factors. He verified his findings through a *Sixteen Personality Factor Questionnaire*, which showed a relationship among the factors.

BIOLOGICAL TRAIT THEORIES

Hans Eysenck believed that people could be described along introversion-extroversion and emotionality-stability dimensions. He defined introverts as people who prefer privacy and extroverts as people who are outgoing and enjoy social settings. He said that people who displayed the characteristics of **emotionality** *were moody and worried*, and that those who displayed **stability** *were calm and relaxed*. Using factor analysis, people would fall between extroversion and introversion, and between emotionality and stability.

THE BIG-FIVE MODEL OF PERSONALITY

Paul Costa and Robert McCrae, in turn, felt that Raymond Cattell identified too many traits and Hans Eysenck too few. As a result, they used factor analysis to develop the big-five model of personality. These factors were openness (to experience), conscientiousness, extraversion, agreeableness, and neuroticism.

- Openness (to experience): curious, insightful, imaginative, structured, creative
- Conscientiousness: organized, reliable, hardworking
- Extraversion: active, energetic, affectionate
- Agreeableness: forgiving, generous, trusting
- Neuroticism: anxious, tense, vulnerable

Nuts and Bolts

A good way to remember the big-five personality factors is to think of the acronym O.C.E.A.N. O: openness to experience, C: conscientiousness, E: extraversion, A: agreeableness, and N: neuroticism.

AP Tip

You may be asked to match the correct trait theory with each of the following trait theorists: Gordon Allport, Raymond Cattell, Hans Eysenck, and Paul Costa and Robert McCrae.

EVALUATION OF THE TRAIT APPROACH

The trait theory is excellent at labeling behavior, but it doesn't explain why a person acts a certain way. As in the example mentioned earlier, a personal ad is good at describing an individual, but fails to explain why the person is caring or helpful. This perspective also does not consider how social situations could affect a person's traits. For example, would a lack of money affect whether a person is dependable? Even though the big-five model of personality is widely accepted by most personality researchers, it fails to explain why a person possesses those traits.

SOCIAL-COGNITIVE APPROACH

The social-cognitive approach explains personality by showing how conscious thoughts influence a person's actions, and vice versa. Specifically, social-cognitive theorists believed personality to be the interaction of cognitive, behavioral, and environmental factors.

Nuts and Bolts

To understand the meaning of the social-cognitive perspective, put the name of the perspective into these sentences: SOCIAL situations affect the way people think (COGNITION).

SOCIAL-COGNITIVE THEORISTS

JULIAN ROTTER

Julian Rotter believed that people's expectations shape behavior and personality. He described those expectations as either **internal or external factors** or i**nternal or external locus of control**. With internal locus of control, *a person believes he or she could control environmental influences.* For example, a person making an effort to prepare for an exam would illustrate an internal locus of control because the person can control his or her level of effort. With external locus of control, *a person believes that he or she cannot control environmental factors.* For example, no matter how hard this person prepares for the exam, he or she cannot control what types of questions will be asked.

ALBERT BANDURA

Albert Bandura believed that personality is the result of the interaction between thoughts, behavior, and environmental situations. He called the way in which these factors constantly influence each other **reciprocal determinism**. For example, environmental factors affect the way you think (cognition), which affects the way you act (behavior). A person who finds a class very interesting (environmental) will think more effectively (cognition) and act more appropriately in the class (behavioral). Another example might be to think about an AP classroom. The environment of an AP classroom tends to be more rigorous and demanding, which affects the way a student acts (behavior) and thinks (cognition).

Bandura also emphasized the importance of **self-efficacy beliefs**, *expectations that play a role in how a person behaves or acts.* For example, people with high self-efficacy will have confidence in their abilities and skills and will feel that they can effectively solve problems. Those with low self-efficacy will be far less confident of their abilities. As another example, if a student believes that he or she could be successful in an AP course, then that student is going to make a good effort. However, if a student does not think he or she will do well, he or she may quickly give up trying.

> ## AP Tip
>
> You may be asked to identify the three parts of reciprocal determinism (cognitive, behavioral, and environmental).

EVALUATION OF THE SOCIAL-COGNITIVE APPROACH

An advantage of the social-cognitive perspective is that it includes cognitive, behavioral, and environmental factors in describing personality. This perspective has been used to help understand how social circumstances influence thought processes and the way a person acts; for example, how does media violence influence children's thoughts and behavior? A disadvantage of this approach is that it does not discuss how the unconscious affects personality.

HUMANISTIC APPROACH

The humanistic approach explains personality by describing how people differ in terms of self-awareness, creativity, decision making, and responsibility. A humanistic psychologist believes that all people have an innate, or inborn, drive that promotes and directs growth. This growth process influences how a person will go about achieving his or her full potential.

HUMANISTIC THEORISTS

CARL ROGERS

Carl Rogers developed his theory of the self based on a belief that people have an **actualizing tendency,** *an innate drive that motivates a person to reach his or her full potential.* For example, many athletic coaches have commented on how hard it can be to motivate players to try their best. Some coaches have concluded that this is something that they cannot teach, that the player either is born with self-motivation or isn't. This is one example of an innate actualizing tendency.

Rogers believed that **self-concept** is *how a person perceives him- or herself.* He said that unconditional positive regard could improve the self-concept. **Unconditional positive regard** is *the acceptance of a person for who he or she is.* When you unconditionally accept someone for who they are, you are accepting that person for what he or she represents, believes in, and characteristically displays. This, in turn, leads to **congruence**, which *occurs when a person can be him- or herself and not worry about trying to impress others with false beliefs or behavior.* In other words, a person's thoughts match, or are congruent with, his actions because he knows that other people are going to accept him as he is. Congruence then leads to a healthy self-concept because the person's thoughts are validated through his behavior.

On the other hand, Rogers believed that conditional love (or conditioned positive regard) could lead to an unhealthy self-concept. This could occur if a person believed that only when certain conditions are met would she be shown approval and affection. For example, a child whose parents only show approval when she is successful in school may be more likely to lie when her parents inquire about school. In other words, this child understands that the only way to achieve approval from her parents is to meet the conditions the parents have set. Rogers believed that this understanding could lead to an unhealthy self-concept, since a person may distort the truth of who he or she is to achieve approval.

Or think of adolescents eager to impress others and gain approval of a particular group. These individuals might pretend to have had certain experiences and admire certain behaviors in order to fit in and be accepted by the group. But even if the group believes these distortions, these young people will not feel good because what they said does not reflect who they really are. In other words, their self-concept is incongruent because what they said does not match what they feel.

ABRAHAM MASLOW

Abraham Maslow believed that the way one tries to achieve **self-actualization**, *the pursuit of fulfilling and realizing one's potential*, could define personality.

According to Maslow, people may lose focus of the pursuit of self-actualization because they strive for materialistic, meaningless goals. He referred to this as "deficiency orientation." "Growth orientation," according to Maslow, occurs when people focus on what they have, how they perform, and the importance of their achievements.

Nuts and Bolts

 To differentiate between deficiency and growth orientation, think about what people stress to measure achievement. A person who emphasizes how you play the game would exhibit growth orientation. On the other hand, a person who believes that it is not how you play the game that is important, but whether you win or lose, would be showing deficiency orientation.

AP Tip

Be prepared to identify self-actualization as the highest level of Maslow's hierarchy of needs.

EVALUATION OF THE HUMANISTIC PERSPECTIVE

The humanistic perspective sees people as unique; this uniqueness is based on the importance they place on events and situations. However, many researchers believe that the humanistic perspective is too naïve and optimistic. Researchers have a hard time believing that each person is inherently good, as held by the humanistic perspective. In addition, critics have noted that the humanistic perspective does not factor in the role played by the situation. For example, if people are all inherently good, as the humanistic perspective states, then why do some commit crimes and blame it on their surroundings and situations?

ASSESSING PERSONALITY

Personality researchers will often use personality tests to gather information. These tests tend to be a better assessment tool than interviews, in which subjects often distort their answers in the presence of a researcher. In addition, interviews can be time-consuming and expensive. Personality tests are standardized, which improves validity, and are easy to administer and score, which saves time. Personality tests are either objective or subjective.

Type of Test	Format	Advantage	Disadvantage	Example
Objective	Multiple-choice, true-false	Questions can be machine scored; saves time and money; ensures reliability. 　A score for each test can be interpreted by the test-giver, providing a label that people can understand.	People can fake responses to answer in a way that is influenced by how they think they should answer. 　Some people may rush through the questions without considering each alternative. 　People may not understand the questions, or may feel the answers don't describe them. 　There may be cultural bias if questions and answers are universal and not culturally specific.	NEO-PI: measures the big-five personality traits MMPI: (Minnesota Multiphasic Personality Inventory): the most widely used personality tests/ 500 true-false questions/ originally designed to measure mental health and detect psychological problems
Projective	Unstructured stimuli that are subjectively scored, based on personal inter-pretation	The psychodynamic approach uses projective per-sonality tests be-cause vague stimuli tend to reveal contents of the unconscious. 　Researchers be-lieve that the ambiguity of vague stimuli make it hard for a person to hide true responses because the individual does not know what the re-searcher is asking.	Researcher's subjective inter-pretation may not describe the individual taking the test. 　Tests are not re-liable because an individual taking the test may interpret pictures or images differently from one viewing to the next.	Thematic Apper-ception Test (TAT), developed by Henry Murray and Christina Morgan, uses picture scenes to measure a per-son's need for achievement. Rorschach Inkblot Test, developed by Hermann Rorschach, instructs a person to respond to what he or she sees in various inkblots.

AP Tip

Be prepared to provide examples of objective and projective personality tests and to explain the advantages of each test.

APPLICATION OF PERSONALITY TESTS

Personality tests are administered for a variety of reasons. Industrial/organizational psychologists, who try to improve work conditions by improving the ways businesses operate and by placing people in jobs that fit their personalities, use such tests to make predictions about potential employees. Sometimes personality tests can be misleading. For example, when a potential employee distorts answers that predict work performance, this distortion is often revealed when the person starts work. In short, personality tests can help employers find the right employee, but actual experience is what truly measures a person's potential and quality.

Multiple-Choice Questions

1. Personality is defined as
    (A) infrequent and often omitted behavior
    (B) a unique and consistent pattern of thinking, feeling, and acting
    (C) a universally accepted way of viewing behavior
    (D) a perception based on past experiences and viewpoints
    (E) something that happens by chance

2. Which of the following discovered that not all disorders could be explained through physical causes?
    (A) Gordon Allport
    (B) Raymond Cattell
    (C) B.F. Skinner
    (D) Sigmund Freud
    (E) Carl Rogers

3. Sigmund Freud believed that a person's thoughts, feelings, and behavior are determined by
    (A) various unconscious influences
    (B) the interaction of thoughts, feelings, and behaviors
    (C) central and secondary traits
    (D) self-actualization
    (E) secondary traits

4. A baby cries in the middle of the night and demands immediate gratification from his or her caregiver. Freud would suggest that this child's immediate gratification is based on the
    (A) reality principle
    (B) pleasure principle
    (C) actualizing tendency
    (D) moral principle
    (E) inferiority complex

5. Suzy was tempted to cheat on her exam, but quickly remembered that cheating is wrong and immoral. Freud would say that the thought that cheating was wrong came from the
   (A) ego
   (B) id
   (C) superego
   (D) collective unconscious
   (E) unconditional positive regard she received as a child

6. Will received an "F" on his exam. He quickly pointed out to fellow classmates that the exam questions were not covered on the review and that the teacher had not indicated that they would be included in the exam. Will is exhibiting which type of defense mechanism?
   (A) Compensation
   (B) Displacement
   (C) Sublimation
   (D) Rationalization
   (E) Regression

7. During which psychosexual stage does a boy develop strong sexual desires for his mother?
   (A) Anal stage
   (B) Oral stage
   (C) Genital stage
   (D) Phallic stage
   (E) Latency stage

8. Stan is the youngest in a very competitive family. As a result, Stan often does not get attention or succeed in family activities. Stan's classmates have noticed that he strives to win at all classroom activities. Which neo-Freudian would state that Stan's competitiveness is in response to his childhood experience?
   (A) Carl Jung
   (B) Karen Horney
   (C) Alfred Adler
   (D) Erik Erikson
   (E) Carl Rogers

9. Everyone who knows him describes Tom as a caring person. No matter what the situation, he is always there to offer support to those who need it. According to Gordon Allport, Tom's display of caring would be an example of what trait?
   (A) Stable
   (B) Central
   (C) Secondary
   (D) Aggressive
   (E) Loving

10. A mathematical formula that is used to describe the relationships among traits is called
    (A) factor analysis
    (B) case study
    (C) naturalistic observation
    (D) correlation study
    (E) survey

11. The big-five traits are conscientiousness, extraversion, agreeableness, neuroticism, and
    (A) optimism
    (B) pessimism
    (C) openness to experience
    (D) happiness
    (E) self-actualization

12. According to Albert Bandura, reciprocal determinism is the combination of thinking, behavior, and
    (A) environment
    (B) verbal skills
    (C) stability
    (D) optimism
    (E) conditions

13. Carl Rogers said that the _____ is (are) an innate drive that motivates all human behavior toward growth.
    (A) unconscious
    (B) central traits
    (C) actualizing tendency
    (D) wish fulfillment
    (E) ego

14. Jane was asked to look at a series of ambiguous pictures and describe what she saw. This would be an example of which type of personality test?
    (A) Case study
    (B) Naturalistic observation
    (C) Surveys
    (D) Projective
    (E) Factored

15. The MMPI is classified as a (an)
    (A) objective test
    (B) projective test
    (C) descriptive study
    (D) interview
    (E) experiment

Free-Response Questions

1. Describe how each of the following perspectives explains personality development.
   (a) Psychodynamic perspective
   (b) Trait perspective
   (c) Social-cognitive perspective
   (d) Humanistic perspective

2. Identify the advantages and disadvantages of administering objective and projective personality tests.

Answers

MULTIPLE-CHOICE QUESTIONS

1. Answer: B. Personality is a unique pattern of thinking, feeling, and acting and is consistent in various situations (*Psychology,* 8th ed. p. 551/9th ed. p. 557).

2. Answer: D. Sigmund Freud believed that some people who displayed neurotic disorders did not have physical causes to explain their behaviors (*Psychology,* 8th ed. p. 553/9th ed. p. 558).

3. Answer: A. Freud believed that unconscious processes, the main influence on a person's thoughts and behaviors, were the underlying causes of personality (*Psychology,* 8th ed. p. 553/9th ed. p. 558).

4. Answer: B. Freud believed that the id operates according to the pleasure principle, which constantly demands gratification (*Psychology,* 8th ed. p. 553/9th ed. p. 559).

5. Answer: C. Freud defined the superego as the part of personality that tells a person what is or is not acceptable, thus serving as a moral guide (*Psychology,* 8th ed. p. 553/9th ed. p. 559).

6. Answer: D. Rationalization provides excuses that justify a wrong decision or act to reduce anxiety (*Psychology,* 8th ed. p. 554/9th ed. p. 560).

7. Answer: D. Freud believed that the Oedipus complex occurs during the phallic stage (*Psychology,* 8th ed. p. 555/9th ed. p. 561).

8. Answer: C. Alfred Adler believed that people have an innate desire to overcome childhood inferiorities in order to gain control over their lives (*Psychology,* 8th ed. p. 556/9th ed. p. 562).

9. Answer: B. Gordon Allport labeled central traits as the traits most easily noticed by others; these traits are in control of behavior in all situations (*Psychology,* 8th ed. pp. 559–560/9th ed. pp. 566–567).

10. Answer: A. Factor analysis was used by trait researchers to establish relationships and predictability among traits (*Psychology*, 8th ed. p. 560/9th ed. p. 567).

11. Answer: C. Openness to experience is the part of the big-five model. This dimension is described as curious, imaginative, and original (*Psychology*, 8th ed. p. 561/9th ed. p. 567).

12. Answer: A. Albert Bandura believed that personality emerges through a combination of thinking, behavior, and environment (*Psychology*, 8th ed. p. 568/9th ed. p. 575).

13. Answer: C. Carl Rogers believed that people have an actualizing tendency that is an innate drive that guides behavior resulting in personality (*Psychology*, 8th ed. p. 572/9th ed. p. 578).

14. Answer: D. In projective tests subjects look at vague stimuli and report their feelings and thoughts (*Psychology*, 8th ed. p. 582/9th ed. p. 586).

15. Answer: A. The MMPI is the most commonly used objective test (*Psychology*, 8th ed. p. 581/9th ed. p. 588).

FREE-RESPONSE QUESTIONS

1. (a) The psychodynamic perspective holds that personality is the result of unconscious interactions expressed through the development of the id, the ego, and the superego. This perspective also emphasizes that personality development occurs through five psychosexual stages.

   (b) The trait perspective describes personality as a combination of traits that people display consistently and through various situations. Traits are helpful for predicting certain behaviors that describe personality.

   (c) The social-cognitive perspective's approach is based on personality being the result of thinking and behavior that is molded over time and through different social experiences. Personality development comes from interaction among people and the experiences of different social situations.

   (d) The humanistic perspective suggests that an innate drive toward growth affects motivation and shapes personality. This is based on uniqueness, self-awareness, creativity, independent decision making, and self-responsibility. A person's unique perceptions of the world and points of interest and importance guide personality development.

2. The advantages of objective tests are as follows: They can be given to many people at the same time and can be machine scored. These tests can save time and money, and are very reliable. There is one correct answer for each question, which allows conclusions to be drawn and then compared to other people's responses to draw inferences. One disadvantage of an objective test is that sometimes

the subject detects a pattern of questions and answers the questions a certain way, thereby not giving a true indication of their personality. Also, with limited answers, a subject may feel that the answers don't describe him or her. In addition, these tests may not take cultural factors into account, thus creating inaccuracies.

An advantage of a projective test is that the ambiguous nature of the questions makes it hard for respondents to report what they think is the best answer, or the answer the researcher is looking for. Projective tests also make it difficult for people to distort their answers because each test is unstructured, allowing researchers to detect personality features that maybe overlooked or misrepresented. One disadvantage of projective tests is that they are subjectively scored, leaving much up to the scorer's interpretation. This interpretation could be biased or inaccurate, thus leading to a false score.

11

ABNORMAL PSYCHOLOGY

Psychopathology refers to *the study of the causes, symptoms, and development of psychological or mental disorders.* **Mental disorders** are *characterized by deviant, maladaptive, or harmful behaviors and disruptive patterns of thinking, feeling, and acting that cause distress and dysfunction and affect the performance of daily functions.* These disorders can also cause distress and discomfort for the people who come in contact with a person displaying a disorder. Surveys have shown that approximately sixty million Americans have at some time displayed or are currently suffering from a mental disorder, and that roughly half of all Americans can expect to experience some type of mental disorder by the time they are seventy-five. Symptoms of mental disorders tend to first be exhibited in childhood, and many affect economic, gender, and ethnic groups equally. However, researchers have determined that some of the studies that provided this information may have been flawed. For example, some surveys only asked participants about certain disorders, and may not have taken into account people who showed only minor symptoms. The occurrence of mental disorders may therefore be even greater than what those surveys reported.

AP Tip

A possible multiple-choice question may ask about the characteristics of a mental disorder in comparison to normal, "everyday" symptoms.

DEFINING ABNORMAL BEHAVIOR

Defining what is abnormal is a complex process that often cannot be accomplished from a single determinant. **Deviant behavior** *is defined as being different from the behavior of most people in a particular culture.* However, cultures define normal behavior differently. What could be considered deviant or unusual in one culture could be seen as normal, everyday behavior in another. In addition, some people who deviate from the norm may end up excelling in certain activities. For example, some athletes who spend more than the expected amount of time practicing may, in turn, play better. Nonetheless, some have concluded that abnormal behavior is synonymous with the violation of social norms. For example, some people consider individuals who do not have good hygiene abnormal. But is this abnormal behavior, or just a case of someone who has not learned proper hygiene? The problem with using social norms to ascertain whether behavior is normal or abnormal is that not every culture has the same established norms.

Statistical infrequency has been used to determine abnormal behavior, meaning that if unusual behaviors are observed infrequently, they are considered "abnormal." The problem with statistical infrequency is that people who do not conform to the standards of society, or "follow the crowd," are then labeled abnormal. People who express opinions or partake in activities that are not considered "mainstream" may be looked at skeptically by others. But are these different opinions or activities a true indication of abnormal behavior, or simple expressions of individuality?

Some believe that personal suffering could be an indication of abnormal behavior. A person who is experiencing extreme distress or discomfort may realize that he or she has a problem and that treatment is necessary. But personal suffering alone cannot determine abnormal behavior, as some people who are experiencing cognitive distortions, or lack of mental functioning, may not have the ability to realize that they are suffering.

A more accurate way of defining abnormal behavior is to examine whether the behavior impairs the person's ability to function. The *practical approach* to defining abnormal behavior examines the behavior being displayed, comparing it to the norms established in the sociocultural context and identifying the consequences associated with the behavior. This approach focuses on how a person's thoughts, feelings, and behavior affect, or interfere with, his or her home life, work, and social functioning. For example, a person who no longer is able to take care of his or her children, who cannot go to work, and who doesn't enjoy social activities is exhibiting signs that might indicate a mental disorder.

EXPLAINING PSYCHOLOGICAL DISORDERS

In the early 1800s, Philippe Pinel of France was one of the first to suggest that mental illness was not the result of demonic possession, but a sickness of the mind. Pinel's theories were reconfirmed by watching the progression of syphilis, which, if left untreated, affected the functioning of the individual's mind, causing "madness" and eventually death. Pinel's efforts and the discovery of the effects of syphilis led to the development of the medical model. The **medical model** *suggests that psychological disorders are actually sicknesses associated with specific symptoms that must be treated medically.* This in turn led to the development of hospitals whose specific intent was to provide treatment for mental disorders.

Researchers now agree that biological, psychological, and sociocultural factors contribute to the development of psychological disorders. There has been some debate about which factor contributes the most, but over time researchers have concluded that each of these factors plays a role. The **neurobiological model**, *a modern name for the medical model, suggests that psychological disorders are the result of biological factors.* This could include imbalances of bodily processes, brain abnormalities, and genetic influences. The **psychological model** *states that psychological disorders are the result of psychological processes.* This may include the interpretation of stressful events, memories from traumatic events and episodes, self-defeating attitudes and thinking patterns, and distorted perceptions. The **sociocultural model** *suggests that psychological disorders result from societal roles and expectations, environmental location, gender, age, ethnicity, and social and cultural definitions of normal and abnormal behavior.* The **biopsychosocial model** *suggests that psychological disorders are the result of the combination and interaction of biological, psychological, and sociocultural factors.*

AP Tip

Be prepared to discuss how the medical and biopsychosocial models explain mental disorders.

DIATHESIS-STRESS MODEL

The biopsychosocial model is useful in identifying factors that could contribute to a psychological disorder, but less so in determining how the interaction of such factors could lead to a psychological disorder. If a person is predisposed (biologically) to certain disorders, then what actually triggers the disorder? The **diathesis-stress approach/model** *suggests that the amount and type of stress play a crucial role in triggering genetic predispositions, which could result in psychological disorders.* For example, let's say two people are equally predisposed (genetically speaking) to depression. According to the diathesis-stress approach, the individual who lives a relatively stress-free life is far less likely to exhibit depressive symptoms than the individual who experiences an enormous amount of stress. Though they began life with the same predisposition (diathesis) for a psychological disorder, it was the amount and type of stress that determined whether they would actually experience that psychological disorder.

AP Tip

Be prepared to explain how stress could contribute to the onset of a mental disorder. Be ready to discuss the diathesis-stress approach in this explanation.

CLASSIFYING PSYCHOLOGICAL DISORDERS

In order for psychologists to study disorders, they must have a common way to classify and organize them. Studying people with similar symptoms allows psychologists to compare family histories, thinking, and behavior, which may help identify causes of a disorder. For example, if a psychologist observes self-defeating thinking patterns in the majority of depressed patients, the psychologist could identify these patterns as a symptom of depression. In 1952, the American Psychological Association published a reference book, the **Diagnostic and Statistical Manual of Mental Disorders, or DSM,** now *used by all psychologists for identifying and classifying psychological disorders.* The latest edition, DSM-IV-TR (*Diagnostic and Statistical Manual,* 4th edition, Text Revision, in use since 2000) includes new disorders and more identifiable causes and symptoms than the original DSM. The DSM-IV-TR provides common language and guidelines that are used by all psychologists to determine the nature and course of psychological disorders. If a person were diagnosed as schizophrenic by one psychologist, another psychologist, using the DSM-IV-TR, would probably also diagnose the same person as schizophrenic.

BREAKING DOWN THE DSM-IV-TR

The DSM-IV-TR was not written by a single individual, but by a group of professionals. Different viewpoints, methods, and approaches were incorporated, resulting in a thorough and comprehensive reference book. The DSM provides specific guidelines that must be met for someone to be diagnosed and labeled with a given disorder. These guidelines list factors identified through the biopsychosocial model, which provides a checklist for psychologists in determining causes of disorders. Psychologists evaluate individuals on five different dimensions represented by five axes.

Axis I	
Clinical Syndromes	**Characteristics**
Disorders displayed in infancy, childhood, and adolescence	Childhood fears, behavioral issues, bed-wetting, autistic disorder (severe impairment in social, behavioral, and language development)

| Axis I | |
Clinical Syndromes	Characteristics
Delirium, dementia, and amnestic and other cognitive disorders	Physical deterioration of the brain from either aging, disease, or drugs that leads to the inability to think straight (delirium) or loss of memory (dementia)
Substance-related disorders	Dependence on chemical substances resulting in increased tolerance, withdrawal symptoms, and impaired functioning
Schizophrenia and other psychotic disorders	Abnormalities in thinking, perception, and emotion characterized by hallucinations (inaccurate perceptions), false beliefs (delusions), and inappropriate displays of emotions
Mood disorders (affective disorders)	Severe impairments in moods, depression and overexcitement, mania
Anxiety disorders	Specific fears: phobias, unexplainable panic attacks, generalized feelings of anxiety, ritualistic thoughts and actions, obsessive-compulsive disorder, anxiety associated with memories and traumatic events, posttraumatic stress disorder
Somatoform disorder	Physical symptoms—e.g., blindness—that have no physical cause, hypochondriasis (fear of being diagnosed with an illness)
Factitious disorders	False mental disorders produced to satisfy some psychological need
Dissociative disorders	Problems of consciousness and self-identification caused by psychological factors resulting in loss of memory (amnesia), or development of more than one identity (multiple personality)
Eating disorders	Anorexia nervosa (obsession with dieting, fear of gaining weight, excessive exercise) Bulimia nervosa (binging and purging through self-induced vomiting)
Sleep disorders	Problems associated with sleep-wake cycle Insomnia (inability to fall asleep) Narcolepsy (difficulty staying awake)

Axis I	
Clinical Syndromes	**Characteristics**
Impulse control disorders	Kleptomania (compulsive gambling, stealing), pyromania (setting fires)
Adjustment disorders	Problems associated with adjusting to stressful events—divorce, financial or family problems

Axis II	**Characteristics**
Personality disorder	Behavioral patterns throughout life that the individual finds not normal and others find disturbing
Mental retardation	Individuals who have an IQ lower than 70 and who experience problems in communication, daily functions, and task performance

Axis III	**Examples**
General medical condition	Hypertension, diabetes, etc.

Axis IV	**Examples**
Psychosocial or environmental problems	Poverty, school issues, environmental stress such as crime, etc.

Axis V	**Scale**
What is the global assessment of this person's current ability to function in daily life? (aka GAF or Global Assessment of Functioning)	Based on a scale of 0–100 91–100: Superior functioning—no problems 51–60: Moderate symptoms—some difficulty functioning 1–10: Danger of hurting self or others—inability to function 0: Not enough information to score

LABELING PSYCHOLOGICAL DISORDERS

Some critics believe that labeling someone with a psychological disorder will cause more harm than good. When a person is labeled, others tend to treat him differently based on the characteristics of the label. For example, when a student is labeled a troublemaker, teachers may treat him or her differently than they do other students. Psychiatrist Thomas Szasz said a label is not the same as a description of a person. A label doesn't include the unique qualities that are often part of the description of a person. Further, people who are labeled with a certain disorder tend to act or live up or down to the expectations and characteristics of that label, which may affect their chances of improvement.

AP Tip

A multiple-choice or free-response question might ask you to explain or identify the structure, advantages, and disadvantages of the DSM-IV-TR. Be sure to identify the five axes, as well as the pros and cons associated with labeling individuals with mental disorders.

ANXIETY DISORDERS

Every person experiences the characteristics of **anxiety**: *worrying, apprehension, and increased physical arousal.* An anxious individual will have a hard time concentrating or relaxing as his or her mind is preoccupied with what is worrying him or her. In time, anxiety-causing stimuli disappear. The individual's body will then return to a relaxed state, and he or she will likely be able to concentrate on other tasks once again. However, anxiety disorders involve more extreme symptoms and do not often just disappear. **Anxiety disorders** *are characterized by extreme feelings of apprehension, which disrupt functioning, and are present for a long time.* People show that they are not able to control their emotions or responses when confronted with anxiety-provoking stimuli. Even if a person understands that the stimuli cannot cause him or her harm, he or she may be unable to relax. Lastly, and sometimes most harmfully, anxiety disorders disrupt daily functioning. A person experiencing an anxiety disorder may not be able to think clearly, take care of himself or herself, maintain relationships, or function properly at work.

TYPES OF ANXIETY DISORDERS

Type	Characteristics	Example
Phobia	Irrational fear of an object or situation that doesn't warrant such fear, resulting in avoidance of the object or situation	Specific phobia: a phobia that involves a particular fear: avoidance of animals, fear of heights (acrophobia), for example Social phobia: irrational fears related to social situations, fear of being criticized by others Agoraphobia: irrational fear of open, public places (from the Greek "agora" or central marketplace) – can lead to one's staying at home all the time
Generalized anxiety disorder	Mild anxiety not connected to any particular object or situation that tends to last for a long period of time Includes fatigue, irritability, and the belief that something terrible is going to happen	General anxiety all the time and in most situations Also referred to as free-floating anxiety
Panic disorder	Involves sudden occurrence of panic attacks: rapid heart rate, heavy breathing, dizziness, sweating, and fainting	Fear that a panic attack is going to happen, increasing the likelihood that one will occur, which can lead to agoraphobia, not leaving home
Obsessive-compulsive disorder (OCD)	Involves repetitive thoughts (obsessions) that often lead to ritualistic and repetitive behaviors (compulsions)	An obsessive thought that one is contaminated with germs may lead to washing one's hands repeatedly and ritualistically (compulsion)
Posttraumatic stress disorder (PTSD)	Symptoms of anxiety in response to extreme physical or psychological trauma, causing the person to avoid any situations that resemble the trauma	Some Vietnam War veterans developed PTSD associated with the trauma from the war and have frequent memory recurrences, avoid situations and stimuli that trigger memories of the war, and experience extreme physical arousal associated with those memories Some cases of PTSD have recently been observed in soldiers returning from the war in Iraq

CAUSES OF ANXIETY DISORDERS

Biologically, most anxiety disorders run in families. People tend to be predisposed to an anxiety disorder if another family member has been diagnosed with one. Studies of twins have shown that if one identical twin develops an anxiety disorder, the other twin has an increased chance of developing one as well. Researchers have found that some people inherit predispositions that cause the autonomic nervous system to overreact to stressful stimuli.

Research has also shown that people with anxiety disorders have predispositions, which affect certain neurotransmitters in the brain. **Norepinephrine**, *a neurotransmitter linked with arousal,* tends to be overactive in people experiencing anxiety disorders. This overactivity could explain the onset of panic attacks. **Serotonin**, *a neurotransmitter involved in the regulation of sleep and mood,* shows a lack of functioning in people exhibiting anxiety disorders. Serotonin has been linked to obsessive-compulsive disorder and social phobias. **GABA**, *an inhibitory neurotransmitter,* has also been implicated in anxiety disorders. There appears to be a deficiency of this neurotransmitter in individuals diagnosed with anxiety disorders, which could account for the racing thoughts.

Psychological factors could also play a role in the onset of anxiety disorders. For example, some parents model the characteristics of anxiety disorders for their children. They may have trouble leaving the house and may be overly concerned about certain events and situations. Through *observational learning,* children, in turn, adopt this behavior. A lack of *perceived control* could lead to symptoms associated with anxiety disorders. People who don't believe they have control over certain events and situations may develop habits associated with isolation or may learn to avoid certain stimuli.

Anxiety disorders could also be the result of conditioning. Watson and Rayner demonstrated with their experiment on "Little Albert" that fear could be conditioned. Albert was conditioned to be fearful of a rat, although he originally did not have this fear. The experiment involved associating a white rat with a stimulus, a loud sound that naturally causes fear. Albert eventually developed a fear of the white rat and any stimuli that resembled a rat. Certain people experiencing anxiety disorders, especially phobias, learned their fear the way Little Albert did. These people developed fears of certain stimuli, which were just associated with, or occurred during, a traumatic experience. In other words, these associated fears were in fact conditioned or learned fears associated with something that naturally caused fear. For example, a person who was in a car accident and developed a resulting fear of driving might also associate the fear with any stimuli that coincided with the accident. This might include avoiding the same route, listening to the radio, or even wearing the same outfit worn on the day of the accident. People also tend to generalize their fears, in the way that Little Albert generalized his fear to any stimuli that resembled a white rat. In short, some people have a biological predisposition to certain anxiety disorders, but psychological factors, such as thinking and learning styles, affect the likelihood of an anxiety disorder actually developing.

SOMATOFORM DISORDERS

Somatoform disorders *occur when people experience psychological problems associated with physical symptoms that are not linked to a physical cause.*

TYPES OF SOMATOFORM DISORDERS

Type	Characteristics
Conversion disorder	Sensory and motor failure, blindness, deafness, or paralyzed limbs with no identifiable physical cause Usually first appears in childhood or adolescence, and under extreme stress Person usually does not show much concern for inoperative sensory and motor functions
Hypochondriasis	Intense feelings of having a physical illness with no justifiable cause Person believes he or she already has disease, whereas people with anxiety disorders have a fear of getting sick Very quickly seek medical treatment
Somatization disorder	People report multiple physical ailments rather than an isolated disease or condition
Pain disorder	Reported severe pain without any known physical cause

CAUSES OF SOMATOFORM DISORDERS

Early on, many children learn that special attention and privileges are granted when they are sick. This rationalization may carry over to adolescence and adulthood; they may hope that if they act sick they will get attention from others. The diathesis-stress model indicates that somatoform disorders are the result of people being overly sensitive to physical sensations, including everyday aches and pains. This usually occurs during long periods of stress.

AP Tip

Be prepared to identify the types and causes of somatoform disorders. Also, be ready to compare and contrast somatoform to other types of disorders.

DISSOCIATIVE DISORDERS

Dissociative disorders *are rare occurrences that involve sudden and mostly temporary disruptions to a person's memory, consciousness, and identity.* For anywhere ranging from a few hours to a few years, a person with a dissociative disorder may experience a loss of memory of who he or she is or where he or she has lived; certain other memories may also be temporarily lost. Limited research has been conducted on dissociative disorders, but certain observations have revealed that some memory loss and other disruptions in identity are legitimate. Controversy and differences of opinion remain among researchers concerning the origins and symptoms of dissociative disorders.

TYPES OF DISSOCIATIVE DISORDERS

Type	Characteristics
Dissociative fugue	Sudden loss of memory resulting in a new identity and moving to a new location (amnesia coupled with active flight)
	Person doesn't have recall of previous life
Dissociative amnesia	A sudden loss of memory
	Person has no recall of previous life, but does not move to a new location as with dissociative fugue
Dissociative identity disorder (DID)—formerly called multiple personality disorder	Person exhibits more than one personality that is unique by style of thinking, speaking, acting, feeling, and memories

CAUSES OF DISSOCIATIVE DISORDERS

Researchers have also suggested that some people experience memory and identity loss as the result of an episodic traumatic event the person did not want to cope with, or could not resolve. For example, severe child abuse has been implicated in the onset of dissociative disorders, particularly DID. Psychodynamic (Freudian) therapists believe that dissociative disorders develop as a result of a defense mechanism, repression, which blocks unwanted impulses and memories from entering consciousness. According to the psychodynamic perspective, a person experiencing dissociative symptoms may have created a "new person" who now acts out the unacceptable impulses and copes with the traumatic events. This, in turn, becomes a dissociative person's way of dealing with conflicts and concerns that he or she could not handle.

Social-cognitive therapists suggest that in any given situation, people act differently depending on both the circumstances and the setting of a situation. A person may become increasingly rowdy at a football game even though such behavior is not in his or her true nature. But for some people, acting like "another person" becomes extreme to the point at which others hardly recognize the individual.

Even though researchers have observed actual dissociative symptoms, questions remain. Dissociative identity disorder is fairly rare. The book and movie *Sybil*, about a woman with multiple personalities, brought multiple personality disorders into public consciousness, which in turn caused clinicians to look for symptoms in their patients. This led to a lot of possible cases of multiple personality disorder, but many were later refuted.

AP Tip

Be ready to discuss why there is controversy associated with dissociative disorders.

MOOD DISORDERS

Mood disorders, *also known as affective disorders, involve extreme mood disruptions, such as depression or mania.* Everyone experiences feelings of being depression, or ecstatic from time to time, but people with mood disorders experience mood disruptions that are not consistent with situational or circumstantial factors, and that often continue for a long time. **Depression** *can range from occasional, manageable sadness to extreme episodes of depression that require hospitalization.* Some people may feel "down" for a few days but then simply feel better, while others don't feel like getting out of bed for several days and will not improve without professional intervention.

TYPES OF DEPRESSIVE DISORDERS

Type	Characteristics
Major depressive disorder Also referred to as unipolar disorder	Person experiences extreme depression, which can last for weeks or months, during which time one or many depressive episodes are experienced; minimum of two weeks of deep depression Changes in activity level, eating habits, and hygiene that could result in rapid weight loss or gain Cognitive problems affecting focusing, remembering, or thinking

Type	Characteristics
	Person feels worthless, hopeless, or inadequate, resulting in an inability to function socially or at work
	Suicidal ideations (thoughts)
Dysthymic disorder	Less intense depression, often of longer duration than major depression
	Person lacks interest in activities, generally feels sad
	Must have depressive symptoms for a longer period than two years to be classified as dysthymic disorder

AP Tip

Be prepared to identify the differences among and symptoms of routine depression, major depression, and dysthymic depression.

BIPOLAR DISORDERS

The polar opposite of depression is **mania**, *which is characterized by extreme enthusiasm, an optimistic outlook, and an energetic state of mind.* When a person alternates between periods of depression and episodes of mania, the behavior is characterized as a bipolar disorder. Bipolar disorders can come in three different forms and vary according to intensity and duration.

TYPES OF BIPOLAR DISORDERS

Type	Characteristic
Bipolar I disorder (previously called manic depressive disorder)	Alternating between periods of deep depression, characterized by major depressive symptoms, and mania (energetic, optimistic, impulsive, has belief he or she can do anything/ polar opposite of depression)
	Brief "normal moods" between periods of depression and mania
	Rare, affecting only 1 percent of adults
	MDD coupled with mania
Bipolar II disorder	Major depressive episodes alternate with periods of **hypomania**, *less severe symptoms of mania compared to Bipolar I*
	Rare: affects only 1 percent of adults

Type	Characteristic
Cyclothymic disorder	Involves alternating periods of depression and mania, but less severe than characteristics associated with Bipolar I

Dysthymic disorder coupled with hypomania |

CAUSES OF MOOD DISORDERS

Mood disorders have been shown to run in families, especially when coupled with bipolar disorders. Researchers studied identical twins and determined that when one twin developed a mood disorder, the other twin was more likely to develop the same disorder. They have also identified a malfunction of *chromosome 13,* which is connected to the production of serotonin, as a possible cause for mood disorders. Serotonin is a neurotransmitter responsible for sleep and mood regulation.

Brain abnormalities (especially in the brain's neurotransmitter systems), endocrine systems, and lack of development in the frontal lobes, hippocampus, amygdala, and other areas of the limbic system have all been connected to mood disorders. The neurotransmitters norepinephrine, serotonin, and dopamine could possibly be linked to the development of mood disorders. Low amounts of these neurotransmitters have resulted in symptoms of depression, whereas overactivity by these neurotransmitters has led to symptoms of mania. Some depressive people have also shown a malfunction in the endocrine system. Studies have demonstrated that people experiencing depression have an excessive release of the stress hormone cortisol, which could be connected to impaired functioning of the hypothalamus and pituitary gland.

Seasonal affective disorder (SAD), *depression that is frequently associated with the darker winter months,* suggests that depression might be related to malfunctions in the body's circadian clock. This could be explained through inaccurate detection of light via the suprachiasmatic nucleus, which may in turn trigger an excessive release of the hormone melatonin, causing a person to become increasingly tired.

Biological factors are only one component of mood disorders; psychological and social factors also play a role. Negative thinking, a pessimistic viewpoint, certain personality traits, and dysfunctional family systems can all contribute to the development of mood disorders. Women have a higher chance than men of developing a mood disorder, and some researchers believe that this is because women are more likely to have experienced a traumatic event, such as child abuse or rape.

Social-cognitive therapists suggest that learned helplessness contributes to mood disorders. People blame themselves for their depression, believing there is no point in trying, thinking life is never going to get better, resulting in their giving up or, in other words, learning to be helpless.

Mood disorders have also been linked to sociological factors such as poverty, high-crime neighborhoods, domestic violence, and other stressful situations. The diathesis-stress model has studied the effects of stress on mood disorders and revealed a positive correlation, which suggests that the more stress there is, the greater the likelihood that a mood disorder will develop, especially for those with a biological predisposition.

AP Tip

A free-response question might ask you to identify the symptoms, types, and causes of mood disorders. Also, be prepared to compare and contrast with other types of disorders.

SCHIZOPHRENIA

Schizophrenia *is a severe and often debilitating disorder that involves patterns of disturbed thinking, perceptions, emotions, and behavior.* It occurs in about one to two percent of the population, and affects minority groups and men and women in equal numbers. Women tend to develop schizophrenia later in life, resulting in less severe symptoms but more effective treatment. Disadvantaged communities report more incidences of schizophrenia than do better-off areas. People with a history of substance abuse problems have a higher risk of developing schizophrenia. For example, cocaine abuse affects the level of dopamine receptors, increasing the chances of schizophrenia.

SYMPTOMS OF SCHIZOPHRENIA

Schizophrenia literally means "split mind," but the term should not indicate a split personality, as characterized by dissociative identity disorder. "Split mind" refers to a splitting of normal mental processes through thought processes, perceptions, and feelings. For example, some schizophrenics might laugh at a funeral. Symptoms of schizophrenia tend to first occur in adolescence and early adulthood. The majority of schizophrenics experience a gradual increase in symptoms, with some occurrences first appearing in childhood. For others, the onset is much more rapid. Roughly 40 percent of all schizophrenics improve with treatment and are able to function well with consistent daily routines; still others may never be able to function properly, requiring hospitalization. Treatment is more effective in those who had high functioning skills, referred to as premorbid functioning, before the first symptoms of schizophrenia appeared.

AP Tip

Be prepared to discriminate between schizophrenia and dissociative disorder.

Symptoms of Schizophrenia

Symptom	Characteristic	Example
Neologisms	Using words that only have meaning to the person saying them	"Sowshost" might have meaning to a schizophrenic person, but not to others
Clang associations	Words based on double meanings or on the way the word sounds	"The snake did brake at a high rate."
Loose associations	One thought doesn't seem to be connected with another	"The car sat down and went to sleep."
Word salad	Repetition of nonmeaningful statements	"John grew the house, the bird flew upside down, and the car did flips in the driveway."
Delusions	False and distorted beliefs	Delusions of influence: the belief that one is being controlled by outside forces such as, e.g., the CIA Delusions of grandeur: exaggerated beliefs about oneself; the belief that one is godlike Delusions of persecution: belief that others are out to get him or her, someone is always following him or her
Hallucinations	False reports of perceptions	Auditory hallucinations are most common: hearing voices Hallucinations may also include seeing, smelling, or feeling things that aren't really there
Inappropriate emotions	Displayed emotions that don't coincide with the situation	Laughing at a funeral Flat affect: not displaying any emotional response to certain stimuli

CATEGORIZING SCHIZOPHRENIA

Schizophrenics are categorized according to the symptoms they display. **Positive symptoms** *include disorganized thoughts, hallucinations, and delusions.* **Negative symptoms** *include a schizophrenic's lack of pleasure and motivation, speech skills, and expression of emotion, or flat affect.* Researchers believe that the causes of schizophrenia can be linked to the symptoms shown; this will also affect the choice of treatment. Each subtype of schizophrenia is defined based on the symptoms present.

Nuts and Bolts

To remember the difference between positive and negative symptoms, recall that positive refers to "in addition"— the addition of the symptoms of delusions, hallucinations, and disorganized thinking classify someone as schizophrenic. Connect the word "missing" with negative symptoms—schizophrenics are <u>missing</u> pleasure and motivation features, speech skills, and expression of emotion.

Schizophrenic subtype	Characteristics	Frequency
Paranoid schizophrenia	First appears around ages 25–30 Delusions of grandeur or persecution Onset often very sudden	Roughly 40 percent of all schizophrenics
Disorganized schizophrenia	Many homeless people affected Delusions Hallucinations Disorganized thinking and speech Neglected hygiene	Roughly 5 percent of all schizophrenics
Catatonic schizophrenia	Odd movements: immobility (stupor)/ unexpected bodily movements Waxy flexibility: body becomes rigid and doesn't change position for long periods	Roughly 8 percent of all schizophrenics

Schizophrenic subtype	Characteristics	Frequency
Undifferentiated schizophrenia	Doesn't fall into any category of schizophrenia because of disordered display of behavior, emotions, and thoughts	Roughly 40 percent of all schizophrenics
Residual schizophrenia	People who once had schizophrenic symptoms but are not presently experiencing or displaying symptoms	Frequency varies

CAUSES OF SCHIZOPHRENIA

Research has shown that schizophrenia runs in families. If one identical twin develops schizophrenia, the other twin has a 40 percent chance of doing so as well. Researchers believe that several genes, rather than just one, are linked to schizophrenia.

Brain abnormalities have also been linked to the development of schizophrenia, including undersized areas of the thalamus, prefrontal cortex, and other cortical areas. There may also be increased size in the ventricles, the fluid-filled spaces in the brain. Abnormalities associated with the prefrontal cortex and enlarged ventricles have been linked with the negative symptoms of schizophrenia. The brains of schizophrenics displaying positive symptoms appear normal, and researchers have concluded that excessive dopamine is connected with the positive symptoms of schizophrenia. Excessive receptor sites for the neurotransmitter dopamine have also been found in schizophrenics. By blocking dopamine via the administration of antipsychotic drugs, researchers have successfully reduced hallucinations and delusions in schizophrenics. This is commonly referred to as the "dopamine hypothesis" and is considered the most credible explanation for the onset of schizophrenia.

Researchers have also looked at the effects of prenatal viruses during the time of fetal development. A pregnant mother who experiences physical trauma or influenza may be putting the fetus at later risk of schizophrenia, especially if she herself has schizophrenia. Parental age may also be a factor for increased chances of a fetus's later developing schizophrenia. There seems to be an increased risk of schizophrenia when the father is older than 45 at the time of conception.

Dysfunctional families and extreme environmental stress may also contribute to schizophrenia. A family member who has schizophrenia shows an increased chance of severity of symptoms when surrounded by family members who are critical and negative.

Similar to the diathesis-stress model, the **vulnerability theory of schizophrenia** *suggests that schizophrenia is the result of a biological predisposition and the amount of stress one encounters.* The vulnerability to develop schizophrenia is based on the strength of the biological predisposition—for example, a person with an identical twin with schizophrenia is more vulnerable to developing it himself or herself. On the other hand, a person who has a moderate biological predisposition, such as a relative who has schizophrenia, but who experiences enormous amounts of stress could have the same chance of developing schizophrenia.

AP Tip

A free-response question might ask you to identify the symptoms, types, and causes of schizophrenia. You should also be able to compare and contrast schizophrenia to other types of disorders.

PERSONALITY DISORDERS

Personality disorders *are enduring or continuous inflexible patterns of thinking, feeling, and acting.* These disorders tend to start in childhood and continue through adolescence and adulthood. The most striking difference between personality disorders (Axis II on the DSM-IV) and clinical disorders (Axis I) is that personality disorders tend to be lifelong, pervasive, and inflexible. Individuals with personality disorders also tend to be more resistant to treatment than those with clinical disorders. Personality disorders are grouped into three clusters: odd-eccentric, dramatic-erratic, and anxious-fearful. The odd-eccentric cluster A includes paranoid, schizoid, and schizotypal personality disorders. The dramatic-erratic cluster B includes histrionic, narcissistic, borderline, and antisocial personality disorders. The anxious-fearful cluster C includes dependent, obsessive-compulsive, and avoidant personality disorders.

CLUSTER A: ODD-ECCENTRIC

Personality disorder	Characteristics
Paranoid	Distrust of others, believe people out to harm them Could react with violence to defend themselves
Schizoid	No social relationships The "hermit"
Schizotypal	Problems with either starting or maintaining relationships Odd perceptions, emotions, thoughts, and behavior

CLUSTER B: DRAMATIC- ERRATIC

Histrionic	Obsessed with being center of attention Very dramatic Emotionally shallow person
Narcissistic	Exaggerated belief that he or she is very important and has achieved much success Arrogant
Borderline	Instability of emotions, impulse control, obsessive fear of being alone, difficulty maintaining relationships and routines
Antisocial	No feelings of regard for others and their welfare Lack of conscience or remorse Most heavily studied personality disorder Sociopath and psychopath have been used to describe this disorder.

CLUSTER C: ANXIOUS-FEARFUL

Dependent	An enormous need to be taken care of Cannot make decisions Very needy
Obsessive-compulsive	Obsession with order and control Perfectionist
Avoidant	Oversensitive to criticism Does not partake in social situations

ANTISOCIAL PERSONALITY DISORDER

The antisocial personality disorder has been extensively researched for its implications and the harm it can cause others. No single gene has been identified that would account for this disorder, but research has shown increased chances when relatives have been diagnosed with antisocial personality disorder. Some behavior associated with this disorder can be traced back to early childhood. Boys who exhibit impulsivity in childhood may display aggressive behavior in adolescence. In fact, children who are diagnosed with a conduct disorder during adolescence are more likely to be diagnosed as antisocial once they reach adulthood. Research has found that people with antisocial personality disorder have reduced activity in the frontal lobe, which is responsible for planning and organization. This may explain why people with antisocial personality disorder are impulsive, not thinking things through. Sociocultural factors including a dysfunctional family, lack of positive parenting, attachment problems that appeared in early childhood, and childhood trauma could contribute to antisocial personality disorder. Living in a high-crime neighborhood or growing up in other negative circumstances can also play a role.

As with many other disorders, the biopsychosocial model suggests that biological, psychological, and environmental factors all play a role in developing antisocial personality disorder.

AP Tip

Be ready to identify the symptoms, types, and causes of personality disorders, and be prepared to compare and contrast them with other types of disorders.

PSYCHOLOGICAL DISORDERS ASSOCIATED WITH CHILDHOOD

Stress affects children differently than it does adults. Not only are children still developing physically, psychologically, and socially, but their strategies for coping with stress are not yet fully developed. Disorders often disrupt their development, which may lead to increased problems in adulthood. Two categories associated with childhood are externalizing and internalizing disorders.

Externalizing disorders *affect people in the child's environment and are linked to conduct issues.* **Conduct disorders**, *a category of externalizing disorders,* are mostly exhibited by boys who demonstrate a lack of obedience to authority figures and act aggressively. Such behavior often results in criminal activity and could then lead to antisocial personality development. With attention deficit hyperactivity disorder (ADHD), another example of an externalizing disorder, children show problems concentrating and exhibit impulsive behaviors. Children who have been diagnosed with ADHD may have problems in school both academically and socially. Research has shown that it is not simple "troublemaker" behavior, but a neurological problem. Deficiencies in the neurotransmitter dopamine, which helps the functioning of the attention system, have been observed in ADHD children. Exposures to lead and other poisons, as well as low birth weight, have been seen among children with ADHD.

Internalizing disorders *can cause children to experience depression and anxiety, and to isolate themselves socially.* An example of this category is **separation anxiety disorder**, *which is characterized by a fear of being lost, left behind, or abandoned.* Such children tend to "cling" to their parents, especially their mothers, and may experience problems adapting to school.

Pervasive developmental disorders, *also known as autistic spectrum disorders, are not categorized as externalizing or internalizing; they are characterized by children who are impaired socially and who show problems communicating.* A prevalent example of pervasive developmental disorder is autism. **Autistic children** *tend to show symptoms a few months after birth, have problems forming* attachments and communicating, and suffer severe cognitive impairments that affect concentration, learning, and social interactions with others.

Asperger's disorder, *a less severe form of autism, causes children to experience problems in social relationships; they also engage in repetitive behaviors.* These repetitive behaviors may include memorizing obscure facts such as numbers in a phone book. Overall, however, Asperger children do not show severe cognitive impairments and often are able to function independently as adults.

Research with autistic children has led to the study of mirror neurons, which are linked to the observation and perception of other people's thoughts and behaviors. Autistic children tend to show a deficit in the functioning of their mirror neurons, which may explain why they seem less interested in what others are thinking or doing.

AP Tip

A multiple-choice or free-response question might ask you to identify and explain different types of childhood disorders. Be prepared to identify the causes of each disorder.

Multiple-Choice Questions

1. Jimmy and Rich are identical twins who share a genetic predisposition for major depression. Jimmy lives a fast-paced lifestyle that involves a challenging career, travel, and not much time for rest and relaxation. Rich, on the other hand, lives a more relaxed life and enjoys a simpler lifestyle. When they turned 35, Jimmy alone showed symptoms of major depression. Which approach may explain why Jimmy, but not Rich, became depressed?
   (A) Medical model
   (B) Diathesis-stress model
   (C) Biological model
   (D) Humanistic model
   (E) Psychodynamic model

2. According to the biopsychosocial model, genetic predispositions would be an example of which factor(s)?
   (A) Biological and social
   (B) Psychological and social
   (C) Biological
   (D) Psychological
   (E) Social

3. Substance-abuse disorders would be listed on which axis in the DSM-IV-TR?
   (A) Axis I
   (B) Axis II
   (C) Axis III
   (D) Axis IV
   (E) Axis V

4. Mental retardation would be listed on which axis in the DSM-IV-TR?
   (A) Axis I
   (B) Axis II
   (C) Axis III
   (D) Axis IV
   (E) Axis V

5. A phobia is
   (A) a repetitive thought followed by a compulsive act
   (B) free-floating anxiety that is displayed in many situations
   (C) a delusional belief that impairs reality
   (D) an inaccurate perception
   (E) an unjustified, irrational fear

6. Sally says she experiences anxiety throughout the day. She has no idea why, and lately it has become more persistent. Sally most likely would be diagnosed with
   (A) a phobia
   (B) obsessive-compulsive disorder
   (C) post-traumatic stress disorder
   (D) generalized anxiety disorder
   (E) schizophrenia

7. Luke experienced a sudden loss of memory that resulted in his forming a new identity, traveling to a new location and beginning a new life with no memory of his previous life. Luke would most likely be diagnosed with
   (A) dissociative identity disorder
   (B) dissociative amnesia
   (C) dissociative fugue
   (D) schizophrenia
   (E) generalized anxiety disorder

8. Dysthymic disorder is characterized by
   (A) major depression, including loss of appetite, feelings of worthlessness, and difficulty functioning at home and at work
   (B) fluctuations between periods of major depression and extreme feelings of euphoria
   (C) delusions and hallucinations
   (D) mild depression that persists for more than two years
   (E) irrational fears with no justifiable cause

9. One difference between bipolar I and bipolar II disorders is that bipolar II disorder includes
(A) a longer period of mania
(B) more severe periods of mania
(C) less severe periods of mania
(D) shorter periods of mania
(E) no periods of mania

10. A problem on chromosome _____ seems to be connected with the production of serotonin, which may be linked to the development of mood disorders.
(A) 13
(B) 12
(C) 14
(D) 8
(E) 7

11. "Split mind," used to describe schizophrenia, refers to
(A) anxiety-arousing thoughts
(B) multiple personalities
(C) disorganized thinking patterns
(D) an inability to function properly
(E) catatonic behavior

12. James believes that he is God and that he therefore has tremendous powers. This would be an example of which characteristic of schizophrenia?
(A) Delusions of grandeur
(B) Delusions of persecution
(C) Clang associations
(D) Hallucinations
(E) Flat affect

13. A type of schizophrenia that is characterized by total immobility and the holding of the body in a fixed position for a long period of time, referred to as waxy flexibility, is _____ schizophrenia.
(A) paranoid
(B) disorganized
(C) undifferentiated
(D) residual
(E) catatonic

14. Excessive receptors of the neurotransmitter _____ have been linked to the development of schizophrenia.
(A) serotonin
(B) GABA
(C) dopamine
(D) glutamate
(E) norepinephrine

15. _____ personality disorder is characterized by an excessive need to be taken care of, difficulty making decisions, and clinging behavior.
    (A) Histrionic
    (B) Antisocial
    (C) Narcissistic
    (D) Dependent
    (E) Obsessive-compulsive

Free-Response Questions

1. Identify the advantages and disadvantages of labeling with psychological disorders. Provide examples that support your response.

2. Explain how the following factors could play a part in the development of schizophrenia.
   a. neurotransmission
   b. brain structure
   c. pregnancy
   d. the environment

Answers

MULTIPLE-CHOICE QUESTIONS

1. Answer: B. The diathesis-stress model suggests that the type and amount of stress play a role in the development of a psychological disorder (*Psychology*, 8th ed. pp. 595–596/9th ed. p. 602).

2. Answer: C. Genetic predispositions, which can affect neural communication, brain anatomy, and the nervous system, are associated with the biological component of the biopsychosocial model (*Psychology*, 8th ed. p. 592/9th ed. pp. 599–600).

3. Answer: A. Substance-abuse disorders would be classified, along with other clinical syndromes, on Axis I (*Psychology*, 8th ed. p. 598/9th ed. p. 605).

4. Answer: B. Personality disorders and mental retardation are listed on Axis II of the DSM-IV-TR (*Psychology*, 8th ed. p. 598/9th ed. p. 605).

5. Answer: E. Phobias are irrational fears that do not warrant a reaction to such intense fear (*Psychology*, 8th ed. pp. 603–604/9th ed. p. 610).

6. Answer: D. Generalized anxiety disorder is characterized by generalized anxiety that accompanies many seemingly unrelated situations and circumstances (*Psychology*, 8th ed. p. 605/9th ed. p. 611).

7. Answer: C. Dissociative fugue is characterized by loss of memory, formation of a new identity, and relocation to a new environment (*Psychology*, 8th ed. p. 612/9th ed. p. 618).

8. Answer: D. Dysthymic disorder is a mood disorder that does not include the extreme characteristics of major depression and tends to last more than two years (*Psychology*, 8th ed. p. 615/9th ed. p. 621).

9. Answer: C. Bipolar II disorder includes less severe periods of mania, referred to as hypomania. Both disorders are characterized by periods of deep depression (MDD) (*Psychology*, 8th ed. p. 617/9th ed. p. 623).

10. Answer: A. Genes associated with chromosome 13 may be linked to the development of mood disorders (*Psychology*, 8th ed. p. 618/9th ed. p. 624).

11. Answer: C. "Split mind" refers to the splitting of thought processes that resemble the disorganized thinking characteristic of schizophrenia (*Psychology*, 8th ed. p. 622/9th ed. pp. 627–628).

12. Answer: A. Delusions of grandeur are a characteristic of schizophrenia that include the belief that one is more important than he or she really is (*Psychology*, 8th ed. p. 607/9th ed. p. 628).

13. Answer: E. Catatonic schizophrenia is characterized by a stupor that represents total immobility and a waxy flexibility in which the individual experiences bodily rigidity (*Psychology*, 8th ed. p. 624/9th ed. p. 630).

14. Answer: C. Excessive dopamine receptors have been linked to the development of schizophrenia. This is referred to as the "dopamine hypothesis" (*Psychology*, 8th ed. p. 626/9th ed. pp. 631–632).

15. Answer: D. Dependent personality disorder is characterized by clinging behavior, a hard time making decisions, and an excessive need to be taken care of (*Psychology*, 8th ed. p. 629/9th ed. p. 634).

FREE-RESPONSE QUESTIONS

1. An advantage of labeling people with psychological disorders is that it helps in the preparation and provision of treatment. If a person is identified and labeled with a certain disorder, than psychologists can compare this person's behavior to that of others who have had similar symptoms, shedding some insight on the causes and helping them select a better method of treatment.

   A disadvantage of providing a label would be that other people might treat the person differently knowing he or she has a psychological disorder. In addition, a person who is labeled with a certain psychological disorder might feel the need to act according to the characteristics of that disorder. In other words, a tentative diagnosis could become a self-fulfilling prophecy.

2. a. Excessive dopamine receptors may contribute to schizophrenia.

   b. Schizophrenics tend to have an undersized thalamus and/or prefrontal cortex, and larger than normal fluid-filled spaces in the brain, ventricles.

   c. If a mother, especially one who has schizophrenia, develops a prenatal virus during pregnancy, the chances that the fetus will develop schizophrenia later in life increase.

   d. Schizophrenics who live in families that are highly critical, disorganized, and not supportive may suffer a more severe version of the disorder. Environmental stress also increases the chances that schizophrenia will develop.

12

METHODS OF THERAPY

The different types of psychological disorders—each with different symptoms—require different therapeutic approaches. Psychotherapy and biomedical therapy are two major types of therapy. **Psychotherapy** *is based on the interaction between a trained therapist, using psychological techniques, and a client, who is experiencing emotional, behavioral, or interpersonal problems.* Psychotherapists usually have a Ph.D. in clinical or counseling psychology and are trained in the techniques of psychotherapy. **Biomedical therapies** *use medications, electroconvulsive therapy, or other medical procedures that directly affect the brain and nervous system of a patient experiencing symptoms associated with a psychological disorder.* Psychiatrists have a medical degree, which allows them to prescribe medication, and have had extensive training in a specialty area. Clinical social workers, substance abuse therapists, and marriage and family counselors are some of the other professionals trained to treat mental-health patients.

The **eclectic approach** *involves using a variety of therapeutic techniques based on the symptoms and needs of the client.* The focus among the different types of therapists is to help clients cope with symptoms associated with the disorder. This may require changing the way a client thinks or behaves.

PSYCHODYNAMIC PSYCHOTHERAPY

Sigmund Freud established the psychodynamic approach to understand the causes of psychological disorders. He was interested in why some of his patients, who were experiencing blindness, paralysis, or other symptoms, had no presenting physical causes. When Freud interviewed those patients, he was astounded by how many reported traumatic childhood episodes. Freud concluded that these conflicts, which occurred during early childhood, would later affect the individual as an adult. He believed that unresolved conflicts, which originated in early childhood, become repressed, or pushed back, into

289

the unconscious. Even though a person is unaware of the content of the unconscious, it could still affect personality development, thoughts, and behavior. Freud developed **psychoanalysis**, *a method of psychotherapy aimed at revealing and resolving conflicts that are in the unconscious*. Psychoanalysis involves only the therapist and the client. The goal is to make connections between modern problems and conflicts and events that occurred in the client's past.

Traditional psychoanalytical sessions are based on first helping the client gain insight and understanding of the conflicts in his or her unconscious. Next, clients are shown how these unconscious conflicts affect their thinking and behavior. Clients may have to meet with the analyst several times a week, over the course of several years.

A psychoanalyst relies on several techniques to reveal and resolve the unconscious. One is **free association**, *a technique that involves the client speaking freely about any topic or image that comes into his or her mind*. The client usually lies on a couch and the psychoanalyst takes notes, looking for any symbolic meaning, and asks questions from time to time to continue the dialogue. During the free association period, if a client stops talking or refuses to comment on a particular topic, the psychoanalyst suggests that the client is demonstrating resistance. **Resistance** *is when the client unconsciously tries to block the process of revealing repressed memories*. Through resistance, the psychoanalyst is able to gain insight into a possible conflict within the client's unconscious. Dream interpretation is another technique used by psychoanalysts. **Dream interpretation** *involves identifying and separating the* **manifest content**, *the portion of the dream that is consciously remembered, and the* **latent content**, *which includes impulses, wishes, and fantasies*. The latent content is of interest to the psychoanalyst because it may shed some insight into the unconscious. Psychoanalysts also pay attention to **Freudian slips**, *which are slips of the tongue, or statements accidentally made by the client, that could reveal what the client is unconsciously thinking*. Transference is perhaps the most important technique. **Transference** *occurs when the patient unconsciously responds to the therapist as though he or she were a significant person in his or her life*. The client will possibly transfer and project past unresolved conflicts from the unconscious onto the therapist, which will result in the client's actively reliving and acting out these past conflicts. This can help the psychoanalyst gain insight and also can help the client address and cope with these conflicts.

AP Tip

A multiple-choice question might ask you to identify some of the techniques associated with psychoanalysis.

CONTEMPORARY PSYCHOANALYSIS

Traditional psychoanalysis is still practiced today, but not as commonly as it once was. Many people find psychoanalysis sessions too long and expensive. The emergence of other types of therapy, along with criticisms of Freud's personality theory, led people to seek therapeutic alternatives. In response to this decline, short-term psychodynamic therapy evolved. An advantage of short-term psychodynamic therapy is that it is less expensive than traditional psychoanalysis, since it is not as time-consuming as traditional psychoanalysis. Clients are given quicker diagnoses, and are not required to continue the therapy for more than a few months. The short-term approach still dives into the conflicts of the unconscious, and uses some of the same techniques, including transference and interpretation. Another psychodynamic approach, **interpersonal therapy**, *helps clients cope with present problems and situations*. An interpersonal therapist helps clients deal with problems that have occurred since childhood, focusing on the conflicts presently facing them. This may include problems associated with work, marital issues, grieving from a loss, or handling stressful encounters and situations.

AP Tip

Be prepared to differentiate between modern approaches and traditional psychoanalysis.

HUMANISTIC PSYCHOTHERAPY

The **humanistic perspective** *emphasizes striving for and reaching human potential*. Humanists believe that people are inherently good and are motivated through a desire to grow psychologically. They believe that the most important feature is a person's **self-concept**, *a person's thoughts or perceptions of him- or herself*. Given the right psychological environment, one that will encourage growth, a person can develop a healthy self-concept and strive to reach his or her potential. Humanists believe disorders develop when a person's growth process is stopped or interfered with by an unhealthy environment, resulting in a negative self-perception. Therapy is aimed not at "curing" an individual, but at helping the individual rediscover thoughts and behavior that will further continue his or her growth process, resulting in an improved self-concept. The therapist tries to establish a therapeutic session that is accepting of the individual, making the client feel secure and comfortable to express him- or herself. Clients, in turn, establish their own thoughts and behavioral patterns.

CLIENT-CENTERED THERAPY

Carl Rogers, once a psychodynamic therapist and later a prominent humanistic therapist, was disenchanted with how formal and detached psychodynamic therapy had become and believed that the client should be more involved and help direct the therapeutic sessions. This involved the therapist not interfering, directing, or judging the client. Rogers wanted to establish a therapeutic environment that encouraged growth and self-discovery by the client. He referred to this approach as **client-centered**, or **person-centered therapy**, *therapies that rely on three guidelines provided by the therapist: unconditional positive regard, empathy, and congruence.*

Client-Centered Therapeutic Techniques	Characteristics
Unconditional positive regard	Treating the client as a valued person
	Listening to the client without being judgmental, interrupting, or expressing opinion
	Trying to accept the client's thoughts and considering the background and setting of the client's history
	Goal: the client will overcome feelings of inferiority
Empathy (active listening)	The therapist tries to see problems from the client's perspective
	Understands what the client is going through and how it is affecting his or her decision-making process
	Use of **reflection**, an example of active listening, *which repeats the client's thoughts and concerns, while adding supportive comments*
Congruence (also called genuineness)	The therapist tries to be consistent with how his or her thoughts and feelings are directed toward the client
	If a therapist does not understand a comment by the client, he or she will inquire, instead of just continuing with the session
	The therapist is open and honest with the client, which promotes trust by the client, resulting in a positive relationship

AP Tip

Be prepared to identify the therapist characteristics associated with client-centered therapy.

GESTALT THERAPY

Fritz Perls and his wife Laura developed Gestalt therapy, another version of humanistic psychotherapy. **Gestalt therapy,** influenced by Gestalt psychology, *believes that people actively process information from the environment, resulting in their own version of reality.* Their version of reality—what they are really aware of—either promotes or prevents psychological growth. For example, some people are not aware of what factors or problems surround them. In other words, they might not be aware that their marriage is suffering, or that they are projecting a negative image. The goal of Gestalt therapy is to make clients aware of their environment, present feelings, and actions. This may involve the therapist questioning what the client is saying if it doesn't match the client's actions. Positive growth can again return, when the client has a more realistic understanding of his or her environment.

In recent years, the many forms of humanistic therapies have declined in popularity. The ideals and viewpoints of Rogers are still present in many modern types of therapy, especially his emphasis on the relationship between the client and therapist.

BEHAVIOR THERAPY

Behavior therapy *proposes that psychological problems originate from learned behaviors.* Behavior therapists believe that learned behaviors that contribute to psychological problems can be unlearned. By addressing these problematic learned behaviors, the behavioral therapist can teach his or her client new, more effective learned behaviors. This type of therapy is based on the principles of the behavioral and social-cognitive approach, incorporating the ideas of John B. Watson, Ivan Pavlov, B. F. Skinner, and Albert Ellis. The process of behavioral therapy would take the approach in the following steps:

1. A behavior therapist first establishes a productive client-therapist relationship.

2. The therapist identifies negative thoughts and behavior, which may have contributed to the client's psychological problems.

3. The therapist then becomes a teacher, or mentor, demonstrating positive learning techniques, which will counteract the client's present thoughts and actions.

4. The therapist continues to monitor the client's progress, checking and reevaluating the techniques, providing helpful suggestions and words of encouragement.

There are different versions of behavioral therapy. Behavior therapy utilizes the principles of classical conditioning. Another version, behavior modification, focuses on the principles of operant conditioning, and a third type, cognitive-behavior therapy, addresses both thoughts and behaviors associated with the problem.

AP Tip

Be prepared to identify the origins of behavioral therapy, and how this type of therapy is different from psychodynamic and humanistic therapy.

BEHAVIOR TECHNIQUES EMPHASIZING CLASSICAL CONDITIONING

Ivan Pavlov demonstrated that a dog, through repeated pairings, could learn to associate the ringing of a bell with food, which would eventually result in the dog's responding—through salivation—solely to the bell. Behavioral therapists believe that association learning does not occur only between natural and unnatural stimuli, but also between stimuli and emotional reactions. For example, Watson was able to show that fears could be conditioned, as demonstrated with "Little Albert." Albert developed a fear of a rat, which he originally did not view as threatening, through repeated pairings with a loud noise, a natural fear-evoking stimulus. Albert not only developed a fear of the rat from associating it with a loud noise, but also a fear of any stimuli that resembled the rat, referred to as stimulus generalization.

Watson never tried to suppress Little Albert's fears. Psychologist Mary Cover Jones contemplated whether a learned fear could be reversed. Jones worked with a little boy named Peter, who was fearful of all furry animals, especially rabbits. Jones used a process called **counterconditioning**, *the learning of a new conditioned response that is the opposite of the original learned response*. In order to establish this new conditioned response, Jones conducted a series of steps. She brought the rabbit, in a cage, into the room, far away from Peter but visible to him. Next she gave Peter his favorite snack, milk and crackers. Jones believed that if Peter were to associate a positive feeling, from eating milk and crackers, with the established, original response of fear associated with the rabbit, that would help to counteract the fear. For about two months, Jones worked with Peter to establish this new response. Jones also used observational learning techniques to help Peter overcome his fear by having him observe other kids playing harmlessly with rabbits. Each day the rabbit was brought closer as Peter ate milk and crackers and observed others playing with rabbits. Eventually Peter was able to hold the rabbit while eating his favorite snack. Peter was able to hold the rabbit because he learned to associate the pleasant feelings of his snack with the rabbit. Jones is acknowledged as one of the first behavioral therapists because of her success with Peter. She paved the way for other behaviorists by demonstrating how counterconditioning could eliminate learned fears.

AP Tip

Be prepared to explain how the contributions of Mary Cover Jones were instrumental in the development of counterconditioning.

SYSTEMATIC DESENSITIZATION AND EXPOSURE TECHNIQUES

Joseph Wolpe developed systematic desensitization to treat phobias and other anxiety disorders. **Systematic desensitization** *involves gradual learning of a new conditioned response that will replace, or inhibit, an established maladaptive response such as fear or anxiety.* There are three progressive steps involved in this process.

1. The patient experiences progressive relaxation, the process of increasing relaxation throughout the body in the presence of a fearful stimulus, as he or she is taught to relax each muscle of his or her body.

2. The patient is then asked to identify and generate a list of all images or stimuli associated with the anxiety-provoking stimulus. The patient ranks these images and thoughts in an anxiety

hierarchy, also called a desensitization hierarchy, ranging from most to least stressful. The patient is also asked to imagine a relaxing moment, referred to as a control scene, to help him or her relax when anxiety arises.

3. The actual process of desensitization involves having the patient, while relaxed, first imagine the least stressful image on the anxiety hierarchy; then, as long as he or she is still relaxed, he or she goes to the next image. If anxiety arises at any point as the patient progresses through the anxiety hierarchy, the patient is told to think about the control scene again to relax.

Once the patient is able to reach the top of the anxiety hierarchy, the therapist will start to introduce the actual feared stimulus. If the patient doesn't exhibit fear, then he or she has acquired a new response—relaxation and comfort—instead of the original maladaptive response. Observational learning is also used to demonstrate that other people are not experiencing harm or discomfort when interacting with the feared object.

A recent application of systematic desensitization, **virtual reality graded exposure**, *allows clients to experience their fears in a controlled computerized setting without a real-world context.* Clients prefer this simulated gradual exposure because they find it prepares them for later real-world exposure.

Exposure techniques *involve direct exposure to the feared image or event.* The patient is positioned in a room face-to-face with the object he fears without the chance of escape, but the patient is never put in real danger. This process is referred to as **flooding**, *which produces constant exposure to the feared object.* After being constantly exposed to the object, the patient learns that nothing harmful will occur. Flooding is similar to going right to the highest step on the anxiety hierarchy in systematic desensitization; as a result, some people may find it too stressful, preferring a more gradual approach.

AVERSION CONDITIONING

Aversion conditioning is also based on the principles of classical conditioning. **Aversion conditioning** *involves pairing a harmful stimulus with an unpleasant stimulus, a distasteful substance.* For example, when a person takes Disulfiram (a drug used in aversion conditioning) and then consumes alcohol, he or she ends up nauseous. The purpose is to have the patient associate nausea (conditioned response) with the alcohol, which hopefully will result in him or her no longer wanting to consume alcohol. Aversion conditioning has not proved as successful as once hoped, as results have only been temporary. The popularity of aversion conditioning has declined because clients often find the process uncomfortable.

BEHAVIORAL THERAPIES THAT EMPHASIZE OPERANT CONDITIONING

Operant conditioning is the belief that behavior is shaped through followed consequences. In turn, **behavioral modification therapists** *believe that maladaptive behavior can also be modified through consequential actions.* Positive reinforcement and extinction are two operant terms that have been applied to the behavioral modification processes. Positive reinforcement is the presentation of a pleasant stimulus after a desired behavior is performed, increasing the chances of that behavior being repeated. For example, **token economies** *operate on the principles of operant conditioning, specifically using the concept of positive reinforcement.* In a token economy, a person is given a token for every desired behavior performed. The tokens can be collected and later used to buy snacks, magazines, or other desirable merchandise. Token economies are often used with severely mentally disabled individuals or in institutional settings, such as rehabilitation centers.

Extinction is another operant technique that is used to extinguish or stop a given undesirable behavior. For example, most people continue to perform an action because they are being rewarded after the behavior. A student may continue to disrupt a class because the student earns laughter and applause from other students, which reinforces the nondesired distraction. Nonreinforcement decreases the undesirable behavior by not providing the expected reinforcement. Parents are told that ignoring a child who is having temper tantrums will decrease the tantrums; showing the child a lot of attention during the tantrum will encourage further bad behavior.

Punishment, based on the premise of operant conditioning, involves the presentation of an unpleasant stimulus in response to an undesirable behavior, which reduces the chances that the behavior will be repeated. For example, if a child throws a toy in anger (undesirable behavior), the parent is told to raise his or her voice and correct the child (unpleasant stimulus).

COGNITIVE-BEHAVIOR THERAPY

Behavioral therapists understand that causes of many disorders are linked to different styles of thinking. **Cognitive behavioral therapy** *utilizes learning principles to change people's negative thought patterns.* When an individual is made aware of certain thoughts that cause him or her to act a certain way, his or her behavior then can be modified so it is more productive. In other words, clients are taught that thoughts are responsible for negative and positive actions.

RATIONAL-EMOTIVE BEHAVIOR THERAPY

Albert Ellis developed **rational-emotive behavior therapy (REBT)**, *based on his belief that distorted expectations and irrational beliefs contribute to psychological disorders.* He said that individuals are under the belief that external events are responsible for how they feel. However, he stated that it is not the external events, but the interpretation of such events, that leads to feelings of despair. This view is explained to clients through the "ABC" model: A = activating event, B = belief, C = Consequences.

ABC Model	Example
Activating Event (A)	The individual can't find a date for the prom.
Belief (B)	"I guess nobody likes me enough to go with me to the prom."
Consequences (C)	Feelings of depression

In this example, common sense would say that most people would attribute depression (consequence) to not finding a date for the prom (activating event). But Ellis would suggest that most people are unaware that depression (consequence) actually is the result of their believing that "nobody likes me enough to go with me to the prom." In the therapy session, Ellis, in a supportive fashion, would explain this to the client, providing him or her with other reasons why he or she doesn't have a date for the prom. For example, maybe other people assumed the person already had a date. Once Ellis was able to make the client aware of these self-defeating thinking patterns and other possible reasons for the outcome, the client would then try to use a more rational, more productive interpretation of all activating events.

Rational-emotive behavior therapy is a popular method because clients find it simple and understandable. It has been effective for people dealing with depression, phobias, and other anxiety disorders.

COGNITIVE THERAPY

Aaron T. Beck, who originally trained as a psychoanalyst, developed cognitive therapy (CT). **Cognitive therapy** *is based on the idea that people have developed cognitive distortions, distorted perceptions, and interpretations of events that contribute to psychological disorders,* *especially depression and anxiety.* He believed that clients tend to "blow out of proportion" outcomes of events. For example, a person may interpret failing a test to mean that as a result he or she will never get into college. In addition, clients tend to overpersonalize events: "Everybody is going to think I'm not smart."

Cognitive therapy is a directive approach. Clients are taught not only to identify negative thoughts, but also to actually go out and test those negative beliefs. For example, a client who believes that nobody likes him will be instructed to engage in conversations with other people. He will then be asked to report back with a log of his experiences. The therapist will build on any positive encounters, encouraging the client and showing him how he can be more successful at making friends. If the client had been unsuccessful, the therapist would address the reasons why, identifying any negative beliefs, while providing a more rational viewpoint or explanation.

AP Tip

Be prepared to explain how rational-emotive and cognitive therapy could alleviate symptoms of psychological disorders.

GROUP THERAPY

Individualized psychotherapy provides a personal relationship between client and therapist, allowing the therapist to focus his or her attention solely on the client. However, the therapist is only able to gain information based on what the client is stating. The therapist is not able to see how the client interacts with other people. **Group therapy** *allows one or more therapists to work with several people at the same time, observing social and interaction skills.* Many health clinics and therapeutic practices have a group therapy session as part of their practice. Group therapy offers several advantages. Therapists are able to work and observe interaction skills among several people (usually experiencing the same problem); it is cost effective for the group's members; and, most important, participants are able to gain support from listening and receiving advice from other members. Participants can empathize with other group members, relating to what they are going through, while also sharing, through personal revelations, what has been successful for them. Group members tend to listen more attentively, understanding that other members have experienced similar problems.

Group therapy is administered and run by a trained mental health professional, while non-health professionals tend to direct support and social groups. A therapist may recommend a social support group, in addition to group therapy, to offer further support and build client confidence. For example, some clients find comfort in the presence of others who have had the same experiences. **Family therapy** *focuses not so much on the individual as in group therapy, but on how each member of the family contributes to the family structure.* The aim of family therapy is to make each member aware of how he or she is part of the family and, in turn, how he or she may be contributing to the problem. Family members are allowed to express their concerns and opinions in a constructive and controlled setting.

Marital and couples therapy is similar to family therapy. During **marital or couples therapy** *each person is made aware of the other person's concerns and the partners discuss how they could improve the relationship.* Communication skills, intimacy, and problem-solving skills are all addressed.

AP Tip

One possible multiple-choice question might ask you to identify the advantages of group therapy.

EVALUATING PSYCHOTHERAPEUTIC APPROACHES

Clients and psychotherapists would both agree that therapy can be a positive and productive experience. Providing experimental research to nullify these opinions has been difficult. Researchers have performed **meta-analysis**, *which gathers large amounts of data from a variety of sources and then presents the data in a single report.* A meta-analysis may include a client's expectations, results, the therapist's opinions, and surveys of various people also involved in the therapeutic process. A meta-analysis may indicate whether therapy is effective, but problems may arise from gathering data dealing with different types of therapy, clients, and treatments. For example, how do you measure a client's willingness to perform in a therapeutic setting? Clients who were "pushed" into therapy, not wanting to go by themselves, may not put their best foot forward when it comes to complying with what the therapist has suggested. This obviously would affect the data of a survey.

Data, however, has provided evidence that cognitive, behavior, and interpersonal therapies have been effective for treating depression. Cognitive, behavior, and exposure therapies have been successful in treating anxiety disorders such as phobias, panic disorder, and obsessive-compulsive disorder. Cognitive-behavior therapy has proven beneficial in treating eating disorders, and behavior modification has been successful for treating bed-wetting.

AP Tip

Be prepared to compare and differentiate among the different types of psychotherapy. Be able to identify contributors, approaches, advantages, and disadvantages.

BIOMEDICAL THERAPY

Psychological disorders, which have physical causes, have been treated with drugs and other medical procedures.

Psychosurgery destroys *tissue in regions of the brain for treating psychological disorders.* Egas Moniz used a procedure called **prefrontal lobotomy**, *which involved inserting a sharp instrument into the front part of the brain and moving it from side to side, severing neural connections between the prefrontal cortex and the rest of the brain.* It was thought that severing these connections would reduce the emotional responses that resulted from increased activity in the frontal cortex. For a period during the 1940s and 1950s, prefrontal lobotomies became routine for treating schizophrenia, depression, and anxiety. Today, psychosurgery is considered risky, often producing side effects that are irreversible; as a result, psychosurgery is rarely practiced.

Electroconvulsive therapy (ECT) *is used for depressive patients who didn't respond to drug treatments; a brief electrical shock was thought to stimulate and increase neural activity in the brain, alleviating symptoms of depression and schizophrenia.* ECT is a risky procedure that sometimes produces memory loss, seizures, speech disorders, and confusion. Another problem associated with ECT is that patients almost always have a relapse. Therapists have tried to improve ECT methods by giving the patient an anesthetic and muscle relaxant to prevent discomfort and to prevent bones from possibly fracturing. The duration of the shock also does not last as long as it used to. ECT is not used as much now—only for severe depression, and then it is usually followed immediately with medication. Nobody is quite sure how ECT works, but in some cases it has been successful, especially when combined with medication.

PSYCHOACTIVE DRUGS

The emergence and increased use of psychoactive drugs has become the most popular biomedical type of therapy. Psychoactive drugs are especially effective for people who have physical and psychological causes associated with their disorder.

NEUROLEPTICS

Neuroleptics, or antipsychotics, *have been used to treat psychotic symptoms related to the positive symptoms of schizophrenia such as hallucinations, delusions, disordered thinking, and confused speech.* Chlorpromazine (thorazine in the United States) and haloperidol are two of the most widely used antipsychotic medications. Haloperidol is similar to chlorpromazine, but does not produce as much sleepiness. Patients taking these drugs have shown improvements, but also experience negative side effects, complaining of dry mouth and dizziness. Other side effects resemble Parkinson's disease and include muscle problems, tremors, agitation, and slowed movement. Some of these side effects could be treated with other medications, but patients who took chlorpromazine and haloperidol for a number of years experienced **tardive dyskinesia**, *an irreversible movement disorder characterized by uncontrollable repetitive actions that involve facial twitching and rapid movements of the arms and legs.*

The newer generation of antipsychotic drugs (also called atypical neuroleptics) causes fewer movement disorders. Clozapine (clozaril) is an example of these newer antipsychotic drugs. Clozapine has been successful for those who did not respond to chlorpromazine and haloperidol. Clozapine has been proven to be successful for controlling the negative symptoms of schizophrenia, such as social withdrawal and lack of emotion. One concern with clozapine is that it may cause a fatal blood disease called agranulocytosis. Use of this medication requires weekly blood tests, which patients may find cost prohibitive.

Lately other atypical neuroleptics including Risperdal, Zyprexa, and Seroquel, which have fewer side effects than clozapine, have been introduced. They also treat the negative symptoms and are effective in controlling the positive symptoms, as clozapine does.

ANTIDEPRESSANTS

Antidepressants, *prescribed to treat depression, increase the amount of the neurotransmitters norepinephrine and serotonin.* Even though these neurotransmitters are quickly increased, people using antidepressants often don't notice improvements for several weeks. The first generation of antidepressants consisted of tricyclics and MAO inhibitors, which immediately affected the production of norepinephrine and serotonin. These drugs were available for several years, but negative side effects included dizziness, dry mouth, and weight gain. In addition, because these drugs affect the cardiovascular system, an overdose could prove fatal.

Second-generation antidepressants, including trazodone and bupropion, produced fewer side effects. Even though these drugs were different from first-generation antidepressants, they were not as effective and the side effects—though fewer—were similar.

The third group of antidepressants has proven more successful. Referred to as **selective serotonin reuptake inbibitors (SSRIs),** *these drugs do not act on multiple neurological pathways, focusing only on serotonin.* SSRIs block the reuptake of serotonin, allowing this neurotransmiter to remain in the synapses, increasing the chances that serotonin will be more available the next time the neuron fires. The resulting increase in serotonin alleviates the symptoms associated with depression. Prozac was one of the first SSRIs to be released; it was quickly followed by the similar drugs Zoloft and Paxil. Prozac is no more effective than the original tricyclics or MAO inhibitors, but has proven to have fewer side effects.

Since the SSRIs, new antidepressant medications, called **dual action antidepressants,** have been released. These newer drugs affect serotonin and norepinephrine levels, but have proven to have more side effects then the original SSRIs.

ANTIANXIETY MEDICATIONS

Antianxiety medications, also referred to as anxiolytics, *are prescribed to help people deal with anxiety.* The most popular types of antianxiety medication are the benzodiazepines, which include Valium and Xanax. These drugs reduce the symptoms of anxiety, nervousness, and sleeping problems by increasing the level of the neurotransmitter GABA. GABA inhibits nerve impulses in the brain, and when released reduces the symptoms of anxiety. Benzodiazepines, like other drugs, have side effects, including reduced coordination, alertness, and reaction time. The drug can also be intensified if combined with alcohol, which could result in death. In addition, these drugs are highly addictive; doctors have to strictly monitor how many prescriptions are being written for them.

A newer antianxiety drug, <u>BuSpar</u>, has fewer side effects. BuSpar still relieves symptoms of anxiety, but doesn't affect alertness. However, BuSpar must be taken for at least a couple of weeks before symptoms are alleviated.

LITHIUM

Lithium *is used to treat bipolar disorder. Lithium is a naturally produced substance that affects both the manic and the depressive symptoms of bipolar disorder.* Lithium first alleviates manic episodes, and then, when taken over time, can prevent reoccurrences of both mania and depression. Lithium levels in the blood must be closely monitored. If lithium levels are too low, manic and depressive episodes could return; if too high, vomiting and muscle weakness could result. Lithium has been effective in controlling the levels of the neurotransmitter glutamate, which produces excitatory effects on the brain. Lithium helps to keep glutamate levels within a normal range.

For people who don't respond to lithium, <u>Depakote</u>, an anticonvulsant medication originally used to prevent seizures, has proven a successful alternative.

AP Tip

A possible multiple-choice question might ask you to match a specific drug with the correct category. For example, valium: antianxiety/ Paxil: antidepressant.

EVALUATING DRUG TREATMENTS

Drug treatments have had success in the management of psychological disorders. However, critics have pointed out several concerns. Even though some psychological disorders have associated physical symptoms, drugs may simply mask the problem without curing it, which some patients believe has happened. Critics are also concerned that some psychiatrists overprescribe these medications. Drugs may be prescribed to people who, even though they may feel sad, may not so urgently need to be put on drug treatments. Side effects are also a risk. Some people may experience minor side effects, while others may have permanent effects, like tardive dyskinesia. Perhaps most important, drugs can cause dependency. Some drugs are psychologically addictive because they do alleviate negative symptoms and improve quality of life. Patients may develop a dependency based on the belief that without the drug they will relapse back to the way they felt before.

Doctors need to provide information to the patient that warns about any possible side effects, what he or she should expect when first taking the drug, and any possibility of addiction.

AP Tip

One free-response question might ask you to identify the criticisms associated with biomedical therapy.

COMMUNITY PSYCHOLOGY

There was a growing concern that individuals were not benefiting from being kept in mental hospitals. This led to **deinstitutionalization,** *the process of releasing patients from hospitals, which in turn led to the shutting down of many mental health hospitals.* Many of these released patients became homeless. This led to **community psychology,** *a movement to decrease or prevent psychological disorders through offerings in community mental health programs.* Community psychologists try to identify symptoms in the earliest stages in hopes of preventing disorders from getting worse. In addition, they provide programs that teach positive social skills, coping strategies, and other methods to build and improve character. Community psychology has successfully addressed poverty, homelessness, substandard living situations, and generally making sure people get the help they need.

Multiple-Choice Questions

1. What type of therapist has a medical degree and therefore is able to prescribe medications?
    (A) Clinical psychologist
    (B) Social worker
    (C) Counselor
    (D) Psychiatrist
    (E) Psychiatric nurse

2. Psychoanalysis is a method of
    (A) treatment that helps patients gain an understanding and possible resolution of conflicts hidden in the unconscious that may be responsible for psychological disorders
    (B) reversing learned behaviors that are now associated with psychological disorders
    (C) developing and promoting a healthy self-concept
    (D) examining thoughts and actions connected with psychological disorders
    (E) group interaction and social skill development

3. The process in psychoanalysis in which a patient reports on whatever thoughts, memories, or concerns come to mind is called
    (A) resistance
    (B) empathy
    (C) transference
    (D) latent content
    (E) free association

4. In a psychoanalytical session, the following dialogue demonstrates which term?

   Psychoanalyst: "Why don't you tell me more about your mother?"

   Patient: "You were never there for me—why did you do the things that you did?"

   (A) Resistance
   (B) Transference
   (C) Empathy
   (D) Unconditional positive regard
   (E) Manifest content

5. Who developed client-centered therapy?
   (A) Sigmund Freud
   (B) Fritz Perls
   (C) Carl Rogers
   (D) B. F. Skinner
   (E) Albert Ellis

6. Suzy doesn't like to make speeches. Every time she gets up in front of people she starts to shake and becomes increasingly nervous. Which therapeutic perspective would explain Suzy's response as a result of negative associations?
   (A) Humanistic
   (B) Psychodynamic
   (C) Cognitive
   (D) Gestalt
   (E) Behavior

7. Who conducted the first research to use the technique of counterconditioning?
   (A) Joseph Wolpe
   (B) Mary Cover Jones
   (C) Carl Rogers
   (D) Fritz Perls
   (E) Margaret Floy Washburn

8. In certain rehabilitation centers, patients are given coupons for good behavior that later can be used to buy desirable merchandise or acquire certain privileges. This process is refereed to as
   (A) systematic desensitization
   (B) client-centered therapy
   (C) Gestalt therapy
   (D) token economies
   (E) transference

9. Facing a fear in a controlled and non-harmful manner is an example of which type of therapy?
   (A) Group therapy
   (B) Exposure therapy
   (C) Psychodynamic therapy
   (D) Client-centered therapy
   (E) Gestalt

10. What factor would Albert Ellis agree could potentially contribute
    to a psychological disorder?
    (A) Learned behaviors
    (B) Conflicts that occur within the unconscious.
    (C) A defeated self-concept.
    (D) Beliefs that surround an event.
    (E) The negative outcome of an event

11. Who would suggest that cognitive distortions or errors in logic
    that are blown out of proportion could lead to psychological
    disorders?
    (A) Sigmund Freud
    (B) Ivan Pavlov
    (C) Carl Rogers
    (D) Aaron Beck
    (E) Mary Cover Jones

12. A form of therapy that tends to be cost effective and involves
    interaction among several people is
    (A) systematic desensitization
    (B) psychodynamic therapy
    (C) client-centered therapy
    (D) Gestalt therapy
    (E) group therapy

13. Prefrontal lobotomies are an example of which type of therapy?
    (A) Psychosurgery
    (B) Electroconvulsive therapy
    (C) Psychodynamic therapy
    (D) Client-centered therapy
    (E) Behavior therapy

14. Which drug has been used as alternative to lithium for treating
    bipolar disorder?
    (A) Thorazine
    (B) Prozac
    (C) Paxil
    (D) Depakote
    (E) Valium

15. Tardive dyskinesia was associated with which type of psychoactive
    drug?
    (A) Antidepessants medications
    (B) Neuroleptics (antipsychotic medications)
    (C) Antianxiety medications
    (D) Lithium
    (E) Tranquilizers

Free-Response Questions

1. (a) Identify how each of the following therapeutic approaches would explain how psychological disorders develop.
        psychodynamic
        humanistic
        behavioral
    (b) Provide one example for each that would show how the disorders develop in accordance with the rationalization of the approach.

2. (a) Identify concerns for prescribing psychoactive drugs to treat psychological disorders.
    (b) Explain how psychiatrists should properly distribute and prescribe medications.

Answers

MULTIPLE-CHOICE QUESTIONS

1. Answer: D. A psychiatrist has a medical degree that allows him or her to prescribe medications to patients (*Psychology*, 8th ed. p. 645/9th ed. p. 652).

2. Answer A. Psychoanalysis identifies and explains possible conflicts that are present in the unconscious and might be at the root of a psychological disorder (*Psychology*, 8th ed. p. 646/9th ed. p. 653).

3. Answer: E. Free association is a psychoanalytical technique in which patients report any thoughts, memories, or concerns that come to mind (*Psychology*, 8th ed. p. 647/9th ed. p. 654).

4. Answer: B. Transference is when a patient transfers his or her feelings from earlier life experiences, which may have involved certain people, onto the therapist (*Psychology*, 8th ed. pp. 647–648/9th ed. p. 654).

5. Answer C. Carl Rogers developed client-centered therapy, which encouraged the client to become more involved in the sessions. This approach helps the client gain insight into his or her problems and their causes (*Psychology*, 8th ed. p. 650/9th ed. p. 657).

6. Answer: E. Behavioral therapy believes that psychological disorders are the result of learned associations between certain stimuli and emotional responses (*Psychology*, 8th ed. p. 653/9th ed. p. 659).

7. Answer B. Through her work with Peter and the rabbit, Mary Cover Jones was able to demonstrate that learned fears could

be counterconditioned (*this material does not appear in either textbook edition*).

8. Answer: D. Token economies involves giving tokens after a desired behavior has been displayed. The tokens can later be used to buy specific merchandise (*Psychology*, 8th ed. p. 657/9th ed. p. 662).

9. Answer: B. Exposure therapy, or flooding, involves patients coming face to face with their fears in a non-harmful manner (*Psychology*, 8th ed. p. 656/9th ed. p. 664).

10. Answer: D. Albert Ellis believed that the negative beliefs that accompany the outcome of an event are responsible for the consequences associated with psychological disorders (*Psychology*, 8th ed. pp. 658–659/9th ed. pp. 665–666).

11. Answer: D. Aaron Beck developed cognitive therapy based on his belief that symptoms associated with psychological disorders, especially depression, could be traced to cognitive distortions that misinterpret events (*Psychology*, 8th ed. pp. 659–660/9th ed. p. 666).

12. Answer: E. Group therapy involves interaction among many people assembled in a setting that encourages sharing and revealing solutions to solve individual problems (*Psychology*, 8th ed. p. 661/9th ed. pp. 667–668).

13. Answer: A. Prefrontal lobotomies are an example of psychosurgery, where neural connections in the frontal lobe were severed to reduce emotional responses (*Psychology*, 8th ed. p. 675/9th ed. p. 682).

14. Answer: D. Depakote has been used as alternative to lithium when lithium has been not been effective in treating bipolar disorder (*Psychology*, 8th ed. p. 679/9th ed. p. 685).

15. Answer: B. Tardive dyskinesia, a condition that resembles Parkinson's disease and produces muscle problems, was one possible side effect of neuroleptics, the first antipsychotic medications to be released (*Psychology*, 8th ed. p. 675/9th ed. p. 683).

FREE-RESPONSE QUESTIONS

1. (a) Proponents of the psychodynamic approach believe that psychological disorders originated from conflicts that occurred during early childhood and were kept in the unconscious.

   The humanistic approach's adherents stress that an unhealthy self-concept affected by a blocked or stopped growth process could contribute to a psychological disorder.

   Psychologists who follow the behavioral approach believe that psychological disorders were the result of negative learned behaviors that were responsible for certain undesirable emotional responses.

(b) Psychodynamic: A child who has suffered a traumatic event may repress or block the event from entering his or her consciousness, resulting in the memory being filed in the unconscious and leading to future problems in thinking and acting.

Humanistic: A person who believes that he or she is not a worthy person develops a negative self-concept, which affects the way he or she pursues goals and often leads to a self-defeating attitude.

Behavioral: A person who has a bad experience may develop anxiety, which then leads to any repeat of that experience resulting in anxiety.

2. (a) People who are prescribed medications to treat the physical causes associated with certain psychological disorders may be thinking that the drugs have cured them, when in fact the drugs are just controlling the symptoms of the disorder. This may lead to the understanding that without the drug a person is not able to experience positive feelings and actions. This could lead to addiction. Side effects are another major concern. Certain drugs are associated with side effects and often either the patient cannot tolerate them or must use other medications to treat them.

(b) Psychiatrists should prescribe medications with proper instructions that explain any possible side effects, including warnings about such possible problems as addiction, and expectations of how and why the prescribed drug is going to make them feel better. Drugs should also be accompanied by psychotherapy to help the patient figure out the proper methods to deal with symptoms associated with the given disorder.

13

SOCIAL PSYCHOLOGY

Social psychology *is the study of how our thoughts, feelings, and behaviors are influenced by the real or imagined presence and influence of others.* Social psychologists are interested in how others can affect what an individual does and how he or she thinks or feels, as well as in how that individual can, in turn, influence others.

AP Tip

Since the first AP psychology exam, one free-response question has inevitably included information from the social psychology chapter.

SOCIAL INFLUENCES ON THE SELF

Social psychologists attempt to address important ideas including **self-concept**, *one's perception of who one is,* and **self-esteem**, *how valuable one feels oneself to be.* Humans are social creatures, and typically enjoy the company of others. However, when we are with other people we often engage in **social comparison**, *comparing ourselves to those around us as a way of judging or evaluating ourselves.* When using social comparison we often judge ourselves based on our **reference group**, *people we use as a comparison to ourselves and with whom we identify most strongly.* Using our reference group to evaluate ourselves may lead to **relative deprivation**, *being denied access to what we feel we are entitled to have,* as well as a sense of inadequacy. However, not all comparison needs to take place around others; we are constantly drawing on **temporal comparisons**, *using our past experiences to judge and evaluate ourselves in the current moment.* Whether it is with our reference group or with our own past behaviors and experiences, we humans are constantly passing judgment on ourselves.

Which group an individual identifies with is an important component of who he or she is. That group is known as the **in-group**, *a group for which the individual has strong feelings of loyalty, respect, and togetherness due to a common feature.* An in-group could be your family, your sports team, or even those who listen to the same kinds of music as you. It is not uncommon for an individual to be a part of several different in-groups. Many times in-group members display **in-group bias**, *showing favoritism toward other members of the same group based on shared feelings and admiration.* The opposite of an in-group is an **out-group**, *a group of people who hold beliefs different from those of the individual and toward whom he or she feels animosity.* An example of an out-group could be a rival team or those who speak a different language. As with an in-group, it is easy for an individual to identify numerous out-groups, or groups to which he does not belong.

Self-schemas, *mental frameworks or blueprints that people have about themselves,* are different for each person. They affect the decisions we make, such as how we dress, what we pay attention to, and what and how we remember or react to another person, as well as our overall behavior. The schemas we hold of others influence our first impressions of others. When we meet a new person, we often employ the schema because we are interested in seeing whether that person will be similar to us in behaviors and thoughts. However, while talking to the person, we may begin to disagree with what he or she is saying, and we accordingly change the schema we initially held. Negative first impressions are much harder to change than positive ones. Our schemas have considerable power over those we encounter each day.

Our schemas can unknowingly influence how we treat a person. If you were told that Christina was a smart and kind young lady, you would most likely behave in a way that reflected what you had been told. The schema you have of Christina influences what you say and how you act around her. Because schemas are powerful and influential, they may lead to a **self-fulfilling prophecy**, when *a person unknowingly behaves in a manner that helps to justify or fulfill the expected outcome.*

Pygmalion Effect / Teacher-Expectancy Effect

Psychologists Robert Rosenthal and Lenore Jacobson (1968) conducted an experiment that demonstrated the power of self-fulfilling prophecies. Rosenthal and Jacobson administered a valid intelligence test to all students at a school at the beginning and the end of the year. They then convinced the elementary school to administer another test that was supposed to predict future academic success. It must be noted that the test given was not valid, nor did it contain any predictive validity; it was simply invented by the researchers for purposes of the experiment. Each teacher was given a list of names that identified which students scored in the top 20 percent of their classes. In reality, the student names that were given were simply chosen at random. Rosenthal and Jacobson observed how each teacher interacted with his or her students, and noted that those who scored in the top 20 percent on the supposed future academic success test had greater expectations placed on them. Teachers spent more time with these students, challenging them and explaining concepts. At the end of the school year, Rosenthal and Jacobson administered the valid intelligence test to see if there were any fluctuations. The results of their research indicated that those students who were in the top 20 percent showed marked gains, whereas other students suffered losses. Rosenthal and Jacobson concluded that the teachers' expectations toward the top 20 percent had caused them to unknowingly behave in a manner that would confirm those beliefs.

Nuts and Bolts

 You can apply self-fulfilling prophecies to yourself as well. If you believe that you are not good at mathematics you will avoid taking any math class, and therefore you will not get better at math. Your behavior, not taking a math class, is being influenced by your belief that you are not good at math. You are unknowingly behaving in a manner that will confirm the prophecy.

EXPLAINING BEHAVIOR

Why do people behave the way they do? Social psychologists study **attributes**, *attempts to explain why a person behaves a certain way,* as a way of understanding how and why individuals explain their own behaviors, as well as the behaviors of others.

ATTRIBUTION THEORIES

People tend to explain behavior in one of two ways: as the result of either **internal (dispositional) factors**, *behavior that is explained as the result of personal (dispositional) characteristics,* or **external (situational) factors**, *behavior that is explained as the result of unavoidable factors or factors out of one's control.* Suppose Jim and his friend are walking down the hallway when another student, whom Jim does not know, bumps into him. Jim says to his friend, "Wow, that guy doesn't know how to walk!" Jim has made an internal (dispositional) attribution by saying that the person who bumped into him doesn't know how to walk. However, if Jim said to his friend, "That guy must have been in a hurry to get to class on time," Jim would have made an external attribution. We all use attributes to explain the behaviors of others, as well as our own behaviors.

ERRORS IN ATTRIBUTION

A common attribution error that people make each day is the **fundamental attribution error (FAE)**, *the tendency to explain the behavior of others as the result of an internal or dispositional factor.* For example, imagine you are driving a car and a person cuts in front of you. In response, you honk the horn and say to yourself, "That guy can't drive!" You are making a fundamental attribution error in assuming that the reason the person cut in front of you was because he doesn't know how to drive. You are trying to explain his erratic behavior by blaming it on dispositional/internal factors. In doing so, you are ignoring any of the myriad situational factors (e.g., he is rushing to the hospital with an injured friend, or he had just been stung by a bee) that could easily account for the behavior.

However, if you suddenly swerved into the next lane because you were trying to avoid hitting a squirrel, you would know to attribute your erratic driving to the situation. Your explanation as to why you cut off the car in the next lane is the result of **actor-observer bias**, *the tendency to explain the behavior of others as the result of internal or dispositional factors while attributing your behavior to external or situational factors.*

A third common error in attribution that many people commit is known as the **self-serving bias**, the tendency to attribute success to internal or dispositional factors, while blaming any failure on external or situational factors. For example, if Ashley received an A on her psychology test, she would likely attribute it to the fact that she knew the material and had studied hard. However, if Ashley received an F on her psychology test, she might blame the grade on the fact that she had had to work late the night before the test or that the test had too many questions on material from previous chapters. Self-serving bias protects our sense of self and self-esteem.

A fourth common error in attribution is known as **unrealistic optimism**, *the belief that favorable events are more likely to occur to you than to other people.* For example, Juan believes that he is more likely than Robert to pick the winning lottery numbers.

A final common error in attribution is known as **self-handicapping**, *limiting one's potential for success by offering explanations for failure before an event even takes place.* For example, Chelsea has an important track meet that she is nervous about. During breakfast she complains to her teammate that her ankle is really hurting, and says she may not be able to run as fast as she could. Chelsea has provided an excuse for herself in case she doesn't run well at the meet. However, if Chelsea does run well, her teammates will look admiringly on her for running despite her injury.

ATTITUDES

Attitudes, *reactions to situations, events, or objects based on previous experiences with them,* affect our lives every day. Imagine a friend asks whether you like a certain band; your response would indicate your attitude toward that band. Attitudes are beliefs (cognitions), feelings (emotions/affect), and behaviors you have toward situations, events, or objects, and are relatively unchanging. (Attitudes can change, but not readily.) Attitudes are also said to predict behavior, but the correlation between attitudes and behavior is weak to moderate; this is known as the **A-B problem**, *one's attitudes do not necessarily predict future behavior.* Just because a person has a particular attitude does not mean she will behave in a manner that is consistent with that attitude. Think of an actor who has spoken out against drug use, but who has then been back in the news because he or she is going to a drug rehabilitation center to resolve an addiction.

Nuts and Bolts

 Don't confuse attitude with rudeness or anger. To say that someone is giving you "attitude" implies that the person is being rude or impolite. But if a person asks your opinion on which shoes you like best in a store window, your answer is essentially your attitude, your feelings about the shoes.

FORMING ATTITUDES

The simplest way to explain the formation of attitudes is through the lens of behaviorism. Many attitudes are formed through conditioning (classical or operant) and modeling. For example, research has shown that participants who were exposed to negative words (such as *anger, hate, fascism*) paired with a particular political party will have a negative attitude toward that party.

Nuts and Bolts

 Political ads use classical conditioning principles to help sway public opinion. By associating opponents with negative words or images, candidates generally hope to instill a negative public attitude toward them.

Many parents model their behaviors and attitudes when raising their children, trying to teach them right from wrong. Children form attitudes by imitating those around them. For example, many elementary schools hold mock presidential elections during election years. Young children do not know enough about politics to make an informed decision; therefore, they rely on what they have heard at home to formulate their attitudes toward particular politicians.

Another way in which attitudes are formed is through the **mere exposure effect**, in which *the more a person is subjected to a novel stimulus, the more he or she will grow to enjoy the stimulus*. Attitudes are often shaped by repeated exposure; this is similar to modeling in that the more one is exposed to an attitude or behavior, the more likely one is to display that exposed attitude or behavior in the future.

Nuts and Bolts

 One way to remember the mere exposure effect is to think of your favorite song or movie. Sometimes the more you hear the song or see the movie, the more you enjoy it.

CHANGING ATTITUDES

Trying to change a person's attitudes is a difficult task. However, there are ways it can be done. The first is through the **elaboration likelihood model of persuasion**, *a persuasion model offering two distinct routes to persuasion: central and peripheral*. The **central route to persuasion** *involves a careful examination of the message to determine the validity of the argument*. An example of the central route to persuasion occurs after you read an article in a magazine and consider the author's different points, trying to decide whether you agree with the article. The **peripheral route to persuasion** *involves the use of outside factors to influence the validity of the argument*. For example, many companies pay celebrities to endorse their products in television commercials. These celebrities make various claims about the products advertised. Does using a celebrity help in selling a product? Yes. When deciding what product to purchase, many people will rely on the most easily accessible information (availability heuristics) to make a decision, and if one company has used a well-known celebrity in its commercials, there is a good chance viewers will remember what the celebrity said—and will then purchase the product.

Nuts and Bolts

An easy way to remember the difference between the central and peripheral routes to persuasion is to recall that "peripheral" means off to the side, whereas "central" means in the middle. So if someone is trying to directly challenge your opinion, he will address that exact position. However, if he is using the peripheral route, he will bring up other issues that may be loosely related to the main issue as a way of getting you to change your opinion or attitude.

Another way to elicit attitude change is through **cognitive dissonance**, *discomfort resulting from conflicting cognitions and behaviors*. Every person experiences cognitive dissonance, and we all seek to reduce the discomfort that results from it. To ease this discomfort a person is more likely to change an attitude than a behavior. For example, Laura believes that people should not download songs illegally off the Internet. However, after hearing a song on the radio she immediately went online and illegally downloaded the song herself. Laura is now experiencing cognitive dissonance because her attitude is different from her behavior. To ease this, Laura convinces herself that what she has done is insignificant because it's only one song, and musical artists make a lot of money from their concerts. Laura's behavior doesn't match her attitude; therefore, she must change her attitude to reduce the discomfort she is experiencing.

Nuts and Bolts

 One of the quickest ways to change a person's attitude is to have him or her change a behavior first.

AP Tip

You should prepare for a free-response question on identifying ways to change behaviors.

PREJUDICE AND STEREOTYPES

Prejudice, *a positive or negative belief about a category of people, refers to prejudging a person because he or she belongs to a specific group.* **Stereotyping** *refers to the generalization of a particular group of people based on a preexisting concept or image; stereotyping involves generalizing an attitude toward a larger segment of the population.* **Discrimination** *is differing treatment toward a category of people.* Discrimination may involve preferential treatment of some good or service to a group of people, typically people of a different ethnicity, religion, or gender. It is important to note that both stereotyping and discrimination can occur in either a positive or a negative manner. The psychology behind prejudice, discrimination, and stereotyping is based on three main factors: motivational, cognitive, and behavioral.

Influencing factors	Definition	Example
Motivational	The belief that prejudice, stereotyping, and discrimination are the result of an underlying reason, such as self-preservation, self-identity, or in-group bias.	Jackie and her friends ridicule a fellow classmate in order to increase their own self-esteem and sense of self-importance.
Cognitive	The use of mental shortcuts (heuristics) to form an impression about a group of people.	Hank's brother wears glasses and reads; therefore, Hank believes that all people who wear glasses like to read.
Behavioral	A person models the behaviors he sees and hears at home, on television, or from his peers.	Max's parents often talk negatively about people who are of a different race. One day at school Max began calling all such students names.

REDUCING PREJUDICE

Because prejudice is often the result of misinformation or lack of contact with another group of people, psychologists have proposed numerous ways to head off prejudice, stereotyping, and discrimination. One of the more important studies on reducing prejudice was conducted by Muzafer Sherif (1954), and took place at the Robbers Cave State Park in Oklahoma. Sherif was interested in seeing how quickly 11-year-old boys could become prejudiced. Two groups, consisting of 11 boys each, were kept separate for a few days to ensure that in-group bonding took place. After a few days, the two groups were to compete for various prizes. The boys were instructed to show support for their respective teams. As the competition grew, so did the boys' ill feelings toward each other. As the feelings of prejudice increased, so, too, did the pranks, or attacks. The groups became more and more physical with each passing day, until the researchers had to separate the two groups into different locations within the state park.

Sherif had been able to successfully institute prejudice in a relatively short amount of time. The researchers now began the task of reducing the prejudice by forcing the contact of the two groups for a series of competitions. This forced contact appeared to do little to lessen the prejudice between the groups. However, Sherif then organized a series of difficult challenges that required the cooperation of all group members. After successful completion of the task, the prejudice had been reduced. The completion of a task that benefited all the boys seemed to reduce the ill feelings the members of the groups had toward each other.

CONFORMITY AND COMPLIANCE

Conformity *is a change in behavior due to real or imagined group pressure.* **Compliance** *is changing behavior due to a direct request.* The difference between conformity and compliance is that conformity occurs when a person simply goes along with the crowd without directly being told to do so, whereas compliance occurs when a person changes a behavior due to a direct request from another. Each day we are exposed to various situations that require conformity, and most of us are willing to follow along. Unwritten rules of conformity in our society are **social norms**, *implicit or explicit rules that guide daily behavior and are based on societal expectancies.* An example of a social norm occurs when riding in an elevator: an unwritten rule is to not speak to anyone and face forward. Breaking this social norm is not a crime, but you may get some looks from the other passengers if you do. To maintain social norms, **reciprocity**, *responding to a behavior with the same behavior,* is often used. For example, if a person holds the door for you, you may then reciprocate by holding the door for the person walking behind you. The behavior helps maintain social order.

Nuts and Bolts

Remember that <u>conforming</u> is done without an expressed request. For example, if you walk into a room and notice everyone is standing up, you will most likely remain standing as well, even though nobody asked you to do so. Complying is done when a person makes a direct request. For example, your teacher asks you to pass your homework to the front of the class, and you do so.

THE ASCH EXPERIMENT

In the 1950s, social psychologist Solomon Asch conducted an experiment to demonstrate the power of conformity. In the experiment, eight people were brought into a room to take part in what they were told was an experiment on visual discrimination. Of the eight participants, seven were **confederates**, *subjects unknown to the actual participants in an experiment assigned by the researcher to influence the experiment*, planted by Asch and instructed to give the wrong response. The eighth participant was in fact the only true subject. The confederates and the subject were shown a series of lines on two large cards. Card A included the standard line, and card B had three comparison lines. The participants were instructed to pick the line on card B that most closely matched the line on card A. Each participant selected and stated out loud the line on card B that most closely resembled the line on card A, with the confederates going first.

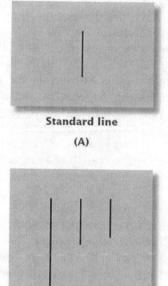

Standard line

(A)

Test lines

(B)

After numerous trials, a pattern began to emerge. The eighth participant (the real test subject) began agreeing with the obviously false line selected by the others. In all, 75 percent of the test subjects agreed with the majority's wrong answer at least once during the experiment. This experiment showed the power of conformity. Although the test subject had the ability to disagree with the other participants, he rarely did so. The test subject felt compelled to agree with the group even if he knew the answer was clearly wrong. Asch's study concluded that people will simply go along with the group, even if there were no direct orders to follow along, thus demonstrating conformity to the group.

Asch began to wonder if the size of the group determined the level of conformity. By varying the number of confederates, Asch noted that if a group was too small, subjects would not comply with it. Asch also noted that when one of the confederates dissented first, the test subject was more likely to dissent, or disagree with the group's decision on which line matched more closely. Having another dissenting voice in the group gave the test subject the courage to speak up and share his disapproval. Some critics believed that gender may influence the level of conformity. According to subsequent studies conducted by Asch, it does not; women are just as likely as men to conform to a group.

INDUCING COMPLIANCE

As mentioned earlier, in the section on persuasion, there are numerous ways to persuade a person to change his or her beliefs or attitudes. There are also a few techniques that can be used to induce compliance, including the foot-in-the-door technique (FITD), the door-in-the-face technique (DIFT), the that's-not-all technique (TNA), and low-balling.

The **foot-in-the-door technique (FITD)** *means getting a person to agree to a substantial request by first having him or her comply with a more modest request.* When an individual agrees with a small, more moderate request, he will then be more likely to comply with the larger request.

A second way to induce compliance is known as the **door-in-the-face technique (DITF)**, which is *asking for a large request first, even though you know it will be turned down, and following it with the smaller, true request.* For example, if you wanted to borrow $20 from your parents, it would be wise to ask to borrow $50, even though you know they would not comply with the request. However, following up the initial request with a more reasonable request of $20 is more likely to elicit compliance.

A third way to induce compliance is using the **that's-not-all technique (TNA)**, *offering an additional product or service to someone before presenting him or her with the actual product, thus enticing him or her by adding more options and, increasing desirability.* For example, suppose you are watching a television commercial late one evening, and the announcer proclaims, "If you act now you can get all of this, a $40 value, for only $19.95! But wait—order within the next ten minutes and we'll throw in two replacements, FREE!" The TNA technique is useful in inducing compliance because the person feels that he is getting a better bargain, but only if he acts quickly.

The final way to induce compliance is known as **low-balling**, *making a request and securing it, and then increasing the fee with hidden costs or unforeseen circumstances.* For example, when you purchase an automobile, the salesperson may quote you a price, which you agree to. Then, just before you sign the paperwork, you notice fees that had not been mentioned before. This increases the price from what you were originally quoted.

OBEDIENCE AND THE POWER OF THE SITUATION

Obedience, *agreeing to an explicit or implicit request because it came from a person of perceived authority,* is one of the ways society functions smoothly. However, in some cases obedience can result in a person behaving differently than normal. Agreeing to clean your room is not the same as agreeing to deliver a potentially fatal shock to a person, yet in both instances a majority of people will do as they are told.

Nuts and Bolts

 Remember that in order for obedience to occur, the request must come from someone of real or perceived authority. For example, if your teacher asks you to stand up, and you do, you are demonstrating obedience.

THE MILGRAM EXPERIMENTS

Social psychologist Stanley Milgram conducted one of psychology's more shocking experiments in 1963 in an effort to understand obedience. Subjects were told that they were participating in a study on punishment and memory. Two subjects were used for the experiment: one was a confederate, while the other was the real test subject. The confederate was assigned the role of "learner," while the subject was assigned the role of "teacher." The teacher watched as the learner was hooked up to a device that was supposed to deliver electrical shocks, and then was led to an adjacent room. The teacher was to administer these electrical shocks from a "shock machine" each time the learner answered incorrectly. In reality, the learner did not receive any shock, nor was the shock machine real. However, Milgram went to great lengths to create the illusion of a working shock machine.

As the experiment progressed, the teacher was instructed by another confederate, who acted as the lead researcher, to increase the intensity of the supposed shock with each wrong answer. The "shock machine" had different levers, each labeled with the amount of voltage the switch supposedly delivered. Before the teacher administered the shock, he or she was to inform the learner of the voltage amount and then quickly deliver the shock. As the experiment progressed, the learner began to express displeasure with the experiment, even explaining that he or she had a heart condition. The teacher was instructed to continue administering shocks despite the pleas. At the conclusion of the experiment, Milgram noted that 65 percent of those who participated in the study delivered the highest level stated on the "shock machine."

According to Milgram, the reason the participants delivered the highest level of shocks was because a perceived authority figure, the researcher, reassured them that they would not be held responsible for any damage that might occur to the learner. Obediently following orders from an authority figure, or someone of perceived authority, is nothing new—students in school do it each and every day. For example, when your teacher says to clear off your desks for an upcoming test, all students obey. Although your teacher is not asking you to do anything so dramatic as administer electrical shocks to a person, you do as you are told.

There are three main factors that affect obedience: the status or prestige of the person giving the order, the behavior of others in the same situation, and the personal characteristics of the individual. Each of these three contributes to whether an individual will blindly obey the orders he or she is given, no matter how strange those orders may be.

AP Tip

The concepts of obedience and compliance can be challenging, and therefore will most likely show up on the multiple-choice section of the exam.

THE POWER OF THE SITUATION

In 1971, Stanford social psychologist Philip Zimbardo conducted his infamous prison study. Zimbardo recruited 24 volunteers to serve as prisoners and guards in his prison simulation experiment. One goal of the experiment was to study the obedience levels of the prisoners. The study was supposed to take place over a span of 14 days. However, the experiment was halted after six days due to the internalization of roles by both "prisoners" and "guards." According to Zimbardo, the guards began to act in ways that degraded and humiliated the prisoners, and he couldn't justify continuing the experiment. The power of the situation and the role each person played became so ingrained in each man that they began to lose touch with reality. Zimbardo's experiment proved that the context, or situation, can and will influence the behavior of the individual.

AGGRESSION

According to psychologists, **aggression**, *any act that is intended to cause harm to another*, can be witnessed throughout the world and in all species of animals. Any time a person willingly and purposefully harms another person or animal, they can be said to be acting aggressively. What causes this behavior? Five theories have been formulated to explain aggression: psychodynamic, biological, evolutionary, behavioral-cognitive, and environmental.

INNATE AGGRESSION

According to the psychodynamic perspective proposed by Sigmund Freud, aggression is instinctive, the result of the unconscious impulses emitted by the id. Freud believed that these impulses must not be allowed to fester and build, because the resulting behavior could be troublesome. Instead, Freud suggested that the impulses should be redirected and channeled through socially acceptable means, which he referred to as **catharsis**, *the release of instinctual aggressive impulses*.

Another theory that suggests that aggression is the result of an innate drive is the biological perspective. According to biological psychologists, aggression is the result of brain structure, hormones, and genetics. As mentioned in the chapter on biological psychology, our frontal lobes play a significant role in inhibiting our behavior. Damage to the frontal lobes often results in impulsive behavior, as well as bouts of anger or aggression. Research has shown that the limbic system is said to be our emotional center and, if damaged, may lead to aggressive behavior. The hormone testosterone has been implicated in aggression as well. As testosterone levels increase, so, too, does aggression. Research on the role of genetics in aggression shows that twins reared separately display similar aggressive characteristics.

Evolutionary psychologists believe that aggression is innate, and serves to further the survival of a species. The more aggressive or defensively aggressive a species is, the greater its chances for long-term survival. The desire to survive is one of the strongest desires a species may have.

NURTURED AGGRESSION

The behavioral-cognitive theory of aggression states that aggressive acts are reinforced, thereby increasing the chances of those aggressive acts to continue. Other behaviorists, such as Albert Bandura (refer to Chapter 8), believe that aggressive behaviors are learned by observing and imitating others.

Environmental psychologists believe that aggression stems from outside factors such as temperature, pollution, and proximity of living arrangements to those of others. As the temperature rises, so does the crime rate. Inhaling pollutants may also lead to more aggressive behavior, possibly because the person is trying to remove himself from a negative situation. Psychologist John Calhoun (1963) investigated the effects of living conditions and levels of aggression in rats. Calhoun found that the more dense the living conditions, the greater the number of aggressive behaviors.

ALTRUISM AND NON-HELPING BEHAVIORS

Why does one individual help someone in distress, while another may ignore the person altogether? **Altruism**, *a genuine concern for the safety and well-being of another*, and what propels a person to commit altruistic acts, has been an area of much interest for social psychologists.

HELPING BEHAVIOR

Why would a person assist someone else? One way to explain altruistic behavior is through the **arousal cost-reward theory,** *weighing several options in order to reduce the unpleasant feeling associated with seeing a person in distress.* According to this theory, if person A sees person B in distress, person A will begin to feel anxious or unpleasant and begin weighing the costs of action against those of inaction. If person A feels that the cost associated with helping person B is relatively low, but the cost of not helping person B is also low, person A is more likely to help the person in distress. However, if the cost associated with helping person B is high, while the cost of not helping person B is low, person A is more likely *not* to help the person in distress. However, not all decisions to act are based on the arousal cost-reward theory.

The decision of whether to help sometimes comes down to whether the person feels he or she will gain some benefit in doing so. **Reciprocal altruism,** *assisting another person with the expectation that that person will repay the deed in the future,* is also known as tit-for-tat. The idea is based on the belief that if you help a person now, they will help you in your time of need—it's sometimes summarized as "If you scratch my back, I'll scratch yours." For example, if Tyler missed some meetings of his psychology class, he might ask Melanie if he could borrow her notes to look over prior to a test. If Melanie agreed on the condition that Tyler would let her do the same later if necessary, she would be likely to let Tyler borrow her notes. However, if Tyler didn't let Melanie borrow his notes to study for the next test, Melanie would be less likely to help Tyler in the future.

NON-HELPING BEHAVIOR

Seeing a person in distress doesn't always produce a helping reaction in people. In some instances, the cost of getting involved is too high. An example of non-helping behavior is known as the **bystander effect (bystander apathy),** *when the presence of others inhibits the helping behavior of an individual.* The bystander effect was first tested by Bibb Latané and John Darley in response to the lack of bystander intervention in the murder of Kitty Genovese. The Genovese murder attracted national interest when it was learned that 38 people witnessed it, yet not one of them called for help. According to Latané and Darley, the reason was simple: the larger the crowd, the less likely a person is to intervene, mainly due to the fact that the person believed that others had already called for help. In the Genovese murder, onlookers experienced what is known as **diffusion of responsibility,** *not intervening in the presence of others because the person thinks that others are going to intervene in the situation. In this kind of situation, people feel they cannot personally be held responsible because there are others around.*

Latané and Darley conducted a series of experiments to demonstrate the bystander effect and diffusion of responsibility. In those experiments, subjects were put in separate rooms and instructed to listen to the words being presented through headphones. While in their individual rooms, the experimenters had a confederate cry for help. To the surprise of the researchers, few subjects exited the rooms and came to the aid of the person in apparent need of help. According to the researchers, each individual felt that another person would intervene and provide help, and therefore did not respond. In another experiment Latané and Darley conducted, participants were asked to sit with others in a waiting room. Unbeknownst to the subjects, the others were in fact study confederates. Researchers then pumped artificial smoke into the room through the vents. The confederates were instructed to ignore the smoke and sit quietly, without reacting. When the actual subjects realized that smoke was coming from the vents, they looked around at the others in the waiting room for a response. Latané and Darley's explanation was that because the confederates did not react in an alarmed manner, the subjects inferred that the situation was not of dire consequence, and therefore displayed a sense of diffusion of responsibility and conformity.

Nuts and Bolts

 An example of the bystander effect and diffusion of responsibility occurs when you drive past a car accident. If you didn't actually witness the accident, but were one of many cars driving by, you might not stop and ask if anyone needed assistance because you would assume that other people had already called for help.

Some factors that contribute to the bystander effect and diffusion of responsibility are that a person might feel incompetent in front of others, may be having a bad day, is in an unfamiliar environment, doesn't realize that the situation is a genuine emergency, or simply doesn't want to be singled out by getting involved. To counter the bystander effect, research suggests that a person should take charge and assign roles to others. Pointing directly to a person and assigning him or her a task ensures that that person, as well as others, will help.

COOPERATION, COMPETITION, AND CONFLICT

When a person decides to help another, it is said that they are cooperating. **Cooperation**, *working with another to obtain a desired goal,* is seen in all settings, whether it be athletics, academics, or society in general. However, when a group of people begins working toward a goal and another group is pursuing the same goal, competition may ensue. **Competition**, *pursuit of a desired outcome while refuting that same outcome to others,* is most commonly seen when two groups are vying for the same goal. Oftentimes during a competition, **conflict**, *opposing members of a group being in direct opposition to another group in accomplishing a similar goal,* may emerge. Cooperation, competition, and conflict often go hand-in-hand and are seen in various aspects of our daily lives. The chart below shows various aspects of cooperation, competition, and conflict.

Cooperation, competition and conflict in action		Explanation	Example
Social dilemmas	Prisoner's dilemma	A desirable outcome is achieved only when both parties cooperate mutually.	
Interpersonal conflict	Zero-sum game	Gains or losses of one person are balanced by gains or losses of another.	Christina and Audrey want the same teddy bear. There is only one bear, so whoever gets the bear will receive a gain, whereas the other will suffer a loss.
Managing Conflict	Bargaining	Both sides attempt to produce a win-win situation, with each giving up a little.	Sarah wants to borrow her parents' car for the evening. Her parents insist that she put gas in the car with her own money if she wants to borrow it.
	Superordinate goals/identity	Realizing that one is involved in a larger goal helps reduce tension or conflict.	Gloria is the president of a car rental company. She agrees not to ask for a pay increase due to the fact that her company is struggling financially.

GROUP PROCESSES

How a group's members interact with one another is often the direct result of leadership style. A charismatic leader can be extremely motivating to a group, while a leader who is disorganized or reserved may be uninspiring. The group itself may promote or discourage certain types of behaviors in its members. In all, leaders and the groups they are in charge of greatly influence the actions of individuals.

LEADERSHIP

With all groups there needs to be a leader, as well as followers. Some are considered **task-oriented leaders**, *leaders who direct strongly,* *and are driven by production and goals.* Task-oriented leaders are often those who discourage discussion within the group because they believe it serves as a distraction to productivity. Leadership that is considered **person oriented** is *concerned more with group harmony than with production.* Such leaders typically seek the advice of their workers.

INFLUENCE OF THE GROUP ON BEHAVIOR

Groups can have tremendous influence on the behavior of individuals. They can aid a person in completing a task, or they can hinder that individual's performance. Because groups provide a sense of anonymity, they can cause their members to undertake behaviors they would not under normal circumstances. Groups provide people with a feeling of togetherness. The following is a list of various ways groups can influence the behaviors of individuals.

Group Influence	Definition	Example
Social-facilitation	Performance improves due to the presence of others.	Haley is an excellent pool player. She plays best when others are watching.
Social-inhibition (evaluation apprehension)	Performance decreases in the presence of others for fear of being embarrassed.	Terry is not very good at juggling. When people are watching, he makes a lot of mistakes.
Social loafing	The larger the group, the less a person feels personally responsible, and therefore doesn't put forth his or her full effort.	Li is participating in a team game of tug-of-war. He is one of 14 members on his team, so he thinks he doesn't need to try very hard.
Group polarization	Having an opinion strengthened after listening to an extreme position that favors that opinion.	Andrea, who cares about the environment, attended an Earth Day rally. After the rally, she was even more strongly committed to the environmental cause.
Groupthink	Members of the group stress unity over potential conflict.	Paul and his friends are trying to figure out what to do for the evening. Paul suggests they see a movie, but his friends want to go to the park. Not wanting to upset and break rank with his friends, Paul agrees to go to the park.
Deindividuation	Lowered sense of self-identity due to the anonymity produced by being in a large crowd.	During her high school's spirit assembly, Kenna throws a paper airplane at the school principal. He is sitting on the lowest level of the crowded bleachers.

Multiple-Choice Questions

1. Which of the following best illustrates the concept of social facilitation?
   (A) Henrik is not confident in his reading abilities, and when he is asked to read a selected passage aloud in class he stutters.
   (B) Juan likes to run by himself because when people are watching he doesn't run smoothly.
   (C) Gloria understands chemistry, yet she almost always fails her chemistry tests.
   (D) Yolanda is a pretty good juggler; when asked to juggle for her class, she performs very well.
   (E) When Clarence fails a test, he blames his teacher for not teaching him properly.

2. While the entire class was singing "Happy Birthday" to Jared, Mica was moving his lips but was not singing. Because there were already 28 people singing, Mica didn't feel that he needed to sing as well. This group phenomenon is known as
   (A) cognitive dissonance
   (B) social facilitation
   (C) social striving
   (D) social loafing
   (E) social normation

3. Kareem recently attended a Halloween party whose invitation specified that everyone was to wear a mask. While at the party, he began yelling obscenities at the other guests because he didn't think anyone would know who was behind the mask. Kareem displayed which social psychological principle?
   (A) Social loafing
   (B) The bystander effect
   (C) Actor-observer bias
   (D) Deindividuation
   (E) Social facilitation

4. Louis was walking through a crowded hallway to his third-period class when the person in front of him stopped short. Louis immediately decided that the person was inconsiderate and mean. Louis was guilty of committing
   (A) the bystander effect
   (B) actor-observer bias
   (C) social facilitation
   (D) the frustration-aggression principle
   (E) the fundamental attribution error

5. Which of the following best illustrates the concept of self-handicapping?
   (A) Joc throws a paper airplane during a crowded school assembly.
   (B) Henry complains of a sore throat an hour before he is scheduled to give a speech.
   (C) Taylor is convinced that she is the only player who can make the winning shot for her basketball team.
   (D) Gavin thinks that all people with glasses are smart.
   (E) Gwen thinks she received an A on the latest psychology test because she is smarter than everyone else.

6. A local sports celebrity is in an advertisement for a car. The celebrity is shown driving the car with many of his friends riding along with him. This advertisement is using which of the following techniques to promote the car?
   (A) Peripheral
   (B) Central
   (C) Outside
   (D) Low-balling
   (E) That's-not-all

7. Terrance is normally quiet and reserved and has said that parties are stupid and pointless. However, this past Saturday Terrance went to a party at his friend's house, where he danced wildly. The next day Terrance said that parties are all right every now and then. Terrance's change in belief could best be explained as
   (A) the actor-observer effect
   (B) bystander apathy
   (C) social referencing
   (D) cognitive dissonance
   (E) diffusion of responsibility

8. Sue believes that her employees should be given orders and kept busy in order to maximize profits for the company. Which leadership style is Sue most likely to agree with?
   (A) Person-oriented
   (B) Task-oriented
   (C) Client-centered
   (D) Cognitive dissonance
   (E) Group polarization

9. Tyler was running late to an appointment when he encountered a person lying on the sidewalk. Tyler noticed that others in the area did not seem to be concerned, and therefore he continued on his way. Which psychological principle did Tyler display?
   (A) Altruism
   (B) Actor-observer effect
   (C) Bystander effect
   (D) Cognitive dissonance
   (E) Compliance

10. The results of Stanley Milgram's shock experiment indicated that
    (A) people will not go against their beliefs just for an experiment
    (B) people will obey others if they perceive them to be authority figures
    (C) if a person is paid enough money, he or she will administer a full range of shocks
    (D) people take credit for their successes, but blame others for their failures
    (E) as the number of people in a setting increases, so does the likelihood that someone will help

11. Which of the following best illustrates the concept of conformity?
    (A) Jose holds open the door for the person behind him.
    (B) Lamar raises his hand when the teacher asks a question.
    (C) Patty wears the same name-brand clothes as her friends.
    (D) Destiny wears shorts in winter.
    (E) Roy buys his friend a birthday present.

12. Professor Jackson is studying the testosterone levels of rats that live in a crowded environment. Professor Jackson believes in which perspective regarding aggression?
    (A) Biological
    (B) Psychodynamic
    (C) Cognitive
    (D) Behavioral
    (E) Humanistic

13. Zoe wants to purchase a new car. The car salesman offers to let Zoe take the car home for the weekend because he knows that she is more likely to purchase the car after driving it for a couple of days. The car salesman is using which approach to influence Zoe's decision?
    (A) Door-in-the-face
    (B) Low-balling
    (C) That's-not-all
    (D) Foot-in-the-door
    (E) Central route to persuasion

14. Which of the following best illustrates the concept of catharsis?
    (A) Fred is cheering for his favorite football team.
    (B) Janice is playing basketball.
    (C) Darnell likes to paint pictures of mountains.
    (D) Claude is an aggressive person who starts fights.
    (E) Rhonda likes to take notes in class.

15. Randall believes he failed the psychology test because he had to work late the night before and so didn't have a chance to study. However, he believes that the other students who failed the test did so because they are stupid. Which psychological principle is Randall demonstrating?
    (A) Fundamental attribution error
    (B) Cognitive dissonance
    (C) Mere-exposure effect
    (D) Actor-observer bias
    (E) Self-handicapping

Free-Response Questions

1. Carlos is the leading scorer on his high school basketball team. On the morning of a big game, Carlos complains of a sore knee. Explain how each of the following factors may affect Carlos.
   - self-fulfilling prophecy
   - self-handicapping
   - social loafing
   - social facilitation

2. Aggression is often linked to violent behavior. Discuss how each of the following psychological perspectives views aggression.
   - psychodynamic
   - biological
   - behavioral
   - evolutionary

Answers

MULTIPLE-CHOICE QUESTIONS

1. Answer: D. Social facilitation happens when someone improves his or her performance in response to the presence of others (*Psychology*, 8th ed. p. 725/9th ed. p. 731).

2. Answer: D. Social loafing occurs when one person doesn't put forth his full effort because there are other people that he assumes will compensate for his slacking off (*Psychology*, 8th ed. p. 725/9th ed. pp. 731–732).

3. Answer: D. According to the theory of deindividuation, a person loses his or her sense of individuality and has an increased feeling of anonymity when in the presence of many others; the individual is confident that he or she will not be noticed or caught (*Psychology*, 8th ed. pp. 723–724/9th ed. pp. 730–731).

4. Answer: E. According to the fundamental attribution error, a person views another's behavior as the result of internal dispositions (*Psychology*, 8th ed. p. 699/9th ed. p. 706).

5. Answer: B. Self-handicapping occurs when a person makes up an excuse prior to a performance in case he or she fails at the task at hand (*this material does not appear in either textbook edition*).

6. Answer: A. The peripheral route to persuasion focuses on outside factors to influence the validity of an argument. The car company is focusing on the popularity of a celebrity to entice a person into buying a particular car. Doing so uses the peripheral route to persuasion (*Psychology*, 8th ed. p. 704/9th ed. p. 710).

7. Answer: D. Cognitive dissonance occurs when discomfort is produced by two conflicting thoughts, or when an action conflicts with a belief (*Psychology*, 8th ed. pp. 704–706/9th ed. pp. 711–712).

8. Answer: B. Task-oriented leaders are those who believe that the final outcome is the most important. They also believe that to be most efficient, people need to be kept busy and told what to do (*Psychology*, 8th ed. p. 756/9th ed. p. 763).

9. Answer: C. Bystander effect (apathy) occurs when a person does not become involved in a situation because he or she experiences a diffusion of responsibility; other people are not helping so the individual decides not to help either (*Psychology*, 8th ed. p. 747/9th ed. p. 753).

10. Answer: B. In Stanley Milgram's experiment, nearly 65 percent of all subjects administered the full range of shocks. The participants were directed by a person of perceived authority and therefore were more likely than not to complete the experiment (*Psychology*, 8th ed. pp. 732–734/9th ed. pp. 738–739).

11. Answer: C. Conformity is when a person goes along with others due to real or perceived pressure, even though no direct order was given (*Psychology*, 8th ed. p. 727/9th ed. p. 733).

12. Answer: A. Biological psychologists are interested in hormone levels in relation to aggressiveness (*Psychology*, 8th ed. pp. 737–738/9th ed. pp. 743–744).

13. Answer: D. The foot-in-the-door approach occurs when a person first agrees to a lesser request and then feels obligated to agree to more extreme subsequent requests (*Psychology*, 8th ed. pp. 729–731/9th ed. p. 736).

14. Answer: A. According to Sigmund Freud, catharsis is the venting of aggressive impulses through socially acceptable means. Cheering on a favorite sports team should allow any

aggressive impulses to subside (*Psychology*, 8th ed. p. 737/9th ed. p. 743).

15. Answer: D. The actor-observer bias occurs when a person attributes the behaviors of others to dispositional or internal factors, while attributing their own behaviors to situational or external factors (*Psychology*, 8th ed. pp. 699–700/9th ed. pp. 706–707).

FREE-RESPONSE QUESTIONS

1. A self-fulfilling prophecy occurs when a person unconsciously behaves in a manner that helps to justify or make an expected outcome happen. Because he complained about his sore knee prior to the game that evening, Carlos may unconsciously perform in a manner that is below his capabilities, thus making his predicted outcome come true. Self-handicapping is when a person makes an excuse that will help justify an outcome prior to the event's taking place. Because Carlos has said that his sore knee may influence his ability in the game that evening, he is making an excuse for his possible poor performance. If he performs poorly that evening, he has already provided an excuse. However, if he performs well that evening, his teammates will think highly of him because he will have played with a sore knee. Social loafing occurs when a person doesn't feel responsible for putting forth his full effort because he is confident that others will pick up the slack and won't notice how he performs. Because Carlos plays a team-oriented sport, he feels that if he has a bad game his fellow teammates will be able to compensate for his lackluster performance. Social facilitation occurs when an individual's performance improves due to the presence of others. Carlos may overcome his sore knee because he will have a crowd watching him play.

2. Psychodynamic psychologists view aggression as the result of the emitting of the id's unconscious impulses that are not confined by the ego or the superego. Biological psychologists view aggression as the result of genetics, an imbalance of chemicals (increase in testosterone, increase in serotonin, or damage to the frontal lobes) that inhibit impulsive behavior. Behavioral psychologists view aggression as the result of reinforcement or observational learning. If a person has been reinforced for past aggressive behavior, she will continue to display that aggressive behavior in the future. If a person has witnessed aggressive behavior by another person, she is likely to display that same aggressive behavior, especially if the behavior has gone unpunished. Evolutionary psychologists believe that aggression is the result of an innate desire for survival. Aggressive species tend to survive, ensuring their long-term survival in nature, thus making it probable that the aggressive behavior will continue.

14

HISTORY OF PSYCHOLOGY

Over time, people have wondered what makes living organisms act and think. Psychology has emerged from the resulting inquiries and findings as the scientific study of behavior and mental processes. The development of the field of psychology has led to a better understanding of what causes various behaviors—an understanding that may enable people to operate more effectively in their environments.

As you read this chapter, you will find that it provides a good review of the concepts and theories discussed throughout this book. Pay particular attention to terminology. If you are unfamiliar with a term or concept, refer back to the chapter where it was discussed in greater detail.

AP Tip

Be prepared to define "psychology."

HISTORY OF PSYCHOLOGY

The modern definition of "psychology" can be traced back through the history and development of past theoretical questions and approaches. In ancient Greece, philosophers, including Socrates, Plato, and Aristotle, debated the respective roles of the mind and body. Socrates and Plato supported **dualism**, *a belief that the mind and body were separate.* From this notion, Socrates and Plato inferred that ideas were innate. Aristotle, on the other hand, believed that the mind was connected to the body and that ideas came from experience. In the 1600s, Rene Descartes developed the concept of **interactive dualism**, *the belief that the mind and body are separate but interact to produce conscious experiences,* including emotions and sensations. These

332

different viewpoints and arguments forged the modern debate of **nature versus nurture**: *are we products of heredity or products of our environment?* Philosophical debate generated questions that sparked an interest in these psychological matters, but physiology, an area of biology that studies the functions and parts of an organism, provided the scientific method and evidence that enabled psychology to become a science.

Francis Bacon, who also lived during the early 1600s, is considered one of the founders of modern science. Bacon believed that research should be based on experimental design and experience. These ideas later led to the use of empirical data to support theories. John Locke, a British philosopher who expanded Bacon's ideas for providing testable data in the seventeenth century, further developed empiricism. **Empiricism** *is the belief that science should be based on knowledge that comes from experience and observation rather than speculation or intuition.* Locke suggested that, at birth, the mind was a blank slate, or *tabula rasa*, on which people "wrote" their experiences as they lived them.

AP Tip

Be prepared to identify philosophy and physiology as the roots of psychology.

CONTRIBUTIONS OF WILHELM WUNDT

Wilhelm Wundt, a German physiologist, is credited as the founder of modern psychology. Wundt was one of the first researchers to apply the laboratory techniques that helped psychology separate from philosophy when, in 1879, he opened the first psychology laboratory in Leipzig, Germany. He was interested in people's sensory reaction times to certain visual and auditory stimuli. He developed a technique called **introspection**, *to look inward, observe and measure conscious experience.* He found that the quality and intensity of a stimulus led to different types of perceptions that accounted for different types of emotions. In his book, *Principles of Physiological Psychology,* he argued that physiology and psychology were related, but that psychology should be a separate science based on experimental techniques used to study mental processes.

AP Tip

Be prepared to connect Wilhelm Wundt with the development of the method of introspection, the writing of *Principles of Physiological Psychology*, and the opening of the first psychology laboratory.

SCHOOL OF STRUCTURALISM

Edward Titchener, a student of Wilhelm Wundt, started the school of thought called structuralism. **Structuralism** *was based on the idea that conscious experiences could be broken down into structures, or parts.* Titchener used introspection to study these structures by asking subjects to view certain stimuli and then later write down what they remembered. Over time, introspection did not prove reliable. Subjects often reported different responses to the presentation of the same stimulus. In addition, introspection could not be used with children or animals, or in any study of learning, personality, or mental disorders. These flaws led to the end of structuralism.

WILLIAM JAMES AND THE SCHOOL OF FUNCTIONALISM

William James began his career as a physiology teacher at Harvard University, but as he continued to teach, his lectures concentrated more on the topics of psychology than on physiology. As he discussed the content of psychology with his students, he also began to write a comprehensive book that would take him close to a decade to finish. In 1890, he released *Principles of Psychology*; it covered a number of topics, including the components of the brain, the role of memory, and the mechanisms of sensation and perception. His book helped to popularize psychology in America, earning him the title of "father of American psychology." James's ideas were important to the formulation of a new school of thought called functionalism.

Nuts and Bolts

 A good way to remember that William James is called the father of American psychology is to think of the American colony of Jamestown. <u>James</u>town was the first American colony; William <u>James</u> was the father (the first) of American psychology.

AP Tip

Be prepared to identify the contributions of William James.

Functionalism *is the study of how an organism functions and adapts to its environment.* Whereas the school of structuralism relied on introspection, which was unreliable and did not provide accurate data, functionalism relied on naturalistic observation. Perhaps the most important element of functionalism was how research data could be applied to a number of areas, including education, work, and family upbringing. In other words, functionalism had a purpose and people found reasons to listen. Even though the school of functionalism doesn't exist today, its ideals can be found in several approaches to modern psychology.

Nuts and Bolts

 To discriminate between structuralism and functionalism, think about working on a car. A structuralist would work on the engine, which is how the car operates (the way a person processes information); also, the engine is hidden, like the brain. A functionalist would be concerned with how the car performs, similar to how people adapt and perform in the environment.

AP Tip

Be prepared to discriminate between the ideals and contributions of structuralism and functionalism.

THE LEGACY OF WILLIAM JAMES

G. Stanley Hall, a student of William James, became the first in the United States to earn a Ph.D. in psychology. In addition to this honor, Hall started the first psychological journal, *American Journal of Psychology* (1887). Perhaps most importantly, Hall was instrumental in the forming of the American Psychology Association (APA), of which he became the first president.

Mary Whiton Calkins was another student of William James. However, Calkins had a tough road in terms of establishing herself in psychology. She completed all of the requirements for her Ph.D. in psychology, but Harvard would not award her the degree because she was a woman. Calkins continued to contribute to psychology and in 1905 became the first woman president of the APA. Margaret Floy Washburn, a student of Edward Titchener's, was the first woman to be awarded a Ph.D. in psychology; she later became the second woman president of the APA.

SIGMUND FREUD

In the early 1900s, new developments challenged the approaches of structuralism and functionalism. Sigmund Freud claimed that personality and behavior could be explained through the role of the unconscious. He believed that the unconscious resides below conscious awareness, making it unknown to the individual. He thought that conflicts that occur in the unconscious, mainly those that are sexual and aggressive in nature, could affect the development of personality and behavior. Through dream analysis, resistance, slips of the tongue, and certain therapeutic techniques, not only could the unconscious be accessed, but inner conflicts could be treated and resolved. Freud's theories led to the development of psychoanalysis, which studied the origins and influences of personality, mental disorders, and the treatment of disorders.

John B. Watson

A major shift in the theoretical viewpoints of psychology occurred with the arrival of behaviorism. In the early 1900s, behaviorists questioned and dismissed the importance of consciousness. They were supported by the schools of structuralism and functionalism as well as by Freud's emphasis on the importance of the unconscious on personality development. But behaviorism placed importance on the study of overt behavior—behavior that could be observed and objectively measured. This premise arose from the work of a Russian physiologist, Ivan Pavlov. Pavlov discovered while studying the digestive tracts of dogs that dogs could learn to associate a neutral stimulus with an automatic and natural stimulus. He was able to condition dogs to associate the sound of a bell with the sight of food, which caused them to salivate; that eventually resulted in the bell alone triggering salivation. Pavlov believed that all learned behaviors were learned through association.

In America, John B. Watson extended Pavlov's theory and applied it to humans. Watson dismissed the ideals of structuralism, especially the method of introspection. He instead focused on how behavior develops and how such behaviors could be modified through environmental stimuli.

Like Watson, B. F. Skinner believed that behavior should be studied overtly. Skinner considered the roles and effects of reinforcement and punishment on the modification and shaping of behavior. Through his work with rats and pigeons Skinner was able to demonstrate how an animal's behavior could be modified by reinforcement and punishment.

Nuts and Bolts

 A good way to remember what John B. Watson contributed to the development of behaviorism is to associate him with Sherlock Holmes and John Watson. Holmes and Watson were detectives who searched for observable clues, much the way that John B. Watson based behaviorism on observable evidence.

Carl Rogers and Abraham Maslow

Behaviorism and psychoanalysis dominated psychology during the first half of the 1900s. In the 1950s, a new school of thought, humanistic psychology, referred to as the "third force of psychology," emerged based on the ideas of Carl Rogers. The humanists believed that not all human behavior and mental processes could be explained by associations, rewards and punishments, or unconscious conflicts, and thus criticized these theories for failing to account for free will and a desire to grow and control one's own future. Rogers was an American psychologist who, like Freud, developed his viewpoint from working with therapy clients. Rogers disagreed with Freud's emphasis on the role of the unconscious, finding more importance in conscious experiences that could be displayed through a person's unique potential and psychological growth. In addition, he disagreed with the behaviorists on how behavior is shaped and modified; he focused instead on how self-determination and free will affect a person's conscious choice to feel and act a certain way.

Abraham Maslow was another influential humanistic psychologist. Utilizing the concepts of the humanistic perspective, Maslow developed a theory of motivation that underlined psychological growth. Maslow believed that the pursuit of self-actualization, self-mastery, could explain motivation and development.

Nuts and Bolts

 A good way to connect Carl Rogers and the humanistic perspective is to remember Mr. Rogers from the children's television show. Mr. Rogers wanted to be your "neighbor"; he stressed the importance of being your unique self and trying to be the best that you can in a way similar to Carl Rogers and the humanistic perspective.

PSYCHOLOGICAL PERSPECTIVES

Over the years, the knowledge base for psychology has grown, resulting in a variety of perspectives. Each perspective differs in how it researches and explains psychological concepts. These different perspectives have shown that there is more than one way to explain mental processes and behavior, resulting in psychology's becoming a diverse science that can be applied to a variety of topics and situations.

Perspective	Origins and Influences	Area of Interest	Possible Research Question
Biological (Neuroscience)	Physiology	Interaction between physical bases—brain, nervous system, endocrine system, immune system—and human behavior	How would a stroke affect a person's speaking and writing skills?
Behavioral Genetics	Nature versus nurture debate	How genes and environment influence our behavior	Are we products of genetics (nature) or the environment (nurture)?

Perspective	Origins and Influences	Area of Interest	Possible Research Question
Psychodynamic	Sigmund Freud	Importance of unconscious influences, early life experiences affecting the unconscious, and personality development and therapeutic methods designed to show and resolve unconscious conflicts and motivations, known as psychoanalysis	Could the memories of child abuse affect personality development?
Behavioral	John B. Watson B. F. Skinner Ivan Pavlov Albert Bandura	Focus on observable behavior through observation and measurement Study how behavior develops and how it could be modified through behavioral techniques such as reinforcement and punishment	Would providing positive reinforcement, such as extra credit, improve a student's academic performance?
Humanistic	Carl Rogers Abraham Maslow	Importance of the self-concept and how the self-concept develops through free will, self-determination, and reaching one's potential	How do a healthy self-concept and improved self-esteem affect performance at work and school?
Cognitive	Development of the first computers in 1950s led to revitalized interest in the role of cognition Jean Piaget Noam Chomsky	Importance of mental processes that include thinking, language development, problem-solving strategies, and memory	Can an improvement in cognitive skills affect language development?

Perspective	Origins and Influences	Area of Interest	Possible Research Question
Cross-Cultural (Sociocultural)	Emerged in the 1980s as psychologists became increasingly interested in the role of diversity	Focus on how thinking and behavior are affected by cultural and environmental factors such as poverty or environmental setting	How can a competitive classroom environment affect a student's school performance?
Evolutionary	Charles Darwin's research, cited in his book *On the Origin of Species by Means of Natural Selection*	How **natural selection**, *the innate necessary characteristics passed from generation to generation that enable survival,* can also affect psychological, or thinking, processes	How does the development of phobias enhance survival?

AP Tip

A possible free-response question could ask you to differentiate among and identify the major viewpoints of the various psychological perspectives. Be prepared to identify the people responsible for the contributions that make up each perspective.

DIFFERENT AREAS OF SPECIALIZATION IN PSYCHOLOGY

There are many specialty research areas that support the various perspectives on psychology. Psychologists perform **basic research**, *studies that enhance the knowledge base of psychology,* and **applied research**, *studies that emphasize solving a practical problem.* Over the years, areas of psychology that specialize in enhancing thinking and functioning have arisen. The following are a few subfields that have proven tremendously beneficial.

Nuts and Bolts

 A good way to remember the difference between basic research and applied research is to think of the following statement: "Basically you have to know the content of psychology before you can apply it."

Specialty Subfields of Psychology	Area of Study	Previous Discussion
Biological psychologist	The relationship between the brain and the nervous system, and how biological factors affect behavior	Chapter 2
Cognitive psychologist	Mental processes such as thinking, language, problem solving and memory	Chapters 4 and 9
Experimental psychologist	Research on psychological topics such as learning, emotion, memory, etc.	Chapter 1
Developmental psychologist	Physical, social, and psychological changes that occur over a lifetime	Chapter 3
Personality psychologist	Origins of personality and why and how people are alike and different	Chapter 10
Health psychologist	Psychological factors that affect a person's health, immune system; treatment strategies aimed at improving a person's lifestyle and health	Chapter 5
Educational/ school psychologist	How people of all ages learn and how a proper educational environment can lead to improved learning	Chapters 3 and 9
Industrial/ organizational psychologist	Proper matching of employees with specific jobs; how to improve working conditions using psychological concepts	Chapter 5
Social psychologist	How certain social and cultural settings affect thinking and behavior	Chapter 13
Clinical psychologist	Identifying causes of psychological disorders, and providing psychological treatments and prevention strategies	Chapter 12
Counseling psychologist	Helping people improve everyday functioning by providing productive and positive thinking and acting skills	Chapter 12

Specialty Subfields of Psychology	Area of Study	Previous Discussion
Psychiatrist	Identifying causes of psychological disorders, and providing treatment and prevention strategies (Psychiatrists have medical degrees in addition to training in psychology, which allows them to prescribe medication. A clinical psychologist, who has a Ph.D. in psychology, does not have a medical degree and can't prescribe medication.)	Chapter 12
Community psychologist	Working to make sure that people who are unable or unwilling to seek psychological treatment receive it	Chapter 12

AP Tip

You may be asked to identify the different areas of psychology. Be prepared to identify the area of specialization for each subfield.

Multiple-Choice Questions

1. Psychology is defined as the scientific study of
   (A) the unconscious mind
   (B) behavior and mental processes
   (C) overt and measurable behavior
   (D) working to reach one's potential
   (E) how nature selects organisms best suited for survival

2. *Tabula rasa* refers to
   (A) the idea that the mind is like a blank slate on which experiences are written
   (B) looking inward at the atoms of the mind
   (C) revealing the wishes and motivations of the unconscious
   (D) a way to reach self-actualization
   (E) how nature selects organisms suited for survival

3. The method Wilhelm Wundt used to study the elements of the mind was called
   (A) observation
   (B) case study
   (C) introspection
   (D) dream analysis
   (E) resistance

4. Sigmund Freud believed that
   (A) research should be based on observable and measurable data
   (B) reaching one's potential by developing a positive self-concept was important
   (C) nature selects organisms best suited for an environment
   (D) cultural and social backgrounds play a crucial role in development
   (E) unconscious motivations and wishes affect personality and psychological well-being

5. Behaviorism was built around the idea that
   (A) research should be based on observable and measurable data
   (B) reaching one's potential by developing a positive self-concept is important
   (C) nature selects organisms best suited for an environment
   (D) cultural and social backgrounds play a crucial role in development
   (E) unconscious motivations and wishes affect personality and psychological well-being

6. Who contributed to the ideas of the evolutionary perspective by suggesting that nature selects organisms best suited for survival in a given environment?
   (A) Charles Darwin
   (B) Sigmund Freud
   (C) John B. Watson
   (D) William James
   (E) Wilhelm Wundt

7. Which school of thought focused on how an organism adapts to the environment?
   (A) Structuralism
   (B) Gestalt
   (C) Psychoanalysis
   (D) Behaviorism
   (E) Functionalism

8. The belief that the brain and nervous system affect behavior is fundamental to which perspective of psychology?
   (A) Evolutionary
   (B) Psychodynamic
   (C) Behavioral
   (D) Cognitive
   (E) Biological

9. Which perspective is concerned with how information is processed in terms of thinking, remembering, and communicating?
   (A) Evolutionary
   (B) Psychodynamic
   (C) Behavioral
   (D) Cognitive
   (E) Biological

10. A researcher supporting which psychological perspective might recite the following quotation: "I believe that the memories and events of early childhood contribute to unconscious development affecting personality"?
    (A) Evolutionary
    (B) Psychodynamic
    (C) Behavioral
    (D) Cognitive
    (E) Biological

11. Carl Rogers and Abraham Maslow developed what perspective?
    (A) Evolutionary
    (B) Psychodynamic
    (C) Behavioral
    (D) Cognitive
    (E) Humanistic

12. The ideas of William James agreed with which psychological school of thought?
    (A) Structuralism
    (B) Functionalism
    (C) Gestalt
    (D) Psychodynamic
    (E) Behaviorism

13. Which subfield of psychology studies how people change over the course of a lifetime?
    (A) Cognitive psychology
    (B) Clinical psychology
    (C) Psychiatry
    (D) Biological psychiatry
    (E) Developmental psychology

14. When describing her job, Jenny says she makes sure that people who need psychological care receive it. Jenny is what type of psychologist?
    (A) Cognitive psychologist
    (B) Clinical psychologist
    (C) Community psychologist
    (D) Biological psychologist
    (E) Developmental psychologist

15. Which subfield of psychology would focus on how a stroke could affect the functioning of the brain?
    (A) Cognitive psychology
    (B) Clinical psychology
    (C) Community psychology
    (D) Biological psychology
    (E) Developmental psychology

Free-Response Questions

1. Tracy has decided to major in psychology, but she's unsure which particular area she wants to specialize in. She's interested in finding out what the following areas of study would focus on:
   (a) cognitive
   (b) biological
   (c) personality
   (d) clinical psychologist

   Provide a brief description of each of these types of psychologist to help Tracy make her decision.

2. Describe the area of interest and key figures identified for each of the following psychological perspectives.
   (a) humanistic
   (b) behavioral
   (c)_ psychodynamic

Answers

MULTIPLE-CHOICE QUESTIONS

1. Answer: B. Psychology is defined as the scientific study of behavior and mental processes (*Psychology*, 8th ed. p. 3/9th ed. p. 4).

2. Answer: A. Empiricists believed that the mind was a blank sheet on which experiences were "written." This idea went against the beliefs of the older philosophers (*Psychology*, 8th ed. p.13/9th ed. p.14).

3. Answer: C. Introspection meant to "look inward" and was a technique relied on by Wundt and the structuralists (*Psychology*, 8th ed. p. 13/9th ed. p. 14).

4. Answer E. Sigmund Freud believed that the unconscious contributes to personality development by providing inner conflicts that must be resolved (*Psychology*, 8th ed. pp. 14–15/9th ed. p. 16).

5. Answer: A. Behaviorism was developed around the idea that research should be based only on data that could be observed and measured (*Psychology*, 8th ed. p. 16/9th ed. p. 17).

6. Answer: A. Charles Darwin theorized natural selection, which is the premise that nature selects organisms best suited for survival in an environment (*Psychology*, 8th ed. p. 18/9th ed. p. 20).

7. Answer: E. Functionalism, a school of thought championed by William James, was predicated on the consideration of how

organisms adapt to the environment (*Psychology*, 8th ed. pp. 15–16/9th ed. pp. 16–17).

8. Answer: E. The biological perspective stated that the brain and nervous system affect the behavior of an organism (*Psychology*, 8th ed. p. 18/9th ed. p. 19).

9. Answer: D. The cognitive perspective is based on research that examines how cognitive processes, such as thinking, remembering, and communicating, occur (*Psychology*, 8th ed. p. 20/9th ed. p. 22).

10. Answer: B. Those supporting the psychodynamic perspective believed that events in early childhood affect the development of the unconscious, which in turn affects how personality develops (*Psychology*, 8th ed. pp. 19–20/9th ed. pp. 20–21).

11. Answer: E. Carl Rogers and Abraham Maslow believed in free will, self-determination, and the importance of the self-concept, which gave rise to the humanistic perspective (*Psychology*, 8th ed. pp. 20–21/9th ed. pp. 22–23).

12. Answer: B. Functionalism was a school of thought that focused on how an organism adapted to enhance its survival in a particular environment. William James rejected the ideas of structuralism and instead concentrated his studies on how organisms adapt and function (*Psychology*, 8th ed. pp. 15–16/9th ed. pp. 16–17).

13. Answer: E. Developmental psychologists study ways in which psychological and physical changes occur over a lifetime (*Psychology*, 8th ed. pp. 4–5/9th ed. p. 6).

14. Answer: C. Community psychologists make sure that people who either cannot seek help or are unwilling to do so receive psychological care (*Psychology*, 8th ed. p. 6/9th ed. p. 7).

15. Answer: D. Biological psychology studies the functioning of the brain and nervous system and how that affects functioning and behavior (*Psychology*, 8th ed. p. 4/9th ed. p. 5).

FREE-RESPONSE QUESTIONS

1. a. A cognitive psychologist studies how mental processes, such as thinking, remembering, and communicating, occur.
   b. A biological psychologist studies how the brain and nervous system affect behavior.
   c. A personality psychologist studies how people are unique, consistent, and different in terms of personality development.
   d. A clinical psychologist studies the causes, symptoms, and treatment of psychological disorders.

2. a. Those supporting the humanistic perspective are concerned with the development and role of the self-concept. They stress the importance of free will, self-determination, achieving one's unique potential, and striving to make positive choices. Carl

Rogers and Abraham Maslow were key figures in the development of the humanistic perspective.

b. The behavioral perspective focused on observable and measurable data. Followers of this perspective believed that behavior could be modified through associations, rewards, and punishments. John B. Watson, B. F. Skinner, and Ivan Pavlov are associated with the behavioral perspective.

c. The psychodynamic perspective stressed the importance of events in early childhood and how they affected the development of the unconscious. Those supporting this perspective believed that conflicts and wishes that originate in the unconscious could affect personality development. Sigmund Freud was the originator of the psychodynamic perspective.

Part III

Practice Tests

Practice Test 1

PSYCHOLOGY
Section I: Multiple-Choice Questions
Time—70 minutes
Number of Questions—100

MULTIPLE-CHOICE QUESTIONS

1. Operational definitions help to
   (A) establish the control group
   (B) clarify the way the researcher will test a hypothesis
   (C) allow for the researcher to establish standardization
   (D) help control for confounding variables
   (E) eliminate the need for a double-blind procedure

2. Which area of the brain is known as the pleasure center?
   (A) The frontal lobes
   (B) The parietal lobes
   (C) The cerebellum
   (D) The thalamus
   (E) The hypothalamus

3. Carl Rogers believed that the client should be treated as a valued person. This is an example of
   (A) empathy
   (B) active listening
   (C) unconditional positive regard
   (D) congruence
   (E) incongruence

4. Which psychological approach suggests that depression is the result of discomfort within the unconscious?
   (A) Behavioral
   (B) Humanistic
   (C) Cognitive
   (D) Psychodynamic
   (E) Biological

5. When he was 40, Rich was asked how he had celebrated his 16th birthday. Which type of memory contains the events that took place on Rich's 16th birthday?
   (A) Encoding
   (B) Semantic
   (C) Procedural
   (D) Episodic
   (E) Visual encoding

6. Which of the following descriptions can be correlated to obesity?
   (A) A BMI of lower than 30
   (B) A very active life-style
   (C) Not linked to diabetes and high blood pressure
   (D) Not prevalent in Western Cultures
   (E) Eat higher amounts of food high in fat

7. Darcy can't seem to get over her break-up with her boyfriend and has been displaying symptoms that resemble major depression. She doesn't want to go to work or interact with friends. Which viewpoint would offer the best explanation for Darcy's behavior?
   (A) Psychological model
   (B) Infrequency
   (C) Biological model
   (D) Diathesis-stress approach
   (E) Norm violations

8. The humanistic approach emphasizes
   - (A) an innate drive directed toward psychological growth
   - (B) unconscious motivations
   - (C) the interaction of social and environmental factors
   - (D) the stability of relationships
   - (E) overcoming childhood inferiorities

9. A rat receives a food pellet for every fifth bar press. This is an example of what type of reinforcement schedule?
   - (A) Fixed-interval
   - (B) Fixed-ratio
   - (C) Variable-interval
   - (D) Variable-ratio
   - (E) Partial reinforcement

10. Paul suffered a stroke that paralyzed his left arm. In what area of the brain did Paul most likely suffer damage?
    - (A) Left motor cortex
    - (B) Right motor cortex
    - (C) Broca's area
    - (D) Wernicke's area
    - (E) Cerebellum

11. Who is credited with creating the first modern intelligence test?
    - (A) Lewis Terman
    - (B) Alfred Binet
    - (C) David Wechsler
    - (D) Ivan Pavlov
    - (E) Howard Gardner

12. The Gestalt principle that says that when objects move in the same direction and at the same speed they are perceived as belonging together. This is known as
    - (A) figure-ground
    - (B) continuity
    - (C) common fate
    - (D) closure
    - (E) similarity

13. High levels of _____ have been linked to many cases of depression.
    - (A) serotonin
    - (B) norepinephrine
    - (C) dopamine
    - (D) cortisol
    - (E) adrenaline

14. What type of memory has information about how to do things such as ride a bike, tie shoelaces, or hit a golf ball?
    - (A) Explicit
    - (B) Semantic
    - (C) Procedural
    - (D) Episodic
    - (E) Flash-bulb

15. A researcher was interested in studying how high school freshman navigated their way through the halls to their classes on the first day of school. Which research method would she most likely use in this study?
    - (A) Experimental method
    - (B) Case study method
    - (C) Correlational method
    - (D) Survey method
    - (E) Naturalistic observation method

16. Which of the following correlational coefficients demonstrates the strongest relationship between variables?
    - (A) +0.23
    - (B) +0.14
    - (C) -0.55
    - (D) -0.78
    - (E) -0.31

17. Edward Thorndike believed that behaviors that were successful in obtaining a reward would be continued, while behaviors that were not successful would not be continued. This is known as the
    - (A) law of classical conditioning
    - (B) law of learned helplessness
    - (C) law of effect
    - (D) law of social proximity
    - (E) law of reward

18. Professor Olsen noted that students who took notes while he lectured earned higher exam scores than students who did not take notes. Professor Olsen concluded that note-taking produces a higher exam score. Which type of correlation is being displayed?
(A) Positive
(B) Negative
(C) Null
(D) Zero
(E) Valid

19. Which of the following theorists believed that language is the result of an inborn communication device?
(A) B. F. Skinner
(B) Benjamin Whorf
(C) Albert Bandura
(D) Noam Chomsky
(E) Elizabeth Loftus

20. Carl noticed that he runs faster when he runs with others rather than alone. This can be explained by the phenomenon known as
(A) social loafing
(B) social inhibition
(C) social facilitation
(D) diffusion of responsibility
(E) group polarization

21. Horace is a skilled musician who has composed more than 100 symphonies, but he has difficulty spelling simple words. According to Robert Sternberg, Horace is considered to possess
(A) analytic intelligence
(B) practical intelligence
(C) creative intelligence
(D) monarchic intelligence
(E) convergent intelligence

22. Albert Ellis theorized in rational emotive behavior therapy that psychological disorders are the result of
(A) unpleasant events and situations
(B) the interpretation of events and situations
(C) unconscious conflicts and motivations
(D) learned tendencies associated with outcomes
(E) a pursuit of self-actualization

23. During a psychoanalytical session, Jenny was asked about her mother. Jenny grew instantly angry and started to talk to the therapist as if she was Jenny's mother, commenting on how she was never there for her and had abandoned Jenny. Jenny's dialogue could be described as
(A) a Freudian slip
(B) transference
(C) manifest content
(D) latent content
(E) resistance

24. Dr. Knight believes that chewing gum increases a person's ability to solve geometry problems. Participants in group A are instructed to chew gum for a half-hour and are then given a geometry test. Participants in group B are instructed to sit quietly for a half-hour and are then given the same test. Which of the following best illustrates a potential confounding variable?
(A) Chewing gum
(B) An individual's prior mathematical ability
(C) The amount of time that passes before the test is given
(D) The number of participants in the experiment
(E) The number of pieces of gum given to the participants

GO ON TO NEXT PAGE

25. Which disorder is caused by an extra 21st chromosome?
    (A) Huntington's disease
    (B) Parkinson's disease
    (C) Down's syndrome
    (D) Alzheimer's disease
    (E) Fetal-alcohol syndrome

26. Tom's counselor told him that he should join the football team because football could serve as an outlet for his aggression. Which defense mechanism is Tom's counselor applying?
    (A) Repression
    (B) Projection
    (C) Denial
    (D) Reaction formation
    (E) Sublimation

27. Jen thought she only experienced anxiety when she had to stand up in front of people and talk. She later realized that she was starting to experience anxiety during other events—virtually everything that she does. Jen could be experiencing
    (A) phobia
    (B) post-traumatic stress disorder
    (C) obsessive-compulsive disorder
    (D) schizophrenia
    (E) generalized anxiety disorder

28. Studies conducted in the United States and Canada that involve using humans as subjects must first be approved by whom?
    (A) American Psychological Association (APA)
    (B) Internet Ethics Committee (IEC)
    (C) Human Participation Research Association (HPRA)
    (D) Fair use of Animals Committee (FAC)
    (E) Institutional Review Board (IRB)

29. Mr. Allen asked his students to turn in their homework. The students lined up at his desk to hand in their papers. This is an example of
    (A) deindividuation
    (B) peer pressure
    (C) groupthink
    (D) group polarization
    (E) obedience

30. A recent poll was administered to people attending the Natural History Museum. Seventy-five percent of the respondents said they enjoyed looking at plants, yet only 15 percent of the same group said they were interested in botany. The reason for this discrepancy is due to what phenomenon?
    (A) The framing effect
    (B) Confirmation bias
    (C) Analogies
    (D) Mental set effect
    (E) Insight

31. Gladys was having a difficult time sleeping. Her doctor suggested she should take medication containing which hormone, to help regulate her circadian rhythm?
    (A) Dopamine
    (B) Testosterone
    (C) Melatonin
    (D) Thyroxin
    (E) Serotonin

32. As a person gets older, his or her _____ intelligence decreases, while his or her _____ intelligence increases.
    (A) fluid; crystallized
    (B) crystallized; fluid
    (C) fluid; fluid
    (D) crystallized; crystallized
    (E) egotistical; moral

33. Professor Thomas believes that proximity of residence has a positive correlation to aggression levels. Professor Thomas's views are best explained by research from which type of psychologist?
    (A) Biological
    (B) Evolutionary
    (C) Environmental
    (D) Cognitive
    (E) Humanistic

34. Ted attributes the A on his calculus test to his superior mathematical abilities, but blames his failing grade in English on his teacher's teaching style. Ted is exhibiting
(A) self-handicapping
(B) self-serving bias
(C) hindsight bias
(D) social loafing
(E) diffusion of responsibility

35. When asked which age group has the highest number of automobile accidents, Manny recalls the person who cut him off on the way to school and raises his hand, shouting, "Old people!" Manny has used what mental shortcut to formulate an answer?
(A) Analogy
(B) Representativeness heuristic
(C) Availability heuristic
(D) Anchoring and adjustment heuristic
(E) Mental set

36. Greg has just completed his first marathon and despite the 26.2-mile run he claims that he does not feel much pain, but rather is excited and numb. Which hormone is responsible for helping the body deal with pain?
(A) Melatonin
(B) Endorphins
(C) Serotonin
(D) Dopamine
(E) GABA

37. Which area of research focuses on the relationship between physical energy from the environment and a person's psychological interpretation of the energy?
(A) Developmental
(B) Biological
(C) Psychophysics
(D) Ecological
(E) Psychodynamic

38. Five-year-old Stanley brings his mother his favorite stuffed animal to comfort her when she is sad. Stanley is displaying behavior commonly found in which of Piaget's developmental stages?
(A) Sensorimotor
(B) Preoperational
(C) Concrete
(D) Operational
(E) Post-operational

39. Which of the following is responsible for the digestion of food, breathing, and the regulation of body temperature?
(A) Autonomic nervous system
(B) Somatic nervous system
(C) Central nervous system
(D) Sympathetic nervous system
(E) Arousal nervous system

40. A disadvantage of an objective personality test is that
(A) the test is machine scored
(B) the test can be given to a large number of people
(C) subjective stimuli can be used for testing
(D) test scores can be compared to those of large groups of people
(E) the questions provide only one correct answer

41. Which of the following provides creditability to the nature view of intelligence?
(A) Lance has the same IQ as his adoptive parents.
(B) Alvin, Simon, and Theodore are brothers, and each has a different IQ.
(C) Calvin and Sally are dizygotic twins. Sally has above-average intelligence and Calvin is considered mentally retarded.
(D) Renee and Michele are monozygotic twins who were raised separately, yet they both have the same IQ as their biological parents.
(E) Cleon and Brittany are a married couple who both have an IQ of less than 80.

GO ON TO NEXT PAGE

42. Which of the following methods allows a researcher to control the environment and manipulate variables to establish cause and effect?
    (A) Correlational method
    (B) Experimental method
    (C) Survey method
    (D) Case study method
    (E) Inferential statistical method

43. The MMPI personality test was originally designed to measure
    (A) extraverted and introverted personality types
    (B) psychological disorders
    (C) personality stability
    (D) job selection based on personality type
    (E) openness to try new experiences and situations

44. While looking at a painting at her high school art show, Gwen commented to her friend that the reason we perceive objects that have less clarity as being farther away is because of which Gestalt principle?
    (A) Texture gradient
    (B) Proximity
    (C) Shadowing
    (D) Shape constancy
    (E) Size constancy

45. Recent research concluded that major league baseball players hit more home runs in July than in June. This is an example of what type of statistic?
    (A) Descriptive
    (B) Inferential
    (C) Quantitative
    (D) Absolute
    (E) Confounding

46. Waxy flexibility is a characteristic of which schizophrenic subtype?
    (A) Paranoid
    (B) Disorganized
    (C) Catatonic
    (D) Undifferentiated
    (E) Residual

47. Which of the following best illustrates the concept of negative reinforcement?
    (A) Turning on the air conditioner when it is hot
    (B) Taking away a child's favorite toy when they misbehave
    (C) Administering a shock for every wrong answer
    (D) Receiving twenty dollars for every A
    (E) Having your car taken away for staying out past curfew

48. In John B. Watson's famous Little Albert experiment, prior to conditioning, the white rat served as the
    (A) unconditioned stimulus (UCS)
    (B) unconditioned response (UCR)
    (C) conditioned stimulus (CS)
    (D) conditioned response (CR)
    (E) neutral stimulus (NS)

49. Clare enjoyed watching the Olympic Games. After seeing the gymnasts perform their routines, Clare went out to her trampoline to replicate what she had seen. According to social-cognitive learning theorists, Clare is demonstrating
    (A) secondary learning
    (B) higher-order conditioning
    (C) modeling
    (D) shaping
    (E) learning by association

50. After looking at a map of the local state park, Grover decided to go on a hiking expedition. While hiking, he accidently dropped his map. However, because he had studied the map, he continued on and was able to arrive safely at his destination. According to cognitive psychologists, Grover was able to complete his expedition because of his
    (A) latent learning
    (B) cognitive map
    (C) incentive level
    (D) learned helplessness
    (E) cognitive introspection

51. While on a trip in the Amazon rain forest, Sonya was bitten by a spider, causing her muscles to contract violently. What neurotransmitter substance was responsible for the spasms?
    (A) Dopamine
    (B) Serotonin
    (C) GABA
    (D) Acetylcholine
    (E) Endorphins

52. Researchers noted that rats that were unable to escape an electrical shock eventually stopped trying. This is known as
    (A) learned avoidance
    (B) learned escape
    (C) learned helplessness
    (D) biofeedback training
    (E) operant conditioning

53. Daryl recently was hit on the head by a baseball. His doctors are concerned that his brain may be swelling and have ordered tests to help determine the extent of his injury. Which brain imaging technique are Daryl's doctors most likely to use?
    (A) Electrocardiogram (EKG)
    (B) Positive Emission Tomography scan (PET scan)
    (C) Electroencelphograph (EEG)
    (D) Transcranial stimulation (TS)
    (E) Computer Aided Tomography scan (CAT scan)

54. Naomi is seeing a therapist in order to overcome her fear of dogs. Her therapist suggests that Naomi visit a kennel with 25 dogs. Naomi's therapist is using which technique to help her overcome her fear of dogs?
    (A) Flooding
    (B) Counter-conditioning
    (C) Systematic desensitization
    (D) Gradual exposure therapy
    (E) Virtual reality therapy

55. Dr. Palmer is studying the effects of grapes on visual acuity. Both groups are first administered a visual acuity test to establish baseline data. Fifty subjects are first given grapes, followed by a visual acuity test. The remaining 50 subjects are not given grapes, but are still required to take the visual acuity test. In Dr. Palmer's study, what is the dependent variable?
    (A) The number of grapes eaten
    (B) The color of the grapes
    (C) The visual acuity improvement
    (D) The size of the grapes
    (E) The number of subjects

56. Individuals tend to attribute dispositional factors to the behaviors of others, while attributing situational factors to their own behavior. This phenomenon is known as
    (A) the bystander effect
    (B) the fundamental attribution error
    (C) the A-B problem
    (D) conformity
    (E) the actor-observer effect

57. In order to allow each participant to have an equal chance of being placed in a particular research group, researchers must use
    (A) random sampling
    (B) random assignment
    (C) participation bias
    (D) hindsight bias
    (E) double-blind design

58. Seth is convinced that he's going to fail his upcoming exam because he has a game the night before it, and he tells himself has no time to study. Consequently, Seth does not study for the test. Seth's behavior can be attributed to
    (A) social loafing
    (B) social inhibition
    (C) diffusion of responsibility
    (D) self-handicapping
    (E) self-serving bias

GO ON TO NEXT PAGE

59. Wilbur recently purchased the car he has been wanting for five years. After driving it for a week in bad weather, Wilbur noticed that the car didn't handle well. However, he justifies his purchase with the great deal he received on the car. Wilbur is experiencing which social psychological phenomenon?
    (A) Social inhibition
    (B) Cognitive dissonance
    (C) Self-handicapping
    (D) Self-serving bias
    (E) Diffusion of responsibility

60. Researchers have trained dolphins to swim through a tube, retrieve a mannequin, and swim to an awaiting Coast Guard boat. They then placed an obstacle in the tube, thus requiring the dolphins to push the obstruction aside to reach the end of the tube, which they did successfully. Researchers concluded that dolphins possess the ability of what cognitive function?
    (A) Incubation
    (B) Mental set
    (C) Natural concepts
    (D) Insight
    (E) Functional fixedness

61. Richard was not paying attention to his teacher and therefore missed the main points of the lecture. Which process of memory would be immediately affected by Richard's lack of attention?
    (A) Retrieval
    (B) Encoding
    (C) Storage
    (D) Maintenance
    (E) Rehearsal

62. B. F. Skinner would most likely say that learning to speak is the result of
    (A) an inborn communication system
    (B) the result of many years of evolution
    (C) the result of reinforcement from others
    (D) the result of unconscious impulses
    (E) the result of cultural influences on vocabulary

63. When an individual only accepts information with which he agrees and ignores information that goes against his beliefs, he is said to be displaying
    (A) a mental set
    (B) an availability heuristic
    (C) insight
    (D) cause and effect
    (E) confirmation bias

64. In order for a cell to "fire" it must enter which phase of neural transmission?
    (A) Action potential
    (B) Recharge threshold
    (C) Refractory period
    (D) Threshold period
    (E) Depolarization

65. Ken is taking his psychology final exam, a cumulative test that will cover all the material presented throughout the semester. This is considered what type of test?
    (A) Intelligence
    (B) Achievement
    (C) Aptitude
    (D) Personality
    (E) Normative

66. Professor Paulson has been using the same final exam for his U.S. history class for the past ten years. Those who have done well on this final exam typically do well on the nationwide examination. Therefore, it is reasonable to conclude that Professor Paulson's tests are considered to possess high
    (A) reliability
    (B) standardization
    (C) face validity
    (D) criterion validity
    (E) normative reliability

67. Which phrase best describes an absolute threshold?
    (A) Maximum level of stimulation necessary to detect a change in a stimulus
    (B) Minimum level of stimulation necessary to detect a stimulus
    (C) Minimum level of stimulation necessary to detect a stimulus percent of the time
    (D) Any stimulus above the minimum level of stimulation that will absolutely be detected
    (E) Any stimulus above the minimum level of stimulation that will absolutely not be detected.

68. Which psychological approach would support the following statement: "If a person were to develop a psychological disorder, it is possible, through proper psychological techniques, that the person could eventually unlearn factors that contributed to the disorder"?
    (A) Psychodyanmic
    (B) Behavioral
    (C) Humanistic
    (D) Cognitive
    (E) Biological

69. If a test accurately measures what it is designed to measure it is said to be
    (A) reliable
    (B) standardized
    (C) normed
    (D) predictable
    (E) valid

70. Which researcher's study of goslings was important in establishing the theory of imprinting?
    (A) Harry Harlow
    (B) Mary Ainsworth
    (C) Diana Baumrind
    (D) Jean Piaget
    (E) Konrad Lorenz

71. Which of the following best demonstrates the long-term effects of authoritative parenting?
    (A) John has been arrested five times, and is currently in prison for armed robbery.
    (B) Clare has a difficult time maintaining relationships with others.
    (C) Andy is uncooperative and will not share his toys with others.
    (D) Allison is quiet and doesn't speak for fear of being yelled at.
    (E) Brian is respectful toward his teachers and other authority figures.

72. A characteristic of the prescription drug buspirone (BuSpar) is that it alleviates
    (A) symptoms of anxiety within days to weeks
    (B) symptoms of bipolar disorder
    (C) the positive symptoms of schizophrenia
    (D) the negative symptoms of schizophrenia
    (E) the symptoms of anxiety immediately

73. Which of the following conditions would cause a rat to eat endlessly?
    (A) Destruction of the ventromedial nucleus of the hypothalamus
    (B) Stimulation of the ventromedial nucleus of the hypothalamus
    (C) Destruction of the lateral hypothalamus
    (D) Stimulation of the ventromedial hypothalamus and stimulation of the lateral hypothalamus
    (E) Stimulation of the ventromedial hypothalamus and destruction of the lateral hypothalamus

GO ON TO NEXT PAGE

74. Professor Welch believes that children with low IQs are more likely to end up in poverty. Which of the following research methods should Professor Welch use when conducting his study?
(A) Case study
(B) Kinship study
(C) Longitudinal method
(D) Cross sectional method
(E) Experimental method

75. Frank is told to go straight to Tommy's house for his birthday party. Along the way Frank sees another child fall off her bicycle, but refuses to stop and help. Which stage of Lawrence Kohlberg's moral development best describes Frank's actions?
(A) Preconventional
(B) Conventional
(C) Postconventional
(D) Preoperational
(E) Concrete

76. Aiden is 16 years old and has recently joined his high school's cross-country team. According to Erik Erikson, which psychosocial stage is Aiden currently in?
(A) Trust versus mistrust
(B) Industry versus inferiority
(C) Identity versus role confusion
(D) Intimacy versus isolation
(E) Generativity versus stagnation

77. Two-year-old Angelica is placed in a room with her mother and a stranger. Her mother leaves the room, leaving Angelica alone with the stranger. Angelica begins to cry when her mother leaves, and when her mother reenters the room Angelica stops crying. According to Mary Ainsworth, Angelica is displaying which attachment style?
(A) Insecure
(B) Secure
(C) Avoidant
(D) Neglectful
(E) Ambivalent

78. Which early school of thought was influenced by Charles Darwin's

theory of evolution and stressed the role of the consciousness?
(A) Structuralism
(B) Gestalt
(C) Functionalism
(D) Psychophysics
(E) Behaviorism

79. Jenny is having a hard time adapting to her new school. She is annoyed that so many people seem concerned only about themselves, and less concerned about others. As an example, Jenny couldn't believe that no one offered to help a student who was struggling in math. When she inquired why, a fellow student said, "That's his problem. I have a good grade." Which sociocultural factor explains Jenny's regard for other people?
(A) Individualistic cultural background
(B) Collectivistic cultural background
(C) High socioeconomic status
(D) Low socioeconomic status
(E) Rural residence

80. The process of deinstitutionalization, which was the shutting down of mental hospitals and the release of many patients, led to the rise of
(A) Gestalt therapy
(B) the biopsychosocial model
(C) the increased use of psychosurgeries
(D) community psychology
(E) eclectic approaches

81. Which sense receives information from receptors located in muscles and joints?
(A) Vestibular
(B) Audtion
(C) Gustation
(D) Olfaction
(E) Kinesthesis

82. What is the characterization of the sleep cycle as a person continues to sleep throughout the night?
(A) NREM stage 2 increases
(B) REM sleep decreases
(C) NREM stage 3 increases
(D) NREM stage 4 increases
(E) NREM stage 2 decreases

83. Baclofen, a drug that enhances the effectiveness of the inhibitory neurotransmitter GABA, is administered to reduce the withdrawal symptoms associated with which psychoactive drug?
(A) Alcohol
(B) Marijuana
(C) Cocaine
(D) LSD
(E) Nicotine

84. As Jim ran in a marathon he grew thirsty, so he stopped for a cup of water. Which biological mechanism was responsible for alerting Jim that he needed to drink water?
(A) Arousal
(B) Homeostasis
(C) Endorphins
(D) Hormones
(E) Adrenaline

85. Tracy had an exhausting day at work. Later that night, she called her friends and told them that she would not being going out, as they had planned. When her friends inquired why, Tracy said that day had been too exhausting and she just wanted to go to bed. Which theory of motivation would account for Tracy's not wanting to go out?
(A) Drive reduction theory
(B) Optimal arousal theory
(C) Instinct theory
(D) Homeostasis
(E) Facial-feedback theory

86. Nancy ate a fattening meal for lunch, and as a result, she wasn't hungry for the remainder of the day. Which hormone reacts to high fat content in food, causing feelings of satiation?
(A) Insulin
(B) Glucose
(C) CCK
(D) Leptin
(E) Orexin

87. At the beginning of the year, Kerri didn't like her psychology teacher. However, as the year progressed, she began to enjoy the class and the teacher more and more. Her change in attitude is the result of what phenomenon?
(A) Conformity
(B) The mere exposure effect
(C) Bystander effect
(D) Actor-observer effect
(E) Fundamental attribution error

88. When Beth got her test back and realized she had failed, she didn't seem upset. A friend later asked Beth why she wasn't disappointed by the test score. Beth replied as though she didn't care about her grade. Which theory of emotion could account for Beth's unresponsive reaction?
(A) Two-factory theory of emotion
(B) Facial-feedback hypothesis
(C) Cannon-Bard theory of emotion
(D) James-Lange theory of emotion
(E) Cognitive appraisal theory of emotion

89. During a stressful event, the pituitary gland stimulates the outer portion of the adrenal glands to release _____, a hormone, which allows the body to release energy supplies, helping to fight inflammation.
(A) catecholamines
(B) corticosteroids
(C) endorphins
(D) adrenaline
(E) noradrenaline

90. Joe is entering late childhood and recently has started to play only with boys. Joe is exhibiting the characteristics of which psychosexual stage?
(A) Oral
(B) Anal
(C) Phallic
(D) Latency
(E) Genital

91. Julian Rotter believed that _____ guide behavior and influence personality.
(A) unconscious motivations
(B) expectancies
(C) social relationships
(D) superiorities
(E) self-efficacy beliefs

GO ON TO NEXT PAGE

92. Carl Rogers believed that personality development began with the realization of positive regard, which is
    (A) the resolving of unconscious motivations
    (B) the addressing of inferiorities from early life
    (C) the need for independence
    (D) the need for other people's approval
    (E) the understanding of cognitive abilities

93. The practical approach for defining abnormal behavior emphasizes
    (A) how the behavior violates norms
    (B) the frequency of the behavior displayed
    (C) the interpretation of family members who are in contact with the displayed behavior
    (D) the amount of stress it causes the family members
    (E) how the behavior impairs one's ability to function

94. _____, a neurotransmitter, which, when prevented from exerting its inhibitory influence, could be responsible for the symptoms related to anxiety disorders.
    (A) Glutamate
    (B) Endorphins
    (C) GABA
    (D) Serotonin
    (E) Dopamine

95. Jerry has complained of experiencing physical problems in multiple places on his body. His doctor explained that even though Jerry feels the pains, there is no physical evidence of anything causing them. Jerry's symptoms are an example of
    (A) Schizophrenia
    (B) Somatization disorder
    (C) Generalized anxiety disorder
    (D) Conversion disorder
    (E) Major depression

96. Fixed, unlearned patterns of behavior best describe which theory of motivation?
    (A) Drive-reduction theory
    (B) Optimal arousal theory
    (C) Instinct theory
    (D) Facial-feedback theory
    (E) Incentive theory

97. The statement, "The car buried itself, then the door answered the cat, and time ran up and down the stairs," is an example of which schizophrenia characteristic?
    (A) Neologisms
    (B) Delusions of grandeur
    (C) Delusions of persecution
    (D) Hallucinations
    (E) Word salad

98. According to the classification of personality disorders, the dramatic-erratic cluster includes
    (A) histrionic, narcissistic, borderline, and antisocial personality disorders
    (B) histrionic, narcissistic, borderline, and schizoid personality disorders
    (C) histrionic, narcissistic, borderline, and schizotypal personality disorders
    (D) borderline, narcissistic, antisocial, and paranoid personality disorders
    (E) avoidant, borderline, antisocial, and paranoid personality disorders

99. As John's father tried to read his newspaper, John continued to display annoying behaviors. Rather than get upset, John's father simply ignored his son, resulting in John's not displaying the annoying behavior further. Which behavioral term describes the situation?
    (A) Token economy
    (B) Applying positive reinforcement
    (C) Applying negative reinforcement
    (D) Punishment
    (E) Extinction

100. Which childhood disorder could indicate the later development of antisocial personality disorder?
    (A) Conduct disorder
    (B) Asperger's disorder
    (C) Separation anxiety disorder
    (D) School phobia
    (E) Autistic disorder

STOP

END OF SECTION I

IF YOU FINISH BEFORE TIME IS CALLED, YOU MAY CHECK YOUR WORK ON THIS SECTION. DO NOT GO ON TO SECTION II UNTIL YOU ARE TOLD TO DO SO.

GO ON TO NEXT PAGE

PSYCHOLOGY
Section II
Time: 50 minutes

1. Define each of the following and explain how each influences perception and memory.
   - (a) Availability heuristics
   - (b) Serial position effect
   - (c) Conformity
   - (d) Acetylcholine
   - (e) Retroactive interference
   - (f) Anterograde amnesia

2. Ray has not felt like himself for weeks. He doesn't know why, or even how to describe the way he feels. He just knows he feels different—not like himself.
   - (a) Identify a symptom from each of the following psychological disorders listed below, to help Ray narrow down the choices and possibly identify the disorder he is experiencing.
     - ▨ Major depressive disorder
     - ▨ Bipolar disorder
     - ▨ Generalized anxiety disorder
     - ▨ Conversion disorder
   - (b) Identify a possible cause that each of the following therapeutic approaches would attribute to the development of a psychological disorder.
     - ▨ Psychodynamic
     - ▨ Humanistic
     - ▨ Behavioral

END OF EXAMINATION

ANSWERS FOR MULTIPLE-CHOICE QUESTIONS

Using the table below, score your test.

Determine how many questions you answered correctly and how many you answered incorrectly. You will find explanations of the answers on the following pages.

1. B	21. C	41. D	61. B	81. E
2. E	22. B	42. B	62. C	82. A
3. C	23. B	43. B	63. E	83. C
4. D	24. B	44. A	64. C	84. B
5. D	25. C	45. A	65. B	85. B
6. E	26. E	46. C	66. D	86. D
7. A	27. E	47. A	67. C	87. B
8. A	28. E	48. E	68. B	88. E
9. B	29. E	49. C	69. E	89. B
10. B	30. A	50. B	70. E	90. D
11. B	31. C	51. D	71. E	91. B
12. C	32. A	52. C	72. A	92. D
13. D	33. C	53. E	73. A	93. E
14. C	34. B	54. A	74. C	94. C
15. E	35. C	55. C	75. A	95. B
16. D	36. B	56. E	76. C	96. C
17. C	37. C	57. B	77. B	97. E
18. A	38. B	58. D	78. C	98. A
19. D	39. A	59. B	79. B	99. E
20. C	40. E	60. D	80. D	100. A

1. Answer: B. Operational definitions allow researchers to clarify how they will go about testing a hypothesis. Operational definitions are important for researchers to define before conducting research (*Psychology,* 8th ed. p. 32/9th ed. p. 34).

2. Answer: E. The hypothalamus is known as the pleasure center of the brain, and is responsible for the regulation of food, fight, flight, body temperature, and sex (*Psychology,* 8th ed. p. 215/9th ed. p. 217).

3. Answer: C. Unconditional positive regard consists of treating the client as a valued person, who—no matter what he or she has done—deserves to be treated without biased judgment. Empathy involves putting yourself in the client's situation and thinking in terms of what the client is experiencing (*Psychology,* 8th ed. pp. 650–651/9th ed. p. 657).

4. Answer: D. The psychodynamic approach stresses that behavior and mental processes are the result of the content of the unconscious. Conflicts that occur within the unconscious affect behavior and mental processes (*Psychology,* 8th ed. p. 19/9th ed. pp. 20–21).

5. Answer: D. Episodic memories contain information that describes events and knowledge a person has actually experienced. Semantic memories contain information relevant

to general knowledge (*Psychology*, 8th ed. p. 239/9th ed. p. 243).

6. Answer: E. Obese people tend to consume foods that are high in fat, contributing to the storage of excess fat, which in turn results in weight gain. A BMI of 30 or higher indicates obesity (*Psychology*, 8th ed. p. 416/9th ed. pp. 425–426).

7. Answer: A. The psychological model emphasizes that psychological factors, such as past memories and thinking styles, contribute to the onset of psychological disorders. The diathesis-stress model emphasizes that the amount and types of stress could affect a genetic predisposition to develop a certain disorder. (*Psychology* 8th ed. pp. 593–594/9th ed. p. 600).

8. Answer: A. The humanistic approach emphasizes that people have an innate drive that directs their behavior toward attaining psychological growth. Alfred Adler stressed that personality development is the overcoming of childhood inferiorities, resulting in a striving to be superior (*Psychology*, 8th ed. p. 571/9th ed. pp. 577–578).

9. Answer: B. Fixed-ratio schedules provide the operant (person/animal) with a reward or punishment after a set number of behaviors has been performed (*Psychology*, 8th ed. p. 212/9th ed. p. 214).

10. Answer: B. The right hemisphere of the brain controls the left side of the body. The motor cortex is vital for movement. Therefore, Paul's stroke must have been localized to his right motor cortex region (*Psychology*, 8th ed. p. 86/9th ed. pp. 88–89).

11. Answer: B. Alfred Binet developed the first standardized modern intelligence test for the French government to help identify special needs students (*Psychology*, 8th ed. p. 367/9th ed. p. 374).

12. Answer: C. The concept of objects appearing to move at the same speed and direction is known by Gestalt psychologists as common fate (*Psychology*, 8th ed. p. 164/9th ed. p. 168).

13. Answer: D. High levels of the stress hormone cortisol have been linked to cases in which individuals show symptoms of depression. Serotonin, norepinephrine, and dopamine appear to be low in relation to symptoms of depression (*Psychology*, 8th ed. p. 619/9th ed. pp. 624–625).

14. Answer: C. Procedural memories contain information that pertains to how to perform specific skills. Episodic memories include information that is relevant to personal experiences, and semantic memories describe general knowledge about the environment and situations (*Psychology*, 8th ed. p. 239/9th ed. p. 243).

15. Answer: E. Naturalistic observation refers to a researcher observing a subject in its natural setting or environment without any interference on the researcher's part *(Psychology,* 8th ed. pp. 34–35/9th ed. p. 37).

16. Answer: D. The closer the correlation coefficient is to +1.00 or −1.00, the stronger the relationship between the variables *(Psychology,* 8th ed. pp. 51–52/9th ed. p. 54).

17. Answer: C. According to Thorndike, the law of effect states that if a behavior successfully lead to a reward it would continue. However, if the behavior did *not* successfully lead to a reward, the behavior would not be displayed in the future *(Psychology,* 8th ed. pp. 205–206/9th ed. p. 208).

18. Answer: A. Positive correlations occur when both variables move in the same direction. Because Professor Olsen's class average increased when students took notes while listening to his lectures, a positive correlation is displayed *(Psychology,* 8th ed. pp. 51–52/9th ed. p. 54).

19. Answer: D. Noam Chomsky said that each human is born with the ability to produce language, due to the language acquisition device (LAD) within the human brain. According to Chomsky, the LAD is what enables humans to produce language *(Psychology,* 8th ed. pp. 316–317/9th ed. p. 321).

20. Answer: C. Social facilitation refers to the increased performance of an individual due to the presence of others *(Psychology,* 8th ed. p. 725/9th ed. p. 731).

21. Answer: C. According to Robert Sternberg, creative intelligence is the ability to create novel ideas in various situations. Because Horace has created numerous symphonies he is said to have creative intelligence *(Psychology,* 8th ed. p. 389/9th ed. p. 396).

22. Answer: B. Ellis believed that people's interpretations of events, rather than the events themselves, were responsible for the symptoms associated with psychological disorders. He said that the tendency to overanalyze the outcomes of situations results in a self-defeating style of thinking. In other words, he believed that irrational or faulty thinking was the root cause of psychological dysfunction *(Psychology,* 8th ed. pp. 658–659/9th ed. pp. 665–666).

23. Answer: B. Transference occurs when the patient directs past feelings and conflicts associated with other people onto the therapist. Transference allows the therapist to identify and understand past conflicts. Resistance occurs when the person does not want to discuss, or shows hostility toward discussing, a topic introduced by the therapist *(Psychology,* 8th ed. pp. 647–648/9th ed. p. 654).

24. Answer: B. A confounding variable is any variable that may influence the outcome of an experiment, and over which the

researcher has no control. In this example, a person's mathematical ability, based on his or her exposure to geometry concepts, may influence the results of the experiment *(Psychology,* 8th ed. pp. 41–44/9th ed. pp. 43–45).

25. Answer: C. Down's syndrome is the result of an extra 21st chromosome *(Psychology,* 8th ed. p. 398/9th ed. pp. 405–406).

26. Answer: E. Sublimation is substituting unacceptable impulses and actions for more acceptable behaviors. Projection is unconsciously attributing guilt and anxiety onto other people *(Psychology,* 8th ed. p. 554/9th ed. p. 560).

27. Answer: E. Generalized anxiety disorder, also referred to as free-floating anxiety, is characterized by feelings of anxiety in all situations and experiences. No identifiable stressor precipitates the anxiety. Obsessive-compulsive disorder is associated with repetitive thoughts and compulsive actions *(Psychology,* 8th ed. p. 605/9th ed. p. 611).

28. Answer: E. The Institutional Review Board must approve experiments when humans are involved. The IRB ensures that participants are not exposed to any painful or lasting effects, while still allowing the researchers to investigate their proposals *(Psychology,* 8th ed. pp. 55–56/9th ed. pp. 57–58).

29. Answer: E. Obedience occurs when a person obeys the command of an actual or perceived authority figure *(Psychology,* 8th ed. p. 731/9th ed. p. 737).

30. Answer: A. The framing effect occurs when words are manipulated to produce a desired response. Participants who said they were interested in plants may have been unaware that botany is the study of plants *(Psychology,* 8th ed. p. 322/9th ed. p. 326).

31. Answer: C. Melatonin is produced by the pineal gland and helps regulate circadian rhythms (sleep/wake cycles) *(Psychology,* 8th ed. pp. 342–343/9th ed. p. 344).

32. Answer: A. As a person ages, fluid intelligence (the ability to quickly process and recall information) decreases, but overall crystallized intelligence (total accumulated knowledge) increases *(Psychology,* 8th ed. pp. 387, 394/9th ed. pp. 394, 401).

33. Answer: C. Environmental psychologists believe that the closer individuals live to each other, the higher the levels of aggression *(Psychology,* 8th ed. p. 743/9th ed. p. 750).

34. Answer: B. With a self-serving bias, individuals take credit for their success, but blame others for their failures *(Psychology,* 8th ed. p. 700/9th ed. p. 707).

35. Answer: C. Availability heuristics are mental short cuts, or rules of thumb, that rely on the judgment or decision to be based on the most easily accessible information the person has

on the subject. Because he was cut off by an elderly person early in the day, Manny based his decision on this information *(Psychology,* 8th ed. p. 294/9th ed. p. 299).

36. Answer: B. Endorphins are the body's natural painkillers *(Psychology,* 8th ed. pp. 98–99/9th ed. pp. 101–102).

37. Answer: C. Psychophysics focuses on the relationship between the physical characteristics of the environment and the individual's subjective interpretation of those characteristics, resulting in perception *(Psychology,* 8th ed. p. 155/9th ed. p. 159).

38. Answer: B. Children in Piaget's preoperational stage display egocentrism. Because Stanley's mother is upset, Stanley brings her his favorite toy in an effort to cheer her up *(Psychology,* 8th ed. pp. 470–471/9th ed. p. 475).

39. Answer: A. The autonomic nervous system is responsible for the body's automatic functions, such as digestion, breathing, heartbeat, and temperature regulation *(Psychology,* 8th ed. pp. 68–69/9th ed. p. 72).

40. Answer: E. A disadvantage of an objective personality test is that there is only one correct answer per question. A test taker might feel that none of the answers accurately described him or her *(Psychology,* 8th ed. p. 580/9th ed. p. 590).

41. Answer: D. Monozygotic twins who were raised separately but have the same IQ provide the best example that IQ is based on genetics, because monozygotic twins share the same genotype, as opposed to the influence of the environment on IQ *(Psychology,* 8th ed. pp. 377–378/9th ed. pp. 384–385).

42. Answer: B. The experimental method of research allows the researcher to control the environment in which the experiment takes place, as well as manipulate the variables being tested. This type of research is also useful in establishing cause and effect *(Psychology,* 8th ed. p. 40/9th ed. p. 42).

43. Answer: B. The MMPI was originally designed to measure the characteristics related to psychological disorders *(Psychology,* 8th ed. p. 581/9th ed. p. 588).

44. Answer: A. According to the Gestalt principle of *texture gradient* the closer an object appears, the more texture gradient, or clarity of detail, you can perceive; the farther away an object appears, the less detail you can perceive *(Psychology,* 8th ed. p. 167/9th ed. p. 171).

45. Answer: A. Descriptive statistics are useful in numerically describing the results for an entire population *(Psychology,* 8th ed. p. 49/9th ed. p. 51).

46. Answer: C. Catatonic schizophrenia is characterized by odd movement, which includes the body's displaying a rigid,

statue-like posture referred to as waxy flexibility (*Psychology*, 8th ed. p. 624/9th ed. p. 630).

47. Answer: A. Negative reinforcement occurs when an aversive (unpleasant) stimulus is removed, causing future behavior to increase. Turning on the air conditioner to remove the aversive stimulus (the heat), will result in the person's repeating this action if he is exposed to heat in the future (*Psychology*, 8th ed. p. 207/9th ed. p. 209).

48. Answer: E. The neutral stimulus is any stimulus that does not elicit a response prior to conditioning. In the case of Little Albert, prior to the conditioning trials the white rat elicited no response (this case study does not appear in the text, but discussion on classical conditioning is found in *Psychology*, 8th ed. p. 198/9th ed. p. 201).

49. Answer: C. Modeling refers to replicating an observed behavior, as Clare tried to do on her trampoline (*Psychology*, 8th ed. pp. 225–226/9th ed. pp. 227–228).

50. Answer: B. Cognitive maps are mental representations of a particular place or situation. Having a good mental map allowed Grover to successfully navigate his way through the state park (*Psychology*, 8th ed. p. 224/9th ed. pp. 225–226).

51. Answer: D. Acetylcholine is responsible for muscle contraction, and when an excess amount is released, it can lead to violent and uncontrollable muscle contractions (*Psychology*, 8th ed. p. 96/9th ed. p. 99).

52. Answer: C. Learned helplessness occurs when someone or something feels that it cannot influence the outcome and simply refuses to try in future (*Psychology*, 8th ed. p. 221/9th ed. p. 223).

53. Answer: E. CAT/CT scans provide a detailed image of the body, and would most likely be used to assess any damage that may have occurred (*Psychology*, 8th ed. p. 327/this material does not appear in 9th ed.).

54. Answer: A. Flooding involves constantly exposing an individual to whatever she fears in hopes of successfully causing extinction between the conditioned stimulus and the conditioned response (*Psychology*, 8th ed. p. 655/9th ed. p. 664).

55. Answer: C. The dependent variable is the measureable outcome of the experiment. Therefore, the dependent variable would be how much a subject increased visual acuity (*Psychology*, 8th ed. pp. 38–39/9th ed. p. 43).

56. Answer: E. Blaming the behaviors of others on dispositional/internal factors while excusing one's own behavior as the result of situational/external factors is known

as the actor-observer effect (*Psychology,* 8th ed. pp. 699–700/9th ed. pp. 706–707).

57. Answer: B. Random assignment of participants ensures that each person has an equal chance of being selected to either the experimental or the control group. Random sampling refers to the entire population's being given an equal chance of being selected to participate in an experiment (*Psychology,* 8th ed. p. 41/9th ed. p. 44).

58. Answer: D. Self-handicapping occurs when an individual excuses future performance in case of failure (*this material does not appear in either textbook edition*).

59. Answer: B. Cognitive dissonance occurs when an individual experiences discomfort as the result of conflicting beliefs, or a conflict between beliefs and behaviors (*Psychology,* 8th ed. pp. 704–705/9th ed. pp. 711–712).

60. Answer: D. Insight is the sudden realization of the solution to a problem. When the dolphins figured out that the obstacle needed to be moved to complete the task, researchers concluded that the dolphin possessed the ability to think logically, thus enabling it to realize the solution to the current problem (*Psychology,* 8th ed. p. 224/9th ed. p. 227).

61. Answer: B. Encoding is a memory process that involves acquiring information, which will later be entered into memory. Selective attention determines whether encoding will take place (*Psychology,* 8th ed. p. 238/9th ed. p. 242).

62. Answer: C. Behaviorists such as Skinner would argue that the development of language is the result of reinforcement from others. If a child pronounces a word correctly, her parents or guardians respond in a positive manner, therefore increasing the chances that she will repeat that word in future (*Psychology,* 8th ed. pp. 315–316/9th ed. pp. 320–321).

63. Answer: E. Confirmation bias occurs when a person ignores or rejects information that contradicts his or her currently held beliefs and looks for or accepts only information with which he or she agrees (*Psychology,* 8th ed. pp. 291–292/9th ed. pp. 305–306).

64. Answer: C. After a neuron has fired it enters the refractory period, which allows the cell to process incoming information and begin the "firing" process all over (*Psychology,* 8th ed. p. 64/9th ed. p. 68).

65. Answer: B. Achievement tests are designed to measure a person's accumulated knowledge on a given subject. Because the test is based on information learned throughout the semester, it would be considered an achievement test. Aptitude tests are used to help predict how well a person will perform in the future (*Psychology,* 8th ed. p. 372/9th ed. p. 378).

66. Answer: D. A test is considered valid if it accurately measures what it is supposed to be testing. Reliability refers to the fact that a test produces the same results after being administered to numerous subjects. Because Professor Paulson has used the same test for the past ten years, and his students perform well on the nationwide exam, we can assume that his test possesses good criterion validity, the ability of a test to predict how well a person will do on future tasks and performances (*Psychology,* 8th ed. pp. 373–374/9th ed. p. 380).

67. Answer: C. The absolute threshold is referred to as the minimum level of stimulation necessary for detection 50 percent of the time. Even though a stimulus could exceed an absolute threshold, it's possible it would not be detected if the person is not paying attention, is not motivated, or is distracted by background noise. If a stimulus that was constantly presented exceeded the absolute threshold, most people would average about half in terms of detection of the stimulus. Half the time they would detect it, and the other half of the time they would not (*Psychology,* 8th ed. p. 156/9th ed. p. 161).

68. Answer: B. The behavioral approach emphasizes the study of observable behavior. Behaviorists believe that behavior is the result of what has been learned, and therefore, that what is learned can be also unlearned. The psychodynamic approach focuses on unconscious conflicts and motivations (*Psychology,* 8th ed. p. 19/9th ed. p. 17).

69. Answer: E. A valid test is one that measures that it was designed to measure (*Psychology,* 8th ed. p. 373/9th ed. p. 380).

70. Answer: E. Konrad Lorenz established the theory of imprinting while conducting research on goslings. Imprinting refers to the establishment of attachment an animal has on the first object it observes moving (*this material does not appear in the either textbook edition*).

71. Answer: E. According to Diana Baumrind, the authoritative parenting style produces well-adjusted and respectful children. Authoritarian and permissive parenting styles produce uncooperative, aggressive and socially inept children (*Psychology,* 8th ed. pp. 485–487/9th ed. pp. 491–492).

72. Answer: A. Buspirone is used to treat symptoms related to anxiety,. However, most people who take it do not feel the effects for days or even weeks (*Psychology,* 8th ed. p. 679/9th ed. p. 685).

73. Answer: A. The ventromedial nucleus is said to be in charge of stopping hunger. If this part of the hypothalamus were destroyed the rat would continue to eat. The lateral hypothalamus is in charge of initiating hunger (*Psychology,* 8th ed. p. 413/9th ed. p. 422).

74. Answer: C. A longitudinal study allows the researcher to observe subjects over an extended period of time (*Psychology,* 8th ed. p. 393/9th ed. p. 400).

75. Answer: A. According to Lawrence Kohlberg, individuals in the preconventional morality stage base their behavior on avoiding punishment or for personal gain. Because Frank is told to go directly to the birthday party he doesn't stop and help because he doesn't want to be punished for stopping along the way (*Psychology,* 8th ed. pp. 499–501/9th ed. pp. 506–507).

76. Answer: C. According to Erik Erikson, Aiden would be at the identity versus role confusion stage of his psychosocial development. By joining a sports team, Aiden is trying to figure out where he belongs and who he fits in and identifies with most (*Psychology,* 8th ed. p. 485/9th ed. p. 490).

77. Answer: B. According to Mary Ainsworth, securely attached children become upset when their parent leaves the room, but return to their passive state upon the return of the parent (*Psychology,* 8th ed. pp. 482–483/9th ed. pp. 487–488).

78. Answer: C. William James, a functionalist, was influenced by Charles Darwin's theory of evolution and was interested in the role of consciousness in directing a person's behavior and cognitive skills. In contrast, structuralism was the study of the mental elements within the brain (*Psychology,* 8th ed. p. 15–16/9th ed. pp. 16–17).

79. Answer: B. A main component of a collectivistic culture is the welfare of the group. In a collectivistic culture, members put the group above themselves. Individualistic cultures place more emphasis on personal happiness and gain (*Psychology,* 8th ed. p. 23/9th ed. p. 25).

80. Answer: D. Community psychology was a movement that originated partly in response to the sudden release of mental patients from mental hospitals. One aim of community psychology is to help patients cope with problems, identify symptoms associated with psychological disorders, and provide alternatives for treatment (*Psychology,* 8th ed. pp. 684–685/9th ed. pp. 690–691).

81. Answer: E. The kinesthetic sense is responsible for the position of body parts in relation to place and movement. Information is received from receptors in the muscles and joints. The vestibular sense receives information from the semicircular canals and vestibular sacs located in the inner ear (*Psychology,* 8th ed. pp. 146–147/9th ed. pp. 150–151).

82. Answer: A. As the sleep cycle continues, NREM stage 2 becomes more frequent, as does REM sleep. NREM stages 3 and 4 actually decrease as a person continues to sleep (*Psychology,* 8th ed. p. 337/9th ed. p. 341).

83. Answer: C. Baclofen is used to increase the effectiveness of the neurotransmitter GABA, which in turn reduces the withdrawal symptoms associated with cocaine (*Psychology,* 8th ed. p. 356/9th ed. p. 361).

84. Answer: B. Homeostasis monitors physiological systems of the body, indicating when there is a fluctuation within these levels (*Psychology,* 8th ed. p. 408/9th ed. p. 417).

85. Answer: B. The optimal arousal theory of motivation suggests that people are motivated to regulate the amount of arousal in a given time period. If a day is boring, someone may need more excitement; however, if the day is too stimulating, rest may be needed (*Psychology,* 8th ed. pp. 409–410/9th ed. p. 418).

86. Answer: D. Leptin is released into the bloodstream in reaction to increases in fat supplies. When leptin is circulated into the bloodstream, messages are sent to the hypothalamus, indicating satiation. The higher the amount of fat in the bloodstream, the more leptin is released, causing longer-lasting feelings of satiation. CCK provides short-term signals of satiation (*Psychology,* 8th ed. p. 413/9th ed. pp. 421–422).

87. Answer: B. The more a person is exposed to a stimulus, the more he or she begins to like the stimulus (*Psychology,* 8th ed. p. 703/9th ed. p. 710).

88. Answer: E. The cognitive appraisal theory of emotion suggests emotion is the result of how an event is perceived. If an event is perceived as not threatening a person's well-being, then emotion is not intensified (*Psychology,* 8th ed. p. 448/9th ed. pp. 455–456).

89. Answer: B. Corticosteroids are released by the outer surface of the adrenal glands, allowing the body to be able to use its energy supplies to fight inflammation that arises in the body. Catecholamines are released by medulla—the inner portion of the adrenal glands—which, in turn, secrete adrenaline and noreadrenaline into the bloodstream (*Psychology,* 8th ed. p. 524/9th ed. pp. 528–529).

90. Answer: D. According to Sigmund Freud, the latency stage begins in late childhood and is characterized by same-sex friendships in which sexual feelings lay dormant. It is not until the genital stage that sexual impulses return at a conscious level (*Psychology,* 8th ed. p. 555/9th ed. p. 561).

91. Answer: B. According to Julian Rotter, a person's expectations, or what the person expects to happen in a given situation, affect behavior, influencing personality development. According to Albert Bandura, self-efficacy beliefs are expectations, which are based on a person's probability of succeeding (*Psychology,* 8th ed. p. 568/9th ed. pp. 574–575).

92. Answer: D. According to Carl Rogers, personality development begins when the child realizes that he or she has a need of

positive regard, which is the approval of other people's opinions and support. For optimal functioning to occur, Rogers stressed the importance of unconditional positive regard, a condition in which others accept and support you for who you are, and don't impose conditions of worth on you *(Psychology,* 8th ed. p. 572/9th ed. p. 578).

93. Answer: E. The practical approach emphasizes how a person's behavior impairs his or her ability to function during daily routines. The violation of norms is not a valid predictor of abnormal behavior because of the diversity of cross-cultural norms *(Psychology,* 8th ed. p. 590/9th ed. p. 598).

94. Answer: C. GABA, an inhibitory neurotransmitter that slows down neural activity in the brain, has been linked to symptoms associated with anxiety disorder. Glutamate, on the other hand, is an excitatory neurotransmitter. Serotonin has been linked to mood disorders. Dopamine is also an excitatory neurotransmitter and has been linked to schizophrenia and Parkinson's disease *(Psychology,* 8th ed. p. 97/9th ed. p. 101).

95. Answer: B. Somatization disorder is characterized by a number of physical ailments that are not isolated to one specific part of the body. There is no physical illness associated with such ailments. Conversion disorder occurs when a person experiences sensory or motor failure without physical cause *(Psychology,* 8th ed. p. 610/9th ed. p. 617).

96. Answer: C. The instinct theory describes motivation as fixed, unlearned behavior patterns to which one is genetically predisposed *(Psychology,* 8th ed. p. 406/9th ed. p. 415).

97. Answer: E. Word salad is a characteristic of schizophrenia. Such statements are chaotic, unordered, and do not make sense to anyone other than the speaker. Neologisms have special meaning only to the person speaking *(Psychology,* 8th ed. p. 622/9th ed. p. 628).

98. Answer: A. The dramatic-erratic cluster includes histrionic, narcissistic, borderline, and antisocial personality disorders *(Psychology,* 8th ed. p. 628/9th ed. p. 634).

99. Answer: E. This situation is an example of extinction. John annoyed his father in order to achieve a desired response. When the father did not deliver the expected response; John's motivation for performing the behavior decreased, or became extinguished. Punishment is the presentation of a negative stimulus or reaction following an undesirable behavior *(Psychology,* 8th ed. p. 657/9th ed. pp. 663–664).

100. Answer: A. Conduct disorder, characterized by a relatively stable pattern of aggression and other destructive behavior, could lead to antisocial personality disorder later in adulthood. Conduct disorder affects mostly boys, who tend to show a lack of control and impulsivity *(Psychology,* 8th ed. p. 633/9th ed. p. 638).

ANSWERS FOR FREE-RESPONSE QUESTIONS

1. Define each of the following and explain how each influences perception and memory.
   (a) Availability heuristics
      - Definition (Point 1)
         1. Using the most easily accessible information to reach a conclusion.
      - Application (Point 2)
         1. If a person is asked which country has more people, Australia or Chile, the person will rely on the information that is most easily accessible, or the country that comes to mind most easily.
   (b) Serial position effect
      - Definition (Point 3)
         1. The tendency to remember items at the beginning or end of a list
         2. Not remembering information presented in the middle
      - Application (Point 4)
         1. Given a list of 20 words, a person is more likely to remember the earliest and most recent items, rather than those presented in the middle.
   (c) Conformity
      - Definition (Point 5)
         1. Changing behavior due to the presence or imagined presence of another person
      - Application (Point 6)
         1. A person is more likely to agree with others even though he or she was not explicitly asked to do so.
         2. An example is following a social norm, such as not facing others in an elevator.
            (Other social norms are acceptable if they show compliance or an unwritten rule is being followed).
   (d) Acetylcholine
      - Definition (Point 7)
         1. Neurotransmitter implicated in memory and muscle movement
      - Application (Point 8)
         1. People who have Alzheimer's disease have a depletion of Ach.
   (e) Retroactive interference
      - Definition (Point 9)
         1. Old information is lost or disrupted due to the presentation of new information
         2. New information disrupts the recall of old information
      - Application (Point 10)
         1. A student has a difficulty remembering the locker combination from last school year because he has memorized a new locker combination this year.
   (f) Anterograde amnesia
      - Definition (Point 11)
         1. Traumatic injury results in the inability to remember information after the incident.
      - Application (Point 12)
         1. An example would be if you were hit in the head and couldn't remember information after the injury.

2. Ray has not felt like himself for weeks. He doesn't know why, or even how to describe the way he feels. He just knows he feels different—not like himself.

(a) Identify a symptom from each of the following psychological disorders listed below, to help Ray narrow down the choices and possibly identify the disorder he is experiencing.

■ Major depressive disorder (Point 1): one symptom from the following: sadness, feelings of worthlessness, fluctuations in eating habits resulting in loss or gain of weight, changes in sleeping habits, loss of interest in activities, trouble performing daily functions, lack of energy

■ Bipolar disorder (Point 2): alternating between periods of mania and periods of deep depression

■ Generalized anxiety disorder (Point 3): one symptom from the following: excessive and long-lasting experiences of anxiety attributed to a variety of situations—not one in particular—apprehension, irritability, trouble sleeping, inability to concentrate, heightened physiological responses including accelerated heart rate, shakes, increased respiration

■ Conversion disorder (Point 4): a deficient sensory or motor ability such as blindness, deafness, use of a limb, no sensation of touch, smell, or taste not connected to any physical cause (must include that it must not be connected to a physical cause to count)

(b) Identify a possible cause that each of the following therapeutic approaches would attribute to the development of a psychological disorder.

■ Psychodynamic (Point 5): Psychodynamic approach—one of the following factors: unresolved conflicts within the unconscious/ traumatic early childhood experiences/ or conflicts between the id and the superego

■ Humanistic (Point 6): one of the following factors: psychological growth process is interfered with or blocked/ negative self-concept/ lack of awareness of feelings/ distorted perceptions or thoughts concerning events and situations

■ Behavioral (Point 7): maladaptive thoughts and actions that a person has learned contribute to psychological disorders

Calculating Your Score

This scoring chart is based on the 2007 AP Psychology released exam. While the AP Grade Conversion Chart is NOT the same for each testing year, it gives you an approximate breakdown.

SCORING THE MULTIPLE-CHOICE SECTION

Use the following formula to calculate your raw score on the multiple-choice section of the exam:

_____ × 1.00 = _____

number correct   weighted Section 1 Score (out of 100)

SCORING THE FREE-RESPONSE SECTION

Question 1   _____ × 2.084 = _____
(out of 12)   (do not round)

Question 2   _____ × 3.572 = _____
(out of 7)   (do not round)

sum = _____

weighted Section II score (do not round)

YOUR COMPOSITE SCORE

_____ + _____ = _____
weighted   weighted   composite score
Section I score   Section II score   (round to nearest whole number)

AP GRADE CONVERSION CHART

Composite Score Range	AP Grade
113 – 150	5
93 – 112	4
77 – 92	3
65 – 76	2
0 – 64	1

PRACTICE TEST 2

PSYCHOLOGY
Section I: Multiple-Choice Questions
Time—70 minutes
Number of Questions—100

MULTIPLE-CHOICE QUESTIONS

1. You are eating dinner with your parents when your father demands that you take off your hat. If you remove your hat you have
   (A) complied
   (B) conformed
   (C) committed a fundamental attribution error
   (D) demonstrated bystander apathy
   (E) displayed the mere-exposure effect

2. Which of the following is used to determine the relationships among traits represented in the big-five personality model?
   (A) Factor analysis
   (B) Objective personality test
   (C) Personal interviews
   (D) Case studies
   (E) Subjective personality test

3. Linda finds that the more she exercises, the less fast food she eats. Based on this information we could expect that what type of correlation would be present?
   (A) Negative
   (B) Positive
   (C) Null
   (D) Standard
   (E) Central

4. After failing his psychology test, George says that he has "a horrible teacher, who doesn't know what he's talking about." George is exhibiting
   (A) self-handicapping
   (B) a self-fulfilling prophecy
   (C) a self-serving bias
   (D) the mere exposure effect
   (E) bystander apathy

5. The development of psychodynamic therapy was in response to psychoanalysis
   (A) not being able to gain insight into the unconscious
   (B) being too long and expensive
   (C) focusing too much on present problems
   (D) addressing present problems instead of childhood events
   (E) involving more than one therapist

6. An agent that could potentially harm the development of a prenatal child is known as
   (A) a side effect
   (B) assimilation
   (C) a teratogen
   (D) an environmental factor
   (E) temperament

GO ON TO NEXT PAGE 377

7. As Nancy started to take a test, she noticed that her heart was racing and her breathing had become more rapid. According to Hans Selye, which stage of the general adaptation syndrome was Nancy experiencing?
   (A) Exhaustion
   (B) Alarm
   (C) Resistance
   (D) Adaptation
   (E) Regression

8. All of the following are characteristics of a panic disorder except
   (A) accelerated heart rate
   (B) increased perspiration
   (C) feelings of dizziness
   (D) knowing the specific causes of the anxiety
   (E) the attacks arrive without warning

9. Which term best explains that a person holding a 25-pound bag of rocks would not feel a three-ounce rock added to the bag?
   (A) Law of effect
   (B) Signal detection theory
   (C) Weber's law
   (D) Transduction
   (E) Selective attention

10. Which region of the brain is considered the switchboard, transmitting information, other than smell, to the correct area of the brain for further processing?
    (A) Hypothalamus
    (B) Hippocampus
    (C) Amygdala
    (D) Thalamus
    (E) Cerebellum

11. Which neo-Freudian would agree with the following statement: "Information stored in the collective unconscious provides an innate predisposition to act a certain way in various situations"?
    (A) Alfred Adler
    (B) Karen Horney
    (C) Carl Jung
    (D) Erik Erikson
    (E) Erich Fromm

12. If a test were designed to predict how well a student would do in his or her first year of college, yet those who took the test did considerably better than their scores had predicted, the test would be considered
    (A) unreliable and invalid
    (B) unreliable, but valid
    (C) reliable, but invalid
    (D) reliable and valid
    (E) predictable, but not reliable

13. Sam believes that one possible explanation for men developing alcoholism at a higher rate than women is that it is more acceptable for men to drink alcohol than it is for women. Which approach would support Sam's opinion?
    (A) Psychodynamic
    (B) Biological
    (C) Sociocultural
    (D) Humanistic
    (E) Behavioral

14. Which part of a neuron is responsible for transmitting information from the nucleus to the axon terminal?
    (A) Myelin
    (B) Axon
    (C) Axon terminal
    (D) Axon hillock
    (E) Dendrite

15. Which of the following best indicates a positive correlation?
    (A) The more fast food a person eats, the more weight he or she gains.
    (B) The longer a person stays in the sun, the less likely he or she is to burn.
    (C) The more sunscreen a person applies, the more he or she will tan.
    (D) The more a person talks on the phone, the less time he or she will spend reading.
    (E) The less expensive a car he or she buys, the more money a person will have.

16. Professor Winkleman is interested in studying the effects of laughter on positive mental health. Which of the following research methods would Professor Winkleman most likely use to determine a cause-and-effect relationship?
    (A) A case study
    (B) Naturalistic observation
    (C) Survey method
    (D) An experiment
    (E) A correlation

17. A worker is paid $15 for each chair he produces, regardless of how long it takes him to do so. This schedule is known as a
    (A) fixed-interval
    (B) fixed-ratio
    (C) variable-interval
    (D) variable-ratio
    (E) standard-ratio

18. Mr. Pearson has been teaching world history for 35 years. His students are amazed by his vast knowledge. Because you have taken AP psychology, you understand that as a person ages, which form of intelligence increases?
    (A) Fluid
    (B) Crystallized
    (C) Worldly
    (D) Instinctive
    (E) Moral

19. Which of the following best illustrates Stanley Milgram's experiment with obedience?
    (A) Terri refuses to help students who are struggling in physics.
    (B) Polly wears a lot of makeup because her friends do.
    (C) Rhonda thinks she is going to fail an upcoming test, so she doesn't bother to study.
    (D) Nick raises his hand when his teacher asks the class a question.
    (E) Al is constantly late to class despite warnings from his teacher that his grade will be affected if he can't be punctual.

20. Dr. Sobe is interested in studying the behavior patterns of adult apes in the wild. Which research method is Dr. Sobe most likely to use?
    (A) A case study
    (B) An experiment
    (C) Naturalistic observation
    (D) A survey
    (E) A correlational study

21. Fluffy, your cat, comes running into the kitchen every time she hears her dry cat food bag being opened. Her vet recently instructed you to switch to canned food. Which of the following is most likely to occur?
    (A) Fluffy will be able to discriminate between the electric can opener and the bag and will still come running when you are preparing her food.
    (B) After a while, the sound of the bag opening will no longer cause Fluffy to come running.
    (C) The can opener will have no effect on Fluffy.
    (D) Fluffy will use spontaneous recovery when you use an electric can opener to open her food.
    (E) Fluffy will refuse to eat any food opened with an electric can opener.

22. According to Edward Tolman, cognitive maps are
    (A) mental representations that help guide behavior
    (B) mental images that serve no purpose
    (C) maps that people use to establish associations
    (D) the result of positive reinforcement
    (E) the result of negative reinforcement

GO ON TO NEXT PAGE

23. Dr. Belltone recently gave a written survey to 1,000 people about their political beliefs. He found that 42 percent of people identified themselves as Democrats, and 42 percent of people identified themselves as Republicans, while 16 percent were "undecided." One potential flaw in Dr. Belltone's study is that those who responded to the survey may have
(A) had knowledge of the experiment beforehand
(B) an interest in politics
(C) been offered monetary compensation
(D) experienced the mere exposure effect
(E) had their surveys filled out for them

24. Dr. Hillburn is interested in studying the effects of the neurotransmitter GABA on memory. Dr. Hillburn most likely follows which psychological perspective?
(A) Behaviorism
(B) Biological
(C) Cognitive
(D) Humanistic
(E) Psychodynamic

25. Neil complains of severe headaches, so his doctor suggests a test that produces an image based on x-rays taken around a single axis point. Knowing a bit about neuroimaging, you understand that the doctor has ordered a(n)
(A) PET scan
(B) CAT scan
(C) MRI
(D) fMRI
(E) EEG

26. Which psychologist would most likely argue that behavior is primarily the result of observational learning?
(A) Ivan Pavlov
(B) B. F. Skinner
(C) John B. Watson
(D) Albert Bandura
(E) Martin Seligman

27. Groupthink occurs when
(A) group members are more concerned with hearing all opinions
(B) group members are more concerned with maintaining a sense of cohesiveness
(C) individuals feel they will not be personally held responsible for the actions of the entire group
(D) an individual is exposed to information that counters his or her beliefs
(E) an individual changes his or her beliefs due to a request from a person of perceived authority

28. Which of the following is not governed by the autonomic nervous system?
(A) an increase in heart rate and blood pressure
(B) sweating after a ten-mile run
(C) digestion of a meal
(D) an increase in respiration rate after walking up a flight of stairs
(E) picking up a pencil after it fell to the floor

29. Bipolar II is different from bipolar I in which way?
(A) Bipolar I includes only depressive episodes and bipolar II includes only episodes of mania.
(B) Bipolar II includes severe depressive episodes whereas bipolar I does not.
(C) Bipolar II has more severe episodes of mania compared to bipolar I.
(D) Bipolar II has less severe episodes of mania compared to bipolar I.
(E) Bipolar I has less severe episodes of mania compared to bipolar II.

30. A problem-solving strategy that uses a rule of thumb is known as a(n)
(A) algorithm
(B) concept
(C) heuristic
(D) prototype
(E) judgment

31. Which therapist would agree with the following statement: "Cognitive distortions, quick and automatic false beliefs, attributed to the outcomes of events, lead to psychological disorders"?
    (A) Aaron Beck
    (B) Alfred Adler
    (C) Sigmund Freud
    (D) Carl Rogers
    (E) Abraham Maslow

32. Which of the following is most likely to occur in a person who has experienced a lesion to the frontal lobe?
    (A) Decreased ability to plan for future events
    (B) Increased short-term memory
    (C) Decreased ability to process auditory information
    (D) Increased ability to process visual information
    (E) Decreased balance and coordination abilities

33. According to cognitive learning theorists, learning is the result of
    (A) the interactions among neurotransmitters and their effect on behavior
    (B) mental representations/connections
    (C) the collective unconscious
    (D) cultural influence
    (E) unconscious beliefs that guide behavior

34. A characteristic of a projective personality test would be
    (A) multiple-choice questions with one correct answer
    (B) that the results are machine scored
    (C) unstructured stimuli
    (D) true-false questions
    (E) reliable results

35. Which hormone is responsible for the body's metabolic rate?
    (A) Dopamine
    (B) Endorphins
    (C) Testosterone
    (D) Estrogen
    (E) Thyroxin

36. Which of the following uses deductive reasoning to reach its conclusion?
    (A) All birds fly. A penguin is a bird. Therefore, penguins must fly.
    (B) All birds fly. Ostriches do not fly. Therefore, ostriches are not birds.
    (C) Joe is tall. Joe is a man. All men are tall.
    (D) Courtney is a blonde. Courtney is smart. All blondes are smart.
    (E) Librarians are females. All females are librarians.

37. An example of a somatoform disorder is
    (A) hypochondriasis
    (B) generalized anxiety disorder
    (C) panic disorder
    (D) major depression
    (E) bipolar disorder

38. _____ psychologists have found evidence that the brain's large, fluid-filled spaces called ventricles may be linked to schizophrenia.
    (A) Developmental
    (B) Cognitive
    (C) Psychodynamic
    (D) Personality
    (E) Biological

39. Jim was reluctant to quit drinking because he enjoyed the way alcohol makes him feel. Jim's wife, who wants Jim to stop drinking, sought clinical advice. She was told that Jim would need to form a new association with alcohol. The clinician further explained that through medication, Jim would learn to associate drinking with an unpleasant response. Which type of therapy was explained to Jim's wife?
    (A) Systematic desensitization
    (B) Exposure therapy
    (C) Client-centered therapy
    (D) Aversion therapy
    (E) Token economics

GO ON TO NEXT PAGE

40. Drew was having a hard time sitting next to a certain person in class, so he asked the teacher to move him. This solution is an example of which type of coping strategy?
    (A) Positive reappraisal
    (B) Wishful thinking
    (C) Problem-focused
    (D) Emotion-focused
    (E) Self-controlling

41. Vlad is playing cards with his friend. He has lost several previous games, and believes that his luck is about to turn. This error in judgment is known as
    (A) a mental set
    (B) functional fixedness
    (C) an error in cognition
    (D) insight
    (E) the gambler's fallacy

42. Which of the following is not considered a primary reinforcer?
    (A) Food
    (B) Water
    (C) Shelter
    (D) Warmth
    (E) Praise

43. Research has indicated that a deficiency of which neurotransmitter has been linked to depression, alcoholism, aggression, and eating disorders?
    (A) Dopamine
    (B) Serotonin
    (C) Acetylcholine
    (D) Endorphins
    (E) GABA

44. Your friend's 18-month-old baby can walk without assistance. Your friend comments repeatedly how advanced her baby is. However, because you have taken AP psychology you understand that this milestone is most likely the result of
    (A) nurturing
    (B) maturation
    (C) superior intellect
    (D) the critical period
    (E) the zone of proximal development

45. Which Freudian defense mechanism could explain the onset of a dissociative disorder?
    (A) Repression
    (B) Regression
    (C) Projection
    (D) Displacement
    (E) Sublimation

46. The humanistic approach has been criticized for all of the following EXCEPT
    (A) uniqueness of an individual
    (B) unconscious motivations
    (C) learning styles
    (D) situational influences
    (E) inherited characteristics

47. Absolute thresholds are affected by a person's _____, which is the ability to detect a particular stimulus.
    (A) response criterion
    (B) sensitivity
    (C) motivation
    (D) imagination
    (E) reluctance

48. While Jill was playing soccer, she grew thirsty. Midway through her game she couldn't run anymore, and she wanted to stop playing. According to this situation, which theory of motivation could account for Jill's wanting to stop playing and get a drink of water?
    (A) Incentive theory
    (B) Homeostasis
    (C) Instinct theory
    (D) Drive-reduction theory
    (E) Arousal theory

49. While walking down the street you pass a chocolate factory. All at once you remember your mother's homemade cookies and your mouth begins to salivate. The smell of the chocolate would be considered a(n)
    (A) unconditioned stimulus
    (B) unconditioned response
    (C) conditioned stimulus
    (D) conditioned response
    (E) neutral stimulus

50. Jodi recently won $2,500 in a raffle. She decides that she is going to give the money to her mother so other people will think she's a good daughter. According to Lawrence Kohlberg, Jodi is currently in what stage of moral development?
(A) Preconventional
(B) Conventional
(C) Postconventional
(D) Concrete
(E) Preoperational

51. Ecstasy (MDMA) increases the activity of the neurotransmitter _____, which is connected to feelings of pleasure.
(A) Dopamine
(B) Serotonin
(C) Glutamate
(D) GABA
(E) Melatonin

52. Jenny tells her friends that she was recently hypnotized and they ask her to explain how a person can be hypnotized. Jenny responded that she just followed the instructions of the hypnotist. Which concept would best support Jenny's explanation of hypnosis?
(A) State theory
(B) Role theory
(C) Repression
(D) Regression
(E) Gate-control theory

53. What type of humanistic therapy focuses on having the client become more aware of his or her feelings in relation to situations and the environment?
(A) Psychodynamic therapy
(B) Rational-emotive therapy
(C) Systematic desensitization
(D) Exposure therapy
(E) Gestalt therapy

54. What percentage of the general population has an IQ below 100?
(A) 85 percent
(B) 15 percent
(C) 50 percent
(D) 68 percent
(E) 34 percent

55. The equivalent of dysthymic disorders for depression would be _____ for bipolar disorder.
(A) cyclothymic disorder
(B) phobias
(C) obsessive-compulsive disorder
(D) somatization disorder
(E) conversion disorder

56. Larry injured his eye during a high school hockey game. His doctors put a patch over Larry's left eye to help the healing process. While trying to parallel park his car Larry hit the car behind him. The reason for Larry's difficulty with depth perception is because he was only using
(A) binocular cues
(B) monocular cues
(C) rods
(D) cones
(E) a blind spot

57. Nightmares, as opposed to night terrors, occur during which stage of sleep?
(A) REM sleep
(B) NREM stage 1 sleep
(C) NREM stage 2 sleep
(D) NREM stage 3 sleep
(E) NREM stage 4 sleep

58. Which psychologist claims that our culture influences our thoughts, which ultimately influence our language?
(A) B. F. Skinner
(B) Noam Chomsky
(C) Albert Bandura
(D) Benjamin Whorf
(E) Jean Piaget

59. An example of an accessory structure associated with vision would be
(A) lens
(B) optic nerve
(C) pupil
(D) ganglion cells
(E) bipolar cells

GO ON TO NEXT PAGE

60. The cerebral management of information received from our senses, which is then transferred into concepts that are used to solve problems and ultimately reach decisions, is known as
    (A) creativity
    (B) thinking
    (C) analogies
    (D) language
    (E) reasoning

61. Which neurons are responsible for the transmission of sensory information to the brain?
    (A) Afferent
    (B) Efferent
    (C) Myelin
    (D) Hillocks
    (E) Central

62. The smallest unit of meaning in language is known as
    (A) an algorithm
    (B) a phoneme
    (C) a morpheme
    (D) syntax
    (E) semantics

63. Rich really likes Marcy, but when Rich is around her he acts rude to her and doesn't show any indication that he likes her. Which defense mechanism is Rich displaying?
    (A) Displacement
    (B) Sublimation
    (C) Reaction formation
    (D) Regression
    (E) Repression

64. Mr. Hill, a high school math teacher, believes that males are more capable than females of learning math. He spends the majority of his class time helping the males in the class. As a result, the males in his class do much better than the females on the final exam. Mr. Hill's behavior best illustrates which social psychological phenomenon?
    (A) Self-handicapping
    (B) Self-fulfilling prophecy
    (C) Self-serving bias
    (D) The mere exposure effect
    (E) The bystander effect

65. Which of the following is not considered an obstacle to problem solving?
    (A) Mental set
    (B) Incubation
    (C) Functional fixedness
    (D) Confirmation bias
    (E) Expertise

66. Voluntary facial expressions are directed by which part of the brain?
    (A) Amygdala
    (B) Hippocampus
    (C) Pyramidal motor system
    (D) Extrapyramidal motor system
    (E) Association areas

67. Which of the following indicates the strongest relationship between two variables?
    (A) +.23
    (B) +.45
    (C) –.13
    (D) –.53
    (E) –.07

68. Professor Collins believes that those who learn meditation strategies at an early age are more likely to be successful in life. To test his hypothesis, Professor Collins studied 1,500 subjects for their first 40 years of life. Which of the following research methods did Professor Collins use?
    (A) Case study
    (B) Naturalistic observation
    (C) Survey
    (D) Longitudinal study
    (E) Experiment

69. All of Ricardo's friends listen to classical music each day after school. Ricardo recently bought some classical music CDs after hearing his friends talk about their favorite composers. Ricardo displayed which social psychological phenomenon?
    (A) Obedience
    (B) Compliance
    (C) Conformity
    (D) Self-serving bias
    (E) Self-handicapping

70. Mike was told that when he brings his dog to agility training, he should be sure the dog is hungry. The trainer explained that dogs respond better to treats for good behavior when they are hungry. Which motivational theory does this example best indicate?
(A) Instinct theory
(B) Arousal theory
(C) Incentive theory
(D) Achievement theory
(E) Intrinsic theory

71. Statistics that are used to draw conclusions about a specific sample of the population are known as
(A) descriptive
(B) inferential
(C) correlational
(D) central
(E) normal

72. Edward Thorndike is best known for his
(A) law of averages
(B) law of behavior
(C) law of aggression
(D) law of effect
(E) token economy theory

73. Manny is watching his high school volleyball team compete. He cheers widely each time they earn a point, and is upset each time the referee makes a call that goes against the team. According to social psychologists, Manny is displaying
(A) the mere-exposure effect
(B) confirmation bias
(C) participation bias
(D) in-group bias
(E) bystander apathy

74. Researchers were interested in studying the effects of classical music on athletic performance. Subjects in group A were exposed to 20 minutes of classical music before an athletic performance. Group B was not exposed to any classical music prior to an athletic performance. Group B would be considered the
(A) dependent variable
(B) independent variable
(C) control group
(D) standard deviate group
(E) confounding variable

75. Jim, a college sophomore, is contemplating a career in psychology. He recently visited his advisor, and she asked him to think about one topic that he found interesting. Jim responded that he has always been interested in how his roommate can remember material more easily than he can. Based on Jim's response, which area of psychology should he pursue?
(A) Biological
(B) Cognitive
(C) Psychodynamic
(D) Humanistic
(E) Behavioral

76. Which of the following is not a criticism of intelligence tests?
(A) IQ is not a good predictor of how successful a person will be.
(B) IQ tests are said to be culturally biased in their questions.
(C) IQ tests only measure a person's analytical intelligence.
(D) IQ tests are given to numerous people, and have been normed.
(E) IQ scores can be influenced by personal motivation.

77. Horace recently received a perfect score on his SAT, but failed his art class. According to Robert Sternberg, Horace displays a high level of
(A) practical intelligence
(B) analytical intelligence
(C) creative intelligence
(D) emotional intelligence
(E) kinesthetic intelligence

GO ON TO NEXT PAGE

78. Trevor recently scored a 100 on his final exam in psychology, and therefore he assumed that he would score a 5 on the AP psychology exam. However, he in fact only scored a 1. Trevor's psychology final exam
    (A) lacks content validity
    (B) lacks criterion validity
    (C) is unreliable
    (D) is not standardized
    (E) is very reliable

79. According to Charles Darwin, evolution occurs through the process of
    (A) unconscious motivations
    (B) natural selection
    (C) learned tendencies
    (D) psychological growth
    (E) family upbringing

80. The AP psychology exam is administered to thousands of students around the world on the same day, and therefore is considered
    (A) a personality test
    (B) standardized
    (C) a good measure of intelligence
    (D) a good measure of criterion validity
    (E) unreliable

81. Which psychologist is considered the pioneering figure in the field of child development?
    (A) Jean Piaget
    (B) Carl Rogers
    (C) Martin Seligman
    (D) Elizabeth Loftus
    (E) Ivan Pavlov

82. Mrs. Feld believes that each student is smart in his or her own way. Which psychologist is Mrs. Feld most likely to agree with?
    (A) Charles Spearman
    (B) Albert Bandura
    (C) Lewis Terman
    (D) Albert Binet
    (E) Howard Gardner

83. Movement within the _____ causes hair cells to move, which allows sounds to be heard.
    (A) auditory nerve
    (B) pinna
    (C) semicircular canals
    (D) basilar membrane
    (E) ear canal

84. Luigi fell off a horse and hit his head on a rock. When he regained consciousness he had a difficult time understanding what others were saying to him. Which area of the brain did Luigi most likely damage?
    (A) The cerebellum
    (B) The frontal lobes
    (C) Wernicke's area
    (D) Broca's area
    (E) The hypothalamus

85. John's wife has been pleading with him to quit smoking. John is convinced he won't be able to start his day without a cigarette. This is an example of
    (A) physical dependency
    (B) withdrawal symptoms
    (C) tolerance
    (D) psychological dependency
    (E) unconscious motivations

86. Clara believes that the reason her friends failed the math test was because they aren't as smart as she is, but blames her own failure on the fact that she worked late the night before and so was unable to study effectively for the test. Clara is displaying which social psychological phenomenon?
    (A) Conformity
    (B) Obedience
    (C) Bystander apathy
    (D) Actor-observer bias
    (E) Mere-exposure effect

87. Which of the following is not associated with bulimia nervosa?
    (A) eating large amounts of food at one time and then purging the food through self-induced vomiting or use of strong laxatives
    (B) usually experienced by females
    (C) preoccupation with eating and dieting that impairs normal functioning
    (D) intestinal damage and dental problems
    (E) do not see their eating habits as a problem

88. Henry has just been informed that he has an inoperable illness. According to Elizabeth Kübler-Ross's theory on dying, what is Henry likely to experience first?
    (A) Acceptance
    (B) Anger
    (C) Depression
    (D) Bargaining
    (E) Denial

89. Jim was attempting to run his first marathon. Around mile 20, with only 6 miles to go, Jim started to think about giving up. Then he remembered what it would mean to him to finish. At that point, Jim picked up his pace and was able to finish. Which type of motivation enabled Jim to finish the marathon?
    (A) Achievement motivation
    (B) Competence (need) motivation
    (C) Instinct motivation
    (D) Incentive motivation
    (E) Extrinsic motivation

90. Gently touching the cheek of an infant will produce the
    (A) rooting reflex
    (B) Moro reflex
    (C) Palmer reflex
    (D) Babinski reflex
    (E) grasping reflex

91. Professor Flemming believes that all freshman are incapable of learning anything, and therefore refuses to answer questions from any freshman. Professor Flemming is exhibiting
    (A) discrimination
    (B) bystander apathy
    (C) mere-exposure bias
    (D) social loafing
    (E) social inhibition

92. The other day, Alberto wanted to recommend a movie he had seen recently to a friend, but he couldn't remember the title. While eating dinner last night, he suddenly remembered it. Alberto experienced a problem-solving strategy known as
    (A) insight
    (B) functional fixedness
    (C) memory impediment
    (D) creativity
    (E) mental set

93. Stella doesn't have a curfew, and her parents don't communicate with her regularly and don't seem overly concerned when she fails a class. According to Diana Baumrind, Stella's parents would most likely be classified as
    (A) authoritarian
    (B) authoritative
    (C) permissive
    (D) understanding
    (E) overbearing

94. Confounding variables
    (A) increase the likelihood that an experiment will produce a desired result
    (B) can be directly controlled by the researcher
    (C) are found in every case study
    (D) allow the researcher to study cause and effect
    (E) may influence the outcome of a study

GO ON TO NEXT PAGE

95. Jenny describes herself as outgoing, likes to go to parties, and occasionally engages in risky behavior, but tends to be moody and worries often. According to Hans Eysenck, how would Jenny be characterized?
    (A) Extraversion; stability
    (B) Introversion; stability
    (C) Extraversion; emotionality
    (D) Introversion; emotionality
    (E) Emotionality; stability

96. Juan recently went to the grocery store to get some pasta for dinner. He had never been to this particular grocery store, so he decided to walk up and down each aisle until he found the pasta. Juan is using a problem-solving strategy known as
    (A) a heuristic
    (B) an analogy
    (C) creativity
    (D) an algorithm
    (E) incubation

97. According to the DSM-IV-TR, which disorders are included on Axis I?
    (A) clinical syndromes
    (B) personality disorders
    (C) mental retardation
    (D) environmental conditions
    (E) global assessment and functioning

98. Max asked his parents if he could borrow the car for the weekend; his parents said no. Max then asked if he could borrow the car for the evening, and his parents agreed. Max was using which method to persuade his parents to let him borrow the car?
    (A) Foot-in-the-door technique
    (B) Low balling technique
    (C) That's-not-all technique
    (D) Door-in-the-face technique
    (E) Not-in-my-backyard technique

99. When Julie was in her early 20s she developed symptoms of schizophrenia. In her 30s, through proper treatment, Julie is symptom-free. Which type of schizophrenia would Julie be presently diagnosed with?
    (A) Paranoid
    (B) Catatonic
    (C) Undifferentiated
    (D) Disorganized
    (E) Residual

100. In order for family therapy to be effective, each member must
    (A) show up independently
    (B) assess blame to other people
    (C) be willing to admit that each individual is a part of the family
    (D) only express an opinion when asked to do so
    (E) be quicker to point out criticisms when noticed

STOP

END OF SECTION I

IF YOU FINISH BEFORE TIME IS CALLED, YOU MAY CHECK YOUR WORK ON THIS SECTION. DO NOT GO ON TO SECTION II UNTIL YOU ARE TOLD TO DO SO.

PSYCHOLOGY
Section II
Time: 50 minutes

1. Psychologists often disagree on the influence of nature and nurture. Using your understanding of each issue, explain how the nature and nurture arguments consider each of the following:
   a. Intelligence
   b. Language
   c. Phobias
   d. Aggression
   e. Mental disorders

2. Jim is unsure whether he wants to take the AP psychology exam. He has developed a mental list of pros and cons to help determine whether he should take it.
   a. Explain how the following could help Jim make a decision. Be sure to relate your answers to the content of the situation.
      - Yerkes-Dodson law
      - Extrinsic motivation
      - Self-efficacy beliefs
      - Conformity
      - Obedience
   b. One of the reasons Jim doesn't want to take the exam is that he believes he has test anxiety. He states that he experiences feelings of sickness, shaky hands, and headaches when he sits down to a test. How could the following terms and theories explain Jim's interpretation of symptoms associated with taking a test?
      - Lazarus's cognitive mediational theory of emotion
      - Hans Selye's General Adaptation Syndrome: Alarm Stage/ Resistive Stage/ Exhaustion Stage
      - positive psychology

END OF EXAMINATION

ANSWERS FOR MULTIPLE-CHOICE QUESTIONS

Using the table below, score your test.

Determine how many questions you answered correctly and how many you answered incorrectly. You will find explanations of the answers on the following pages.

1. A	21. B	41. E	61. A	81. A
2. A	22. A	42. E	62. C	82. E
3. A	23. B	43. B	63. C	83. D
4. C	24. B	44. B	64. B	84. C
5. B	25. B	45. A	65. B	85. D
6. C	26. D	46. A	66. C	86. D
7. B	27. B	47. B	67. D	87. E
8. D	28. D	48. D	68. D	88. E
9. C	29. D	49. C	69. C	89. B
10. D	30. C	50. B	70. C	90. A
11. C	31. A	51. A	71. B	91. A
12. A	32. A	52. B	72. D	92. A
13. C	33. B	53. E	73. D	93. C
14. B	34. C	54. C	74. C	94. E
15. A	35. E	55. A	75. B	95. C
16. D	36. A	56. B	76. D	96. D
17. B	37. A	57. A	77. B	97. A
18. B	38. E	58. D	78. B	98. D
19. D	39. D	59. A	79. B	99. E
20. C	40. C	60. B	80. B	100. C

1. Answer: A. Compliance occurs when a person demonstrates a requested behavior, even if he does not change his belief *(Psychology,* 8th ed. p. 727/9th ed. p. 733).

2. Answer: A. Paul Costa and Robert McCrae conducted a factor analysis, which is a mathematical formula used to determine factors, or traits that predict one another *(Psychology,* 8th ed. p. 560/9th ed. p. 567).

3. Answer: A. Negative correlations are when one variable increases and another variable decreases *(Psychology,* 8th ed. p. 51/9th ed. p. 54).

4. Answer: C. Self-serving bias occurs when a person takes credit for his or her successes but blames others for his or her failures *(Psychology,* 8th ed. p. 700/9th ed. p. 707).

5. Answer: B. Psychodynamic therapeutic sessions are not as long, and thus are less expensive compared to psychoanalysis. Psychodynamic therapy still focuses on the role of, and resolving conflicts within the unconscious *(Psychology,* 8th ed. pp. 648–649/9th ed. pp. 655–656).

6. Answer: C. Teratogens are agents that could possibly harm the development of a child. Some teratogens include alcohol,

caffeine, and nicotine (*Psychology,* 8th ed. p. 460/9th ed. p. 469).

7. Answer: B. According to Hans Selye, the alarm stage of the general adaptation syndrome is characterized by experiences similar to the fight-or-flight syndrome. This includes the hypothalamus triggering the sympathetic nervous system, which signals the adrenal glands to release catecholamines, which activate internal organs (*Psychology,* 8th ed. pp. 523–524/9th ed. pp. 528–529).

8. Answer: D. A person experiencing a panic disorder does not know what causes the disorder. Panic disorders tend to come about with no warning signs, resulting in an increase in perspiration, heart rate, and dizziness (*Psychology,* 8th ed. pp. 605–606/9th ed. p. 612).

9. Answer: C. Weber's law states that the ability to detect a difference between stimuli depends on the intensity of the original stimulus. As the intensity of the original stimulus increases, so must the strength of the second stimulus, in order to be detected. Transduction involves the conversion of stimulus energy into neural code, enabling the brain to process the information (*Psychology,* 8th ed. p. 161/9th ed. p. 165).

10. Answer: D. The thalamus is responsible for transmitting information, other than smell, to the appropriate area of the brain for further processing (*Psychology,* 8th ed. pp. 79–80/9th ed. p. 82).

11. Answer: C. Carl Jung believed that each person has a collective unconscious, where information is inherited from human and nonhuman ancestors. This information unconsciously affects people's decisions and actions. Alfred Adler believed that people have an innate desire to overcome childhood inferiorities (*Psychology,* 8th ed. pp. 555–556/9th ed. p. 562).

12. Answer: A. Tests that accurately predict how well a student will do the first year in college would be considered valid. A test that yielded consistent results over numerous trials would be considered reliable (*Psychology,* 8th ed. pp. 372–374/9th ed. p. 380).

13. Answer: C. The sociocultural model for explaining psychological disorders suggests that social and cultural expectations and norms contribute to psychological disorders. Expectations of genders could contribute to the onset of certain psychological disorders. Behaviorists believe that maladaptive learning patterns contribute to psychological disorders (*Psychology,* 8th ed. pp. 594–595/9th ed. pp. 601–602).

14. Answer: B. The axon is responsible for sending information from the nucleus to the axon terminal, where it "fires" and releases neurotransmitters to an awaiting neuron (*Psychology,* 8th ed. p. 62/9th ed. p. 66).

15. Answer: A. In a positive correlation, both variables move in the same direction (*Psychology*, 8th ed. p. 51/9th ed. p. 54).

16. Answer: D. The experimental method allows researchers the opportunity to actively manipulate the variables in a controlled setting, and is the only method from which a cause-and-effect relationship can be inferred. Professor Winkleman would benefit from being allowed to determine which groups received the treatment and which did not (*Psychology*, 8th ed. pp. 40–41/9th ed. pp. 42–43).

17. Answer: B. A fixed ratio occurs when a subject is rewarded after a set number of responses or behaviors are performed (*Psychology*, 8th ed. p. 212/9th ed. p. 214).

18. Answer: B. As a person ages, crystallized intelligence (accumulated knowledge) increases, while fluid (mental quickness/cognitive flexibility) decreases (*Psychology*, 8th ed. p. 387/9th ed. p. 394).

19. Answer: D. Stanley Milgram's experiment on obedience concluded that people obey those they perceive to be authority figures (*Psychology*, 8th ed. pp. 731–735/9th ed. pp. 739–741).

20. Answer: C. Naturalistic observation is used to study subjects in their natural environments. This allows the researcher to witness both how the subjects interact and their behaviors without interfering or controlling the environment (*Psychology*, 8th ed. pp. 34–35/9th ed. p. 37).

21. Answer: B. After enough trials, the sound of the bag opening will no longer cause Fluffy to come running and the behavior will become extinct. According to the principles of operant conditioning, positive reinforcement (Fluffy being rewarded each time she hears the bag of food being opened) increases the chance that behavior will be performed in the future. By no longer rewarding Fluffy with the food when the bag opens, negative punishment (omission) has occurred, and Fluffy will no longer display the behavior (*Psychology*, 8th ed. p. 199/9th ed. p. 215).

22. Answer: A. Cognitive maps are mental representations that help guide a person's behavior (*Psychology*, 8th ed. p. 224/9th ed. p. 225).

23. Answer: B. Participants who returned the survey may have had an interest in politics and were more inclined to answer the survey questions, which may influence the results of the study (*Psychology*, 8th ed. pp. 41–42/9th ed. pp. 40–41).

24. Answer: B. Researchers who follow the biological perspective are interested in studying the inner workings of the brain, including hormones and neurotransmitters (*Psychology*, 8th ed. p. 18/9th ed. p. 19).

25. Answer: B. CAT/CT scans are x-ray images that involve imaging techniques that rotate around a single axis point. They are useful in detecting abnormalities within a targeted area (*This material does not appear in either textbook edition*).

26. Answer: D. Albert Bandura conducted numerous studies on the influence of violent television programs on individual aggression levels. He noted that people are more likely to act in an aggressive manner after viewing another person act in such way (*Psychology*, 8th ed. pp. 225–226/9th ed. pp. 227–228).

27. Answer: B. Groupthink occurs when individuals are concerned with maintaining a group's cohesive structure, and so don't want to deviate from the group (*Psychology*, 8th ed. pp. 757–758/9th ed. p. 764).

28. Answer: D. The somatic nervous system deals with information pertaining to sight, sound, smell, taste, and touch, and is also responsible for voluntary muscle movement (*Psychology*, 8th ed. pp. 67–68/9th ed. pp. 71–72).

29. Answer: D. In bipolar II, episodes of mania are less severe, referred to as hypomania, in comparison to bipolar I (*Psychology*, 8th ed. p. 617/9th ed. p. 623).

30. Answer: C. A heuristic is a rule of thumb or shortcut that relies on the most accessible information to help solve a problem (*Psychology*, 8th ed. p. 292/9th ed. p. 298).

31. Answer: A. Aaron Beck believed that psychological disorders could be traced to an individual's false beliefs, which through repetition become almost automatic. Beck suggested that actively having the client test those false beliefs in various situations would help the client realize that he or she was rushing to conclusions without taking in all of the factors (*Psychology*, 8th ed. pp. 659–660/9th ed. pp. 666–667).

32. Answer: A. The frontal lobes are responsible for inhibitions, planning for future tasks, and short-term memory (*Psychology*, 8th ed. pp. 79–80/9th ed. p. 90).

33. Answer: B. A cognitive psychologist believes that learning is the result of mental connections from previous experiences that help guide current and future behavior (*Psychology*, 8th ed. pp. 220–221/9th ed. pp. 222–223).

34. Answer: C. Projective personality tests use unstructured stimuli, like inkblots, to assess the content of the unconscious. However, interpretations are subjective, based on the researcher's opinions, which can be unreliable in comparison to an objective personality test (*Psychology*, 8th ed. pp. 582–583/9th ed. pp. 586).

35. Answer: E. Thyroxin, produced in the thyroid gland, is responsible for the body's basal metabolic rate (BMR) (*Psychology*, 8th ed. p. 100/9th ed. p. 103).

36. Answer: A. According to deductive reasoning, if the premise is true, the conclusion must be true (*Psychology*, 8th ed. pp. 290–291/9th ed. p. 296).

37. Answer: A. Hypochondriasis, along with conversion disorders, somatization disorder, and pain disorder, are all classified as somatoform disorders (*Psychology*, 8th ed. p. 610/9th ed. pp. 616–617).

38. Answer: E. Biological psychologists study how the interaction of the brain and the nervous system affects, and is influenced by, mental processes and behavior (*Psychology*, 8th ed. p. 4/9th ed. p. 5).

39. Answer: D. Aversion therapy uses classical conditioning to associate a new, unpleasant response—in contrast to the original response—with a specific stimulus. Systematic desensitization involves classical conditioning, but by associating a new, pleasant response—in comparison to a maladaptive response—with a specific stimulus (*Psychology*, 8th ed. p. 657/9th ed. p. 664).

40. Answer: C. Problem-focused coping involves addressing the problem associated with the stress. Emotion-focused coping involves addressing emotions, or feelings, associated with the problem. If Drew were to try and be more positive around this person, that would be an example of emotion-focused coping (*Psychology*, 8th ed. pp. 530–531/9th ed. p. 536).

41. Answer: E. The gambler's fallacy occurs when an individual believes that the probability of a random sequence is determined by previous behaviors. Since Vlad believes that his luck will turn around, because he lost the previous games, he is committing this fallacy (*Psychology*, 8th ed. p. 306/9th ed. p. 312).

42. Answer: E. Praise is not considered a primary reinforcer because it is not a biological necessity—it is not essential to the survival of a species (*Psychology*, 8th ed. pp. 210–211/9th ed. p. 213).

43. Answer: B. A serotonin deficiency has been linked to depression, alcoholism, aggression, and eating disorders. To treat these disorders, psychiatrists prescribe selective serotonin reuptake inhibitors, which increase the amount of serotonin available in the synapse (*Psychology*, 8th ed. p. 97/9th ed. p. 100).

44. Answer: B. An overwhelming majority of toddlers can walk unassisted by the age of 18 months; this is simply due to the natural maturing of the child (*Psychology*, 8th ed. p. 458/9th ed. p. 471).

45. Answer: A. Repression is the unconscious blocking of traumatic memories. Dissociative disorders are characterized by sudden and temporary disruptions in memory and identity.

Repression could explain why people are unable to remember previous memories and identities (*Psychology*, 8th ed. p. 613/9th ed. p. 619).

46. Answer: A. The humanistic approach emphasizes the uniqueness of each individual in terms of determining psychological growth and a healthy self-concept. The humanistic approach does not take into consideration unconscious motivation, learning styles, situations, and inherited characteristics (*Psychology*, 8th ed. pp. 574–575/9th ed. pp. 580–581).

47. Answer: B. Sensitivity refers to a person's ability to detect a stimulus, which is influenced by the intensity of the stimulus, functioning of a person's sensory systems, and amount of background noise expressed through the signal detection theory. Response criterion is also included in the signal detection theory, but emphasizes a person's willingness to respond to a stimulus (*Psychology*, 8th ed. p. 158/9th ed. p. 162).

48. Answer: D. According to the drive-reduction theory, homeostasis monitors the internal conditions of the body. When physiological systems fall beneath desired levels, drives such as thirst are produced and then direct behavior to reduce the drive (*Psychology*, 8th ed. p. 408/9th ed. p. 417).

49. Answer: C. A conditioned stimulus produces a conditioned response. Because you have had chocolate before, and you salivated while eating chocolate before, the smell of chocolate becomes a conditioned stimulus (*Psychology*, 8th ed. p. 198/9th ed. p. 202).

50. Answer: B. According to Lawrence Kohlberg, a person who makes a decision based on how others will view him or her is operating at the conventional level of morality (*Psychology*, 8th ed. pp. 499–501/9th ed. p. 506).

51. Answer: A. Ecstasy heightens the activity of dopamine-releasing neurons, which are connected to feelings of pleasure—similar to cocaine and amphetamines. Ecstasy acts as an agonist for serotonin, which may explain why people experience hallucinations while taking this drug (*Psychology*, 8th ed. p. 357/9th ed. pp. 362–363).

52. Answer: B. Role theory suggests that people who are hypnotized play a special role that includes acting in accordance to certain suggestions made by the hypnotist. The state theory suggests that hypnosis is an altered state of consciousness (*Psychology*, 8th ed. p. 348/9th ed. p. 352).

53. Answer: E. Gestalt therapy is a type of humanistic therapy that emphasizes to clients that psychological growth can only occur when one is aware of the environment in relation to how one forms an interpretation of environmental and situational factors. When a person loses touch with reality in terms of

what is happening around him or her, psychological growth is prevented. (*Psychology,* 8th ed. pp. 652–653/9th ed. p. 659).

54. Answer: C. The mean, or average, IQ is 100. In normal distributions, 50 percent of the scores will be below the mean and 50 percent of the scores will be above it (*Psychology,* 8th ed. p. A13/9th ed. p. 378).

55. Answer: A. Cyclothymic disorder involves less severe symptoms of mania and depressions associated with bipolar disorder. In comparison, dysthymic disorder involves less severe symptoms of depression (*Psychology,* 8th ed. p. 618/9th ed. p. 623).

56. Answer: B. Monocular cues are not useful in judging depth perception. For accurate depth perception, both eyes would be needed to make appropriate use of binocular cues (*Psychology,* 8th ed. pp. 166–169/9th ed. pp. 170–173).

57. Answer: A. Nightmares are frightening dreams that occur during REM sleep. Night terrors are often not recalled by the child in the morning and occur during NREM stage 4 sleep (*Psychology,* 8th ed. p. 341/9th ed. p. 348).

58. Answer: D. According to Benjamin Whorf, culture influences language. One's culture influences ones thoughts, which in turn influence language. If a person lives in a culture that has numerous words for "time," he is more likely to use more words describing the concept of time when speaking (*Psychology,* 8th ed. pp. 320–321/9th ed. pp. 325–326).

59. Answer: A. The lens of an eye is considered an accessory structure that modifies the energy of a stimulus in order for it to be processed. The pupil, controlled by the iris, is responsible for allowing light to enter the eye (*Psychology,* 8th ed. p. 108/9th ed. pp. 121–122).

60. Answer: B. Managing information that is received from our senses and transferring the information into concepts used to solve problems and reach conclusions is known as thinking (*Psychology,* 8th ed. p. 282/9th ed. p. 287).

61. Answer: A. Afferent neurons are responsible for transmitting sensory information to the brain to be processed, while efferent neurons are responsible for transmitting information from the brain to the organs and muscles (*Psychology,* 8th ed. p. 70/9th ed. p. 73).

62. Answer: C. The smallest unit of meaning in a language is the morpheme. Phonemes are the sounds produced in a language (*Psychology,* 8th ed. p. 310/9th ed. p. 315).

63. Answer: C. Reaction formation is doing the opposite in terms of feelings and thoughts associated with unacceptable thoughts and impulses. Sublimation involves converting unacceptable

impulses into favorable, acceptable behaviors (*Psychology*, 8th ed. p. 554/9th ed. p. 560).

64. Answer: B. Self-fulfilling prophecy occurs when the unconscious behaviors of a person influence the outcome (*Psychology*, 8th ed. p. 383/9th ed. p.390).

65. Answer: B. Incubation refers to the process of allowing a problem to work itself out, while stepping back or walking away from the problem. This allows the individual to break the mental set that may be inhibiting the problem solving. If a person has expertise regarding the problem being solved, it is more likely that he or she will, in fact, solve the problem (*Psychology*, 8th ed. p. 295/9th ed. pp. 300–301).

66. Answer: C. The pyramidal motor system is responsible for an individual's voluntarily making a facial expression; the extrapyramidal motor system is responsible for natural, involuntary facial expressions (*Psychology*, 8th ed. p. 439/9th ed. p. 447).

67. Answer: D. The closer a number is to +1.00 or –1.00 the stronger the relationship between the two variables. Whatever number has an absolute value closer to 1.00 is considered to have a stronger relationship (*Psychology*, 8th ed. p. 51/9th ed. p. 54).

68. Answer: D. A longitudinal study examines subjects throughout a set time period. Because Professor Collins believes that people who meditate will be more successful, he used a longitudinal study (*Psychology*, 8th ed. p. 393/9th ed. pp. 400–401).

69. Answer: C. Conformity occurs when a person changes a behavior to coincide with that of others, even though no direct request was made (*Psychology*, 8th ed. p. 727/9th ed. p. 733).

70. Answer: C. The incentive theory states that behavior is aimed at obtaining desirable stimuli, such as a treat, and escaping unwanted stimuli. Incentives are influenced by biological factors, so if the dog is hungry, it will make the treat even more appealing (*Psychology*, 8th ed. pp. 410–411/9th ed. pp. 418–420).

71. Answer: B. Inferential statistics are used when a researcher is trying to draw a conclusion that generalizes findings (*Psychology*, 8th ed. p. 49/9th ed. p. 55).

72. Answer: D. Thorndike was responsible for establishing the law of effect, which says that behaviors that result in a reward will be "stamped in," whereas behaviors that do not result in a reward will be "stamped out" (*Psychology*, 8th ed. pp. 205–206/9th ed. p. 208).

73. Answer: D. In-group bias refers to the tendency to show favoritism toward other members of the same group due to shared admiration (*Psychology*, 8th ed. p. 699/9th ed. p. 706).

74. Answer: C. A control group is a group that is not exposed to the independent variable, and is used as a basis of comparison for the experimental/treatment group (*Psychology*, 8th ed. p. 40/9th ed. p. 43).

75. Answer: B. The cognitive approach emphasizes cognitive abilities associated with encoding, manipulating, storing, and retrieving information. Cognitive psychologists are interested in how cognitive processes affect behavior. Behavioral psychologists study observable behavior in terms of how learning develops and could be modified (*Psychology*, 8th ed. p. 20/9th ed. p. 21).

76. Answer: D. Critics claim that IQ tests are culturally biased, cannot predict future success, only measure analytical intelligence, and can be influenced by personal motivation. However, because IQ tests have been given to numerous people they are said to be normed, or standardized (*Psychology*, 8th ed. pp. 374–376/9th ed. p. 379).

77. Answer: B. According to Robert Sternberg, a person who does well on standardized tests has high analytical intelligence (book smarts) (*Psychology*, 8th ed. p. 389/9th ed. p. 396).

78. Answer: B. Criterion validity refers to how well a test predicts future behavior. If a test lacks criterion validity it is said to be unable to predict future behavior (*Psychology*, 8th ed. p. 373/9th ed. p. 380).

79. Answer: B. According to Charles Darwin, evolution occurs through natural selection, which is the tendency for nature to select organisms that are best suited for survival. This may include genes that have mutated or evolved to encourage adaptation in certain environments (*Psychology*, 8th ed. p. 18/9th ed. p. 20).

80. Answer: B. Standardized tests are administered to numerous people on the same day. Standardized tests have been tested and retested to check for any potential bias that might occur (*Psychology*, 8th ed. p. 372/9th ed. p. 379).

81. Answer: A. Jean Piaget is considered the most influential psychologist in the field of child development. His research inspired many other psychologists to study child development (*Psychology*, 8th ed. p. 459/9th ed. p. 467).

82. Answer: E. Howard Gardner's theory of multiple intelligences states that each person is intelligent in a specific area (*Psychology*, 8th ed. pp. 391–392/9th ed. pp. 398–399).

83. Answer: D. The basilar membrane forms the bottom of the cochlea. When fluid moves throughout the cochlea, it causes

the basilar membrane to move, in turn causing hair cells to be stimulated, allowing the individual to hear (*Psychology*, 8th ed. p. 113/9th ed. p. 115).

84. Answer: C. Wernicke's area is responsible for processing auditory information. It allows a person to understand what others are saying. Broca's area is responsible for speech production and articulation (*Psychology*, 8th ed. p. 86/9th ed. p. 90).

85. Answer: D. Psychological dependency involves a mental preoccupation with the consumption of a drug, despite adverse warnings, resulting in a strong desire to take the drug to maintain a sense of well-being (*Psychology*, 8th ed. p. 352/9th ed. p. 356).

86. Answer: D. The actor-observer bias occurs when a person attributes the behaviors of others to internal or dispositional factors while attributing their own behaviors to external or situational factors (*Psychology*, 8th ed. p. 700/9th ed. p. 706).

87. Answer: E. One difference between anorexics and bulimics is that bulimics do see the binge-purge method as a problem, whereas anorexics do not believe there is a problem with the way they diet or exercise (*Psychology*, 8th ed. pp. 418–419/9th ed. pp. 427–428).

88. Answer: E. According to Elizabeth Kübler-Ross's theory of death and dying, a person will experience the following, in order: denial, anger, bargaining, depression, and acceptance (*this material does not appear in either textbook edition*).

89. Answer: B. Competence (need) motivation is reflected in meeting or surpassing a personal goal, which will accompany feelings of satisfaction. Achievement motivation is characterized by a desire to outperform others in terms of achieving satisfaction (*Psychology*, 8th ed. pp. 428–429/9th ed. pp. 436–438).

90. Answer: A. The rooting reflex occurs when an infant's cheek is touched. This reflex enables the infant to turn his or her head in response to touch, in search of the nipple that provides food (*Psychology*, 8th ed. p. 463/9th ed. p. 471).

91. Answer: A. Discrimination occurs when a person displays adverse treatment toward a category of people because of stereotypes they have of those people (*Psychology*, 8th ed. p. 708/9th ed. p. 715).

92. Answer: A. Insight is the sudden realization of a solution to a problem. Insight typically occurs after a period of incubation (*Psychology*, 8th ed. p. 224/9th ed. p. 227).

93. Answer: C. According to Diana Baumrind, permissive parents don't communicate with their children, set very few—if any—

rules, and allow their children to fend for themselves (*Psychology,* 8th ed. pp. 485–487/9th ed. pp. 491–492).

94. Answer: E. Confounding variables cannot be controlled for by the researcher, and may influence the overall results of a study (*Psychology,* 8th ed. p. 41/9th ed. pp. 43–44).

95. Answer: C. Extraversion is characterized by sociable behavior, enjoyment of social activities and excitement and change. Emotionality is characterized by moodiness, restlessness, and feelings of anxiety. Introversion is characterized by people who enjoy isolation, nonsocial involvement, and thoughtful. Stability is characterized by calmness and relaxed feelings (*Psychology,* 8th ed. pp. 561–562/9th ed. p. 568).

96. Answer: D. An algorithm is a systematic procedure that guarantees the correct solution to a problem. Although this procedure may take longer, it always leads to the correct answer (*Psychology,* 8th ed. p. 290/9th ed. p. 295).

97. Answer: A. In the DSM-IV-TR, Axis I includes clinical syndromes, such as childhood disorders, dissociative disorders, and sleep disorders. Axis II includes personality disorders and mental retardation, Axis III includes medical conditions, Axis IV includes situational and environmental factors, and Axis V includes a global assessment correlated to functioning (*Psychology,* 8th ed. pp. 597–598/9th ed. p. 604).

98. Answer: D. The door-in-the-face persuasion technique/procedure occurs when the initial request is one that is much larger than the actual desired request. Max knows that the larger request will be denied, but that his actual request will then seem reasonable in comparison (*Psychology,* 8th ed. pp. 730–731/9th ed. pp. 736–737).

99. Answer: E. Residual schizophrenia is a term that applies to people who have experienced symptoms of schizophrenia but are no longer experiencing the symptoms (*Psychology,* 8th ed. p. 624/9th ed. p. 630).

100. Answer: C. The focus of family therapy is to have each member of the family realize that he or she is part of the family structure. This includes respecting other family members, listening to others attentively, and increasing communications (*Psychology,* 8th ed. pp. 662–663/9th ed. pp. 669–670).

ANSWERS FOR FREE-RESPONSE QUESTIONS

1. Psychologists often disagree as to the influence of nature and nurture. Using your understanding of each issue explain how the nature and nurture arguments attempt to explain each of the following:
   a. Intelligence
      i. Nature (**Point 1**)
         - Genetic/family/kinship studies attempt to draw the conclusion that intelligence is hereditary.
         - Studies show that adopted children have IQs similar to those of their birth parents.
         - Monozygotic twins show a moderate correlation in their IQ levels.
         - Sir Francis Galton first proposed intelligence to be genetic, due to his kinship studies.
      ii. Nurture (**Point 2**)
         - Adoptee studies have demonstrated the effects of environment on IQ. Adopted children have been shown to have IQs similar to those of their adopted parents.
         - Exposure to new situations and better schooling have been shown to increase IQ.
   b. Language
      iii. Nature (**Point 3**)
         - According to Noam Chomsky, humans are born with the innate ability to develop language.
         - oNoam Chomsky's language acquisition device (LAD) helps foster the development of language.
         - Infants throughout the world babble the same (no dialect is found between children prior to development of language).
         - Children throughout the world develop language in roughly the same timeframe.
      iv. Nurture (**Point 4**)
         - If a child is neglected/abused/isolated and not exposed to language past the critical language period (approximately 12 years of age), the chances of the child fully developing true language are diminished.
         - Genie case study (must be explained and related to the absence of her ability to speak due to isolation and missing the critical window for language)
   c. Phobias
      v. Nature (**Point 5**)
         - Evolutionary psychologists believe phobias of certain animals/insects/reptiles serve a purpose to help further the likelihood of survival of a species.
      vi. Nurture (**Point 6**)
         - According to the classical conditioning model, phobias are learned through association (must correctly apply UCS, UCR, NS, CS, CR terms to show how a phobia could be developed).
         - According to the operant conditioning model, phobias are learned through negative reinforcement (removal of aversive stimulus will increase future behavior).
         - According to social-cognitivists, phobias are the result of observational learning (must provide an example clearly demonstrating an understanding of how this leads to the formation of a phobia).

    d. Aggression
      vii. Nature (**Point 7**)
- Biological psychologists believe that a decrease in serotonin leads to aggressive behaviors.
- Biological psychologists believe that an increase in testosterone leads to aggressive behaviors.
- Evolutionary psychologists argue that aggression helps increase the chances of survival of a species.

      viii. Nurture (**Point 8**)
- Social cognitivists believe that observational learning of aggressive behavior leads to aggression.
- Albert Bandura's Bobo doll study is evidence that aggression is learned through observational learning.
- According to behaviorists, aggressive behavior is the result of operant conditioning (must explain how positive reinforcement may lead to aggression)

    e. Mental disorders
      ix. Nature (**Point 9**)
- Biological psychologists view mental disorders as the result of a deficiency or excess of neurotransmitter substances (must match deficiency or excess neurotransmitter substance with mental disorder correctly—for example, excess dopamine has been linked with the onset of schizophrenia).

      x. Nurture (**Point 10**)
- Behaviorists view the development of mental disorders as the result of reinforcement of a behavior associated with a given mental disorder (i.e., attention for acting a particular way).
- Social cognitivists believe that mental disorders develop through observational learning.

2. Jim is unsure if he wants to take the AP Psychology Exam. He has developed a mental list of pros and cons to help determine if he should take the exam. Explain how the following terms could help Jim make a decision. Be sure to relate your answers to the content of the situation..

- Yerkes-Dodson law (**Point 1**)
  - Yerkes-Dodson law states that the degree of psychological arousal helps performance, but only to a certain degree. If Jimmy thinks the test is too hard he may not take the exam, especially if he is facing other demands such as term papers and projects. Jimmy needs to be moderately aroused to perform optimally on the exam.
- Extrinsic motivation (**Point 2**)
  - A desire to perform a behavior because of external rewards—Jimmy may take the exam because his parents promised him a new car.
- Self-efficacy beliefs (**Point 3**)
  - Beliefs or expectations about one's abilities—Depending on how Jimmy views his own abilities, whether positive or negative, will play a role in Jimmy's decision. With high self-efficacy, Jimmy will likely take the exam.
- Conformity (**Point 4**)
  - Changing one's behavior to meet the demands of the group—Jimmy may feel pressure to take the exam because all his friends are taking it.
- Obedience (**Point 5**)
  - Tendency to comply with orders from someone in a perceived position of authority—Jimmy may feel pressure to take the exam if his parents or teacher tell him to.

b.

- Lazarus's cognitive mediational theory of emotion (**Point 6**)
    - Lazarus's cognitive mediational theory of emotion states that emotion is the result of cognitive interpretation or appraisal. Jimmy could assume that the test is going to be too difficult and that he won't be able to pass it.
- Hans Selye General Adaptation Syndrome: Alarm Stage/ Resistive Stage/ Exhaustion Stage (**Point 7**)
    - Alarm stage: Fight or flight syndrome is the outpouring of stress hormones epinephrine and norepinephrine, which trigger the sympathetic nervous system, which elevates breathing, heart rate, and perspiration, and slows down digestion. Jimmy will naturally experience increased arousal from the presence of the exam.
    - Resistive stage: Cortisol is a hormone released to help fight stress by releasing stored energy in the body.
    - Exhaustion stage occurs when body's reserves becomes depleted. If Jimmy got to this stage then he might get sick or feel mentally exhausted.
- Positive psychology (**Point 8**)
    - Area of psychology that focuses on optimal human functioning and the factors that allow individuals to thrive—Jimmy may want to read some of Martin Seligman's research to help him raise his self-esteem and develop the confidence he needs to take exams successfully.

Calculating Your Score

This scoring chart is based on the 2007 AP Psychology released exam. While the AP Grade Conversion Chart is NOT the same for each testing year, it gives you an approximate breakdown.

SCORING THE MULTIPLE-CHOICE SECTION

Use the following formula to calculate your raw score on the multiple-choice section of the exam:

$$\underline{\hspace{3cm}} \times 1.00 = \underline{\hspace{3cm}}$$

number correct   weighted Section 1 Score (out of 100)

Scoring the Free-Response Section

Question 1 $\underline{\hspace{2cm}} \times 2.5$ = $\underline{\hspace{3cm}}$
(out of 10)   (do not round)

Question 2 $\underline{\hspace{2cm}} \times 3.125$ = $\underline{\hspace{3cm}}$
(out of 8)   (do not round)

sum = $\underline{\hspace{3cm}}$

weighted Section II score (do not round)

YOUR COMPOSITE SCORE

$$\underline{\hspace{2.5cm}} + \underline{\hspace{2.5cm}} = \underline{\hspace{3cm}}$$

weighted Section I score   weighted Section II score   composite score (round to nearest whole number)

AP GRADE CONVERSION CHART

Composite Score Range	AP Grade
113 – 150	5
93 – 112	4
77 – 92	3
65 – 76	2
0 – 64	1

CPSIA information can be obtained
at www.ICGtesting.com
Printed in the USA
FFOW01n0515300616
25521FF